CRIMINAL LAW

CRIMINAL LAW

MODEL PROBLEMS AND OUTSTANDING ANSWERS

Kathryn Christopher

and

Russell Christopher

OXFORD
UNIVERSITY PRESS

OXFORD
UNIVERSITY PRESS

*Oxford University Press, Inc., publishes works that further Oxford University's objective of excellence
in research, scholarship, and education.*

Oxford   New York
Auckland   Cape Town   Dar es Salaam   Hong Kong   Karachi   Kuala Lumpur   Madrid   Melbourne
Mexico City   Nairobi   New Delhi   Shanghai   Taipei   Toronto

With offices in
Argentina   Austria   Brazil   Chile   Czech Republic   France   Greece   Guatemala   Hungary   Italy
Japan   Poland   Portugal   Singapore   South Korea   Switzerland   Thailand   Turkey   Ukraine
Vietnam

Library of Congress Cataloging-in-Publication Data

Christopher, Kathryn H.
  Criminal law : model problems and outstanding answers / Kathryn H. Christopher, Russell L. Christopher.
     p. cm. — (Model problems and outstanding answers)
  Includes bibliographical references and index.
  ISBN 978-0-19-539177-0 ((pbk.) : alk. paper)
  1. Criminal law—United States—Examinations, questions, etc.
  2. Criminal procedure—United States—Examinations, questions, etc. I. Christopher, Russell L. II. Title.
  KF9219.85.C48 2012
  345.730076—dc23   2011022498

Note to Readers

This publication is designed to provide accurate and authoritative information in regard to the subject
matter covered. It is based upon sources believed to be accurate and reliable and is intended to be current
as of the time it was written. It is sold with the understanding that the publisher is not engaged in rendering
legal, accounting, or other professional services. If legal advice or other expert assistance is required,
the services of a competent professional person should be sought. Also, to confirm that the information has
not been affected or changed by recent developments, traditional legal research techniques should be used,
including checking primary sources where appropriate.

*(Based on the Declaration of Principles jointly adopted by a Committee of the
American Bar Association and a Committee of Publishers and Associations.)*

You may order this or any other Oxford University Press publication by
visiting the Oxford University Press website at www.oup.com

CONTENTS

ACKNOWLEDGMENTS

We are indebted to Whitney Davis, Ken Levy, Dan Markel, Eric Reynolds, Peter Westen, Sam Wiseman, Vicki Limas, Paul Marcus, Markus Dubber, Jim Tomkovicz, and Ken Simons for painstakingly reading drafts of chapters and suggesting much needed improvements. Thanks to The University of Tulsa College of Law for providing a research grant that greatly facilitated the development of this project. We are grateful to Steve Sheppard for inviting us to write this book. Many thanks to the outside reviewers for their helpful comments, suggestions, and perceptive critiques. The editors at Oxford University Press tirelessly reviewed and scrutinized every word of multiple rough drafts of this volume, making the book the best that it could be. Any errors, of course, are our own. We also thank our students for their insights and feedback on these hypotheticals—they were the guinea pigs. We dedicate this book to our parents, Albert & Thelma, and Donna & Tom. Thanks for your love and support.

ABOUT THE AUTHORS

Russell Christopher is Professor of Law at the University of Tulsa College of Law, where he teaches and conducts research in the area of criminal law and criminal procedure. Kathryn Christopher was Visiting Assistant Professor, teaching criminal law, at the University of Tulsa College of Law. In addition to this book, they have enjoyed collaborating on a number of projects. They have co-authored articles appearing in *Northwestern University Law Review* and *Indiana Law Journal*, they have co-presented at numerous universities including Oxford University and the University of Arizona, and they have even taught classes together, both in America and England. Additionally, the authors have published separately in numerous journals including *Arizona State Law Journal, Cardozo Law Review, Georgetown Law Journal, Fordham Law Review, Ohio State Law Journal, Oxford Journal of Legal Studies*, and *Philosophy & Public Affairs*.

INTRODUCTION

It is not enough to know the criminal law. You have to be able to apply it. As many 1st year law students find out too late, abstract knowledge of the rules, principles, and doctrines embodying the criminal law is not enough. Proficiency in criminal law requires, and law school exams test, the ability to apply that knowledge to complicated, confusing, counter-intuitive, challenging, red-herring-filled hypothetical fact-patterns. The book that you are holding takes the obvious but nonetheless novel approach that the best way to learn how to apply the criminal law is to practice applying it. Rather than passive rote-memorization, you need to actively practice applying the rules and principles of criminal law to the type of hypothetical fact-patterns that you will confront on an exam.

While knowledge of the criminal law is not sufficient, it is necessary. In order to apply the criminal law, one must have sufficient knowledge of the criminal law. Interestingly enough, the best way to learn the criminal law so that you can apply it is also through applying the criminal law.

It is still not enough to know the criminal law and to be able to apply it. You have to be able to convey what you know and demonstrate your ability to analyze and apply law to facts through a well-reasoned, well-organized, and well-written essay. And again, the best way to develop this proficiency in essay writing is by practicing writing essays that apply your knowledge of the criminal law to the sort of fact-patterns that you will encounter on an actual exam. The three rules of criminal law proficiency are application, application, and application.

This volume facilitates learning the various principles and doctrines of criminal law through the vehicle of writing essays to the type of problems, hypotheticals, or fact-patterns you are likely to confront on an exam. For each major topic in criminal law, a hypothetical problem is presented followed by a model answer. The model answer is not meant to reflect what a typical, or even a very good, law student would produce, but instead is aspirational or exemplary. That is, it presents what would easily be an "A" answer. The advantage of this approach is two-fold. First, it provides a better means for you to learn—completely, comprehensively, and exhaustively—the criminal law. Second, it supplies a model to which you may aspire. It reveals the type of answer that your professor is looking for. In short, this book is not designed simply to prepare you for a law school exam in criminal law. Rather, it is designed to make you *more than prepared*.

While the problems are challenging and the model answers rigorous, the hypothetical fact-patterns are interesting and accessible. Many of them are loosely based on crime dramas such as *Se7en, Reservoir Dogs*, and *Memento*. While there are, of course, the obligatory high-brow allusions to Shakespearean characters, there are also several hypotheticals based on Will Ferrell comedies and there is even one involving the beloved Sesame Street characters showing their dark and twisted sides, doing unspeakable acts to one another.

After each model answer is a Tools section supplying the means by which you can assess how well you did on your answer as well as explain how you might improve. One of the most valuable features of this section is a meticulous, step-by-step flow chart revealing the best mode of analyzing the problem presented as well as any other problem on that topic.

Another valuable feature focuses on how to organize and structure your essay. It demonstrates the underlying structure of the model answer as well as presents alternative organizational schemes side-by-side. This facilitates mastery in how to organize and structure any essay answer.

The organization of the chapters in this book is much like your casebook. Chapters 1–5 present the fundamental elements of any crime, Chapters 6–10 cover the specific crimes of homicide and rape, Chapters 11–14 involve defenses, Chapters 15–16 treat attempts, and Chapters 17–18 address group criminality—accomplice liability and conspiracy.

But this book diverges from the typical approach in two ways. First, the most difficult areas of criminal law are covered more expansively. Felony murder and impossible attempts are the subjects of their own separate chapters. These subjects are defanged and demystified by simpler explanations, practical strategies, and clarifying charts. Second, the final chapter of the book ties together many of the areas of criminal law by providing an overview on mistakes. The problem of mistake is pervasive in criminal law. Exculpatory mistakes of fact and law may provide the basis for a defense by negating mens rea, mistakes pertaining to a defense (e.g., self-defense) may bear on the validity of the defense, and inculpatory mistakes are central to understanding impossible attempts. Typically criminal law courses study these different mistakes separately, as if in a vacuum. But on a fact-pattern in an exam, these different types of mistake are not presented pre-identified and it is easy to confuse them. This Mistake Overview chapter provides the key tools to differentiate between these disparate types of mistake and avoid getting confused.

While the special sanction or remedy of punishment is often said to be the distinguishing feature of criminal law, the study of criminal law should not be a punishing experience. Hopefully the novel approach of this book will make your study of criminal law a little less cruel, even if a little more unusual. As a former gang member, upon his release from prison, says to Otto, the lead character in the 80s cult classic, *Repo Man*, "Let's Do Crimes!"

Kathryn Christopher
Russell Christopher
Tulsa, Oklahoma

CRIMINAL LAW

ACTUS REUS:

ACTS AND OMISSIONS

INTRODUCTION

Any criminal offense consists of mens rea or a guilty mind (see Ch. 2), actus reus or a guilty act, and their concurrence. The actus reus is expansively defined to include the conduct of the actor, any relevant circumstances, a harmful result, and that the actor's conduct caused the result. While not all offenses include circumstance, result, and causation elements, all offenses do include a conduct element. The conduct of an actor consists of what the actor has done or not done. This conduct element is termed the act requirement. The act requirement may be satisfied in either of two ways: (i) a voluntary act or (ii) an omission—a failure to act when there is a duty to act.

An act is often defined as a bodily movement. But merely committing an act does not suffice: the act must be voluntary. Though notoriously elusive to define, perhaps it can be most simply expressed as a willed bodily movement. Another approach is to define a voluntary act in terms of what it is not. A voluntary act is not an involuntary act. The Model Penal Code (MPC) includes the following examples of involuntary acts: reflexes, convulsions, and bodily movements during unconsciousness, sleep, or hypnosis, or more generally, those that are "not a product of the effort or determination of the actor." MPC § 2.01(2).

Where all of the actor's conduct is voluntary or where none of it is, the analysis of whether the requirement is satisfied is clear. As we will see, the difficulty lies where some of the actor's relevant conduct is voluntary, and some of it is involuntary. Different jurisdictions employ different approaches to this situation of mixed—voluntary and involuntary—conduct.

Generally, the criminal law does not punish people for their failures to act. At any one time, each of us is necessarily failing to do an infinite number of acts. For example, at this moment you are failing to trek across the Sahara Desert, paddle a canoe down the Amazon River, climb Mt. Everest, etc. The failures to act that do satisfy the act requirement and do subject people to criminal liability are limited to those that violate a duty to act. While the criminal law demands that we refrain from many actions—murdering, raping, robbing, etc., the criminal law imposes comparatively fewer duties to affirmatively act. The only such duties to act arise from one of the following: (i) statute, (ii) status relationship, (iii) contract, (iv) voluntary assumption of care and seclusion, or (v) creation of peril. Even though a failure to act can cause the same harm as an affirmative act, we do not have a general duty to render aid, prevent harm, or be a good Samaritan apart from the above five bases.

The act requirement ensures that our criminal justice system punishes people neither for their thoughts alone nor for their status. For example, neither merely thinking about robbing a bank nor being a drug addict is a criminal offense. The act requirement limits the scope of the criminal law's application to what we do (or do not do) and excludes what we think and who we are. To criminalize one's thoughts or status is to criminalize that which is outside of one's control. And we are not culpable or responsible for that which is outside of our control. For this reason, the law punishes only that over which one has control—what we do or fail to do.

PROBLEM

Bert and Ernie arrive in Florida for Spring Break. To obtain a rental car, each one signs the rental contract obligating them to make a good faith effort to return the car undamaged. They immediately proceed from the airport to a bar and spend the next several hours drinking. They both become intoxicated. Then Bert decides they should take the car out for a spin. And Bert, who is driving, decides that he wants to stop at a convenience store that sits atop a hill to buy some Cheesy Poofs for snacking.

Ernie, still quite intoxicated, decides to remain in the passenger seat and maybe grab a quick nap. After about ten minutes, feeling something amiss, Ernie wakes up and realizes that the car is rolling down the hill. Ernie sees people in the crosswalk at the bottom of the hill. He also sees his hated enemy Grover. Grover is voluntarily walking in the crosswalk with the knowledge that he (Grover) is prone to epileptic seizures when startled. Behind Grover, there is a group of schoolchildren on a field trip; and behind them, much to Ernie's surprise, is Ernie's fiancée, Lola, walking arm-in-arm with Biff. Ernie could stop the car by moving from the passenger seat to the driver seat and depressing the brake pedal, but Ernie believes this would be a great opportunity to kill Grover and Lola and get away with it.

Everyone in the crosswalk sees the car bearing down on them. Grover immediately succumbs to an epileptic seizure during which he knocks several schoolchildren down and falls on top of them. Lola realizes that Ernie is in the car, so she shoves Biff and runs away, hoping Ernie did not see her. Biff trips as a result of Lola's shove, knocks the rest of the schoolchildren down, and falls on top of them. Grover regains consciousness and gets out of the way of the oncoming car. Grover realizes that he could help the children that he knocked down evade the oncoming car, but he decides instead to run off. The children die immediately upon impact with the car. Biff and the children he fell on were hopelessly tangled in a heap and were not able to get out of the way of the car. Biff miraculously only sustains a few scratches and cuts, but the children sustain serious injuries from which they will die if they do not receive immediate aid. Rather than render aid, Biff runs off, and the children die. Ernie, now concerned about the mayhem, flees. The rental car is fairly badly damaged as a result of colliding with the pedestrians.

The jurisdiction includes the following statute. *Driver Leaving the Scene of an Accident*: It shall be a felony for a driver of a vehicle to leave the scene of an accident arising out of the operation of a vehicle without rendering or obtaining aid for any injured person.

Ernie is charged with the murder of the children, attempted murder of Lola, Grover, and Biff, and Driver Leaving the Scene of an Accident. Grover is charged with the murder of the children that he knocked down. Lola is charged with assault and battery of Biff and the murder of the children that Biff knocked down. Biff is charged with the murder of the children that he knocked down.

Analyze and discuss whether Ernie, Lola, Biff, and Grover satisfy the act require-ment for their respective offenses under both the common law and the MPC.

LIST OF READINGS

Martin v. State, 17 So.2d 427 (1944)
People v. Decina, 138 N.E.2d 799 (1956)
Jones v. United States, 308 F.2d 307 (1962)
People v. Beardsley, 113 N.W. 1128 (1907)
MODEL PENAL CODE § 2.01 (Official Code and Revised Comments 1985)

ESSAY

Remember: This essay raises many issues, and a good student, even the good lawyer, might not have seen all of them in the first effort at analysis. Do not be discouraged if you do not spot all of the issues. The Essay is designed both to supply a model and to aid a full understanding of the relevant principles.

Lola probably does, Ernie possibly does, Grover probably does not, and Biff most likely does not, satisfy the act requirement for their respective offenses.

Ernie

COMMON LAW

[1] In order to satisfy the act requirement of an offense, an actor must either commit a voluntary act or fail to act where the actor is under a duty to act. The voluntary act or failure to act must be relevant to or pertain to the offense charged.

[2] Ernie did engage in a number of voluntary acts. For example, Ernie volun-tarily flew to Florida, rented a car with Bert, got into the car, and went to a bar. But none of these voluntary acts is relevant to the charged offenses. They are nei-ther the acts that possibly caused harm to the victims, attempted harm to the victims, nor are they the conduct described in the leaving the scene of the accident statute. Ernie's relevant conduct is being in the car when it rolled down the hill, running over various people. Because Ernie was merely a passenger in the car, his presence therein was no act at all. Sitting passively in a car is not an affirmative act, whether voluntary or involuntary. Because it is not a bodily movement, it is not an affirmative act.

[3] Even if Ernie committed no relevant affirmative act, Ernie may have failed to act where he was under a duty to act. Generally, actors are not subject to crimi-nal liability for failures to act. There are, however, five bases for a duty to act to arise: (i) status relationship, (ii) contract, (iii) statute, (iv) voluntary assumption of care and seclusion, and (v) creation of peril. The failure to fulfill a duty to act may result in omission liability.

[4] The first basis creates a duty to act where an actor stands in a special status relationship to the person in peril. The principal status relationships are a spouse to a spouse and a parent to his or her minor child. Such a relationship gives rise to a duty to prevent harm to or aid the person in peril. Here, the only victim with whom Ernie might be said to have a special status relationship is Lola. Under the traditional rule, Ernie would only have a duty to prevent harm to Lola if she was his spouse. But the more modern trend is to expand the duty beyond spouses to sometimes include persons in long-term relationships. Depending on factors

such as the length of the relationship or cohabitation, Ernie might have a duty to act to prevent harm to Lola. If Ernie actually does have such a duty, he violated it by failing to stop the car as it careened toward Lola. As a result, Ernie may have satisfied the act requirement for the attempted murder of Lola.

[5] The second basis creates a duty to act if a contract imposes such a duty. The only contract in this hypothetical is the contract between the car rental agency and Bert and Ernie. The contract imposes a duty on Bert and Ernie to make a good faith effort not to damage the car. Ernie violated this duty by failing to avoid damaging the car—by failing to avoid colliding with the pedestrians. Is this contractual duty to act sufficient to support criminal omission liability for failure to avoid harm to the pedestrians? It is not entirely clear. Generally, a contractual duty sufficient to support criminal omission liability involves a contractual duty to render aid or prevent harm. For example, a lifeguard, nurse, or nanny has a contractual duty to prevent harm to the *people* specified in the contract. In contrast, Ernie's specific contractual duty was to prevent harm not to people, but to a thing—the car. On this basis, Ernie's contractual duty to prevent harm to the car does not suffice to support criminal omission liability.

But one might argue Ernie's contractual duty does suffice for criminal omission liability. Ernie had a contractual duty to avoid damage to the car. The car colliding with pedestrians is one way to damage the car. Therefore, Ernie had a contractual duty to avoid colliding with pedestrians. In a sense, the duty with respect to the car entailed a duty with respect to pedestrians. A contractual duty may support criminal omission liability even if the contractual duty is owed to a party different than the criminal victim. For example, suppose a mother contracts with a nanny to render care to an infant, but the nanny fails to do so and the infant dies. The nanny may be criminally liable for the death of the infant even though the contractual duty (to care for the infant) was owed not to the infant but to the mother. (In contract terms, the mother is the obligee to whom a duty of performance was owed.) Similarly, Ernie may be criminally liable for an omission for the deaths of the children and the attempted murder of others even though the contractual duty was owed not to the victims but to the car rental agency (the obligee). While the criminal law duty is owed to the victims, the contractual duty is owed to the obligees. On this basis, Ernie's contractual duty to prevent harm to the car does suffice to support criminal omission liability.

On balance, it is not clear whether the contractual duty to the rental car company creates a duty to act that supports criminal omission liability.

[6] The third basis creates a duty to act if a statute imposes such a duty. For example, a statute imposes the duty to pay income tax. Failure to comply with such a statute results in criminal liability. The only statute at issue here, Driver Leaving the Scene of an Accident, applies to drivers of automobiles, not passengers. Because Ernie was never a driver or operator of the vehicle, but always a passenger, he was not under that statutory duty. This third basis fails to support omission liability for Ernie.

[7] The fourth basis creates a duty to act if an actor voluntarily undertakes the assumption of care of another and secludes him or her. Ernie did not voluntarily undertake to aid any of the victims here, so he will not incur omission liability for this reason. This fourth basis fails to support omission liability for Ernie.

[8] The fifth basis creates a duty to act if through an affirmative act an actor places another into peril. Although Ernie did commit a number of affirmative acts, none of them imperiled another. Even Ernie's affirmative act of fleeing the mayhem did not imperil anyone. His victims were already in peril prior to his flight from the scene. Ernie's only conduct that placed others into peril was not an affirmative act but rather a failure to act. But the duty to act stemming from a creation of a peril most likely requires an affirmative act that creates the peril. A failure to act that creates the peril is insufficient. This fifth basis fails to support omission liability for Ernie.

MODEL PENAL CODE
[9] Under the MPC, Ernie similarly fails to commit a relevant affirmative act. As to omission liability, the MPC defaults to the common law position.

CONCLUSION
[10] Ernie fails to satisfy the act requirement of any of his charged offenses on the basis of an affirmative voluntary act. Ernie possibly satisfies the act requirement for all his charged offenses (excepting Driver Leaving the Scene of an Accident) through an omission.

Grover
COMMON LAW
[11] Grover's affirmative act of knocking the children down and into the path of the car was involuntary because it occurred during an epileptic seizure. Conduct during an epileptic seizure is a paradigmatic example of an involuntary act. On this basis, Grover's conduct would not support liability for the deaths of the children because it was involuntary. But arguably, Grover's relevant conduct includes voluntary pre-seizure acts as well. Prior to his seizure, Grover was voluntarily walking.

[12] When an actor's relevant conduct includes both voluntary and involuntary actions, different courts and jurisdictions take three different approaches. First, all of an actor's relevant acts must be voluntary. Because Grover's affirmative act of colliding with the children was involuntary, he would not satisfy the act requirement under this approach.

[13] Second, if an actor's relevant acts include a voluntary act, the actor satisfies the act requirement. If Grover's pre-seizure conduct of voluntarily walking in the crosswalk can be construed as part of his relevant conduct, then Grover would satisfy the act requirement under this approach. In *Decina*, the court found that a driver who killed pedestrians during an epileptic seizure did involve a voluntary act—the defendant voluntarily decided to drive with the knowledge that he was prone to seizures. Based on *Decina*, one might argue Grover's pre-seizure conduct of voluntarily walking or deciding to walk with the knowledge that he was prone to seizures might also support liability. Though tracking the reasoning of *Decina*, this argument is weak and will most likely fail. The reasoning of *Decina* is most likely disanalogous to cases involving comparatively less dangerous conduct like walking.

[14] Third, only the most important or essential aspect of an actor's relevant conduct must be voluntary in order to satisfy the voluntary act requirement. If Grover's voluntary pre-seizure conduct could be construed to be more important

or essential than his involuntary conduct during his seizure, then Grover would satisfy the act requirement under this approach. But determining which aspect of an actor's conduct is most important or essential is elusive and unclear. Only a very weak argument could be made that Grover's innocuous voluntary pre-seizure conduct was comparatively more important or essential than his conduct during the seizure (that immediately preceded the harm to the children). But, of course, this is the very argument of *Decina*.

[15] Some commentators attempt to describe how courts analyze whether an actor satisfies the act requirement through use of the explanatory device termed "time-framing." Courts, intentionally or unintentionally, select a broad or narrow time frame within which to determine whether an actor has committed a voluntary act. By selecting a broad time frame, a court will go farther back in time to find a voluntary act. Using a narrow time frame, on the other hand, will include less conduct so the court is less likely to find a voluntary act. As a result, the selection of the time frame will largely determine whether the actor satisfies the act requirement. For example, *Decina* employed a broad time frame. Despite Decina acting involuntarily during the seizure when his car collided with the victims, the court went backward in time until it found a voluntary act—Decina's decision to drive. Here, using a broad time frame would encompass Grover's voluntary pre-seizure act of walking, where using a narrow time frame would only include Grover's involuntary act during the seizure.

[16] Even if Grover has not committed a relevant voluntary act, a failure to act where there is a duty to act equally satisfies the act requirement. Grover failed to save the children (that he knocked down) from being run over by Ernie's car. The only possible basis for Grover to owe a duty to save the children is creation of a peril. Grover's involuntary act of knocking down the children placed them into the peril posed by Ernie's onrushing car. Most jurisdictions, however, would probably not find that Grover had a duty to act. As opposed to a criminal act that creates a peril, Grover created a peril through an involuntary act, which is the weakest basis for omission liability via creation of a peril. If Grover did have a duty to act based an involuntary act creating a peril, then he would satisfy the act requirement by his omission. But he most likely does not have a duty to act, and thus he does not satisfy the act requirement by an omission.

MODEL PENAL CODE

[17] The MPC seems to only require that an actor's conduct include a voluntary act in order to satisfy the act requirement. As discussed above in [13], Grover's relevant conduct probably does not include a voluntary act. The MPC defaults to the common law's analysis of omission liability. As discussed above in [16], Grover most likely does not owe a duty to the children to save them from Ernie's onrushing car. As a result, Grover probably neither commits a voluntary act nor violates a duty to act and thus probably does not satisfy the act requirement.

CONCLUSION

[18] Grover probably fails to satisfy the act requirement of any charged offense based on an affirmative voluntary act. He probably also fails to satisfy the act requirement based on an omission.

Lola

COMMON LAW

[19] Lola's voluntary affirmative act of pushing Biff will most certainly support criminal liability. Lola has satisfied the act requirement for assault and battery upon Biff. Lola's voluntary act may also satisfy the act requirement for homicide of the children. (Whether Lola is ultimately liable may depend on a causation analysis.) (See Ch. 5.)

[20] Lola also satisfies the act requirement by an omission. Lola's criminal act of pushing Biff, who in turn fell on the children, placed the children in peril. Because the act creating the peril was a criminal act, there is a particularly strong basis on which to find that Lola owed a duty to the children. By fleeing, Lola violated her duty to render aid to the injured children. (But again, whether she will ultimately be liable for the homicides will depend on a causation analysis.)

MODEL PENAL CODE

[21] The MPC analysis would not differ from that discussed above in [19]–[20].

CONCLUSION

[22] Lola clearly satisfies the act requirement for assault and battery of Biff by her voluntary act of pushing Biff. By that same act, she most likely satisfies the act requirement for murder of the children. Lola also satisfies the act requirement for murder of the children by omission.

Biff

COMMON LAW

[23] Biff's affirmative conduct that contributed to the deaths of the children was involuntary. Biff was pushed by Lola and as a result trips and falls on top of the children. As a result, Biff's involuntary act would not satisfy the act requirement.

[24] Biff may, however, satisfy the act requirement through an omission. His involuntary act of falling on top of the children placed the children in peril from Ernie's onrushing car. An involuntary act that places another in peril is the weakest creation of peril basis for a duty to aid to arise. Even if a court would find that Biff owed a duty to aid, the facts state that Biff was physically unable to save the children from the collision with the car. Therefore, he did not violate his duty to prevent them from being hit by the car. However, after the children are hit, Biff is physically able to render aid to the injured children. If he has a duty to aid, he violates it by fleeing. But Biff most likely does not satisfy the act requirement by an omission because creation of peril via an involuntary act probably does not give rise to a duty to act.

MODEL PENAL CODE

[25] The MPC analysis would not differ from that discussed above in [23]–[24].

CONCLUSION

[26] Biff clearly did not satisfy the act requirement through affirmative conduct and most likely does not satisfy the act requirement through an omission.

Conclusion

Ernie: Ernie clearly does not satisfy the act requirement through affirmative voluntary conduct but possibly satisfies the act requirement through an omission for all charged offenses (excepting Driver Leaving the Scene of an Accident).

Grover: Grover probably fails to satisfy the act requirement.

Lola: Lola probably or clearly (depending on the offense charged) satisfies the act requirement through her affirmative voluntary act and clearly satisfies the act requirement through her omission.

Biff: Biff clearly did not satisfy the act requirement through an affirmative voluntary act and most likely does not satisfy the act requirement through an omission.

TOOLS FOR SELF-ASSESSMENT

Go back to your written answer. Look for the issues identified in paragraphs [1]–[26] above. Look also for the analysis that follows each issue, and mark your essay where you locate it. Do you fully describe the issue, identify the precise legal standard that applies, list the relevant facts, and show how the facts and law support a conclusion for each issue in a separate paragraph? Mark each conclusion in your essay. Are there sufficient reasons in the law and in the facts to support the conclusion?

1.   Do what you are told. Here you are to analyze whether Ernie, Lola, Biff, and Grover satisfy the act requirement of an offense. A complete answer would include whether each committed a voluntary act relevant to an offense and whether each violated a duty to act.

2.   Always analyze under the MPC unless you are instructed otherwise.

3.   State the best possible arguments for alternative conclusions. Even as you reject possible conclusions as to whether an actor commits a voluntary act or omission, make the best possible argument first, and only then reject that possibility.

4.   Be on the alert for red herrings. Some information in the fact pattern of a hypothetical is irrelevant or even included so as to mislead you. For example, whether Ernie hopes or intends that Lola and Grover die is irrelevant as to whether Ernie committed a voluntary act or omission.

5.   Do not miss the small things. For example, it might seem that the analysis of Grover and Biff is the same because both create a peril to children via their involuntary acts. But there is a crucial difference that is easy to overlook. Grover was capable of rescuing the children from the oncoming car; Biff was not. As a result, only Grover violated any applicable duty to prevent the children from being hit.

6.   Organization is key. In a hypothetical with multiple perpetrators committing multiple crimes against multiple victims, it is easy to get confused and to miss key components of the analysis. To avoid this, pick one actor, and analyze his or her satisfaction of the act requirement before moving on to the next actor. There are a number of possible ways to decide with which actor to begin your analysis. For example, you might choose the actor who has committed the acts or omissions involving the most serious crime/s. Or, you might proceed chronologically, starting with the first actor who has possibly committed an act or omission and then proceed to the next one, and so on. The latter approach, as exemplified by the above Essay, is preferable for two reasons. First, the chronological ordering of

events is particularly important in the hypothetical. Second, each of the actors roughly committed equally serious crimes. Be flexible in choosing the organizational structure that best fits the hypothetical you are analyzing. What follows are three possible organizational structures. Structure 1 illustrates the organization of the above Essay that structures the essay primarily by actor. Alternatively, Structure 2 organizes the essay by the two different ways of satisfying the act requirement—by voluntary act and omission. One further alternative possibility, as depicted by Structure 3, is to organize primarily by legal approach—common law and MPC.

Structure #1	Structure #2	Structure #3
Introduction	Introduction	Introduction
Ernie	Voluntary Act	Common Law
Common Law	Ernie	Ernie
Model Penal Code	Common Law	Grover
Grover	Model Penal Code	Lola
Common Law	Grover	Biff
Model Penal Code	Common Law	Model Penal Code
Lola	Model Penal Code	Ernie
Common Law	Lola	Grover
Model Penal Code	Common Law	Lola
Biff	Model Penal Code	Biff
Common Law	Biff	Conclusion
Model Penal Code	Common Law	
Conclusion	Model Penal Code	
	Omission	
	Ernie	
	Common Law	
	Model Penal Code	
	Grover	
	Common Law	
	Model Penal Code	
	Lola	
	Common Law	
	Model Penal Code	
	Biff	
	Common Law	
	Model Penal Code	
	Conclusion	

7. The following steps reveal the progression of the above Essay's analysis of each actor's satisfaction of the act requirement. These steps are somewhat over-simplified so as to afford a better view of the forest without the obstruction of

the trees. But this should neither be mistaken for nor taken as a substitute for in-depth knowledge of the trees. Perhaps with some modification, these steps could be utilized in answering Variations on the Theme.

Voluntary Act

i. Did the actor commit an (affirmative) act?

ii. If no, go to OMISSION analysis below.

iii. If yes, is the act relevant to the offense charged?

iv. If no, then this act does not satisfy the act requirement. (Go back to step i., and analyze any other acts committed by the actor.)

v. If yes, is the act voluntary?

vi. If no, then this act does not satisfy the act requirement. (Go back to step i., and analyze any other acts committed by the actor.)

vii. If yes, is all of the actor's relevant conduct voluntary?

viii. If yes, then the actor satisfies the act requirement. Go to OMISSION analysis below.

ix. If no, is it a jurisdiction requiring that all of the relevant conduct be voluntary?

x. If yes, then the actor may still satisfy the act requirement by an omission. Go to OMISSION analysis below.

xi. If no, then is it a jurisdiction which requires that only the most important act (for the charged offense) be voluntary?

xii. If no, then go to xv.

xiii. If yes, is the actor's voluntary act the most important act?

xiv. If yes, then the actor satisfies the act requirement. Go to OMISSION analysis below.

xv. If no, then is it a jurisdiction that requires the actor's conduct include merely a single voluntary act?

xvi. If yes, then the actor satisfies the act requirement. Go to OMISSION analysis below.

xvii. If no, go to OMISSION analysis below.

Regardless of whether the actor satisfies the act requirement through his or her voluntary actions, proceed to the next stage of the act requirement analysis to determine whether the actor has committed an omission.

Omission

i. Did the actor have a duty to act? There are five possible bases under which an actor will have a duty to act:

   a. **Status Relationship:** does the actor share a special relationship with the victim (e.g., spouse to spouse or parent to minor child)?

   b. **Contractual Obligation:** is the actor obligated under a contract?

   c. **Statutory Duty:** is there a statute that imposes a duty to act?

   d. **Voluntary Assumption of Care & Seclusion:** did the actor voluntarily assume care of the victim and then either literally or constructively seclude the victim?

   e. **Creation of Peril:** by an affirmative act, did the actor create a peril for the victim?

ii. If yes, to any of the questions, a–d, then the actor has a duty to act. Go to vi.

iii. If no, what was the answer to e?

iv. If no, then the actor has no duty to act and thus no omission liability.

v. If yes, the actor may have a duty to act depending on the jurisdiction and depending on whether the act was criminal, innocent, justified, or involuntary. (If criminal, most likely to establish a duty; if innocent or justified, courts are split; if involuntary, least likely to establish a duty.)

vi. If the actor was under a duty to act, then did the actor fail to act when s/he was able to act?

vii. If no, then the actor did not violate the duty to act and has no omission liability.

viii. If yes, does the actor's violation of the duty satisfy the act requirement of the offense charged?

ix. If no, then the actor has no omission liability for that offense.

x. If yes, then the actor is eligible for omission liability for that offense.

8. Is it all of, one of, or the most important of the acts that must be voluntary? Jurisdictions and courts differ as to how much or what part of the actor's conduct must be voluntary to satisfy the act requirement.

9. In contrast to satisfying the act requirement via voluntary acts, a single failure to act when one is under a duty to act satisfies the requirement in all jurisdictions.

10. Keep in mind the concept of time-framing. First, time-framing is a description of what commentators believe courts are doing in analyzing the act requirement. It is not a formal approach that courts or jurisdictions would overtly and explicitly adopt. Second, typically but perhaps not invariably, the broader the time-frame utilized, the more likely a voluntary act will be found thereby satisfying the act requirement. The narrower the time-frame utilized, the less likely a voluntary act will be found. While detractors of courts' use of time-framing object that it is an impermissible manipulation of the act requirement, proponents argue that courts are using it in good faith to ensure a fair and just outcome.

11. For a duty to act to arise from creation of a peril, most likely only an affirmative act may create the peril. A failure to act that creates a peril does not suffice. (Otherwise, omission liability would be founded on a double failure to act.)

12. Keep in mind that with respect to omission liability arising from an actor's voluntary care and seclusion, there are three components that must be satisfied: (i) the actor must assume the care of the victim, (ii) that assumption of care must be voluntarily undertaken, **and** (iii) the actor must seclude the victim. This simplistic account, however, needs refinement. Consider *Beardsley* where the defendant and his nonspouse lover spent a weekend alone together at the defendant's house. While there, Beardsley's lover overdosed on morphine, and Beardsley failed to call a doctor. Although Beardsley was acquitted of omission liability because he had no duty to render aid to a nonspouse based on a status relationship, did Beardsley have a duty based on voluntary assumption of care and seclusion? While arguably Beardsley secluded the victim, the seclusion occurred *prior* to the victim's need for care and aid. Keep in mind that for a duty to arise under this basis for omission liability, the actor must seclude a victim that is *already* helpless or in need of aid.

13. With respect to omission liability arising from an actor's voluntary assumption of care and seclusion, be sure to consider constructive seclusion. The seclusion component may be satisfied without a literal seclusion of the victim. Constructive seclusion may suffice. Constructive seclusion occurs when an actor undertakes to aid the victim and, as a result, no one else renders aid. The actor has thus made the victim worse off by "secluding" the victim from receiving assistance from others. To illustrate constructive seclusion, compare the following two examples:

Example 1: A and B are sitting on the beach when C starts to drown. A informs B that A will rescue C and, based on that representation, B does nothing. A swims out to drowning C, decides on a whim not to render aid, and C drowns.

Analysis: A constructively secluded C without literally secluding C. Why? Because A's act of undertaking to save C prevented any action on B's part. A constructively or effectively secluded C from receiving assistance from B. A is eligible for omission liability for C's death.

Example 2: The same facts occur except that neither B nor anyone else was present.

Analysis: A's identical conduct would not result in omission liability because A would not have constructively secluded C by precluding assistance from others.

Perhaps the best test to use in determining whether such an actor has secluded the victim is to ask the following question: *By the actor's conduct or presence did the actor make the victim worse off?* If yes, then the actor may have secluded the victim. If no, the actor did not. (A's conduct made C worse off in Example 1, but not in Example 2.)

14. In some cases it will be difficult to determine whether the actor has committed an affirmative act or failed to act. Courts may construe an affirmative voluntary act as a failure to act and vice-versa. For example, in *Barber v. Superior Court*, 195 Cal. Rptr. 484 (1983), Barber, the victim's treating physician, removed the intravenous tubes that provided hydration and nourishment to the comatose victim, thus ending his life. The court construed the defendant's seemingly affirmative act of removing the life-sustaining tubes as a failure to act. Because the court found that the doctor did not have a legal duty to save the victim, the doctor's failure to act did not result in omission liability for the victim's death. And in *Fagan v. Commissioner of Metropolitan Police*, [1969] 1 Q.B. 439, a court did the converse. The court construed what was seemingly the failure to remove a car tire from on top of the victim's foot as an affirmative act.

But such instances of the conflation of the distinction between affirmative acts and failures to act are very limited, fact-specific, and should not be extended to a general rule. When the distinction is conflated, it is typically done so in the interest of fairness and justice.

15. Keep in mind the distinction between statutes imposing a *specific* duty to act or prevent harm and the so-called "Good Samaritan" statutes imposing a *general* duty to prevent harm or render aid. While the violation of either type of statute

may only be a comparatively minor crime or misdemeanor, the violation of the former type may serve as the basis for omission liability for a much more serious crime, such as murder. In contrast, the Good Samaritan statutes, which apply in only a very small number of jurisdictions, presumably cannot serve as the basis for omission liability for a much more serious offense.

VARIATIONS ON THE THEME

For the following variations, assume that all of the facts from the original hypothetical obtain except as noted.

1. While walking on the sidewalk, Little Granny is unlawfully attacked by Oscar who is trying to kill her. Little Granny's well-placed defensive kick causes Oscar to tumble into the street and into the path of Bert and Ernie's fast moving car. Oscar is hit and badly injured by the car. Little Granny declines to offer aid to Oscar, who eventually dies from his injuries.

2. One of the children is seriously injured but still alive after the car comes to a stop. Grover has his cell phone but instead of calling 911 he sends a text message to his mother to see if she would like him to get her a smoothie while he is out. The child dies due to lack of medical attention.

3. Elmo is out shopping and sees the accident. He sees that one of the children is injured but alive, so he rushes to help however he can. He carefully picks up the child and carries her onto the sidewalk. Deciding that it is too hot with the sun beating down, Elmo carries the child into the woods where there is considerable shade. Once they arrive in the woods, Elmo changes his mind and leaves the child in the woods without providing any aid. The child dies.

4. Patty Passerby sees that one of the children in the crosswalk is badly injured and rushes toward the child with the purpose of rendering aid. As a result of Patty's conduct, Paul Passerby decides not to aid and keeps walking. Before Patty reaches the child, she changes her mind and walks away. The injured child dies.

5. Victor Volunteer voluntarily goes to aid one of the injured children. Victor gets tired and stops. One second later, a doctor comes by and performs beneficial aid to the child, but the child dies.

6. Rather than Lola being Ernie's fiancée, she is his wife.

7. Sam Sleepwalker voluntarily decides to take an afternoon nap with the knowledge that he is prone to sleepwalking. Sleepwalker starts sleepwalking during his afternoon nap, gets into Bert and Ernie's car, where Ernie is in the passenger seat sleeping, and starts "sleep driving." As the car is moving, Ernie awakens, but Sleepwalker does not, and the car hits and kills Kenny.

For the following scenarios below, none of the facts in the Problem obtain:

8. Hal is driving back from an appointment with his cardiologist who has just informed him that he must immediately eliminate junk food, smoking, and drinking alcohol because he fears that Hal is dangerously close to a massive heart attack. Hal, a little bit angry about this news, drives straight to McDonald's, "supersizes" his value meal, pours a double shot of whiskey into his Coke, and heads home. Of course, he lights up a Marlboro to puff between bites of his Big Mac. Hal suffers a massive heart attack while driving and runs over Kenny.

9.   Kitty, who is terrified of bees, is driving along with her windows down without a care in the world. A bee flies into the car while Kitty is driving and stings her on the arm. As a result, Kitty loses control of the car and runs over Kenny.

10.   Homer, who has been driving for the last ten hours, is in a hurry to get home so he does not want to take the time to pull over and rest, despite how difficult it has become to keep his eyes open. Homer eventually falls asleep while driving. While Homer is asleep at the wheel, the car hits and kills Kenny.

ADDITIONAL READINGS

Leo Katz, Bad Acts and Guilty Minds: Conundrums of the Criminal Law 82–164 (1987)

Michael Moore, Act and Crime: The Philosophy of Action and Its Implications for the Criminal Law (1993)

Larry Alexander, *Criminal Liability for Omissions: An Inventory of Issues in Criminal Law Theory*, in Criminal Law Theory: Doctrines of the General Part 121 (Stephen Shute & A.P. Simester eds., 2002)

Andrew Ashworth, *The Scope of Criminal Liability for Omissions*, 105 Law Q. Rev. 424 (1989)

Michael Corrado, *Is There an Act Requirement in the Criminal Law?*, 142 U. Pa. L. Rev. 1529 (1994)

Deborah W. Denno, *Crime and Consciousness: Science and Involuntary Acts*, 87 Minn. L. Rev. 269 (2002)

Joshua Dressler, *Some Brief Thoughts (Mostly Negative) About "Bad Samaritan" Laws*, 40 Santa Clara L. Rev. 971 (2000)

George P. Fletcher, *On the Moral Irrelevance of Bodily Movements*, 142 U. Pa. L. Rev. 1443 (1994)

Douglas N. Husak, *Rethinking the Act Requirement*, 28 Cardozo L. Rev. 2437 (2007)

Douglas N. Husak & Brian P. McLaughlin, *Time-Frames, Voluntary Acts, and Strict Liability*, 12 Law & Phil. 95 (1993)

Ken Levy, *Killing, Letting Die, and the Case for Mildly Punishing Bad Samaritanism*, 44 Georgia L. Rev. 607 (2010)

MENS REA

2

INTRODUCTION

Criminal liability generally requires mens rea, that is, a guilty mind. Causing harm or committing wrongdoing unaccompanied by a culpable and blameworthy state of mind typically does not result in criminal liability. As the Supreme Court has loftily intoned, "[t]he contention that an injury can amount to a crime only when inflicted by intention is no provincial or transient notion. It is . . . universal and persistent in mature systems of law. . . ."[1] Strict liability, or the absence of mens rea, is widely condemned for almost all serious crimes. Rape and statutory rape are notable exceptions. However, these well-known exceptions serve to prove the rule because even these offenses require mens rea for some (but not all) of their elements.

Mens rea is required for a number of reasons. First, it ensures that an offender is sufficiently morally deserving of the stigma of a criminal conviction and punishment. Second, the deterrent function of punishment is inefficacious, absent an actor who realizes that her conduct is wrong. That is, the threat of punishment cannot deter people from accidentally committing crimes. Third, the various levels or types of mens rea, correlating with greater and lesser degrees of blameworthiness and severity of punishment, afford a fine-tuned calibration of an offender's culpability and matching punishment.

Terminological confusion has beset the development of mens rea throughout the history of the criminal law. There has been a bewildering variety of exotic types of mens rea, such as being "wicked," "malicious," or having a "depraved and malignant heart." And even seemingly simple terms, such as intent, seldom have the same meaning from jurisdiction to jurisdiction and even from case to case. For example, distinguishing between specific intent and general intent continues to bedevil courts, commentators, and students alike. Perhaps the MPC's most influential contribution has been to dramatically simplify and streamline the levels and types of mens rea to only four—purpose, knowledge, recklessness, and negligence. Notice that the MPC does not include the mental state of intention. To avoid the sometimes maddening multiplicity of meanings of intent, the MPC assigns two different mental states, purpose and knowledge, to capture the two core meanings of common law intention. Purpose approximately correlates with the narrow meaning of intent, and knowledge roughly correlates with the broad meaning of intent. Although the MPC mental states have been adopted in whole or in part in over 40 jurisdictions, non-MPC mental states such as intent, malice, and wilfulness persist.

---

[1] Morissette v. United States, 342 U.S. 246, 251 (1952).

The primary task in analyzing mens rea is identifying, recognizing, and distinguishing between the various types of mens rea. One must differentiate purpose versus intent versus knowledge, knowledge versus recklessness, and recklessness versus negligence. In addition, one must understand some special doctrines of mens rea. The doctrine of transferred intent sometimes allows the mens rea for a crime committed against one victim to transfer to another, unanticipated victim. The rule of conditional intent explains which conditions placed on an actor's intent negate the intent and which types of conditional intent suffice as the requisite intent. And the principle of wilful ignorance determines when an actor's avoidance of knowledge might nonetheless suffice for knowledge.

PROBLEM

Ordell, an illegal gun dealer, wants to drum up interest in a new high-powered assault rifle, with telescopic sight, that he is selling. He decides to give out samples to members of a criminal organization. He gives the guns to Beaumont, Brown, and Livingston, the three top lieutenants in the organization. The gun requires highly specialized and very expensive "full metal jacket" ammunition. Ordell truthfully tells all three that they are getting these guns mostly to get a feel for them, and that only one of the guns has ammunition.

Beaumont lives one mile away from Jackie, his hated enemy, and desires nothing more than to kill her. Jackie's neighborhood is quite festive at this time of year, with many carolers and Christmas shoppers walking about. Beaumont realizes that Jackie's annual Christmas party is tonight, and he has planted a time bomb inside her house. Although Beaumont is very sure that all 100 people in Jackie's house will die when the bomb detonates, he really only wants to kill Jackie and hopes that Jackie's 99 party guests will somehow survive.

Not willing to wait for the bomb to explode, Beaumont decides to give his new rifle a try. Knowing that he has very poor aim and believing very strongly that he will not succeed, Beaumont nonetheless decides to shoot at Jackie from his own balcony one mile away. After reading in his beloved *Soldier of Fortune* magazine that members of execution squads often do not know which one of the members' guns contain live ammunition, Beaumont decides that he also does not want to know whether his gun contains ammunition, so he does not look in the chamber. Believing that his gun does not contain ammunition (because, as the facts state above, only one of the three guns has ammunition), Beaumont takes aim and fires at Jackie. In fact, Beaumont's gun was loaded.

The bullet hits Jackie in the heart, passes through her, and lodges in the head of Melanie, a caroler in the street. Jackie and Melanie both die instantly from the gunshot wounds. Seconds later, the bomb detonates, killing all 99 of Jackie's party guests.

Analyze and discuss Beaumont's mens rea with respect to the deaths of Jackie, Melanie, and Jackie's 99 party guests under both the common law and the MPC.

LIST OF READINGS

United States v. Jewell, 532 F.2d 697 (9th Cir. 1976)
People v. Scott, 927 P.2d 288 (Cal. 1996)
MODEL PENAL CODE §2.02, 2.03(2)(a) (Official Code and Revised
    Comments 1985)

ESSAY

Because Beaumont desires to kill Jackie and only Jackie, the mens rea analysis with respect to Jackie will turn primarily on whether Beaumont acts with purpose (under the MPC) and intent (under the common law). The analysis with respect to the death of Melanie hinges on whether the doctrine of transferred intent applies. The mens rea analysis regarding the deaths of the 99 party guests will turn on the degree of Beaumont's certainty or awareness of risk to these victims.

Bombing of 99 Party Guests

COMMON LAW

[1] Intent is narrowly defined as the desire, purpose, or conscious object to cause the prohibited result or engage in the prohibited conduct. With respect to the conduct element of a homicide charge for the death of the 99 party guests, Beaumont clearly intentionally detonated the bomb. But with respect to the result element of causing their deaths, he did not desire the deaths of all 99. Moreover, the facts state that he hoped that somehow they would survive the bombing. Thus, Beaumont fails to satisfy the narrow meaning of intention with respect to the result element.

[2] Although Beaumont fails to satisfy the narrow meaning of intention with respect to the result element, he possibly satisfies the broad meaning of intention (or knowledge). An actor satisfies the broad meaning if he acts with the belief that the prohibited result, even if not desired, is virtually certain to occur. Beaumont is "very sure" that all 100 people in Jackie's house will die from the explosion of the bomb. Being "very sure" most likely suffices as being virtually certain that the prohibited result will occur. Thus, Beaumont satisfies the broad meaning of intention (or knowledge) with respect to the result element.

[3] Some common law courts and jurisdictions divide mens rea into specific intent and general intent. Although the distinction is ambiguous and has a number of different meanings, as it is used here, specific intent approximately correlates with purpose and the narrow meaning of intention. General intent approximately correlates with knowledge (or a lesser mental state) and the broad meaning of intention. Because Beaumont did not desire the deaths of the 99 guests, he lacked specific intent with respect to the element of the prohibited result. But because he was virtually certain that they would die, he does satisfy general intent. (In contrast, he did desire the death of Jackie. Had the bomb and not the bullet killed Jackie, Beaumont would have specific intent with respect to Jackie's death.)

MODEL PENAL CODE

[4] Purpose is defined as an actor's conscious object to engage in the conduct or to cause the prohibited result. With respect to the conduct element, Beaumont clearly had the conscious object to detonate the bomb. But with respect to the result element of causing the deaths of the 99 party guests, he did not have the conscious object of causing their deaths. He hopes that the 99 party guests survive. Thus, while Beaumont satisfies the mens rea of purpose for the conduct element, he fails to satisfy the mens rea of purpose for the result element. (In contrast, Beaumont did have the conscious object to cause Jackie's death. Had the bomb

and not the bullet killed Jackie, he would have the mens rea of purpose with respect to the result element of Jackie's death.)

[5] Although Beaumont fails to satisfy purpose with respect to the result element, he possibly satisfies the mens rea of knowledge. As pertaining to a result element, knowledge requires that the actor be practically certain that the prohibited result will occur. Beaumont is "very sure" that all 99 party guests will die from the bomb. His being very sure clearly establishes that he was practically certain. As a result, Beaumont satisfies the mens rea of knowledge with respect to the result element.

Shooting Death of Jackie
COMMON LAW

[6] Because Beaumont has the conscious object, desire, and purpose to shoot at and cause the death of Jackie, he most likely satisfies the narrow meaning of intention as discussed in [1] above.

[7] However, some possible obstacles to concluding that Beaumont intentionally killed Jackie remain. He was practically certain that he could not kill Jackie by firing his rifle. This raises the issue of whether one can intend to do that which one knows one cannot do. (Note that it is not merely the case that Beaumont lacks positive knowledge that he will succeed. Rather, he is practically certain, and thus knows, that he will not succeed.)

[8] Another possible obstacle concerns the distinction between intention and hope. Some courts have held that mere hopes do not rise to the level of intention. Arguably a person with very poor aim trying to kill another a mile away is hoping to kill rather than intending to kill. However, it is exceedingly difficult to distinguish precisely between hope and intention.

[9] Although it is somewhat unclear, courts would probably find that Beaumont did intentionally kill Jackie, despite the possible obstacles discussed above in [7]–[8].

[10] If, however, Beaumont fails to satisfy the narrow meaning of intent, the next step in the analysis considers whether he satisfies the broad meaning of intention (or knowledge). The broad meaning of intention (or knowledge) requires that the actor be virtually certain that the prohibited result will occur. Because of his poor aim, the target being a great distance away, and his strong belief that he will not kill Jackie, Beaumont clearly lacks virtual certainty. As a result, he fails to satisfy the broad meaning of intention (or knowledge). An additional factor further supports this conclusion—Beaumont believes that the gun is unloaded (making his ability to kill Jackie even more uncertain).

[11] Beaumont's belief that the gun is unloaded raises the issue of wilful ignorance. The wilful ignorance or wilful blindness doctrine establishes knowledge as to a material fact if the actor was deliberately ignorant or consciously avoided knowledge. He does not merely not know whether the gun is loaded; rather, he chooses not to know. By deliberately not looking to see if his gun was loaded, the wilful ignorance rule establishes that Beaumont had knowledge that his gun was loaded.

[12] Although Beaumont's knowledge that the gun is loaded is a necessary condition to establish the broad meaning of intention (or knowledge) with respect to Jackie's death, it is not sufficient. Despite knowing that the gun was loaded

(via the wilful ignorance rule), he is "very sure" that he will not succeed. His poor aim and the substantial distance between himself and the target make his failure likely and preclude his knowledge. Establishing his knowledge as to the fact that his gun was loaded does not by itself suffice to establish the broad meaning of intention (or knowledge) as to the prohibited result. As a result, Beaumont clearly fails to satisfy the broad meaning of intention (or knowledge) with respect to Jackie's death.

[13] Because Beaumont does not clearly satisfy either meaning of intention or knowledge, the next mens rea to consider is recklessness. Recklessness is defined as consciously disregarding a substantial and unjustifiable risk constituting a gross deviation from the standard of conduct of a reasonable person. As to the consciously disregarding a substantial risk component, Beaumont might argue that given his poor aim and his great distance away from Jackie, the risk to Jackie was insubstantial. Perhaps he might argue that it was a "one in a million" shot. This argument, however, will most likely be unsuccessful. The substantiality of the risk is not merely based on the probability, but also on the degree, of harm. Because shooting a high-powered assault rifle could cause serious harm, doing so most likely poses a substantial risk. And even if the risk were insufficiently substantial with respect to Jackie, it most likely was not insubstantial with respect to the many other persons near Jackie. As a result, Beaumont would most likely satisfy the mens rea of recklessness.

[14] If Beaumont does not satisfy recklessness only due to an insufficiently substantial risk, then he would also not satisfy the mens rea of negligence. The requirement of a substantial risk is equally required for negligence. However, as discussed above in [13], most likely the risk is sufficiently substantial. As a result, Beaumont would most likely satisfy the mens rea of negligence.

[15] Because Beaumont most likely shoots at and kills Jackie with intent (the narrow meaning), Beaumont most likely kills Jackie with specific intent. If he fails to satisfy the narrow meaning of intention, he most likely kills Jackie with recklessness. Killing Jackie recklessly would suffice as general intent under some meanings of the term.

MODEL PENAL CODE

[16] Because Beaumont's conscious object and desire is to kill Jackie, he most likely satisfies the mens rea of purpose under the MPC.

[17] As discussed above in [7], one possible obstacle to Beaumont satisfying the mens rea of purpose is that he was practically certain that he could not kill Jackie. That is, can one purposefully do that which one knows one cannot do?

[18] Under the MPC, one possible resolution of this issue is the rule that a higher level of mens rea suffices for a lower level. Because purpose is a higher level of mens rea than knowledge, satisfying purpose satisfies knowledge. (MPC §2.02(5)). This rule, however, may not clearly resolve the issue because it begs the question of whether Beaumont's lack of knowledge prevents his acting with purpose.

[19] The possible common law approach to this issue—treating Beaumont as having the nonculpable mental state of a mere hope (as discussed above in [8])—may be unavailable under the MPC. The MPC specifically uses the term hope in its very definition of acting purposefully. MPC §2.02(2)(a)(ii).

[20] If Beaumont lacks purpose, the next mens rea to consider is knowledge. As discussed above in [10]–[12], he lacks knowledge.

[21] As discussed above in [11]–[12], Beaumont's choice not to know whether the gun is loaded triggers the application of the MPC's correlate principle to the wilful ignorance doctrine. Under the MPC, knowledge of a particular fact "is established if a person is aware of a high probability of its existence, unless he actually believes that it does not exist." MPC 2.02(7). He realizes that there is a one-in-three probability that the gun is loaded, but he believes that the gun is not. Whether a one-in-three probability qualifies as the requisite "high" probability is unclear. Nonetheless, Beaumont would not satisfy the knowledge standard under the MPC because he actually believes that the gun is unloaded.

[22] If he lacks knowledge, the next mens rea to consider is recklessness. For the same reasons as discussed above in [13], Beaumont most likely satisfies the mens rea of recklessness.

[23] If he does not satisfy the mens rea of recklessness, the next mens rea to consider is negligence. For the same reasons as discussed above in [14], Beaumont most likely satisfies the mens rea of negligence.

Shooting Death of Melanie

COMMON LAW

[24] Though Beaumont did not kill Melanie with the narrow form of intent, Melanie's death does raise the issue of transferred intent. If he intentionally killed Jackie, then that same mens rea may transfer to Melanie's death as well. Under the common law doctrine of transferred intent, the intent with respect to the intended target may transfer to the actual target. In the paradigmatic example, when A intentionally shoots at B but misses and accidentally hits and kills C, A may be held liable for the intentional homicide of C. If, contrary to the actual facts, Beaumont had intentionally shot at Jackie but missed, and the bullet accidentally hit Melanie, his intent to kill Jackie would clearly transfer to his killing of Melanie. In contrast to the paradigmatic example of the application of the doctrine, here, Beaumont kills the intended target as well. There is a split among jurisdictions as to whether the transferred intent doctrine would apply here. Under one approach, the transferred intent doctrine does not apply under the theory that the actor's intent has been used up and cannot therefore be transferred. That is, Beaumont had the intent to kill just one person (Jackie) and by killing that one person, the intent is used up, and there is no intent left to transfer. Under this approach, he only had the intent to kill Jackie but not Melanie. Under the other approach, the intent, even if only to kill one person, is inexhaustible and can transfer to multiple victims. As a result, Beaumont intentionally killed both Jackie and Melanie.

[25] In a jurisdiction that does not transfer Beaumont's intent to the killing of Melanie, he may nonetheless satisfy a lesser mens rea. If he shot his gun with the virtual certainty that he would hit Melanie or some other passerby, Beaumont acted with knowledge or the broad meaning of intent. However, there is no evidence that he was virtually certain that his shot would hit and kill Melanie or anyone else. Therefore, Beaumont does not satisfy the mens rea of knowledge or the broad form of intent.

[26] Beaumont, however, most likely does satisfy recklessness. The analysis of his killing Jackie with recklessness (as discussed in [13] above) equally applies here.

One might argue that Beaumont was not reckless because he did not consciously disregard a risk to Melanie—he had no awareness of Melanie at all. Under this argument, he would only be negligent, which does not require that the actor consciously disregard or be aware of a risk. This argument, however, would most likely fail. In order to be reckless, one need only consciously disregard a risk to a person; one need not consciously disregard a risk to a specific person.

[27] If Beaumont does not satisfy recklessness only due to a lack of conscious awareness, then he would satisfy the mens rea of negligence.

[28] In a jurisdiction in which Beaumont's specific intent to kill Jackie transfers to his killing of Melanie, he would have specific intent with respect to Melanie's death. In a jurisdiction in which Beaumont's specific intent to kill Jackie does not transfer, he most likely kills Melanie with recklessness. Killing Melanie recklessly would suffice as general intent under some meanings of the term.

MODEL PENAL CODE

[29] Although not explicitly stated as such, in effect the MPC utilizes a version of the doctrine of transferred intent. The MPC states that purpose transfers if "the injury or harm designed or contemplated would have been more serious or more extensive than that caused." MPC 2.03(2)(a). Here, the injury Beaumont contemplated (the death of Jackie) is less serious than what he caused (the deaths of Jackie and Melanie). As a result, the mens rea of purpose with respect to Jackie's death does not transfer to Melanie's death.

[30] As discussed above in [10]–[12] and [20]–[21], Beaumont lacks the mens rea of knowledge.

[31] As discussed above in [13]–[14] and [22]–[23], Beaumont most likely satisfies the mens rea of both recklessness and negligence.

Conclusion

With respect to the deaths of the 99 party guests, under the common law, Beaumont clearly satisfies the broad form of intention (or knowledge). Under the MPC, he clearly satisfies the mens rea of knowledge. With respect to the death of Jackie, he most likely satisfies the narrow form of intention under the common law and purpose under the MPC. With respect to the death of Melanie, under the common law, depending on the jurisdiction, he most likely either satisfies the narrow form of intention or recklessness. Under the MPC, Beaumont most likely satisfies recklessness.

TOOLS FOR SELF-ASSESSMENT

Go back to your written answer. Look for the issues identified in paragraphs [1]–[31] in the above Essay. Look also for the analysis that follows each issue, and mark your essay where you locate it. Do you fully describe the issue, identify the precise legal standard that applies, list the relevant facts, and show how the facts and law support a conclusion for each issue in a separate paragraph? Mark each conclusion in your essay. Are there sufficient reasons in the law and in the facts to support the conclusion?

1. Do what you are told. Here, you are to analyze Beaumont's mens rea with respect to the deaths of Jackie, Melanie, and Jackie's 99 party guests.

2. Always analyze under the MPC unless you are instructed otherwise. This is especially true with respect to analyzing mens rea. Mens rea is perhaps the area of the MPC's greatest influence. Over 40 states have adopted in whole or in part the MPC provisions on mens rea.

3. State the best possible arguments for alternative conclusions. Even as you reject possible conclusions as to whether an actor satisfies a particular mental state, make the best possible argument first, and only then reject that possibility.

4. Organization is key. It is very easy to get confused because Beaumont has different mental states with regard to the different victims. He also has different mental states with regard to the different means employed to cause death. To avoid getting confused and to ensure that you do not inadvertently neglect to analyze the death of a victim and/or an additional cause of death, proper organization of your essay is crucially important. The above Essay is organized chronologically in order of the formations of Beaumont's mens rea with respect to the following: (i) detonating the bomb, (ii) shooting Jackie, and (iii) the unanticipated death of Melanie. This ordering also has the virtue of addressing what may be the easiest issue first and then progressing to the more complicated issues. But there is no one right way to organize this or any other essay. For example, you might organize your essay chronologically in order of the victims' deaths. Under that approach, you would first analyze Beaumont's mens rea with respect to Jackie, then Melanie, and then the 99 party guests.

5. Start at the top. In analyzing what mens rea, if any, an actor has, begin with the highest level of mens rea. This is helpful for a couple of reasons. First, under the MPC, a higher level of mens rea suffices for any lower level. But a lower level of mens rea does not suffice for a higher level. As a result, purpose suffices for knowledge, recklessness, and negligence. Negligence, however, suffices for neither recklessness, knowledge, nor purpose. Second, this approach will save you time. Once you determine the highest level of mens rea that an actor *clearly* satisfies, you may stop your analysis there.

6. The following steps reveal the above Essay's analysis of Beaumont's mens rea for the deaths of the various victims. These steps are somewhat oversimplified so as to afford a better view of the forest without the obstruction of the trees. But this should not be mistaken for, or taken as a substitute for, in-depth knowledge of the trees. Perhaps with some modification, these steps could be utilized in answering Variations on the Theme.

      i.   Has the actor possibly committed an offense that requires mens rea?
      ii. If no, then the actor may still be liable if the offense is one of strict liability.
      iii. If yes, was the actor's conscious object to engage in the conduct or to cause the result?
      iv. If yes, under the MPC, then the actor's mens rea is purpose.
      v.   If yes, under the common law, did the actor merely have a hope or wish?
            a. If no, then the actor's mens rea is intent.
            b. If yes, then the actor's mens rea is not intent. Go to x.

vi. If no to the question in iii, does the common law transferred intent rule or the MPC equivalent—§ 2.03(2)(a)—establish the actor's intent or purpose?

vii. If yes, then the actor satisfies the mens rea of intent or purpose.

viii. If no, under the MPC, then go to x.

ix. If no, under the common law, did the actor intentionally commit conduct with the virtual certainty that the prohibited result would occur?
    a. If yes, then the actor may satisfy intention (the broad meaning).
    b. If no, then go to x.

x. Was the actor aware of the nature of his or her conduct, or was the actor practically certain that his or her conduct would cause the prohibited result?

xi. If yes, then the actor's mens rea is knowledge under the MPC and common law.

xii. If no, under the common law, did the actor deliberately choose to avoid knowledge?
    a. If yes, then the actor satisfies knowledge under the wilful ignorance rule.
    b. If no, then the actor's mens rea is not knowledge. Go to xiv.

xiii. If no, under the MPC, was the actor aware of a high probability of the fact's existence?
    a. If no, then the actor does not have knowledge of the fact's existence. Go to xiv.
    b. If yes, did the actor actually believe that it does not exist?
    c. If no, then the actor has knowledge of the fact's existence.
    d. If yes, then the actor does not have knowledge of the fact's existence. Go to xiv.

xiv. Did the actor consciously disregard a substantial and unjustifiable risk that the material element exists or would result from his or her conduct?

xv. If yes, was the risk of such a degree that its disregard involves a gross deviation from the standard of conduct that a law-abiding person would observe in the actor's situation?

xvi. If yes, then the actor's mens rea is recklessness.

xvii. If no to either of the questions in xiv or xv, then should the actor have been aware of a substantial and unjustifiable risk that the material element exists or would result from his or her conduct?

xviii. If yes, was the actor's failure to perceive the risk a gross deviation from the standard of care that a reasonable person would observe in the actor's situation?

xix. If yes, the actor's mens rea is negligence.

xx. If no to either of the questions in xvii or xviii, then the actor may lack mens rea.

7. Distinguish specific intent offenses or elements from general intent offenses or elements under the common law. (The MPC does not utilize this distinction.) It is easy to get confused about this distinction because it has a variety of different meanings. Different courts and jurisdictions will use the distinction in different ways.

After explaining how to draw the distinction, the utility of the distinction will be explored.

There are three principal meanings of the distinction. First, when an offense specifically refers to a mens rea in the definition of the offense it is specific intent; when it does not, it is general intent. Historically, common law offenses typically did not specify a particular mens rea for the offense or its elements. Thus, most offenses were general intent. When an offense atypically did specify a mens rea, the offense was specific intent. For example, compare the offense of assault and battery with the offense of assault with an intent to kill. The offense of assault and battery, despite requiring that an actor intentionally strike the victim, is general intent. In contrast, the offense of assault with an intent to kill is specific intent because the offense specifies the type of mens rea for one of the elements. The actor not only must intentionally strike the victim but also must do so with the intent to kill her. The element of killing the victim specifies a particular mens rea—intent.

Second, under more modern law, specific intent is typically purpose, and general intent is typically any lesser mens rea, such as knowledge, recklessness, or negligence. In contrast to the historical approach, modern law more typically specifies the mens rea required for an offense and for elements of the offense. As a result, the test under the historical approach is no longer as applicable. The specification of mens rea is no longer a reliable guide that the offense or element is specific intent. Likewise, the absence of a specification of the mens rea required no longer ensures that the offense is general intent.

Third, two special categories of offenses or elements comprise specific intent; everything else is general intent. The first special category of specific intent offenses or elements is where a special purpose or motive is required beyond the mens rea required for committing the actus reus of the offense. Again, assault with an intent to kill is an example. Beyond the mens rea required for striking the victim, the actor must have the purpose or motive of killing the victim while the actor intentionally strikes the victim. Burglary is another example. Burglary is typically defined as breaking and entering into the dwelling or structure of another with the intent to commit a felony inside. Beyond the mens rea required for breaking and entering, the actor must have the purpose or motive of committing a felony inside while the actor effects the breaking and entering. The intent to commit the felony inside is a specific intent element. Larceny is yet another example. Larceny is traditionally defined as taking and carrying away the property of another with the intent to permanently deprive that person of it. The intent to permanently deprive is a specific intent element.

The second special category is an offense that requires knowledge or subjective awareness of a fact or circumstance element. For example, consider the offense of receipt of stolen property with the knowledge that the property is stolen. The element that the property is stolen is specific intent because it is a circumstance element that requires knowledge or subjective awareness. (Confusingly, the element of the receipt of the property might require intention but still be a general intent element. But the element that the property be stolen requires a lesser mens rea—knowledge—but is nonetheless considered a specific intent element.)

What is the utility of the distinction? There are two uses. First, and most importantly, the distinction is used to determine what sorts of mistakes of fact and law will be defenses to what sorts of mens rea. Any honest relevant mistake—reasonable or unreasonable—might be a defense to a specific intent offense or element. But only a reasonable mistake is eligible to be a defense to a general intent offense. (This will be further discussed in the next two chapters.) Second, understanding whether an offense or element is specific or general intent may aid in determining what particular mens rea or mental state must be established to render the actor eligible for liability.

8.   Distinguish among the various types of mens rea. Perhaps the most important aspect of both understanding mens rea and applying this understanding on an exam is the ability to distinguish between the different types. Purpose/intent (in the narrow form) involves a desire or conscious object to engage in the conduct or cause the prohibited result. In contrast, with knowledge or the broad form of intent, an actor may engage in the conduct or cause the prohibited result with indifference. The distinction between knowledge and recklessness is based on the actor's degree of certainty. Knowledge entails a higher degree of certainty—practical certainty or high probability—whereas recklessness merely involves the actor's awareness of a substantial risk. The distinction between recklessness and negligence hinges on whether the actor is aware or unaware of the risk. An actor's awareness of the risk is a feature of recklessness. If the actor is unaware (but should have been aware) of the risk, then the actor may qualify as negligent.

9.   Carefully distinguish the two different senses of intention (apart from specific and general intent) under the common law. The narrow meaning of intention is purpose; the broad meaning of intention is knowledge. As discussed in the above Essay, Beaumont desires to kill Jackie, hopes the other party guests somehow survive the bombing, but is very sure that the party guests will die. He satisfies the narrow meaning of intention with respect to Jackie. Because Beaumont knows that the other party guests will die, he satisfies the broad meaning of intention with respect to the deaths of the other party guests.

The MPC sought to avoid this confusion and ambiguity by eliminating the mental state of intention precisely because there are two (or more) meanings of intention. The MPC separated these meanings into two different mental states—purpose and knowledge.

10. Do not overapply the transferred intent doctrine. In addition to the limitations on the doctrine discussed in the above Essay, the doctrine is also limited to transferring intent only within the same type of attempted harm. For example, my intent to shoot an insect will not transfer to the shooting of a human being. And the attempt to commit one type of crime does not transfer to another type of crime. For example, my intent to shoot a human being will not transfer to the breaking of a window caused by my missed shot. In addition, the MPC bars the doctrine when the harm caused is more serious than designed or contemplated. MPC §2.02(3)(a).

11. Appreciate the distinction between the common law and MPC approaches to wilful ignorance. Under the MPC, knowledge of a particular fact "is established if a person is aware of a high probability of its existence, unless he actually believes that it does not exist." MPC §2.02(7). In contrast, under the common law wilful ignorance doctrine, knowledge is established by deliberately or consciously avoiding knowledge. The MPC requires subjective awareness of a high probability

that the fact obtains. In contrast, the common law may not require any awareness. Another difference is that, under the MPC, an actor's subjective belief that the fact does not obtain precludes an inference that the actor had knowledge. In contrast, under the common law, such a belief would not necessarily preclude an inference of knowledge. In sum, the MPC approach focuses on what the actor did or did not believe, and the common law focuses on what the actor did or failed to do that precluded specific knowledge.

12. Did you make the mistake of concluding that Beaumont caused the prohibited result with knowledge because of the common law's wilful ignorance doctrine? It is easy to assume that because the doctrine establishes that Beaumont had knowledge of a fact, the doctrine also establishes that he caused a prohibited result with knowledge. But this is incorrect. That Beaumont had knowledge, under the doctrine, that the gun was loaded, fails to establish that Beaumont was virtually certain that he would kill Jackie.

13. Recognize synonyms for mental states. In a hypothetical or exam question, various words will be used to describe what various actors are thinking, feeling, or trying to do. A hypothetical will rarely explicitly state that the actor committed some crime with purpose, negligence, etc. Rather, different words will be used to describe the actors' mental states. From these descriptions you must infer the actor's mens rea, if any. So, it is helpful to recognize and appreciate typical synonyms or descriptors that almost serve as proxies for mental states. For example, the Problem states that Beaumont is "very sure" that all 100 people in the house will die from the bomb. "[V]ery sure" serves as a synonym or proxy for the mens rea of knowledge. Other terms which may signal knowledge include high probability or certainty. That Beaumont "wants" and "desires" to kill Jackie serves as a synonym or proxy for purpose or intent. The terms goal and conscious object also may signal purpose or intent. Know and appreciate these synonyms and proxies; perhaps even underline these words in a hypothetical or exam question as you are reading it.

14. Look for conditional intent or purpose. Though the Problem did not include it, an actor's intent/purpose may often be subject to one or more conditions. The issue becomes whether the actor's conditional intent/purpose suffices as the requisite intent/purpose. The common law approach is not precisely articulated and may vary depending on the facts. Factors considered include the high or low probability of the condition arising and the intent of the drafters of the statute.

The MPC has a clearly articulated rule but one which is difficult to understand and apply. A conditional purpose does suffice as the requisite purpose "unless the condition negatives the harm or evil sought to be prevented by the law defining the offense." MPC § 2.02(6). In other words, conditional purpose suffices as actual purpose unless the nature of the condition suggests that the actor's conduct is not wrongful or harmful. Even when rephrased, the MPC test may still be difficult to understand and apply. If so, consider using the following alternative test that will most likely yield the same outcomes. Given an actor placing conditions on her purpose, ask yourself whether this is the conduct of a good or a bad person. If it is that of a good person, then the condition does negate the harm or evil of the offense, and the conditional purpose does *not* suffice for the requisite purpose. If instead this is the conduct of a bad person, then the condition does not negate the harm or evil of the offense, and the conditional purpose does suffice for the requisite purpose. Consider the following examples:

1) Beaumont conditions his desire to kill Jackie on the nonappearance of an even-more hated enemy than Jackie.
2) Beaumont conditions his desire to keep a $20 bill he finds outside his home on the condition that it turns out to be the $20 bill he lost a week ago.

In the first example, killing one enemy on the condition of the nonappearance of an even-more hated enemy is obviously not the conduct of a good person. Because this is the conduct of a bad person, the condition does not negate the harm or evil sought to be prohibited by the offense of homicide, and therefore the conditional purpose suffices as the requisite purpose. In the second example, however, purposefully keeping property on the condition that it turns out to be one's own property is the conduct of a good person. As a result, the condition does negate the harm or evil sought to be prevented by the offense of larceny or theft, and therefore the conditional purpose does not suffice as the requisite purpose.

VARIATIONS ON THE THEME
For the following variations, assume all of the facts from the original hypothetical obtain unless otherwise noted.

1.   Beaumont is aware that carolers are present on the street.
2.   Beaumont is unaware that carolers are present on the street.
3.   Jackie does not die from the gunshot wound.
4.   Beaumont's intent to kill Jackie is conditioned on Jackie not apologizing for a Christmas-related slight from years past.
5.   Rather than Beaumont being "very sure" that the bomb will kill all 99 guests, he believes that there is "some chance" that it will do so.
6.   Beaumont is unaware that the bomb could kill all 99 party guests.
7.   Beaumont does desire to kill all of the party guests.
8.   Beaumont does believe that the gun is loaded.
9.   Beaumont does believe that his marksmanship is good enough that he could hit Jackie from one mile away.
10. Beaumont is unaware that he has an assault rifle, and the jurisdiction contains the following statute:
    It shall be a felony to intentionally fire certain specified "assault rifles" inside the city limits.
11. Beaumont is unaware that he has an assault rifle, and the jurisdiction contains the following statute:
    It shall be a felony to fire an assault rifle.

ADDITIONAL READINGS
George Fletcher, Basic Concepts of Criminal Law 111–29 (1998)
Leo Katz, Bad Acts and Guilty Minds: Conundrums of the Criminal Law 165–209 (1987)

Larry Alexander & Kimberly Kessler Ferzan, *Against Negligence Liability, in* CRIMINAL LAW CONVERSATIONS 273–94 (Paul H. Robinson, Stephen P. Garvey & Kimberly Kessler Ferzan eds., 2009) (with comments by Leo Zaibert, Michelle Madden Dempsey, Alan Brudner, Stephen P. Garvey, Andrew E. Taslitz, and Kenneth W. Simons)

Anthony M. Dillof, *Transferred Intent: An Inquiry Into the Nature of Criminal Culpability*, 1 BUFF. CRIM. L. REV. 501 (1998)

Heidi M. Hurd, *The Deontology of Negligence*, 76 B.U. L. REV. 249 (1996)

Douglas N. Husak & Craig Callender, *Willful Ignorance, Knowledge, and the "Equal Culpability Thesis": A Study of the Deeper Significance of the Principle of Legality*, WIS. L. REV. 26 (1994)

Alan C. Michaels, *Acceptance: The Missing Mental State*, 71 S. CAL. L. REV. 953 (1998)

Paul H. Robinson & Jane A. Grall, *Element Analysis in Defining Criminal Liability: The Model Penal Code and Beyond*, 35 STAN. L. REV. 681 (1983)

Kenneth W. Simons, *Rethinking Mental States*, 72 B.U. L. REV. 463 (1992)

Kenneth W. Simons, *Should the Model Penal Code's Mens Rea Provisions Be Amended?*, 1 OHIO ST. CRIM. L.J. 179 (2003)

MISTAKE OF FACT

3

INTRODUCTION

The effect of an actor's mistake(s) on his or her criminal liability has long bedeviled courts and commentators alike. In part, this stems from the wide variety of mistakes an actor might make. The particular type of mistake that is the focus of this chapter is an exculpatory mistake of fact pertaining to one or more elements of an offense. Other types of mistake will be addressed in later chapters. Exculpatory mistakes of law will be covered in the next chapter, Chapter 4. Inculpatory mistakes of both fact and law are addressed in Chapter 16 on "Impossible Attempts." Both exculpatory and inculpatory mistakes pertain to elements of the offense. But other mistakes pertain to aspects of a defense—a justification or excuse—and are subject to different rules than those regarding offenses. Distinguishing mistakes from accidents and ignorance, as well as recognizing and identifying which type of mistake one is facing in a hypothetical or exam question that involves multiple mistakes of different types, will itself be the subject of Chapter 19, "Mistake Overview." But this more complicated analysis will come only after individual chapters have previously addressed each type of mistake in turn.

Mistakes of fact are relevant and important because they affect or negate at least one of the two senses of mens rea. Under the traditional common law, or culpability approach, mens rea is understood to be a sufficient degree of general blameworthiness or culpability. A mistake of fact exculpates to the extent that it makes the actor insufficiently culpable. Whether a mistake does so is a function of policy judgments and arbitrary rules. Under the MPC, or elemental approach, mistakes and mental states share a logical relationship. If a mistake negates the requisite mental state, the mistake will exculpate. If it does not negate the mental state, then it will not exculpate.

Under both the common law and the MPC, however, whether a mistake of fact provides a defense will depend on the relationship between the type of mistake and the requisite mens rea. In general, even an unreasonable mistake will provide a defense to an offense with an element requiring a high level of mens rea—specific intent under the common law, and purpose or knowledge under the MPC. But only a reasonable mistake will provide a defense, if at all, to an offense with an element requiring a lower level of mens rea—general intent under the common law and negligence under the MPC. And any mistake must be honest in order to supply a defense. But no mistake of fact will exculpate if it pertains to a strict liability element. This underscores the relationship between mistakes and mens rea: exculpatory mistakes of fact are only a defense to the extent that they establish that the defendant is insufficiently culpable or did not have the requisite mental state.

One of the more difficult aspects of mistakes of fact are the special rules—the Moral Wrong and Legal Wrong doctrines and the MPC's correlative doctrine—dealing with the effect of a mistake on the actor's liability where the actor would be guilty of some other offense, even under the facts as s/he believes them to be. This chapter will help you understand and master these and other puzzling features of the law of mistake of fact.

PROBLEM

Ms. Alabama Drexel, who mistakenly believes that she has only been a drug dealer for three days (in fact, it has been four days), is on an errand one night to buy some cleaning supplies requested by her new husband, Floyd. On the way back, Alabama stops by what she unreasonably and mistakenly, but honestly, believes is Floyd's bachelor apartment (and thus now her apartment as well because of her marriage to Floyd) to retrieve his suitcase full of clothes and steal the package of drugs belonging to Blue Lou Blitzer that Blue Lou entrusted to Floyd. Finding that the key does not work, she momentarily wonders whether this is the correct apartment but decides that it must be and decides to pick the lock. All she finds inside the apartment is what she unreasonably and mistakenly, but honestly, believes is Floyd's suitcase. Alabama takes the suitcase back to Floyd. Upon seeing and opening the suitcase, Floyd declares that neither the suitcase nor its contents—a number of baggies with twistix ties containing white powder—are his. Floyd confidently identifies some of the baggies as containing Panda heroin from Germany, some containing Bahba heroin from Mexico, and some containing Chohko heroin from the Hartz Mountains. But believing that she knows better, Alabama identifies all of the bags as containing baby powder that is slightly past its expiration date. Deciding to sell the powder-filled baggies, they agree that Alabama should take somewhat more than a kilo and Floyd somewhat less than a kilo. Alabama decides to try to pass off her entire amount of white powder as cocaine in one big sale to the famed movie producer Clarence Donowitz. Alabama and Floyd are each honestly mistaken as to the identity of the powder—it is actually cocaine.[1] The jurisdiction includes the following offenses:

1. Possession of a kilo or more of cocaine with the intent to distribute cocaine within 100 meters of a school
2. Possession of cocaine with the intent to distribute cocaine
3. Possession of less than a kilo of heroin
4. Possession of more than a kilo of cocaine
5. Possession of less than a kilo of cocaine
6. Possession of a controlled substance (e.g., heroin, cocaine, marijuana, etc.) with the intent to distribute a controlled substance
7. Burglary: Breaking and entering the dwelling of another with the intent to commit a felony inside
8. Larceny: The taking and carrying away of the property of another with the intent to permanently deprive the person of the property

---

[1] Aspects of the Problem are inspired by the film, TRUE ROMANCE (Warner Bothers 1993).

Analyze and discuss how the various mistakes affect the criminal liability, if any, of Alabama and Floyd for the above offenses under both the common law and MPC. The offenses above do not necessarily specify all the applicable mens rea for each element of the offenses. To the extent to which the statute fails to indicate the requisite mens rea for an element, analyze the effect of the mistakes, if any, on all possible mens rea. (That is, do not apply the MPC provisions on statutory construction—§ 2.02(3)–(4).)

LIST OF READINGS

MODEL PENAL CODE §§ 2.02, 2.04(1)–(2) (Official Code and Revised
    Comments 1985)
State v. Sexton, 733 A.2d 1125 (N.J. 1999)
Regina v. Prince, L.R. 2 Cr. Cas. Res. 154 (1875)

ESSAY

Under the common law and MPC, Alabama is not liable for larceny, but she may be liable for burglary and some of the drug offenses. Under the common law and MPC, Floyd may be liable for some of the drug offenses. Under the MPC, however, Floyd will be subject to punishment for at least one drug charge.

Alabama's Burglary

[1] The mistake relevant to Alabama's possible liability for burglary pertains to whose dwelling she has broken into and entered. She honestly but unreasonably believes that it is her and Floyd's apartment, but it is not. In order to determine whether this mistake will exculpate Alabama, the mens rea of the particular element of the offense of burglary to which the mistake pertains must be considered. The mistake does not pertain to the elements of breaking and entering or committing a felony inside. Rather, the mistake pertains to the element of dwelling of another.

COMMON LAW

[2] Because the mens rea for the element of dwelling of another is unknown, the mistake will be assessed under all the possibilities under the common law. If the element requires specific intent, then any relevant honest mistake—reasonable or unreasonable—will exculpate. Alabama's honest and unreasonable mistake thereby provides a defense.

[3] If the element requires general intent, then only an honest and reasonable mistake is eligible to provide a defense. If the mistake is honest and reasonable, courts will apply one of the following approaches: (i) an honest and reasonable mistake exculpates; (ii) the moral wrong doctrine, which considers whether the actor's conduct is immoral under the facts as s/he believed them to be; or (iii) the legal wrong doctrine, which considers whether the actor's conduct is criminal under the facts as s/he believed them to be. If an actor's mistake is either dishonest or unreasonable, the mistake does not provide a defense. Because Alabama's mistake is unreasonable, her mistake will not provide a defense.

[4] If the element is one of strict liability, no mistake of fact will exculpate. Alabama's mistake thus does not provide a defense.

MODEL PENAL CODE

[5] Under the MPC, an honest mistake will provide a defense if the mistake negates the requisite mens rea. Whether such a mistake will negate the requisite mens rea depends on the particular mens rea and the type of mistake. If the requisite mens rea is purpose or knowledge, then any honest relevant mistake—reasonable or unreasonable—may negate it. A mens rea of recklessness is only negated by such a mistake that is either reasonable or negligent. If the mens rea is negligence, then such a mistake must be reasonable.

[6] If the element of dwelling of another requires purpose or knowledge, then Alabama's honest and unreasonable mistake would negate either mens rea. Alabama cannot break and enter with the purpose or knowledge that the dwelling is of another if she believes that it is her own (because it is Floyd's) dwelling.

[7] If the element requires recklessness, then Alabama's unreasonable mistake will not negate the mens rea unless the mistake is negligent. Because Alabama briefly wondered whether she might have the wrong apartment and then disregarded that possibility, her unreasonable mistake is reckless and not negligent. As a result, Alabama's mistake does not negate the mens rea of recklessness.

[8] If the element requires negligence, then Alabama's unreasonable mistake will not negate the mens rea.

[9] With very few exceptions, the MPC does not include strict liability offenses (and burglary is not one of the exceptions). In any event, if the element of dwelling of another requires strict liability, then Alabama's mistake would not negate it.

[10] Even when an actor's mistake negates a requisite mens rea, that mistake does not completely relieve an actor of liability if the mistaken actor would still be committing a crime under the facts as s/he believes them to be. In such a case, the actor may only be punished for the offense "of which he would be guilty had the situation been as he supposed." MPC § 2.04(2). (Because this provision only applies where an actor's mistake otherwise negates the requisite mens rea, this provision would only apply here if the mens rea for the element of dwelling of another is purpose or knowledge. Only these two mental states are negated by Alabama's unreasonable mistake, as discussed in [6].) Under the facts as Alabama believes them to be, one might argue, she is lawfully entering her own dwelling, which is not a crime. If so, the provision does not impose any liability on Alabama. However, under a more complete description of the facts as Alabama believes them to be, perhaps she would be committing a crime. She believes that she is lawfully entering her own property with the intent of committing a felony inside—theft of the drugs. This possibly constitutes attempted theft. If so, then her mistake precludes liability for burglary, but she would be subject to punishment for some type of attempted theft.

CONCLUSION

Under the common law, Alabama's mistake as to the identity of the dwelling provides a defense if the element requires specific intent but does not provide one if the element requires general intent or strict liability. Under the MPC, the mistake is a defense if the element requires purpose or knowledge but does not provide one if the element requires recklessness, negligence, or strict liability. (However, she may be liable for another crime—some form of attempted theft.)

Alabama's Larceny

[11] The mistake relevant to Alabama's possible liability for larceny pertains to the identity of the owner of the property that she has taken. She honestly but unreasonably believes that the suitcase is Floyd's (and thus via marriage, her suitcase as well). In order to determine whether this mistake will exculpate, the mens rea of the particular element(s) of the offense of larceny to which the mistake pertains must be considered. The mistake does not pertain to the elements of (i) taking and (ii) carrying away. Rather, the mistake pertains to the elements of (iii) property of another and (iv) permanently depriving that person of their property. (If Alabama mistakenly believes that the property—the suitcase—is Floyd's (and thus her property), that will be relevant in assessing whether she had the mens rea to permanently deprive another of his or her suitcase.)

COMMON LAW

[12] As the larceny statute indicates by express language, the element of permanent deprivation of another's property requires specific intent. As discussed above in [2], Alabama's honest and unreasonable mistake regarding the identity of the owner of the suitcase will be a defense to an offense with a specific intent element to which the mistake pertains. Alabama cannot have the specific intent to permanently deprive another of his or her property when she believes that it is her property.

[13] The larceny statute does not indicate whether element (iii) requires specific intent, general intent, or strict liability. But an analysis of the effect of Alabama's mistake on this element is unnecessary because Alabama's mistake clearly provides a defense to larceny with respect to element (iv).

MODEL PENAL CODE

[14] Analyzing the larceny offense under MPC principles is somewhat problematic because the MPC does not include the mens rea of intent, as the statute specifies for element (iv) but rather uses the mens rea of purpose and knowledge to capture the various meanings of common law intent. The common law mens rea of specific intent required by element (iv) would most closely correlate with purpose under the MPC. In any event, as discussed in [5] and [6], Alabama's honest and unreasonable mistake would negate purpose as well as knowledge. Alabama's belief that she is taking her own property negates a purposeful or knowing permanent deprivation of another's property.

[15] Analysis of the effect of Alabama's mistake regarding element (iii) under the MPC is unnecessary because the effect of the mistake regarding element (iv) clearly provides a defense to larceny.

[16] As discussed in [10], consideration must still be given to whether Alabama is committing a crime under the facts as she believes them to be. Under the facts as Alabama believes them to be, she is taking her own property. Taking one's own property is not a crime. On this basis, then, the MPC's doctrine embodied in § 2.04(2) does not support criminal liability for Alabama under the facts as she believes them to be. One might argue, however, that she intended to take Blue Lou's property and ultimately did take what was perhaps Blue Lou's property. Nonetheless, at the time she did take the property, she believed that she was

taking her own property. As a result, under the facts as Alabama believed them to be, she was not committing a crime, and § 2.04(2) does not provide a basis for holding Alabama criminally liable.

CONCLUSION

Under the common law, Alabama's honest and unreasonable mistake provides a defense to larceny because the element of permanent deprivation requires specific intent. Under the MPC, Alabama's mistake also provides a defense by negating the purpose (as well as knowledge) required by the element.

Alabama's Drug Liability

[17] A number of drug-related offenses may be excluded from the analysis. Because she possesses more than a kilo of cocaine, offenses 3 and 5 are eliminated. And since there is no evidence that she is distributing or has the intent to distribute within 100 meters of a school, offense 1 is eliminated. This leaves offenses 2, 4, and 6 to consider.

[18] The mistake relevant to Alabama's possible liability for the various drug offenses pertains to the type of white powder she possesses. She believes that the white powder is expired baby powder, but it is cocaine. The facts fail to state whether the mistake is reasonable or unreasonable. In order to determine whether this mistake will exculpate, the mens rea of the particular element(s) of the drug offenses to which the mistake pertains must be considered. The mistake pertains to the possession elements of 2, 4, and 6 as well as the intent to distribute elements of 2 and 6. (Because Alabama mistakenly believes that the powder is baby powder, the mistake will be relevant in assessing whether she had the mens rea to distribute cocaine or a controlled substance.)

COMMON LAW

[19] As offenses 2 and 6 indicate by their express language, the element of distribution requires specific intent under the common law. (See [12].) As discussed above in [2], Alabama's honest mistake—whether reasonable or unreasonable—will be a defense to an offense with a specific intent element to which the mistake pertains. Alabama has the specific intent to distribute neither cocaine nor a controlled substance when she believes that she is distributing baby powder. Alabama's mistake regarding the type of powder will be a defense to offenses 2 and 6.

[20] Offense 4 fails to indicate whether the possession element requires specific intent, general intent, or strict liability. If it requires specific intent, then Alabama's mistake will be a defense.

[21] If the possession element requires general intent, whether the mistake will provide a defense depends, in part, on whether the mistake is reasonable or unreasonable. The facts neither state nor allow an inference as to whether Alabama's mistake is reasonable or unreasonable. If her mistake is unreasonable, it will not provide a defense. If it is reasonable, then the mistake may provide one. Where the mistake is reasonable, courts take one of three possible approaches, as discussed in [3].

[22] Under the first approach, Alabama's honest mistake, if reasonable, would be a defense.

[23] Under the second approach, the moral wrong doctrine, Alabama's mistake only provides a defense if, under the facts as she believes them to be, she is not committing a moral wrong. Under the facts as she believes them to be, Alabama possesses baby powder that has passed its expiration date and that she plans to distribute as cocaine. Is that morally wrongful conduct? Although what conduct is morally wrong may engender considerably more disagreement than what conduct is unlawful, intending to distribute baby powder—whether expired or not—as cocaine is fraudulent and thus perhaps morally wrongful. On this basis, then, Alabama's mistake would not provide a defense.

Alabama, however, might argue that the moral wrong doctrine assesses whether what she did was morally wrong, not whether her thoughts were morally wrong. Had she completed the sale or attempted the sale, her conduct would surely be morally wrongful. But merely having the intent to defraud might well be morally wrongful thoughts, but it is not morally wrongful conduct. The possession of the powder is conduct, but possession of powder believed to be baby powder (even if believed to be past its expiration date) is not morally wrongful conduct. On this basis, then, Alabama's mistake does constitute a defense. Probably the best interpretation of the moral wrong doctrine is that it assesses conduct and not mere thoughts. Thus, Alabama's mistake probably does provide a defense.

[24] Under the third approach, the legal wrong doctrine, Alabama's mistake provides a defense only if under the facts as she believes them to be, her conduct does not constitute a crime. Possessing a lawful substance with the intent to fraudulently distribute it as an unlawful substance most likely does not constitute a crime. Had she completed the sale or attempted the sale, her conduct would surely be criminal as fraud under the facts as she believed them to be. But her mere intent to defraud fails to constitute a crime. As a result, Alabama's mistake would provide a defense in a jurisdiction employing the legal wrong doctrine.

[25] If the possession element requires strict liability, then the mistake will not provide a defense, regardless of whether the mistake is reasonable or unreasonable. (See [4].)

MODEL PENAL CODE

[26] The distribution element of drug offenses 2 and 6 requires specific intent and would be treated as purpose (or possibly knowledge) under the MPC, as discussed in [14]. Alabama's honest mistake—whether reasonable or unreasonable—as to the type of powder that she plans to distribute would negate purpose and knowledge. Alabama's belief that she possesses baby powder negates her purposeful or knowing distribution of cocaine or an illegal drug.

[27] Offense 4 fails to indicate the requisite mens rea for the possession element. If the possession element requires purpose or knowledge, then Alabama's honest mistake—whether reasonable or unreasonable—negates it.

[28] If the element requires recklessness, then whether Alabama's mistake negates that mens rea depends, in part, on whether the mistake is reasonable or unreasonable. If the mistake is reasonable, then the mistake negates recklessness. If the mistake is unreasonable, it will only negate recklessness if the mistake is negligent. Because the facts do not provide any evidence that Alabama was aware that the powder might be cocaine or a controlled substance, Alabama's mistake

was not reckless and thus, if unreasonable, it would be negligent. As a result, Alabama's mistake would negate the mens rea of recklessness.

[29] If the element requires negligence, then whether Alabama's mistake negates that mens rea depends on whether the mistake is reasonable or unreasonable. If the mistake is reasonable, then the mistake negates negligence. If the mistake is unreasonable, then the mistake will not negate negligence.

[30] With very few exceptions, the MPC does not include strict liability offenses (and possession offenses are not among the exceptions). In any event, if the possession element requires strict liability, then Alabama's mistake would not negate it.

[31] As discussed in [10], consideration must still be given to whether Alabama is committing a crime under the facts as she believes them to be. Alabama believes that she possesses more than a kilo of baby powder slightly past its expiration date that she plans to distribute as cocaine. Possessing baby powder past its expiration date with a plan of distributing it is not a crime as discussed in [24]. On this basis, then, the MPC's § 2.04(2) doctrine does not support criminal liability for Alabama under the facts as she believes them to be.

CONCLUSION

Under the common law, Alabama's mistake—whether reasonable or unreasonable—is a defense to offenses 2 and 6. If the possession element of offense 4 requires specific intent, Alabama's mistake—whether reasonable or unreasonable—provides a defense. If the element requires general intent, Alabama's mistake will only provide a defense if it is reasonable. If the element requires strict liability, the mistake will not provide a defense, regardless of whether it is reasonable or unreasonable. Under the MPC, Alabama's mistake—whether reasonable or unreasonable—is a defense to offenses 2 and 6. If the possession element of offense 4 requires purpose, knowledge, or recklessness, then Alabama's mistake—whether reasonable or unreasonable—provides a defense. If the element requires negligence, then Alabama's mistake will provide a defense only if it is reasonable. If possession is a strict liability element (though unlikely under MPC principles), then the mistake would not provide a defense, regardless of whether the mistake was reasonable or unreasonable.

Floyd's Drug Liability

[32] A number of offenses may be excluded from the analysis. Because he possesses less than a kilo of cocaine, offenses 1 and 4 are eliminated. Offense 3 is eliminated because he actually possesses cocaine. And offenses 7 and 8 are inapplicable. This leaves offenses 2, 5, and 6 to consider.

[33] The mistake relevant to Floyd's possible liability for the various drug offenses pertains to the type of white powder that he possesses. He believes that the white powder is heroin, but rather it is cocaine. The facts fail to state whether his mistake is reasonable or unreasonable.

[34] Regardless of the type of mistake, Floyd's mistake will not provide a defense to offense 6. Floyd believes that he possesses heroin, which is a controlled substance, but he actually possesses cocaine, which is also a controlled substance. As a result, despite being mistaken about the type of powder that he possesses, Floyd is not mistaken that he possesses a controlled substance. Floyd's mistake—even if honest and reasonable—does not provide a defense to offense 6.

[35] In order to determine whether Floyd's mistake provides a defense for offenses 2 and 5, the mens rea of the particular element(s) of the drug offenses to which the mistake pertains must be considered. The mistake pertains to the possession elements of 2 and 5, as well as the distribution element of 2. (Because Floyd mistakenly believes that the powder is heroin, the mistake will be relevant in assessing whether he had the mens rea to distribute cocaine.)

COMMON LAW

[36] As offense 2 indicates by its express language, the element of distribution requires specific intent under the common law. As discussed above in [2], Floyd's honest mistake—whether reasonable or unreasonable—will be a defense to an offense with a specific intent element to which the mistake pertains. Floyd lacks the specific intent to distribute cocaine because he believes that he would be distributing heroin. Floyd's mistake regarding the type of powder will be a defense to offense 2.

[37] Offense 5 fails to indicate whether the possession element requires specific intent, general intent, or strict liability. If it requires specific intent, then Floyd's mistake will be a defense.

[38] If the possession element requires general intent, whether the mistake will provide a defense depends, in part, on whether the mistake is reasonable or unreasonable. The facts neither state nor allow an inference as to whether Floyd's mistake is reasonable or unreasonable. If his mistake is unreasonable, it will not provide a defense. If it is reasonable, then the mistake may provide a defense. Where the mistake is reasonable, courts take one of three possible approaches, as discussed in [3].

[39] Under the first approach, Floyd's honest mistake, if reasonable, would be a defense.

[40] Under the second approach, the moral wrong doctrine, Floyd's mistake only provides a defense if under the facts as he believes them to be he is not committing a moral wrong. Under the facts as he believes them to be, Floyd possesses heroin that he plans to distribute. Is that morally wrongful conduct? Although what conduct is morally wrong may be less clear than what conduct is unlawful, possessing heroin with the plan to distribute it will most likely be viewed as morally wrongful conduct. On this basis, Floyd's mistake would not provide a defense.

[41] Under the third approach, the legal wrong doctrine, Floyd's mistake provides a defense only if under the facts as he believes them to be, his conduct does not constitute a crime. Possessing heroin with the plan to distribute it clearly constitutes a crime. (See offenses 3 and 6.) As a result, Floyd's mistake would not provide a defense in a jurisdiction employing the legal wrong doctrine.

[42] If the possession element requires strict liability, then the mistake will not provide a defense, regardless of whether the mistake is reasonable or unreasonable.

MODEL PENAL CODE

[43] As discussed in [26], an honest mistake—whether reasonable or unreasonable—as to the type of powder would negate the mens rea of purpose as well as knowledge required by the distribution element of offense 2 under the MPC.

Floyd's belief that the substance that he plans to distribute is heroin would negate a purpose to distribute, or knowledge that he would be distributing, cocaine.

[44] Offense 5 fails to indicate the requisite mens rea for the possession element. If the possession element requires purpose or knowledge, then Floyd's honest mistake—whether reasonable or unreasonable—negates it.

[45] If the element requires recklessness, then whether Floyd's mistake negates that mens rea depends, in part, on whether the mistake is reasonable or unreasonable. If the mistake is reasonable, then it negates recklessness. If the mistake is unreasonable, it will only negate recklessness if it is negligent. Because the facts do not provide any evidence that Floyd was aware that the powder might be cocaine, Floyd's mistake was not reckless and thus, if unreasonable, would be negligent. As a result, Floyd's mistake would negate the mens rea of recklessness.

[46] If the element requires negligence, then whether Floyd's mistake negates that mens rea depends on whether the mistake is reasonable or unreasonable. If the mistake is reasonable, then the mistake negates negligence. If the mistake is unreasonable, then the mistake will not negate negligence.

[47] With very few exceptions, the MPC does not include strict liability offenses (and possession offenses are not among the exceptions). In any event, if the possession element requires strict liability, then Floyd's mistake would not negate it.

[48] As discussed in [10], consideration must still be given to whether Floyd is committing a crime under the facts as he believes them to be. Floyd believes that he possesses less than a kilo of heroin that he plans to distribute. Possessing heroin with a plan of distributing it is clearly a crime as discussed in [41]. On this basis, to the extent that Floyd's mistake provides a defense to either offense 2 or 5, the MPC's § 2.04(2) doctrine would support punishment of Floyd for offense 3.

CONCLUSION

Under the common law, Floyd's mistake—whether reasonable or unreasonable—is a defense to offense 2. If the possession element of offense 5 requires specific intent, Floyd's mistake—whether reasonable or unreasonable—provides a defense. If the element requires general intent, Floyd's mistake will not provide a defense if it is unreasonable. If it is reasonable, Floyd's mistake may provide a defense, depending on the approach that a court adopts. Under the first approach, requiring an honest and reasonable mistake, Floyd would have a defense. Under the second and third approaches, employing the moral wrong and legal wrong doctrines, respectively, Floyd's mistake would not provide a defense. If the element requires strict liability, the mistake will not provide a defense, regardless of whether it is reasonable or unreasonable.

Under the MPC, Floyd's mistake—whether reasonable or unreasonable—is a defense to offense 2. If the possession element of offense 5 requires purpose, knowledge, or recklessness, then Floyd's mistake—whether reasonable or unreasonable—provides a defense. If the element requires negligence, then Floyd's mistake will provide a defense only if it is reasonable. If possession is a strict liability element (though unlikely under MPC principles), then the mistake would not provide a defense, regardless of whether the mistake was reasonable or unreasonable. To the extent that Floyd's mistake provides a defense to either offense 2 or 5, Floyd would nonetheless be subject to punishment for offense 3.

Conclusion

Alabama's Burglary: Under the common law and MPC, Alabama's mistake provides a defense depending on the requisite mens rea for the element of dwelling of another.

Alabama's Larceny: Under the common law and MPC, Alabama's mistake pertaining to the element of permanent deprivation of another's property supplies a defense to larceny.

Alabama's Drug Liability: Under the common law and MPC, Alabama's mistake as to the nature of the white powder is a defense to offenses 2 and 6. The mistake is a defense to offense 4, depending both on the requisite mens rea for the possession element and the nature of the mistake.

Floyd's Drug Liability: Under the common law and MPC, Floyd's mistake as to the nature of the white powder is a defense to offense 2. Under the common law and MPC, the mistake is a defense to offense 5 depending both on the requisite mens rea for the possession element and the nature of the mistake. Under the MPC, however, even if the mistake is a defense to offense 5, Floyd would nonetheless be subject to punishment for offense 3.

TOOLS FOR SELF-ASSESSMENT

Go back to your written answer. Look for the issues identified in paragraphs [1]–[48] in the above Essay. Look also for the analysis that follows each issue, and mark your essay where you locate it. Do you fully describe the issue, identify the precise legal standard that applies, list the relevant facts, and show how the facts and law support a conclusion for each issue in a separate paragraph? Mark each conclusion in your essay. Are there sufficient reasons in the law and in the facts to support the conclusion?

1.   Do what you are told. Here you are to analyze the effects of Alabama's and Floyd's mistakes on each actor's criminal liability, if any, for the listed offenses.

2.   State the best possible arguments for alternative conclusions. Even as you reject possible conclusions as to whether an actor's mistake will provide a defense or negate her mens rea make the best possible argument first and only then reject that possibility.

3.   Always analyze under the MPC unless you are instructed otherwise.

4.   Be on the alert for red herrings. Some information in the fact pattern of a hypothetical is irrelevant or even included to mislead you or to throw you off track. For example, the amount of time Alabama has been a drug dealer is irrelevant as to whether any of her mistakes will provide a defense.

5.   Organization is key. In a hypothetical containing numerous offenses and actors, each making numerous mistakes pertaining to different elements in each offense, it is very easy to become confused and/or overlook all or part of an analysis. The above Essay addresses the various crimes committed in the chronological order in which they were committed in the Problem. The analysis of the effect of the actor's mistake or mistakes on the actor's liability for each crime is analyzed first under the common law and then the MPC. But rather than analyzing each drug offense independently, the drug offenses possibly committed by each actor are analyzed collectively because each actor makes only one mistake pertaining to the drug offenses—the nature of the white powder.

Alternatively, one might organize the essay by first analyzing all of the offenses under the common law and then all of the offenses under the MPC. The disadvantage of this approach is that similarities between the common law and MPC are obscured.

6.   What follows is a step-by-step process by which the above Problem and most any mistake of fact problem can be analyzed. This transparently reveals each step in the chain of reasoning in analyzing an actor's mistake of fact.

   i.   Identify each offense the actor possibly committed.
   ii.   Identify each exculpatory (as opposed to inculpatory) honest mistake of fact the actor committed regarding an offense.
   iii.   Determine to which element(s) of the offense each mistake pertains.
   iv.   Determine the requisite mens rea, if any, for that element or elements.
   v.   Determine whether each mistake is relevant. A mistake may be irrelevant in any of the three following ways:
     a. It does not affect the actor's culpability or mens rea for that element (see Tool #13 below).
     b. The mistake regards a jurisdictional element (see Tool #14 below).
     c. The mistake regards a strict liability element.
   vi.   Analyze each relevant mistake's effect on the actor's culpability or mens rea under common law principles and the MPC as set below:

> **COMMON LAW**—If the mens rea is not specified, analyze under both specific intent and general intent mens rea.
>   *SPECIFIC INTENT*—The mistake, whether reasonable or unreasonable, will provide a defense.
>   *GENERAL INTENT*
>   a. Is the mistake reasonable?
>   b. If no, the mistake will not provide a defense.
>   c. If yes, courts apply one of the following approaches:
>   1. Reasonable mistake is a defense.
>   2. The Moral Wrong Doctrine.
>   a. If the facts were as the actor believed them to be, would the actor's conduct constitute a moral wrong?
>   b. If yes, then the mistake is not a defense.
>   c. If no, the mistake is a defense.
>   3. The Legal Wrong Doctrine.
>   a. If the facts were as the actor believed them to be, would the actor's conduct constitute a legal wrong, i.e., a crime?
>   b. If yes, then the mistake is not a defense.
>   c. If no, then the mistake is a defense.

> **MODEL PENAL CODE**—If the mens rea is not specified, analyze under each of the mental states.
>   *PURPOSE OR KNOWLEDGE*—The mistake, whether reasonable or unreasonable, negates either mental state and thus provides a defense subject to the applicability of § 2.04(2) below.

RECKLESSNESS
    a. Is the mistake reasonable?
    b. If yes, the mistake negates the mens rea and thus provides a defense subject to the applicability of § 2.04(2) below.
    c. If no, then was the mistake merely negligent?
    d. If yes, the mistake negates the mens rea and thus provides a defense subject to the applicability of § 2.04(2) below.
    e. If no, the mistake does not negate the mens rea and thus does not provide a defense.

NEGLIGENCE—Only a reasonable mistake will negate the mens rea and thus provide a defense, subject to the applicability of § 2.04(2) below.

§ 2.04(2)—Even if the mistake would otherwise provide a defense, does the actor's conduct constitute an offense under the facts as the actor believes them to be? (For further explanation, see Tools #10–11 below.)
    a. If no, then the mistake provides a defense.
    b. If yes, then the actor will be punished only for that offense (that the actor commits under the facts as s/he believes them to be).

7.   Remember, when analyzing an offense containing an element requiring intent, the MPC does not include a mens rea of intent but that the mental states of purpose and knowledge roughly correlate to the various meanings of the common law concept of intent.

8.   Keep in mind that some crimes requiring specific intent, such as burglary and larceny, will so indicate in the statutory definition of the offense. (See offenses 7 and 8 in the Hypothetical.) Typically, such an explicit articulation of intent is interpreted to require specific intent. But other specific intent crimes, such as attempt under the majority view, do not explicitly state an intent requirement.

9.   What counts as a moral wrong under the moral wrong doctrine? What constitutes a moral wrong is considerably less clear than what constitutes a crime. As a result, application of the moral wrong doctrine may potentially be more difficult than application of the legal wrong doctrine or MPC § 2.04(2). In many cases, whether an actor's conduct is a moral wrong will be obvious. In those instances where it is unclear, merely assume it one way or the other, and then continue with your analysis. For example, state "Assuming the actor's conduct is a moral wrong, then. . . ." or "Assuming the actor's conduct is not a moral wrong, then. . . ."

10. Consider the relationship between moral and legal wrongs. Moral wrongs probably make up the larger category. If something is a crime it will most likely be a moral wrong. However, the reverse is not true. If something is a moral wrong, it is not the case that it will most likely be a crime. For an example of a crime that is *arguably* not a moral wrong, consider drug possession.

11. The precise specification of the moral wrong, legal wrong, and the MPC § 2.04(2) doctrines seem to assess whether, under the facts as the actor believes them to be, an actor's *conduct* or what the actor has done is a moral wrong or crime. So, if the actor merely intended to commit a crime (but did not commit it),

the mere intention would not constitute "conduct" qualifying as a moral wrong or crime.

12. Keep in mind the differing ramifications of the moral wrong, legal wrong, and MPC § 2.04(2) doctrines. If the actor would be committing a moral wrong or crime, respectively, under the facts as s/he believed them to be, the results will differ, depending on the doctrine. Under the moral wrong and legal wrong doctrines, the actor will generally be liable for a greater crime than the actor committed under the facts as s/he believed them to be. The actor will be liable for the crime of which the actor commits the actus reus. Under the MPC, however, such an actor will be subject to punishment for the crime which the actor would have committed under the facts as s/he believed them to be. The actor will be subject to punishment for the crime of which the actor satisfies the requisite mens rea. This will generally be a lesser crime.

Notice that under all three doctrines, however, the actor will be punished for a crime for which the actor lacks, in a sense, either the requisite actus reus or mens rea. Under the moral and legal wrong doctrines, the actor is held liable for a greater crime by satisfying the actus reus of the greater crime but the mens rea of a lesser crime. In contrast, under the MPC doctrine, the actor is subject to punishment for a lesser crime by satisfying the actus reus of the greater crime and the mens rea of the lesser crime. Under all three doctrines, an actor is subject to punishment for a crime despite not satisfying, in a sense, either the requisite actus reus or mens rea.

13. Be on the lookout for mistakes that pertain to an element of the offense but may be irrelevant. For example, suppose Alabama possesses three kilos of cocaine but honestly and reasonably believes that she possesses only two kilos. If charged with offense 4 above (possession of a kilo or more of cocaine), her mistake is irrelevant. Despite it being an exculpatory, honest, and reasonable mistake of fact pertaining to an element of an offense that does not require strict liability, her mistake would be irrelevant. It does nothing to undermine her mens rea or mental state regarding her possession of a kilo or more of cocaine. Rather, the mistake only serves to bolster or even establish her mens rea. Regardless of her mistake, she nonetheless believes that she possesses more than a kilo of cocaine.

14. Be on the lookout for mistakes that do *not* pertain to an element of the offense and are thus irrelevant. For example, in the Problem, Alabama is honestly and reasonably mistaken as to how long she has been a drug dealer. She believes that she has been a drug dealer for only three days, but, in fact, she has been a drug dealer for four. Even though this might be an honest and reasonable mistake of fact, it is irrelevant because it does not pertain to an element of any offense with which Alabama might be charged.

15. Mistakes pertaining to what may be considered jurisdictional elements will generally be treated as irrelevant. For example, an actor mistakenly believes that she commits a crime in New York, but in fact she commits it in New Jersey. That mistake will be irrelevant if she is charged with that crime in New Jersey. Or, suppose an actor mistakenly believes that he is assaulting a state officer but is in fact assaulting a federal officer. That mistake may be treated as irrelevant in a prosecution for the crime in a federal court.

16. Do not be careless with recklessness. The mental state of recklessness under the MPC is negated by either of two types of mistakes: (i) an honest and reasonable

mistake and (ii) an honest and merely negligent mistake. A merely negligent mistake may also be understood as an unreasonable nonreckless mistake.

What is the difference between a reckless and a negligent mistake? Both are unreasonable. A reckless mistake, however, involves the actor's conscious awareness of the risk of being mistaken. In contrast, with a negligent mistake, the actor is unaware of any risk of being mistaken.

17. Keep in mind the notable strict liability offenses. Although most strict liability offenses are public welfare or regulatory offenses, you should be aware of the notable exceptions. As to the element of the age of the victim in statutory rape, the majority view is strict liability. As to the element of nonconsent of the victim in rape, the minority rule is strict liability. The MPC generally disfavors strict liability for any criminal offense. One notable exception is the element of a sexual offense victim being less than ten years old. That element is strict liability.

VARIATIONS ON THE THEME

For the following variations, assume all of the facts from the original Problem obtain unless otherwise noted.

1.   Alabama is mistaken as to the quantity of powder that she possesses. She actually has less than a kilo.

2.   In deciding to make one big sale to Clarence Donowitz, Alabama and Donowitz agree to conduct the transaction in a parking lot, which Alabama mistakenly believes is one mile from the renowned Donowitz & Worley Film School. In fact, the parking lot is 50 meters away.

3.   Floyd is mistaken as to the quantity of the powder that he possesses. He actually has more than a kilo.

4.   Alabama believes that she possesses baby powder that has not yet expired.

5.   Floyd mistakenly believes that it is only a crime in America to sell American heroin.

6.   Rather than Alabama possessing cocaine and believing that it is baby powder, Alabama possesses baby powder and believes that it is cocaine and intends to distribute it as cocaine.

7.   Floyd mistakenly believes that he took possession of the drugs in Kansas City, Kansas. In fact, he took possession in Kansas City, Missouri. (Floyd is prosecuted in Missouri.)

ADDITIONAL READINGS

GEORGE FLETCHER, RETHINKING CRIMINAL LAW 683–730 (1978)

JOSHUA DRESSLER, UNDERSTANDING CRIMINAL LAW 153–65 (5th ed. 2009)

PAUL ROBINSON, CRIMINAL LAW 259–65 (1997)

Larry Alexander, *Inculpatory and Exculpatory Mistakes and the Fact/Law Distinction: An Essay in Memory of Myke Balyes*, 12 LAW & PHIL. 33 (1993)

Catherine L. Carpenter, *On Statutory Rape, Strict Liability, and the Public Welfare Offense Model*, 53 AM. U. L. REV. 313 (2003)

George P. Fletcher, *Mistake in the Model Penal Code: A False, False Problem*, 19 RUTGERS L.J. 649 (1988)

Douglas N. Husak & George C. Thomas III, *Date Rape, Social Convention, and Reasonable Mistakes*, 11 LAW & PHIL. 95 (1992)

Peter W. Low, *The Model Penal Code, the Common Law, and Mistakes of Fact: Recklessness, Negligence, or Strict Liability?*, 19 RUTGERS L.J. 539 (1988)

Benjamin B. Sendor, *Mistakes of Fact: A Study in the Structure of Criminal Conduct*, 25 WAKE FOREST L. REV. 707 (1990)

Kenneth W. Simons, *Mistake and Impossibility, Law and Fact, and Culpability: A Speculative Essay*, 81 J. CRIMINAL LAW & CRIMINOLOGY 447 (1990)

MISTAKE OF LAW

4

INTRODUCTION

The maxim that ignorance of the law is no excuse is one of the few doctrines of criminal law known by lawyers and nonlawyers alike and "is deeply rooted in the American legal system."[1] Why this is so is less clear. The doctrinal explanation is that most criminal offenses simply do not have a mens rea element as to the actor's awareness that his or her conduct constitutes an offense. In other words, with respect to the commission of most criminal offenses, the actor's knowledge that he or she was in fact committing an offense need not be proven in order to hold the actor criminally liable.

Underlying the doctrinal explanation are numerous historical rationales offered for the criminal law's antipathy toward recognizing, significantly more so than mistakes of fact, mistakes of law as a defense. First, "[b]ased on the notion that the law is definite and knowable, the common law presumed that every person knew the law. . . ."[2] Second, if mistakes of law exculpated, then the law would lose its objectivity and become completely subjective. The law would become whatever anyone believed it to be. As a result, "the exception would swallow the rule."[3] Third, if recognized as a valid defense, defendants would proffer fraudulent mistake of law claims that would be too difficult for the prosecution to disprove. Finally, disallowing mistake of law defenses discourages ignorance of the law; it encourages knowledge of the law.

At a time when all offenses were *malum in se*, and their number was few, the presumption and expectation of complete knowledge of the criminal law was reasonable. Now, however, with the proliferation of offenses numbering in the thousands and the rise of *malum prohibitum* crimes, the hard and fast rule denying mistake of law defenses has softened. Three principal exceptions to the general rule have emerged: (i) reasonable reliance on an official statement of law that is afterward determined to be invalid or erroneous, (ii) ignorance or mistake of law that negates the mens rea of the charged offense, and (iii) lack of fair notice. But even these exceptions have been crafted and construed quite narrowly.

The analysis of these three mistake of law defenses shares aspects of the analysis of both mens rea and excuses. Although mistake of law is typically studied as an aspect of the analysis of mens rea, only one of these three mistake of law defenses pertain to mens rea—a mistake of law that negates the requisite mens rea of the offense charged. Neither the lack of fair notice nor the reasonable reliance mistake of law defense negates the requisite mens rea of the offense charged. In that they do not negate mens rea, these mistake of law defenses are

---

[1] Cheek v. United States, 498 U.S. 192 (1991).

[2] *Id.*

[3] People v. Marrero, 507 N.E.2d 1068 (N.Y. 1987).

more appropriately considered as excuses. (Other excuse defenses, such as duress, insanity, intoxication, and diminished capacity (which may be a partial excuse), are discussed in later chapters.)

PROBLEM

Roman is a convicted sex offender subject to the requirements of the Sex Offender Registration Act (hereinafter SORA). One of the provisions of SORA prohibits a convicted sex offender from residing within 500 feet of a church or school. Roman resides in an apartment that is just over 700 feet away from a school, and he is in full compliance with SORA.

Some months later, on July 1, 2010, the jurisdiction amends SORA. Included among the changes is a provision prohibiting a convicted sex offender from residing within 1000 feet of a church or school. This is a strict liability offense. That same day, the legislature faxes to every bar library and law school library in the jurisdiction a copy of the new legislation.

On July 2, 2010, the new legislation is inserted into the appropriate statute books in all of the above libraries. In addition, a legal notice of these changes is published in the Legal Notice section of the Classifieds of all of the jurisdiction's major newspapers.

The effective date of this new legislation is July 3, 2010.

On July 4, 2010, unaware of this new provision, Roman is arrested and charged with residing within 1000 feet of a school or church in violation of the new SORA provision (which became effective the previous day, July 3).

Roman moves to a new location which he believes is not within 1000 feet of a school or church.

One week later, Roman hears a loud noise at the front door and believing that someone has broken into his apartment, grabs his gun. Despite seeing that the intruder, Cindy, an elderly retired school librarian, is unarmed and poses little threat to his safety, Roman shoots her because, after all, she has unlawfully entered his dwelling. Cindy dies.

Roman is charged with two additional offenses. The first is "wilfully violating the sex offender registration act" by residing 900 feet from a "church." (The offense defines wilfully as knowingly violating a known legal duty.) Roman denies that he is within 1000 feet of a church. The prosecutor explains that 900 feet from Roman's apartment, there is a charity soup kitchen owned and operated by a local church. The prosecutor further explains that the term "church" is defined in § 231 of the civil Property Code as including "any place of worship or structure housing a religiously affiliated charitable organization." Roman argues that he did not realize that the soup kitchen qualified as a church.

The second offense charged is murder, which the jurisdiction defines as "intentionally causing the death of another." However, a "Make My Day" provision in the murder statute supplies an exemption for "occupants who kill someone unlawfully entering their dwelling." The term occupant is defined in § 103 of the civil Property Code as a "homeowner or apartment tenant." Roman claims that as an apartment tenant, he is an occupant who has killed a person who has unlawfully entered his dwelling and thus is not guilty of the murder. After Roman is charged, the trial court interprets the provision defining an occupant as limited to only "lawful" occupants. Applying this interpretation of the provision to Roman, the court finds that Roman is not a lawful occupant because he is living within 1000 feet of a church in violation of SORA.

Analyze and discuss whether Roman could obtain a mistake of law defense to each of the three charged offenses.

LIST OF READINGS

Cheek v. United States, 498 U.S. 102 (1991)

Lambert v. California, 355 U.S. 225 (1957)

People v. Marrero, 507 N.E.2d 1068 (N.Y. 1987)

MODEL PENAL CODE § 2.04 (Official Code and Revised Comments 1985)

ESSAY

Roman's mistake of law defense to the charge of residing within 1000 feet of a school will possibly succeed. Roman's mistake of law defense to the charge of wilfully violating SORA (by residing within 1000 feet of a church) will most likely succeed. Finally, Roman's mistake of law defense to the charge of murder will be unsuccessful.

There are three exceptions to the general rule that ignorance of the law is no defense: (i) reasonable reliance on an official statement of law later determined invalid or erroneous, (ii) a mistake of law that negates the mens rea of the offense charged, and (iii) lack of fair notice. These will provide the basis for Roman's mistake of law claims.

Violation of SORA–Living within 1000 Feet of a School

COMMON LAW

[1] Roman's best mistake of law defense to this offense is based on lack of fair notice. Although he is unaware of the new provision at the time he violates it, the general rule is that citizens are presumed to know the criminal law. Generally, publication of a criminal statute in the jurisdiction's official Code or Reporter constitutes fair notice. Here, the jurisdiction did provide notice of the new provision. The issue, however, is whether this notice was fair.

[2] The leading case, *Lambert*, addresses this issue of the fairness of the notice. The defendant, Lambert, claimed lack of fair notice as a defense to the charge of being in Los Angeles and failing to register as a convicted felon. The Court relied on four factors in finding that Lambert was entitled to the defense: (i) the defendant was actually unaware of the provision, (ii) violation of the law's provisions was accomplished by an omission (mere failure to register), (iii) the provision was based on the defendant's status (being in LA), and (iv) the offense was *malum prohibitum* and thus the defendant had no reason to know of its existence.

[3] Roman most likely satisfies the first three factors and possibly satisfies the fourth. As to the first factor, the facts state that Roman was unaware of the new provision at the time he violated it. As to the second factor, his violation was accomplished by omission in that he failed to move after the law was changed and prior to the effective date. As to the third factor, the SORA provision implicates Roman's status as a sex offender. As to the fourth factor, Roman's offense is *malum prohibitum*, but it is not entirely clear that he had no reason to know of its existence.

With the proliferation of sex offender registration requirements, almost anyone, particularly a sex offender, would have reason to know of their general existence. But Roman perhaps did not have reason to know of this particular provision's existence, especially given the exceedingly short time frame between publication and its effective date.

[4] Whether Roman satisfies the four-factor *Lambert* test is not dispositive as to whether his mistake of law defense will succeed. *Lambert* has been much criticized. The *Lambert* dissent's prediction that the holding will have little precedential value has proven correct. Generally, official publication of a validly promulgated statute constitutes fair notice.

[5] More relevant to the analysis of Roman's mistake of law defense than whether Roman satisfies the four-factor *Lambert* test is the temporal component of the fairness of the notice. Generally, the temporal fairness of the notice is satisfied by a reasonable period of time between the publication and the effective date of the provision. Here, publication occurred on July 2, and the effective date was July 3. While it is unclear what minimally suffices as a reasonable period of time, the time interval here—one day—is possibly insufficient for the notice to be fair.

MODEL PENAL CODE

[6] The elements of this mistake of law defense under MPC § 2.04(3)(a) are as follows: (i) the statute is unknown to the actor and either (ii) not published or (iii) not made reasonably available. Roman was unaware of the new provision. Although the new provision had been published (and official publication generally constitutes reasonable availability), Roman would have a strong argument that its publication one day prior to his violation of it does not constitute making the provision reasonably available. The temporally insufficient fairness of the notice possibly fails to make the provision reasonably available to him.

Wilfully Violating SORA by Living within 1000 Feet of a Church
COMMON LAW

[7] Roman's only plausible mistake of law defense to this charge is based on a mistake of law that negates the requisite mens rea of the offense charged. A mistake of law pertaining to a specific intent offense or element may negate that specific intent and provide a defense. If the mistake pertains to a general intent element or offense, the mistake most likely is not eligible to exculpate. The offense with which Roman is charged, requiring that an actor wilfully violate SORA, is a specific intent offense.

[8] Roman is mistaken about the legal meaning of the term "church." He is unaware that the term includes charity soup kitchens. Because Roman is unaware that the charity soup kitchen within 1000 feet of his residence legally qualifies as a church, he was unaware that he was violating the SORA provision. Lacking awareness that he was violating the SORA provision, he was not wilfully violating SORA. As a result, Roman's mistake of law about the legal meaning of the term church negates the specific intent mens rea of the offense with which he is charged, and thus his mistake of law defense will most likely succeed.

MODEL PENAL CODE

[9] Under § 2.04(1)(a), the MPC also recognizes a mistake of law defense based on the mistake negating the requisite mens rea of the offense charged. Roman's mistake

of law regarding the legal meaning of the term "church" negates his capacity to wilfully violate SORA.[4] As a result, Roman's mistake of law claim would most likely be a successful defense, subject to the application of § 2.04(2).

Section 2.04(2) assesses whether the actor "would be guilty of another offense had the situation been as he supposed." If so, the mistake defense is not available but the actor's liability is mitigated to the grade and degree of offense of which he would have been guilty had the situation been as he supposed. Under the situation as Roman supposes, Roman is living more than 1000 feet away from a church. Roman living more than 1000 feet away from a church is not a criminal offense. Therefore, § 2.04(2) does not bar Roman's mistake of law defense.

Murder

[10] Roman's best mistake of law defense to this charge is based on the reasonable reliance exception to the general rule that mistake of law is no defense. The reasonable reliance exception is nearly identical under the MPC and the common law. An actor obtains this defense if "he acts in reasonable reliance upon an official statement of the law, afterward determined invalid or erroneous...." MPC § 2.04(3)(b). This reasonable reliance exception contains the following elements: (i) acting in reliance, (ii) on an official statement of law, (iii) the reliance is reasonable, and (iv) the official statement of law is later determined invalid or erroneous.

[11] As to the first element, the facts state that Roman invoked the exemption to the murder statute as a basis for the killing being lawful. There is no evidence that he was unaware of the exemption and did not act in reliance on it at the time of the killing. If Roman asserted that he did rely on the exemption, as defendants typically would do, the prosecution would be hard-pressed to rebut it. As a result, courts would possibly presume that he acted in reliance on the exemption, thereby satisfying the first element.

[12] As to the second element, official statements of the law include statutes. MPC § 2.04(3)(b)(i). In killing Cindy, the source of law on which he relied was a statute. As a result, the source of law on which Roman acted in reliance was an official statement of law, thereby satisfying this element.

[13] As to the third element, the reliance is reasonable if the official statement of law upon which the actor relies provides a basis for the actor to reasonably believe that his conduct is lawful. The specific portion of the statute on which Roman relies is the exemption. The exemption applies to an occupant of a dwelling who kills an unlawful intruder. Occupant is defined as a homeowner or apartment tenant. Roman believes that as an apartment tenant, he is an occupant and that Cindy has unlawfully entered his dwelling. Believing he has satisfied the exemption, Roman believes that he is not guilty of murder. Because Roman is an apartment tenant in the dwelling that Cindy did unlawfully enter, his belief that he satisfied the exemption is entirely reasonable. His belief accords with the very plain language of the statute—an apartment tenant is an occupant.

---

[4] Under MPC § 2.02(8), a mens rea of wilfulness is satisfied by knowledge unless otherwise specified in the provision. Because the facts state that the provision specifically defines wilfulness, this mens rea is not satisfied by mere knowledge. See also MPC § 2.02(9).

[14] Despite satisfying the first three elements of the defense, Roman does not satisfy the fourth element—that the official statement of law be ruled invalid or erroneous subsequent to his conduct. True, the definition of occupant was, subsequent to Roman's conduct, interpreted to include only lawful occupants. But this interpretation of a valid and correct definition contained in the statutory exemption does not constitute a ruling that the statutory definition of occupant was invalid or erroneous. That is, the interpretation of the statutory language did not invalidate the statutory language. As a result, the official statement of law—the definition of the term occupant referred to in the murder exemption—upon which Roman acted in reasonable reliance was not subsequently determined to be invalid or erroneous. Thus, Roman's mistake of law defense based on the reasonable reliance exception would succeed neither under the common law nor the MPC.

[15] One might argue that Roman could plausibly raise a different mistake of law defense—a mistake of law negating the requisite mens rea. The argument would be that Roman is not mistaken about the offense with which he is charged. He is entirely aware that it is a crime to intentionally cause the death of another, that is, to commit murder. Rather, his mistake of law concerns the legal meaning of the term "occupant" and, as such, is a mistake of nongoverning law. A mistake of nongoverning law may provide a defense if it negates a specific intent element or offense. If the mistake pertains to a general intent element or offense, the mistake most likely is not eligible to exculpate. Murder, requiring that the actor "intentionally" kill, is perhaps a specific intent offense. As a result, one might argue, Roman's mistake of nongoverning law negates the mens rea of the specific intent offense with which he is charged and thus provides a defense.

However, even assuming that Roman has made a mistake of nongoverning law with respect to a specific intent offense, the argument still fails. Roman's mistake does not negate the mens rea of the offense. Regardless of whether Roman is or is not a legal occupant, he nonetheless kills intentionally (purposefully under the MPC). His mistake of law does not pertain to whether he is killing and thus does not negate his intention/purpose to kill. By failing to negate the mens rea of the offense, Roman's mistake of law claim fails under both the common law and the MPC.

Conclusion

Roman's mistake of law claims will possibly succeed as defenses to both SORA offenses but will fail with respect to the murder charge. Roman's mistake of law defense based on lack of fair notice will possibly succeed as a defense to the offense of living within 1000 feet of a school. His mistake of law claim based on a mistake negating the requisite mens rea will most likely succeed as a defense to the offense of wilfully violating SORA. Neither reasonable reliance nor mistake negating the requisite mens rea provides the basis for a successful mistake of law defense to the murder charge.

TOOLS FOR SELF-ASSESSMENT

Go back to your written answer. Look for the issues identified in paragraphs numbered [1]–[15] above. Look also for the analysis that follows each issue, and mark your essay where you locate it. Do you fully describe the issue, identify the precise legal standard that applies, list the relevant facts, and show how the facts and law support a conclusion for each issue? Mark each conclusion in your essay. Are there sufficient reasons in the law and in the facts to support each conclusion?

1. Do what you are told. Here, you are to analyze the possible mistake of law claims that Roman might have for each of the three criminal offenses under both common law as well as MPC principles.

2. Do not analyze what is unnecessary. For example, do not discuss issues arising out of Roman's arrest, the legitimacy of sex offender registration laws, or defenses he might have other than mistake of law.

3. Always analyze under the MPC as well as the common law unless you are instructed otherwise.

4. State the best possible arguments for alternative conclusions. If, for example, you determine that Roman is not entitled to a mistake of law defense for a particular offense, present the best argument that he is entitled to the defense. It is possible that you will be unable to reach a conclusion if, for example, the case law is particularly unclear or if case law is scant on a particular issue. If so, it becomes even more important that you clearly set out possible alternative arguments. Ultimately you should indicate how you think a court will most likely rule.

5. Did reading the Problem make you feel overwhelmed at first? This Problem was dense with information and perhaps confusing. The key to preventing feeling overwhelmed is to have a firm grasp of the organization of your analysis. Realizing that there are only three offenses and, at most, three types of mistake of law claims makes it more manageable. Start with the first offense and analyze which, if any, mistake of law defenses might be applicable. In a sense, the Problem itself may be more difficult than its analysis.

6. The following is an oversimplified, for purposes of brevity, step-by-step template that breaks down each step used to analyze the three mistake of law defenses:

Reasonable Reliance on an Official Statement of Law Afterward Determined to be Invalid or Erroneous

(The following analysis is the same under both common law and MPC.)

    i. Did the actor act in reliance?
    ii. If no, then the exception is inapplicable.
    iii. If yes, did the actor rely on an official statement of law?
    iv. If no, then the exception is inapplicable.
    v. If yes, was the actor's reliance reasonable?
    vi. If no, then the exception is inapplicable.
    vii. If yes, was the law later determined to be invalid or erroneous?
    viii. If no, then the exception is inapplicable.
    ix. If yes, then the exception does apply.

Mistake Negates Requisite Mens Rea
COMMON LAW
    i. Did the actor make an honest mistake of law?
    ii. If no, then the exception is inapplicable.
    iii. If yes, does the mistake pertain to a strict liability offense or element?
    iv. If yes, then the exception is inapplicable.
    v. If no, does the mistake pertain to a general intent offense or element?
    vi. If no, then go to x.

    vii.   If yes, does the mistake negate the mens rea?

   viii.   If no, then the exception is inapplicable.

     ix.   If yes, then the exception is possibly applicable, but it is still probably inapplicable.

      x.   If the mistake pertains to a specific intent offense or element, does the mistake negate the mens rea?

     xi.   If no, then the exception is inapplicable.

    xii.   If yes, then the exception does apply.

MODEL PENAL CODE

      i.   Did the actor make an honest mistake of law?

     ii.   If no, then the exception is inapplicable.

    iii.   If yes, does the mistake pertain to a strict liability offense or element?

    iv.   If yes, then the exception is inapplicable.

     v.   If no, does the mistake negate the mens rea?

    vi.   If no, then the exception is inapplicable.

    vii.   If yes, then the exception is applicable.

   viii.   Is the defendant committing a crime under the situation as he believes it to be?

     ix.   If no, then the defendant has no criminal liability.

      x.   If yes, then the defendant is liable for the crime committed under the situation as he believed it to be.

Lack of Fair Notice

COMMON LAW

      i.   Was the actor aware of the law's existence?

     ii.   If yes, then the exception is inapplicable.

    iii.   If no, was the law officially published?

    iv.   If no, then the exception does apply.

     v.   If yes, was there fair notice?

    vi.   If yes, the exception is inapplicable.

    vii.   If no, the exception does apply.

MODEL PENAL CODE

      i.   Was the actor aware of the law's existence?

     ii.   If yes, then the exception is inapplicable.

    iii.   If no, was the law published?

    iv.   If no, then the exception does apply.

     v.   If yes, was the law made reasonably available?

    vi.   If yes, then the exception is inapplicable.

    vii.   If no, then the exception does apply.

7.   Note the conceptual difference between the reasonable reliance and the lack of fair notice exceptions versus the mistake negating mens rea exception. The mistake negating mens rea exception is not technically a defense (that is, it is not an affirmative defense) because if the exception applies, then the prosecution has not proven all of the elements of the offense. In a sense, a failure of proof is not a

defense. In contrast, the reasonable reliance and lack of fair notice exceptions are technically defenses (and thus affirmative defenses) because they do not negate an element of the offense. Both are excuse defenses.

8. The conceptual difference in Tool #7 above matters. By understanding the conceptual difference, it should make more sense to you that the reasonable reliance and fair notice exceptions are possible defenses to almost any type of offense, including strict liability, general intent, and specific intent offenses. These two exceptions have no bearing on mens rea; they are more concerned with basic fairness. In contrast, the mistake negating mens rea exception is generally only applicable to specific intent offenses (under the common law) and never applicable to strict liability offenses.

9. One might be tempted to argue that because Roman likely has a valid mistake of law defense to the offense of wilfully violating SORA, then he is in fact a legal occupant. However, a finding that he did not wilfully violate SORA does not make him a lawful occupant. Roman is not a lawful occupant because although he did not wilfully violate SORA, he nonetheless violates SORA because he is living within 1000 feet of a church.

10. Regarding the mistake negating mens rea exception, it is helpful to keep in mind two different types of offenses and two different types of mistakes of law that might negate mens rea. The first type of offense requires an actor's awareness that his or her conduct constitutes a crime. For example, in *Cheek*, the charged offense required that the defendant wilfully commit the offense. Wilfully was defined as the violation of a known legal duty. This offense requires the defendant to intend or know that his conduct constitutes the crime charged. The second type of offense is a specific intent offense that does *not* require the actor's awareness that his or her conduct constitutes a crime. That is, it does not require the mens rea of the first type of offense above. An example of this type of offense is burglary—defined as breaking and entering the dwelling of another with the intent to commit a felony.

There are two principal types of mistake of law that may negate the mens rea of one or both of the above two types of offenses. The first type is variously termed a mistake of governing law or same law. This is a mistake about the existence of the crime charged. That is, when charged with an offense, the actor claims "Oh, I didn't realize that was a crime." The second type of mistake is variously termed a mistake of nongoverning law or different law. The actor is not mistaken about the existence of the offense charged but rather is mistaken about law other than the offense charged. For example, the defendant in *Cheek* is not mistaken about the existence of the crime under which he is charged. He is entirely aware that it is a crime to fail to pay taxes on earned income. Rather, he mistakenly believes that his wages as an airline pilot do not constitute income. This mistake is neither about the offense charged nor even about criminal law. He is mistaken about tax law—whether wages constitute income.

Much of the difficulty in applying the mistake negating mens rea exception can be avoided by keeping in mind how these two types of offenses and two types of mistakes interrelate. With respect to the first type of offense, requiring an actor's awareness that his or her conduct constitutes a crime, either of the above two types of mistake may negate the requisite mens rea and form the basis for a successful mistake of law defense. Take the offense in *Cheek* for example: either an honest claim that Cheek was unaware of the existence of this crime or an honest claim that he did not realize that wages constituted income would negate the requisite mens rea of knowingly violating the legal duty to pay taxes on earned income.

With respect to the second type of offense, a specific intent offense that does not require the actor's awareness that his or her conduct constitutes a crime, the first type of mistake will not be eligible to negate the requisite mens rea, but the second type of mistake will be eligible. As an example, suppose a defendant is charged with the offense of larceny, defined as intentionally taking and carrying away the property of another with the intent to permanently deprive the owner of the property. The element of permanently depriving the owner of the property requires specific intent. Because the statute does not require the actor to know or intend that his or her conduct be unlawful, the defendant's claim that she did not know of the existence of the offense of larceny—the first type of mistake—will not negate the requisite mens rea and will not succeed as a mistake of law defense. In contrast, the defendant's honest, but mistaken, belief that the property is his under that jurisdiction's adverse possession laws would be eligible to negate the requisite mens rea. The defendant is not mistaken about the offense charged but rather, about property law—the law that determines the operation of adverse possession. Because he believes the property to be his own, he cannot intend to permanently deprive the actual owner of the property. The defendant's mistake of property law is a mistake of different law or nongoverning law that negates the specific intent element of permanently depriving the owner of the property.

In short, either type of mistake may negate the requisite mens rea of the first type of offense and succeed as a mistake of law defense. But only the second type of mistake (of these two types) will negate the requisite mens rea of the second type of offense and succeed as a mistake of law defense.

Note that while these two types of offenses and mistakes do not necessarily exhaust all of the possibilities, they are the most important types to know and understand. Hybrid forms of both mistakes and both offenses, combining features of each type, occasionally arise, but the law's treatment of them is not entirely clear. In part, this lack of clarity is due to the difficulty of precisely distinguishing, for all possible cases, the distinction between governing and nongoverning law mistakes.

The above analysis is depicted in the following chart:

Types of Elements/Offenses	Types of Mistakes That Negate Mens Rea	
	Governing/same law	*Nongoverning/different law*
Specific Intent requiring awareness that conduct is a crime	May Negate	May Negate
Specific Intent NOT requiring awareness that conduct is a crime	Does Not Negate	May Negate

11. An alternative way of explaining why Roman fails to satisfy the reasonable reliance exception, discussed above in [14] in the above Essay, is that Roman relied on a personal, however reasonable, but erroneous interpretation of an official statement of law. What this mistake of law defense requires is for Roman to make a correct interpretation of an official statement of law (that is later found to be invalid). At the time of Roman's conduct, the relied-upon official statement of law must, in fact, authorize Roman's conduct. It did not. As a result, Roman's mistake of law claim based on the reasonable reliance exception fails.

VARIATIONS ON THE THEME
For the following variations, assume all of the facts from the original Problem obtain unless otherwise noted.

Violation of SORA–Residing within 1000 Feet of a School
1.   Suppose that before Roman moved into the apartment, he heard rumors that the legislature was meeting to change the provisions involving the housing restrictions. He asked his friend, the city councilman in his district, about the new law. The councilman told Roman that the rumors were false and that SORA was not changed. In reliance on this statement, Roman moved into the apartment 700 feet away from a school. The councilman was wrong, and Roman was arrested for violating SORA.
2.   Residing within 1000 feet of a school is a general intent element of the offense.
3.   Roman is charged with intentionally living within 1000 feet of a school.
4.   Roman is charged with knowingly violating the provision prohibiting living within 1000 feet of a school.
5.   The effective date of the new provision is not July 3, 2010, but rather July 10, 2010. Rather than being arrested on July 4, 2010, Roman is arrested on July 11, 2010.

Wilfully Violating SORA by Living within 1000 Feet of a Church
6.   Roman is charged with the general intent offense of violating SORA.
7.   Roman is charged with the strict liability offense of violating SORA.

Murder
8.   Roman is charged with involuntary manslaughter (a reckless or negligent homicide) for the death of Cindy.
9.   The assistant district attorney informed Roman that he (Roman) was, in fact, an occupant under the law. Roman relied on this statement.
10.   Rather than interpreting its meaning, the court invalidated the provision defining occupant and supplied a new definition.
11.   After Roman shot Cindy, and after the court interpreted the meaning of the term occupant, the exemption was invalidated.
12.   Roman was unaware of the "Make My Day" exemption.
13.   In both the country and culture in which Roman grew up, it was not only legally permissible but culturally obligatory to use all possible force, including lethal force, against those who unlawfully enter another's dwelling.

ADDITIONAL READINGS

JOSHUA DRESSLER, UNDERSTANDING CRIMINAL LAW 167–80 (5th ed. 2009)

GEORGE P. FLETCHER, BASIC CONCEPTS OF CRIMINAL LAW 156–58 (1998)

GEORGE P. FLETCHER, RETHINKING CRIMINAL LAW 736–58 (1978)

PAUL H. ROBINSON, CRIMINAL LAW 264–68, 544–54 (1997)

Douglas N. Husak & Andrew von Hirsch, *Culpability and Mistake of Law*, in ACTION AND VALUE IN CRIMINAL LAW (Steven Shute, John Gardner, and Jeremy Horder eds., 1993)

Andrew Ashworth, *Excusable Mistake of Law*, CRIM. L. REV. 652 (1974)

Sharon L. Davies, *The Jurisprudence of Willfulness: An Evolving Theory of Excusable Ignorance*, 48 DUKE L.J. 341 (1998)

Dan M. Kahan, *Ignorance of the Law Is an Excuse—But Only for the Virtuous*, 96 MICH. L. REV. 127 (1997)

John T. Parry, *Culpability, Mistake, and Official Interpretations of Law*, 25 AM. J. CRIM. L. 1 (1997)

Kenneth W. Simons, *Mistake of Fact or Mistake of Criminal Law? Explaining and Defending the Distinction*, 3 CRIMINAL LAW & PHILOSOPHY 213 (2009)

Kenneth W. Simons, *Ignorance and Mistake of Criminal Law, Noncriminal Law, and Fact*, __OHIO ST. J. CRIM. L.__(forthcoming 2012)

CAUSATION

5

INTRODUCTION

Causation is a required element for all result crimes—criminal offenses that include a prohibited result. But causation is not a required element for conduct crimes—for example, attempts. The most typical category of criminal offense in which causation is a significant issue is homicide. In order for the defendant to be found guilty of the murder or manslaughter, as the case may be, the prosecution must prove that the defendant's conduct was the cause of the victim's death. The rules and doctrines of causation supply the link between the actor's voluntary act or omission and the prohibited result.

Causation consists of two prongs, both of which must be satisfied for the defendant to be the cause of the prohibited result. The first prong is but-for causation, also called factual or actual causation. The test for but-for causation is as follows: But-for the defendant's conduct, would the prohibited result or harm have occurred? If that question is answered "yes," then the defendant's conduct is not the but-for cause, and the defendant is excluded from liability for the result crime. If that question is answered "no," then the defendant's conduct is the but-for cause. In particularly challenging types of cases, the above but-for causation test is too simple and must be modified as follows: But-for the defendant's conduct, would the injury have occurred when it did and as it did? But even this modified test is not sophisticated enough to precisely capture all but-for causes and exclude all non-but-for causes.

The second prong is proximate or legal causation. Proximate causation analysis determines which of the perhaps many but-for causes should bear responsibility for the prohibited result. Proximate causation is easy with respect to some types of causes. A but-for cause in which no other but-for causes intervene between it and the prohibited result is a direct cause. A direct cause is generally a proximate cause. The more difficult issues of proximate causation arise when a but-for cause intervenes between the original or a previous but-for cause and the prohibited result. Some intervening causes do not preclude the original or previous but-for cause from being the proximate cause. Other intervening causes are said to break the causal chain between the original or previous but-for cause and the prohibited result. By breaking the causal chain, such an intervening cause precludes the original or previous but-for cause from being the proximate cause. Such intervening causes are termed supervening or superseding causes.

While the analysis of but-for causation is empirical and factual, the analysis of proximate causation is normative. That is, but-for causation focuses on whether the defendant's conduct actually made a causal contribution to bringing about the prohibited result. In contrast, proximate causation focuses on whether a defendant's conduct constituting a but-for cause *should* or *deserves* to contribute to the defendant's legal responsibility for the prohibited result. In the words of the

MPC, the issue is whether the prohibited result of the defendant's conduct is "not too remote or accidental in its occurrence to have a just bearing on the actor's liability." That is, the defendant's conduct must have a sufficiently close relationship to the prohibited result for the defendant to be sufficiently blameworthy and legally responsible. Because what constitutes "sufficiently close" is ambiguous and elusive, there are few bright-line rules in proximate causation.

This chapter helps you navigate through the confusing aspects of causation by not forcing more precision on the topic than the topic allows. Because bright-line rules are few, especially with respect to proximate causation, this chapter instead utilizes a balancing of factors approach. The rules of proximate causation embody a hodgepodge of common sense, moral intuitions, fairness, expediency, and public policy concerns. Because of the presence of this hodgepodge of considerations and the absence of bright-line rules, the chapter identifies and applies a number of factors that can be sensitively and flexibly applied to a myriad of factual situations.

PROBLEM

Vera offers George a first-class airplane ticket to Tahiti, intending that the plane will crash and that George will die. (Vera has no particular reason to believe that George's flight will crash; she simply realizes that statistically 1 in every 500,000 flights crash.) Happy to get the free flight that he could not otherwise afford, George accepts the ticket, unaware of Vera's intention. With George on the way to the airport to catch his predawn flight, the furnace in George's apartment building explodes, killing all the still-sleeping occupants. That afternoon, over the South Pacific, George's plane is struck by lightning and crashes into the sea. George is seriously injured. A flight attendant refuses to aid George. George quickly drowns and dies.[1]

Analyze and discuss whether Vera is the cause of George's death.

LIST OF READINGS

People v. Acosta, 284 Cal. Rptr. 117 (Cal. Ct. App. 1991)
People v. Campbell, 335 N.W.2d 27 (Mich. Ct. App. 1983)
Regina v. Michael, 169 Eng. Rep. 48 (1840)
MODEL PENAL CODE § 2.03 (Official Code and Revised Comments 1985)
JOSHUA DRESSLER, UNDERSTANDING CRIMINAL LAW 181–97 (5th ed. 2009)

ESSAY

Vera satisfies the technical tests for but-for causation, but there is a fairly persuasive argument that Vera should not be the but-for cause. Vera satisfies some of the tests for proximate causation but not others. Whether Vera is the proximate cause is unclear, but perhaps most courts would not find Vera as the proximate cause. As a result, Vera is probably not the cause of George's death.

---

[1] Aspects of the Problem were inspired by a hypothetical in Sanford H. Kadish, Stephen J. Schulhofer & Carol S. Steiker, CRIMINAL LAW AND ITS PROCESSES: CASES AND MATERIALS 227–28 (8th ed. 2007).

But-for Cause

[1] The simple or general test for but-for causation is as follows: But-for the actor's conduct, would the prohibited result/injury have occurred? Answering that question "yes" means that the actor is not the but-for cause. Answering that question "no" means that the actor is the but-for cause. Applying this test to Vera's conduct, Vera is not the but-for cause. Even if Vera had not given George the ticket, George would have died from the furnace explosion. When the simple but-for test does not yield an outcome that the actor is the but-for cause, application of a revised but-for test should be considered.

[2] Where, as here, there are *multiple* sufficient causes of a victim's death, the simple but-for test requires revision. The revised test is as follows: But-for the actor's conduct, would the prohibited result/injury have occurred when it did? (Where, unlike here, there are *simultaneous* sufficient causes, the test may again require revision as follows: But-for the actor's conduct would the prohibited result/injury have occurred when it did and as it did?) Applying the revised test to Vera, without Vera giving George the ticket, George would have died at a different time—in the morning furnace blast rather than the afternoon plane crash. Because George would not have died when he did without Vera's conduct, Vera is the but-for cause under the revised test.

[3] Even without multiple sufficient causes, we can understand the basis for the necessity of the revised test because, as mortal humans, we will all die eventually. Taking human mortality into account, technically no one would ever be the but-for cause of a victim's death under the simple test. That is, but-for any actor's conduct, the victim would have died eventually—even if only from natural causes. As a result, the answer to the question raised by the simple but-for test—but-for the actor's conduct would the prohibited result of the victim's death have occurred—would always be "yes," meaning that no actor would ever be the but-for cause. Because we will all die eventually, what the revised but-for test is really assessing is whether an actor has accelerated a victim's (inevitable) death. Any act that accelerates a victim's death is a but-for cause of that victim's death. This is sometimes termed the "acceleration doctrine."

[4] Based on this deeper understanding of the revised but-for test, an argument against Vera being the but-for cause emerges. Despite satisfying the revised but-for test, Vera arguably should not be considered the but-for cause of George's death because she did not accelerate George's death. But-for Vera's conduct, George would not have died later than he actually did. Rather, but-for Vera's conduct, George would have died sooner than he actually did. Vera saved George's life; Vera saved George from dying in the morning furnace explosion. Vera did not accelerate George's death; she decelerated it. Vera did not shorten George's life; she prolonged it. As a result, despite technically satisfying the revised but-for test, Vera arguably should not be the but-for cause of George's death. This issue of but-for causation—when the actual cause of death has prolonged life—is considered perhaps the most difficult issue of but-for causation and is perhaps still unresolved by the law of causation.

[5] But-for causation under the MPC is similar to the general, simple test above. MPC § 2.03(1) states as follows: "Conduct is the cause of a result when: (a) it is an

antecedent but-for which the result would not have occurred. . . ." Applying this test to Vera, because George would have died from the furnace blast even without Vera giving George a plane ticket, Vera is not the cause of George's death. The MPC provision might be understood to produce the same result as the revised test above by redescribing the "result" more precisely. Let us say the "result" is not simply George dying, but rather, George dying from a plane crash. Under that redescription of the "result," Vera is the antecedent cause.

However, one might argue that the common law acceleration doctrine should also apply under the MPC. It is not clear whether it applies, but let us assume that it does. Because Vera did not accelerate George's death (rather she decelerated or deferred it), the same argument above in [4] would also apply. Under the MPC as well, Vera arguably should not be considered the but-for cause of George's death.

CONCLUSION

[6] Vera satisfies the technical tests for but-for causation under both the common law and the MPC. However, there is a fairly persuasive argument that she should not be held as the but-for cause of George's death because she did not accelerate his death, but rather, she extended his life. If Vera is not the but-for cause, then she cannot be the cause of George's death, and proximate causation analysis is irrelevant. But in the event that her technical satisfaction of the but-for causation tests suffices for her to be the but-for cause, the next step is to determine if Vera is the proximate cause. (To be the cause of George's death, Vera must be both the but-for and proximate cause.)

Proximate Cause

COMMON LAW

[7] If the defendant is the direct cause of the prohibited result, there is little difficulty in establishing proximate causation. A direct cause produces the prohibited result with no causes intervening between the but-for cause and the prohibited result. Generally, a direct cause is a proximate cause. Vera is not a direct cause. There are a number of intervening causes between Vera giving George the ticket and George's death by drowning. George getting on the plane, the lightning that causes the plane to crash, and the flight attendant's failure to save George are all intervening causes that come between Vera's possible but-for cause and George's death. Despite these intervening causes, Vera may still be the proximate cause if none of these intervening causes are superseding. Superseding intervening causes break the causal chain and relieve the previous but-for cause from being a proximate cause. But not all intervening causes are superseding. Determining which intervening causes supersede and break the causal chain and which do not comprise the bulk of proximate causation analysis.

[8] Apart from direct causes being proximate causes, there are few clear, bright-line rules in analyzing proximate causation. Because most jurisdictions have not codified the rules of proximate causation, courts have considerable latitude to analyze proximate causation in light of common sense, expediency, fairness, and intuition. Given the lack of clarity and the wide variety of approaches to proximate causation, perhaps the best approach is to consider the analysis as

consisting of not a set of rigid rules but flexible factors. One scholar, Joshua Dressler, has helpfully identified a multifactor test that courts might consider.[2]

[9] Perhaps the most important, the most broadly applicable, and the factor virtually every court would use is foreseeability. Simply put, if the prohibited result is foreseeable as a result of the defendant's but-for cause, then the defendant is the proximate cause. If the prohibited result is unforeseeable, then the defendant is not the proximate cause. While the probability of a plane crashing and a passenger dying is extremely low, it is not clearly unforeseeable. Planes do crash periodically, killing the passengers. Moreover, in *Acosta*, two police helicopters colliding and killing the occupants was ruled to be foreseeable despite having never previously occurred. As a result, George's death might well be foreseeable.

[10] Alternatively, foreseeability is framed in terms of the intervening causes. If the intervening causes were foreseeable as a result of the but-for cause, then the but-for cause is the proximate cause. If the intervening causes were not foreseeable as a result of the but-for cause, then the but-for cause is not the proximate cause. To aid in determining whether the intervening causes were foreseeable, courts often utilize the distinction between responsive or dependent intervening causes and coincidental or independent intervening causes. A responsive or dependent intervening cause is in response to or dependent on the but-for cause. In contrast, a coincidental or independent intervening cause occurs coincidentally to and is independent from the but-for cause. Responsive or dependent intervening causes are not supervening, do not break the causal chain, and do not relieve the defendant from criminal liability. But coincidental or independent intervening causes are supervening, do break the causal chain, and do relieve the defendant of criminal liability. The lightning striking the plane and the plane crashing are coincidental to and independent from Vera's act of giving George a plane ticket. Presumably, the lightning would have struck the plane, and the plane would have crashed, regardless of whether Vera gave George a ticket. Framing the analysis of foreseeability in this way supports Vera as not being the proximate cause.

[11] The two different approaches to foreseeability conflict. The foreseeability of the result supports Vera as the proximate cause. The unforeseeability of the intervening cause of the lightning striking the plane and the plane crashing does not support Vera as the proximate cause. Different courts might take either one of the above approaches. As a result, the factor of foreseeability is perhaps inconclusive.

[12] Subsequent human conduct is another factor. Human conduct subsequent to the defendant's but-for cause that is voluntary, knowing, intelligent, and free from coercion is superseding (also called supervening), breaks the causal chain, and relieves the defendant from being the proximate cause. Subsequent human conduct that does not meet the above criteria is not superseding, does not break the causal chain and allows the defendant's but-for cause to be the proximate cause. George's subsequent conduct of accepting the plane ticket and boarding the plane is an intervening cause. If voluntary etc., it would be a supervening cause, thereby relieving Vera from being the proximate cause of George's death.

---

[2] For a court employing Dressler's multifactor test, see People v. Rideout, 727 N.W.2d 630 (Mich. Ct. App. 2006).

If involuntary etc., it would not supervene and not relieve Vera from eligibility for being the proximate cause of George's death.

[13] That George gladly accepts the ticket and boards the plane indicates that he does so voluntarily. On this basis, the intervening cause of George's subsequent conduct is supervening, breaks the causal chain, and relieves Vera from being the proximate cause. But an argument could be made that George's subsequent conduct is not knowing and intelligent. He acts without full knowledge of the circumstances surrounding Vera's gift of the ticket. George is unaware of Vera's intent that the plane crashes and he dies. On this basis, George's subsequent conduct is unknowing and thus is not a supervening cause.

[14] One still might argue that despite acting without full knowledge of the circumstances, George lacks knowledge of only irrelevant circumstances. Vera's intent, despite being unknown, plays no role in the plane crashing and George's death. While lacking knowledge of some irrelevant circumstances, George does act with the full knowledge of all relevant circumstances. As a result, arguably George has sufficient knowledge and his subsequent conduct remains a supervening cause.

[15] There are two problems with the above argument in [14]. First, it is not clear that only lack of knowledge of *relevant* circumstances will preclude an actor's subsequent conduct from being a superseding cause. The test is typically formulated as lack of full knowledge of the circumstances without the further specification of relevant circumstances. Second, Vera's intent might well be a relevant circumstance. Might it not affect George's decision whether to accept the ticket and board the plane? Would not a reasonable person refuse to accept a ticket and board a plane when the ticket giver wishes the recipient to die in a plane crash? Even if convinced that Vera's intent does not increase the chances of a plane crash, George might understandably (and reasonably, albeit irrationally) forego the ticket under such circumstances. If so, the circumstances are entirely relevant. As a result, George arguably does not act with full knowledge of the circumstances; his subsequent human conduct fails to supervene and fails to relieve Vera from being the proximate cause.

[16] Because there are plausible arguments that George's subsequent conduct does and does not supervene, the subsequent human conduct factor is arguably inconclusive.

[17] Another factor is omissions. If an intervening actor fails to act, that failure is generally not a supervening cause. The flight attendant's failure to save George from drowning is an intervening cause, but it fails to supervene. This rule holds even if the intervening actor, like the flight attendant, had a duty to render aid to passengers of the plane. Viewed alternatively, intervening failures to act, even when one is under a duty to act, are entirely foreseeable and do not supersede. As a result, the omissions factor does not relieve Vera from being the proximate cause.

[18] The de minimis contribution factor perhaps best captures our intuitions about the facts. Under this factor, if a defendant's but-for cause makes too small a contribution to the victim's injury or the prohibited result, it is not the proximate cause. Under this factor, arguably Vera's causal contribution was minimal. It only placed George on the plane where the lightning actually caused the plane to crash. Vera's giving George the plane ticket played no role in the plane crash. The lightning had a far greater causal contribution to George's death.

[19] One possible problem with applying the de minimis factor in this way is that it proves too much. Both Vera's conduct and the lightning are necessary but-for causes of George's death. If Vera's conduct is necessary, then precisely why is the lightning a greater cause? According to the above analysis in [18], the lightning is the greater cause because it actually caused the plane to crash, whereas Vera's conduct did not. But under that analysis, Vera's conduct is not merely de minimis in George's death but nonexistent. The casual contribution of Vera's conduct cannot be nonexistent because it is clearly a necessary but-for cause. Arguably, if the only basis by which Vera's conduct is to be viewed as de minimis also proves that her causal contribution is nonexistent, then that basis must be incorrect because Vera is a necessary but-for cause.

[20] Though somewhat problematic, the de minimis factor most likely supports Vera as not being the proximate cause.

[21] The final factor applicable to these facts is the intended consequences doctrine. If an actor intends a consequence and that consequence occurs, the actor may be the proximate cause of the consequence. As is sometimes said, "intended consequences can never be too remote." That is, intended consequences are foreseeable. This rule particularly applies if both the result and the means of effecting the result were both intended. Applying the doctrine here, by Vera giving George the plane ticket, Vera intended that George die, and George did so. Moreover, George not only died as intended but also died by the means that Vera intended— by a plane crash. As a result, the factor of the intended consequences doctrine supports Vera as the proximate cause.

[22] One possible problem with the above analysis in [21] is whether Vera truly intended that George die. In some jurisdictions and in some courts, Vera might be said to have a wish or a hope that George dies rather than a real intention. Arguably, one cannot intend that which one knows will not occur. Arguably, given the odds that George's plane will crash is 1 in 500,000 and that Vera is not doing anything to shorten those odds, Vera might be said to know to a practical certainty that George's plane will not crash. As a result, Vera cannot truly intend that George die. This view might be mistaken, however, in that it seems to conflate knowledge with intention. An actor might well have an intention even without having knowledge. Moreover, the distinction between hopes and wishes on the one hand and real intentions on the other is quite difficult to draw.

[23] The multifactor test for proximate causation is inconclusive. Depending on how the foreseeability and subsequent human conduct factors are understood, Vera either is or is not the proximate cause. The application of the omissions factor is clear but neither precludes Vera from being the proximate cause nor establishes her as the proximate cause. Although not entirely clear, the de minimis factor most likely precludes Vera from being the proximate cause. Also not entirely clear, the factor of the intended consequences doctrine most likely establishes Vera as the proximate cause. Of the five factors analyzed, three are inconclusive, one most likely establishes Vera as the proximate cause, and one precludes her from being the proximate cause.

[24] When the factors conflict, as they do here, it is unpredictable how a court would hold. But there are a number of possible interpretative strategies. First, the most important and fundamental of the factors—foreseeability—would control. As applied here, that strategy is unhelpful because foreseeability itself

is inconclusive. Second, the more specific and narrow factors should control over the more general and broad factors. Perhaps the intended consequences doctrine is the narrowest and most-specific factor. Thus, under the second interpretative strategy, Vera most likely is the proximate cause because she intended that George die in a plane crash. Third, one might simply compare the number of factors that support proximate causation versus the number that preclude it. Whichever has the numerical preponderance of factors determines the answer. Here that strategy is inconclusive because the number of factors supporting and precluding proximate causation are tied—one to one. Fourth, given the prosecution's burden of persuasion in establishing causation beyond a reasonable doubt, an inconclusive assessment of whether the defendant is the proximate cause indicates that the prosecution cannot establish the requisite burden of persuasion, and the defendant cannot be the proximate cause.

[25] Here, even the interpretive strategies for handling conflicts among the factors do not all point toward the same outcome. Two of the interpretive strategies are inconclusive, and two point toward Vera as not the proximate cause. On this basis, perhaps Vera is not the proximate cause.

MODEL PENAL CODE

[26] Under the MPC, proximate causation is treated as an aspect of mens rea. If an offense contains an element requiring that the defendant purposely or knowingly caused the result, that element is satisfied if the actual result is within the purpose or contemplation of the actor. Here, the actual result of George's death by a plane crash is within the purpose and contemplation of Vera. As a result, Vera would satisfy an element requiring that she purposely caused the result. (Because Vera does not have knowledge that George's plane would crash, knowledge seems inappropriate.) If an offense contains an element requiring that the defendant recklessly or negligently caused the result, that element is satisfied if the actor is aware of the risk that the actual result might occur or should have been aware of the risk. Here, Vera was aware of the risk that George's plane might crash and George might die. As a result, Vera might also satisfy an element that she recklessly caused George's death. (Because Vera should not have known that George's plan would crash, negligence seems inappropriate.) Of course, because a higher level of mens rea suffices for or establishes a lower level mens rea, Vera purposefully causing the result would suffice for or establish all the other mental states. As a result, Vera would satisfy proximate causation under the MPC.

Conclusion

[27] Under the common law, it is not clear whether Vera is the proximate cause. Under the multifactor test, some factors are inconclusive, one supports Vera as the proximate cause, and one does not. Even the interpretive strategies for handling conflicts among the factors conflict. Two are inconclusive, and two preclude Vera from being the proximate cause. On this basis, Vera is perhaps not the proximate cause. As a result, under the common law, Vera is perhaps not the cause of George's death. Proximate causation under the MPC functions differently than under the common law and is somewhat an aspect of mens rea. Under the MPC, Vera purposely and perhaps recklessly caused the result of George's death.

TOOLS FOR SELF-ASSESSMENT

Go back to your written answer. Look for the issues identified in paragraphs [1]–[27] in the above Essay. Look also for the analysis that follows each issue, and mark your essay where you locate it. Do you fully describe the issue, identify the precise legal standard that applies, list the relevant facts, and show how the facts and law support a conclusion for each issue in a separate paragraph? Mark each conclusion in your essay. Are there sufficient reasons in the law and in the facts to support the conclusion?

1. Do what you are told. In the instructions to the Problem, you are asked to analyze and discuss whether Vera is the cause of George's death. You need not analyze whether Vera will ultimately be held criminally liable for the homicide of George as that would require an analysis of the other elements of homicide apart from causation.

2. Do not analyze what is unnecessary. For example, it might be tempting to analyze what are the other but-for causes of George's death besides Vera's conduct. Do not do so. If you determine that Vera is not the proximate cause of George's death, it might also be tempting to analyze who is the proximate cause. Do not do so. It is not necessary under the instructions following the Problem.

3. Always remember to include an analysis under the MPC unless you are instructed otherwise.

4. State the best possible arguments for alternative conclusions. Even as you reject possible conclusions as to why Vera is or is not the but-for cause and why Vera is or is not the proximate cause, make the best possible argument first, and only then explain why you are rejecting that conclusion.

5. Be on the alert for red herrings. Some information in the fact pattern of a hypothetical may be irrelevant or even designed to mislead you. For example, that the plane ticket is for a first-class seat and that the destination is Tahiti are irrelevant to your analysis.

6. Be aware of the similarities and differences of causation analysis under the common law and the MPC. Under the common law, causation is a two-part test. The defendant must be both the but-for cause and the proximate cause of the prohibited result. Under the MPC § 2.03(1), an actor being the but-for cause establishes the actor as the cause of the prohibited result. The MPC's somewhat equivalent rules to proximate causation, § 2.03(2)(b) and (3)(b), are more precisely an aspect of mens rea or culpability analysis. But the analysis of whether an actor is the but-for cause is largely the same under both the common law and the MPC. The MPC's approach to proximate causation as an aspect of mens rea has not been very influential on the courts, and your casebook and instructor may not even address it.

7. Apply the two-step test in order. That is, first analyze but-for causation, and then analyze proximate causation. There are a number of reasons why this order is preferable and helpful for you. First, because only but-for causes are eligible to be proximate causes, determining but-for causation will help narrow the possible candidates for proximate cause. Second, issues of but-for causation are generally easier. It would waste precious exam time to undertake a lengthy and perhaps difficult proximate causation analysis only to later determine that the proximate cause candidate was not a but-for cause.

8. Do not be confused by the traditional articulation of the but-for test. It asks, "But-for the defendant's conduct would the harm or prohibited result have

occurred?" A positive answer of "yes" yields the negative outcome that the defendant is *not* the but-for cause. And a negative answer of "no" yields the positive outcome that the defendant *is* the but-for cause. This is potentially confusing and may easily lead to getting the diametrically opposite conclusion than is correct, especially under the time pressure of an exam.

9. Consider using a less confusing but-for causation test as a check to make sure that you do not invert the answer to the traditional test with its outcome. The alternative test is as follows: "Was the defendant's conduct necessary for the occurrence of the harm, injury, or prohibited result?" Under this alternative test, a positive answer of "yes" leads to the positive outcome that the defendant's conduct *is* a but-for cause. And a negative answer of "no" leads to the negative outcome that the defendant's conduct is *not* a but-for cause. But remember to only use this test as a check on your analysis of the traditional test—the traditional test is what courts actually employ.

10. The simple but-for test may be too simple in some cases. If after applying the simple but-for test you conclude that the defendant's conduct is not the but-for cause, you should apply the following revised but-for test: "But-for the defendant's conduct would the harm, injury, or prohibited result have occurred *when it did*?" This revised test establishes but-for causation (when the simple but-for test would not) where the harm or result would have occurred even without the defendant's conduct, but the defendant's conduct makes it happen sooner. For example, the defendant shoots and kills a victim who already is about to die from other causes. This revised test may be more informally understood as the acceleration doctrine. That which accelerates the occurrence of a harm, injury, or result that would have independently occurred later is a but-for cause. If after applying this revised test you conclude that the defendant is not a but-for cause, you should apply the following twice-revised test: "But-for the defendant's conduct, would the injury, harm, or prohibited result have occurred when it did *and as it did*?" This twice-revised test establishes but-for causation (when neither the simple nor revised test would) where the harm or result would have occurred and would have occurred when it did but not in the same way. For example, *A* and *B* simultaneously shoot *C*, and *C* dies instantly. But *C* would also have died instantly from either shot alone. Under both the simple and revised tests, neither *A* nor *B* is a but-for cause. But under the twice-revised test, both *A* and *B* are but-for causes of *C* dying the way *C* died—from two mortal wounds.

11. There are some cases for which perhaps not even the twice-revised but-for test yields the correct answer. Perhaps the most notoriously difficult issue in but-for causation is where an actor is clearly the but-for cause under existing but-for causation tests despite delaying the occurrence of the harm or prohibited result. Consider the example in the Problem—by giving George the plane ticket, Vera is a but-for cause of his death under the existing tests despite lengthening his life by saving him from an earlier furnace explosion. Despite being a but-for cause under some but-for tests, there is a basis for concluding that such an actor should not be the but-for cause. If anything that accelerates a harm or result is a but-for cause of that harm or result, then arguably anything which delays or decelerates a harm or result should not be a but-for cause.

12. In applying the multifactor test for proximate causation, keep in mind that only some, but not all, of the factors are applicable in any given case. The six

factors identified by Joshua Dressler are as follows: (i) de minimis causal contribution, (ii) foreseeability, (iii) intended consequences doctrine, (iv) apparent safety doctrine, (v) subsequent human conduct, and (vi) omissions. Not all of the factors applied to the facts of the Problem. The fourth factor did not apply. Vera did not set into motion a dangerous force that ceased being dangerous once the victim reached a position of apparent safety. But in other cases or hypotheticals, a different factor or factors might be inapplicable. Perhaps the one factor that will always be applicable is foreseeability. That is why courts will almost invariably assess foreseeability and why it is the most fundamental and important factor. But as the most fundamental factor, it is also the broadest and arguably should be trumped by a narrower factor if they conflict. In this way, foreseeability might be viewed as the general rule, and the other factors are exceptions to the general rule.

13. Note that not all of the factors either support or preclude proximate causation. The omissions factor neither establishes nor undermines a given but-for cause as the proximate cause. The factor merely states that an actor's failure to act will generally not be a supervening cause. At most, the factor allows for a previous but-for cause to remain eligible to be a proximate cause.

14. Depending on the nature of the subsequent human conduct, it either will or will not be a supervening cause. Generally, human conduct is conceived to spring from our free will, and thus human conduct subsequent to a previous but-for cause will break the causal chain and supervene. But some types of intervening human conduct are not free, do not break the causal chain, and do not supervene. Examples of this latter type include (i) literally involuntary actions like a spasm or reflex, (ii) conduct under a duty, (iii) conduct under duress, (iv) conduct in self-defense, (v) conduct without full knowledge of the circumstances, (vi) conduct under the influence of drugs or while intoxicated, and (vii) irrational conduct or conduct while under a depression or mental disturbance.

15. The best strategy in analyzing causation is to neutrally apply the rules, principles, and factors to the facts of the case or hypothetical and reach a tentative conclusion. If, however, the outcome of those neutrally applied rules seems clearly unjust, unfair, or impractical, then make a public policy argument as to why the outcome dictated by the neutral application of the rules is wrong. Such arguments are particularly relevant in causation because courts and commentators freely concede that the rules and principles of causation are not precise enough to yield the correct outcome in every case. The doctrines of causation, more than most areas of criminal law, are themselves a hodgepodge of intuition, common sense, expediency, and fairness, rather than a matter of bright-line rules and formal logic. As a result, this hodgepodge of rules must be supplemented by our intuitions and common sense.

VARIATIONS ON THE THEME

1. Rather than a flight attendant who fails to render aid to George after the crash, George's wife fails to render aid.

2. Rather than George accepting the ticket without knowing Vera's intention that he die in a plane crash, George does know Vera's intention.

3. Rather than the furnace in George's apartment building exploding and killing all of the still sleeping occupants, the furnace does not explode, and no one in George's apartment building is killed.

4.   Rather than the plane crashing because of being hit by lightning, the plane crashes because of mechanical difficulties.

5.   Rather than Vera intending that the plane will crash and that George die, Vera is merely aware of the statistical risk that the plane could crash and that George would die.

6.   George initially refuses to accept the ticket. Vera threatens to kill him unless he accepts the ticket and boards the plane.

7.   George is terrified of flying and initially refuses to accept the ticket. Vera drugs George with massive doses of Prozac, an anti-anxiety drug, both before George ultimately does accept the ticket and before George boards the plane.

8.   Rather than a flight attendant refusing to render aid to George and George subsequently dying, George dies immediately upon impact of the crash.

9.   Rather than a flight attendant refusing to render aid, a flight attendant rescues George and rushes him to a hospital. A doctor informs George that he has lost a lot of blood, and a blood transfusion is required to save his life. George refuses on religious grounds and subsequently dies from loss of blood.

10. Rather than George being seriously injured by the crash, George only sustains a few nicks and bruises. But George has an extremely rare preexisting and hidden genetic disease—sodium imbalance syndrome—making additional amounts of sodium toxic to his system. When the plane crashes into the ocean, George involuntarily swallows some salt water from the ocean and subsequently dies.

ADDITIONAL READINGS

People v. Rideout, 727 N.W.2d 630 (Mich. Ct. App. 2006)

GEORGE FLETCHER, BASIC CONCEPTS OF CRIMINAL LAW 59–72 (1998)

GEORGE FLETCHER, RETHINKING CRIMINAL LAW 360–72 (1978)

H.L.A. HART & TONY HONORE, CAUSATION IN THE LAW (2d ed. 1985)

LEO KATZ, BAD ACTS AND GUILTY MINDS: CONUNDRUMS OF THE CRIMINAL LAW 210–51 (1987)

PAUL ROBINSON, CRIMINAL LAW 153–73 (1997)

Larry Alexander & Kimberly Kessler Ferzan, *Results Don't Matter, in* CRIMINAL LAW CONVERSATIONS 147 (Paul H. Robinson, Stephen P. Garvey & Kimberly Kessler Ferzan eds., 2009) (with comments by Gerald Leonard, Peter Westen, Thomas Morawetz, and Jeremy Horder)

Michael Moore, *Causation, in* 1 ENCYCLOPEDIA OF CRIME AND JUSTICE 150 (Joshua Dressler ed., 2nd ed. 2002)

Michael Moore, *The Metaphysics of Causal Intervention*, 88 CAL. L. REV. 827 (2000)

Stephen J. Schulhofer, *Harm and Punishment: A Critique of Emphasis on the Results of Conduct in the Criminal Law*, 122 U. PA. L. REV. 1497 (1974)

HOMICIDE I:

MURDER AND MANSLAUGHTER

6

INTRODUCTION

Homicide is not a specific crime but a category of crimes involving the unlawful killing of a human being (or fetus). This category includes a confusing variety of specific crimes under the common law—murder, voluntary manslaughter, and involuntary manslaughter—and MPC—murder, manslaughter, and negligent homicide. Compounding the confusion is that each of these crimes split into additional crimes. For example, a jurisdiction may subdivide murder into premeditated murder, intentional murder, depraved heart murder, and felony murder. And many jurisdictions, but not the MPC, distinguish between numeric degrees of murder—murder in the first degree, second degree, etc.

The historical reason for this proliferation of different types of homicide is that in the early days of the common law, any homicide was subject to capital punishment. Over time, courts and legislatures found that some homicides were not sufficiently blameworthy to warrant capital punishment and carved out lesser types and degrees of homicide not subject to the death penalty. Today, even in jurisdictions not imposing capital punishment, these different qualitative types and quantitative degrees persist and serve to precisely calibrate the degree of the offender's blameworthiness and match it with the commensurate degree of deserved punishment.

Unlike other crimes, the principal issue in analyzing homicide will not be so much whether a homicide has occurred but rather which type. The primary sorting mechanism for determining the specific type of homicide, and any subdivision or degree within that crime, is the perpetrator's mens rea. Under the common law, a homicide committed with premeditation and deliberation, intention, or gross recklessness is murder. A homicide committed with (simple) recklessness or negligence may be termed involuntary manslaughter. Under the MPC, a homicide committed with purpose, knowledge, or a special type of (gross) recklessness is murder. A homicide committed with (simple) recklessness is manslaughter; a homicide committed with negligence is termed, not surprisingly, negligent homicide.

There are two important special types of homicide that are not exclusively determined by the actor's mens rea. Felony murder and voluntary manslaughter (the MPC uses different terms) feature a number of specialized doctrines and rules and will each be the subject of separate chapters. (Ch. 7, "Homicide II: Provocation/ Extreme Mental or Emotional Disturbance"; Ch. 8, "Homicide III: Felony Murder & Misdemeanor Manslaughter.") Another important issue that arises principally in homicide cases—causation—was the focus of the previous chapter. (Ch. 5, "Causation.")

This chapter will help you meet the challenges of analyzing homicide in two steps. Given a fact pattern in which a perpetrator has caused the death of a human being, which of the many types of homicide has the actor committed? First, determine the perpetrator's mens rea. This chapter will supply clear bases for differentiating between the different types of mens rea. Suppose, for example, that you determine the actor's mens rea to be recklessness. With this determination of the actor's mens rea, the second step is to precisely categorize the specific homicide crime that the perpetrator has committed both under the MPC and the common law. The chapter will provide the tools to organize and manage the confusing and overlapping categories, enabling you to clearly ascertain the appropriate specific homicide crime. Applying these tools allows you to conclude that a homicide committed with the mens rea of recklessness constitutes the common law crime of Involuntary Manslaughter and the MPC crime of Manslaughter. Although perhaps not all cases will be this easy, this two-step approach lends considerable analytic clarity.

PROBLEM

Chip, the grandfather of Walker and Texas Ranger, has been living with a great deal of pain since enduring treatments for bone cancer and has, in fact, been bed-ridden for the last six months. Both Walker and Texas Ranger love and adore their grandfather and it has been quite painful for them to watch him suffer as his quality of life has steadily decreased. They finally decide that rather than watch Chip suffer another day, they will end his life. Walker and Texas Ranger obtain highly toxic spider monkey venom sufficient to kill Chip quickly, painlessly, and with dignity. The boys hug and kiss their grandfather and inject him with enough venom to bring about Chip's death.

Meanwhile, Walker and Texas Ranger's father, Ricky Booby, a world-renowned race car driver who likes to go fast and is known for his Shake 'n Bake routine, is celebrating his recent NASCAR victory at home with a bottle of tequila. After having half a dozen shots, Ricky is feeling quite intoxicated. He walks into Chip's room just after the boys have injected Chip with the venom. Ricky does not want Chip to die and realizes he needs immediate medical attention if he is going to survive the venom. Although Ricky knows that he is intoxicated and could call for an ambulance, he also knows that he is a highly skilled driver. He decides that if Chip is going to live, he must drive him to the emergency room himself. As he is racing through the streets at 100 mph (more than twice the speed limit), he loses control of his car and runs over and kills a pizza delivery boy (Pizza Boy) who was carefully riding his bike in an authorized bicycle lane. Ricky also runs over and kills a crêpe delivery boy (Crêpe Boy) who was passed out in the road from drinking too much French wine.

Ricky arrives at the hospital while Chip is still alive. He rushes Chip to a doctor only to learn that the effects of the spider monkey venom are irreversible, and there is nothing that can be done for Chip. Chip dies quietly later that night.[1]

Analyze and discuss Walker and Texas Ranger's homicide liability, if any, for the death of Chip under the common law and MPC. Analyze and discuss Ricky's homicide

---

[1] Aspects of this Problem are inspired by the film, TALLADEGA NIGHTS: THE BALLAD OF RICKY BOBBY (Columbia 2006).

liability, if any, for the deaths of Pizza Boy and Crêpe Boy under the common law and MPC. (You need not analyze the other elements necessary for liability such as the actus reus, causation, etc.)

LIST OF READINGS

People v. Hall, 999 P.2d 207 (Co. 2000)

Commonwealth v. Carroll, 194 A.2d 911 (Pa. 1963)

State v. Guthrie, 461 S.E. 2d 163 (W. Va. 1995)

MODEL PENAL CODE §§ 2.02(2), 210.2(1)(a)–(b), 210.3(1)(a), and 210.4(1)

(Official Code and Revised Comments 1985)

ESSAY

Regarding Chip, under the common law, Walker and Texas Ranger will be liable for first or second-degree murder depending on the jurisdiction. Under the MPC, Walker and Texas Ranger will be liable for murder.

Regarding Pizza Boy, under the common law, Ricky will possibly be liable for gross reckless murder and most likely be liable for involuntary manslaughter. Under the MPC, Ricky will possibly be liable for murder and manslaughter; he will most likely be liable for negligent homicide.

Regarding Crêpe Boy, under the common law, Ricky will possibly be liable for gross reckless murder and most likely be liable for involuntary manslaughter. Under the MPC, Ricky will possibly be liable for murder and manslaughter; he will most likely be liable for negligent homicide.

Walker and Texas Ranger's Homicide Liability for Chip's Death

COMMON LAW

[1] Murder is traditionally defined as the killing of another human being with malice aforethought. Malice aforethought is a catch-all term for whatever mens rea suffices for murder. There are a number of different types and degrees of murder. In the majority of jurisdictions, first-degree murder is an intentional murder committed with premeditation and deliberation. Generally, second-degree murder is the intentional killing of another human being.

[2] Among the jurisdictions requiring premeditation and deliberation for first-degree murder, there is a split as to what qualifies as premeditation and deliberation. Under one approach, there is no set time period prior to a killing during which the killer must premeditate and deliberate. Premeditation and deliberation may occur as late as while the killer is, for example, pulling the trigger. Under this approach, there is little, if any, difference between premeditation/deliberation and intent. At the time Walker and Texas Ranger injected Chip with the venom, if not before, they intended to kill Chip. As a result, under this approach, they would be criminally liable for first-degree murder of Chip.

[3] Under the other approach, premeditation and deliberation require a sufficient period of time to elapse between the formation of the intent to kill and the actual killing for the premeditation and deliberation to occur. This time period allows an opportunity for reflection on the intention to kill, indicating the killing is by prior calculation and design. While there has been considerable debate over exactly what type of evidence supports a finding of premeditation and exactly how much time must lapse between formation of the intent and the actual killing, Walker and

Texas Ranger clearly displayed premeditation and deliberation in that they "finally" decided that they would kill Chip—indicating that there had been at least some thought about it sometime prior to obtaining the serum and injecting Chip. There was obviously some planning involved as spider monkey venom is presumably not easy to come by. These factors, taken together, support a finding that a sufficient amount of time elapsed between the formation of the intent to kill and the killing. As a result, there probably was sufficient premeditation and deliberation, and Walker and Texas Ranger would probably be liable for first-degree murder.

[4] A minority of jurisdictions do not recognize an intentional murder committed with premeditation and deliberation as first-degree murder. In these jurisdictions, first-degree murder includes an intentional murder committed under special circumstances, such as if the victim is a police officer or correctional facility employee. In some of these jurisdictions, felony murder is also considered first-degree murder. Walker and Texas Ranger neither kill Chip under the requisite special circumstances nor do they satisfy the felony murder rule. (See Ch. 8 for further explanation of the felony murder rule.) But they would be liable for killing Chip with intent rendering them most likely liable for second-degree murder.

[5] One might argue that Walker and Texas Ranger's motive for killing Chip might relieve or mitigate their murder liability. However, the general rule is that an actor's motive is irrelevant. Whether one intentionally kills for love, money, self-preservation, or revenge, one nonetheless kills intentionally and the motive—good or bad—is irrelevant. Here mercy motivates Walker and Texas Ranger to intentionally kill Chip. But even this good motive neither supplies a defense nor mitigates their level of homicide liability.

MODEL PENAL CODE

[6] The MPC defines murder as causing the death of another human being with purpose, knowledge, or a special form of gross recklessness. Purpose as to a result element, such as the death of a human being, is the conscious object to cause death. Walker and Texas Ranger injected Chip with the venom, with the conscious object of killing him. As a result, Walker and Texas Ranger killed with purpose, thereby committing murder.

Ricky's Liability for Pizza Boy's Death

COMMON LAW

[7] Under the common law, Ricky is potentially subject to murder liability for the death of Pizza Boy. Because Ricky did not desire or have as a goal Pizza Boy's death, he does not commit intentional murder. But murder can also be committed unintentionally if the actor kills with gross recklessness exhibiting a depraved or malignant heart, or depraved indifference to the value of human life, if (i) death is likely to result from the actor's conduct, (ii) the actor consciously disregards the risk to life that his or her conduct poses, and (iii) the risk is unjustified. Ricky's conduct of driving at a high rate of speed while considerably intoxicated could be viewed as such gross recklessness. As to the first element, the likelihood of someone dying as a result of Ricky's conduct is sufficiently high to plausibly qualify as "likely." The standard of "likely" does not require that the death be more likely than not. The standard is also somewhat a function of the gravity of harm. Where the

gravity of harm is high, even a relatively low probability of death may rise to the level of "likely" to result. While there is no specific evidence in the facts that Ricky consciously disregarded a risk, conscious awareness of the risk is often presumed merely from the widely known hazardous nature of speeding while intoxicated. Speeding while intoxicated, resulting in another's death, is routinely considered gross reckless murder. On this basis, Ricky might be found liable for gross reckless murder.

[8] There are two distinct facts, however, that complicate the analysis of Ricky's gross reckless murder liability. First, Ricky is a world-renowned driver with extraordinary driving skills. The very same conduct that would be life threatening if undertaken by an ordinary driver might not pose much of a risk at all when undertaken by an extraordinary driver. Moreover, given his extraordinary driving skills, Ricky's conduct of speeding while intoxicated may pose even less of a risk than the conduct of an ordinary, sober driver adhering to the speed limit. If true, this argument would undermine a number of the elements of gross reckless murder. Ricky would lack depraved indifference, and death would not be "likely" to result. And even if the argument is false, Ricky's extraordinary driving skills might lead him to not appreciate the riskiness of his speeding while intoxicated so that he had no conscious awareness that his conduct did actually pose a risk. Either way, whether his extraordinary driving skills objectively preclude the risk or whether they subjectively blind him to awareness of the risk, Ricky possibly does not satisfy the elements of gross reckless murder.

Of course, one might make the opposite argument. Ricky's status as a professional driver cuts both ways. Ricky might pose an even greater danger than the nonprofessional, speeding drunk driver because he believes he is an extraordinary driver that does not have to use the same care as a nonprofessional. And, precisely because he is a professional driver, Ricky surely is consciously aware of the risks inherent in speeding while intoxicated. As a professional driver he has, in effect, a heightened awareness of the dangers of his conduct.

[9] Second, Ricky was rushing Chip to the hospital in an attempt to save his life. This undermines element (iii)—that the risk is unjustified. One approximate measure of whether a risk is unjustified is whether the importance of the actor's objective is less than or disproportional to the magnitude of the risk. Because the importance of Ricky's objective—saving Chip's life—was very high, it might well be greater than or, at least, proportional to the magnitude of the risk. As a result, even if Ricky's conduct is viewed as very dangerous and risky, the risk that he imposed might be justified. And, as justified, Ricky's conduct fails to qualify for gross reckless murder.

[10] Ricky might lose his justification, however, given the number of victims that he kills. While the importance of the objective of saving Chip might be proportional to the magnitude of the risk imposed on Pizza Boy, it might be disproportional to the magnitude of the risk imposed on both Pizza Boy and Crêpe Boy. While the importance of Ricky's objective remains high, as a sufficient number of victims pile up the magnitude of the risk of Ricky's conduct disproportionally exceeds the importance of the objective. Given that he kills two in the attempt to save one, Ricky's conduct may well be unjustified. It is unclear whether the deaths of each victim can be aggregated so that he is justified with respect to neither victim. Or perhaps he is justified with respect to one victim but not the other.

[11] Ricky's attempt to save Chip's life might also serve to undermine the element of depraved indifference to the value of human life. That Ricky values Chip's life so highly demonstrates that Ricky does not exhibit a callous disregard and indifference to the value of human life. However, this argument may not be entirely persuasive. That Ricky values some life (Chip's) does not preclude a finding that he exhibits depraved indifference toward another's life (for example, Pizza Boy). Gross reckless murder may only require a showing that the defendant had a depraved indifference—not to all human life but rather merely to the victim's life (Pizza Boy).

[12] Even if Ricky is not liable for murder under the common law, he might be liable for involuntary manslaughter. Involuntary manslaughter is a form of unintentional homicide committed with either recklessness or negligence.

[13] Recklessness is defined as consciously disregarding a substantial and unjustifiable risk constituting a gross deviation from what a reasonable person would do in the defendant's situation. The difference between gross reckless murder and reckless involuntary manslaughter is a matter of degree. In gross reckless murder, the disregard for human life exhibits a depraved indifference that is likely to result in death; in reckless involuntary manslaughter, the level of recklessness merely involves a conscious disregard of a substantial risk to life. Requiring a comparatively lower standard, reckless involuntary manslaughter is comparatively easier to establish than gross reckless murder.

Even so, the same two facts that may preclude Ricky's liability for gross reckless murder may also preclude Ricky's liability for the recklessness variant of involuntary manslaughter. (See analysis in [8]–[9] above.)

[14] Even if Ricky is not liable for the recklessness variant of involuntary manslaughter, he might be liable for the negligence variant. In the negligence variant, the actor should be aware that his or her conduct creates a substantial and unjustifiable risk. Otherwise, the analysis is the same. Consequently, if Ricky escapes liability for reckless involuntary manslaughter for reasons apart from lacking conscious awareness of the risk, then he will also not be liable for the negligence variant. But, if instead, Ricky escapes liability for the recklessness variant only because he lacks conscious awareness of the risk, he might still be held liable for the negligence variant. If the latter, Ricky would be liable for the negligent variant of involuntary manslaughter if he should have been aware of the risk. Although Ricky's professional driving skills could support an argument either way (see [8] above), most likely he should have been aware of the risk precisely because he is a professional driver who knows all too well the hazards of driving under optimal circumstances, let alone under the suboptimal conditions of speeding and intoxication.

MODEL PENAL CODE
[15] Under the MPC, Ricky possibly commits the gross reckless variant of murder. The elements of the offense are satisfied by an actor killing recklessly under circumstances manifesting an extreme indifference to the value of human life. The analysis is largely the same as for gross recklessness under the common law (see [7]–[11] above). One difference, however, is that the MPC formulation lacks the requirement that death is likely to result. But if conduct is likely to result in death, then it manifests extreme indifference to human life, thereby making the two standards substantively identical. To the extent that the two standards are substantively

different, the MPC formulation, by lacking the additional element, will be comparatively easier to establish. Though easier to establish, Ricky may not be liable for the recklessness variant of murder under the MPC for the same reasons that he might not be liable for gross reckless murder under the common law (see [8]–[11] above).

[16] Even if Ricky is not liable for the recklessness variant of murder, Ricky may be liable for the recklessness variant of manslaughter under the MPC. It is satisfied in much the same way as the recklessness variant of involuntary manslaughter under the common law (see [12]–[13] above). On this basis, to the extent that Ricky is liable for the recklessness variant of involuntary manslaughter under the common law, he would also be liable for the recklessness variant of manslaughter under the MPC.

[17] There is one possible difference between the recklessness variant of involuntary manslaughter under the common law and the recklessness variant of manslaughter under the MPC. While courts are fuzzy about the exact elements, the common law appears to require the following: (i) conscious awareness of a risk, (ii) that the risk be objectively substantial, and (iii) that the risk be objectively unjustified. The MPC formulation is also ambiguous but may require those elements as well as the following additional elements: (iv) conscious awareness that the risk is substantial, and (v) conscious awareness that the risk is unjustified. If so, it may be more difficult to establish liability for Ricky for the recklessness variant of manslaughter under the MPC than for the recklessness variant of involuntary manslaughter under the common law. Ricky might well satisfy elements (i)–(iii) and thus be liable for the common law crime, but not satisfy elements (iv)–(v) and thus not be liable for the MPC crime.

[18] Even if Ricky is not liable for the recklessness variant of manslaughter, he may be liable for negligent homicide under the MPC. It is satisfied in much the same way as the negligence variant of involuntary manslaughter under the common law (see [14] above).

[19] There is one possible difference between involuntary manslaughter under the common law and the MPC crimes of the recklessness variant of manslaughter and negligent homicide. The MPC crimes formally require that, "considering the nature and purpose of the actor's conduct and the circumstances known to him . . . disregard [of the risk] involves a gross deviation from the standard of care that a reasonable person [or law-abiding person] would observe in the actor's situation." MPC § 2.02(2)(c)–(d). The language of "in the actor's situation" partially subjectivizes the otherwise objective reasonable person standard. As a result, the MPC may subjectivize the reasonable person standard to a greater degree than the common law. To that extent, it may be more difficult to establish liability for Ricky under the MPC for manslaughter/negligent homicide than for involuntary manslaughter under the common law. If Ricky's extraordinary driving ability is construed as part of Ricky's "situation" from which the reasonableness of his conduct is to be judged, he may escape liability. Rather than be judged by whether his conduct constitutes a gross deviation from what an ordinary reasonable person would do, instead it would be this: does his conduct constitute a gross deviation from what a reasonable person with world-class driving skills would do? Under this latter standard, Ricky's conduct would be comparatively much less likely to constitute a gross deviation. Although the MPC provides some guidance as to what should and what

should not be included as part of an actor's "situation," it is not clear whether extraordinary driving skills are part of an actor's situation. If they are not part of an actor's situation, then this possible difference between the MPC and common law crimes involving reckless and negligent killings does not apply.

Ricky's Liability for Crêpe Boy's Death

[20] Ricky's liability for the death of Crêpe Boy would be subject to largely the same analysis as for Pizza Boy. The only difference is that Pizza Boy was not at fault but Crêpe Boy was at fault for being passed out in the middle of the road and is, at least partially, at fault for being run over and killed by Ricky. One might argue that Crêpe Boy's contributory negligence should be a defense for Ricky to a charge of homicide liability for Crêpe Boy's death. However, a victim's contributory negligence is not a defense.

[21] That Crêpe Boy's contributory negligence is not per se a defense does not preclude it from being relevant to analyzing Ricky's homicide liability. It could be relevant if running over and killing someone lying unexpectedly in the road was neither reckless nor negligent. One might argue that if Ricky could not have avoided running over and killing Crêpe Boy even if Ricky had not been speeding and intoxicated, then Ricky may lack depraved indifference or extreme indifference to the value of human life. As a result, Ricky would be liable for neither gross reckless murder under the common law nor the recklessness variant of murder under the MPC. If even a reasonable or law-abiding person who was neither speeding nor intoxicated could not have avoided running over and killing Crêpe Boy, then Ricky's conduct would not qualify as a gross deviation from the expected standard of care. As a result, Ricky would neither be reckless nor negligent and would thus be liable for neither form of involuntary manslaughter under the common law. He would likewise be neither liable for manslaughter nor negligent homicide under the MPC.

But this argument will likely fail. That even someone who was not speeding and drinking could not have avoided running over and killing Crêpe Boy does not preclude Ricky's conduct from being grossly reckless/reckless/negligent. While killing someone in a nonblameworthy manner may avoid criminal liability, killing someone while acting in a blameworthy manner may render the actor subject to criminal liability. Ricky acted in a blameworthy manner and killed Crêpe Boy. That a nonblameworthy actor would also have run over and killed Crêpe Boy may be irrelevant.

(Note: Perhaps the better argument for Ricky would be to deny causation. His admittedly gross reckless/reckless/negligent conduct was not the cause of Crêpe Boy's death. Crêpe Boy lying in the middle of the road was arguably unforeseeable and, on that basis, Ricky would not be the proximate cause. (See Ch. 5 for further discussion of Causation.).)

Conclusion

Walker and Texas Ranger: Under the common law, Walker and Texas Ranger will be subject to first-degree murder liability for Chip's death in a majority of jurisdictions. In a minority of jurisdictions, they will only be liable for second-degree murder. Under the MPC, Walker and Texas Ranger will be liable for murder.

Ricky: Regarding Pizza Boy, under the common law, Ricky will possibly be liable for gross reckless murder and the recklessness variant of involuntary manslaughter.

He will most likely be liable for the negligence variant of involuntary manslaughter. Under the MPC, Ricky will possibly be liable for the recklessness variants of both murder and manslaughter. He will most likely be liable for negligent homicide.

Regarding Crêpe Boy, under the common law, Ricky will possibly be liable for gross reckless murder and the recklessness variant of involuntary manslaughter. He will most likely be liable for the negligence variant of involuntary manslaughter. Under the MPC, Ricky will possibly be liable for the recklessness variants of murder and manslaughter. He will most likely be liable for negligent homicide.

However, under both the common law and the MPC, the case for Ricky's homicide liability is weaker for Crêpe Boy than for Pizza Boy. As a result, Ricky may be liable for Pizza Boy's death and either liable for a lower grade of homicide for Crêpe Boy or not liable at all.

TOOLS FOR SELF-ASSESSMENT
Go back to your written answer. Look for the issues identified in paragraphs [1]–[21] in the above Essay. Look also for the analysis that follows each issue, and mark your essay where you locate it. Do you fully describe the issue, identify the precise legal standard that applies, list the relevant facts, and show how the facts and law support a conclusion for each issue in a separate paragraph? Mark each conclusion in your essay. Are there sufficient reasons in the law and in the facts to support the conclusion?

1.   Do what you are told. In the Problem, you are asked to analyze and discuss the criminal liability of Walker and Texas Ranger for the death of Chip and the criminal liability of Ricky for the deaths of Pizza Boy and Crêpe Boy. You are to identify which type or types of homicide each actor commits as well as any applicable defenses.

2.   Do not analyze what is unnecessary. For example, it might be tempting to analyze Walker and Texas Ranger's liability for the deaths of Pizza and Crêpe Boy and likewise to analyze Ricky's liability for the death of Chip. Regardless of any temptation to do so, it is not necessary under the instructions following the Problem.

3.   Always analyze under the MPC unless you are instructed otherwise.

4.   State the best possible arguments for alternative conclusions. Even as you reject possible conclusions as to whether an actor may have satisfied an element or may have a defense, make the best possible argument first and only then explain why you are rejecting that conclusion.

5.   Be on the alert for red herrings. Some information in the fact pattern of a hypothetical may be irrelevant or even designed to mislead you. For example, that Chip is in pain, bedridden, and that his grandchildren love him very much is evidence of the killers' good motive. However tempting it may be to conclude that they cannot be liable for a mercy killing, their motive is irrelevant.

6.   The best strategy to employ in analyzing criminal liability for homicide involves two steps. First, determine the actor's mens rea. This narrows the number of possible specific homicide crimes. Second, determine which specific homicide crime or crimes under both the common law and MPC the actor may have committed, given your determination of the actor's mens rea. With Chart I below, you can see which specific types of homicide may be committed under the common law and the MPC

when an actor has a given mens rea. Chart II depicts largely the same information but in a different way. Chart I matches various mens rea with corresponding types of homicide. In contrast, Chart II begins with types of homicide and then depicts the corresponding requisite mens rea. At the outset, use Chart I to familiarize yourself with the two-step process of identifying the actor's mens rea and then determining the corresponding type of homicide. Use Chart II to supplement your

Chart I

Mens Rea	Type of Homicide	
	COMMON LAW	*MPC*
PURPOSE	————	Murder
INTENTION	Murder	————
KNOWLEDGE	————	Murder
GROSS RECKLESSNESS	Murder	Murder
MALICE AFORETHOUGHT	Murder	————
MURDER + PROVOCATION	Voluntary Manslaughter	————
MURDER + EMED	Voluntary Manslaughter (or Manslaughter)	Manslaughter
RECKLESSNESS	Involuntary Manslaughter (or Manslaughter)	Manslaughter
NEGLIGENCE	Involuntary Manslaughter (or Negligent Homicide)	Negligent Homicide

Chart II

Type of Homicide	Mens Rea Required	
	COMMON LAW	*MPC*
MURDER	Premeditation/Deliberation	Purpose
	Intent + Special Circumstances	Knowledge
	Intention	Gross Recklessness
	Gross Recklessness	(direct)
	Malice Aforethought	Gross Recklessness
	(Felony Murder Rule)	(via enumerated felony)
VOLUNTARY MANSLAUGHTER	Murder + Provocation	————
	Imperfect Self-Defense	
MANSLAUGHTER	Recklessness	Murder + EMED
		Recklessness
INVOLUNTARY MANSLAUGHTER	Recklessness	————
	Negligence	
	(Misdemeanor Manslaughter Rule)	
NEGLIGENT HOMICIDE	Negligence	Negligence

management and mastery of the overlapping categories of homicide under both the common law and MPC. These charts do not provide an analytical framework within which to solve a homicide problem. For that, go to Tools #7–9.

7.   Under the common law, you should start your analysis of determining the actor's mens rea by analyzing whether the actor acted intentionally or unintentionally. If intentionally, then the possibility of murder is included, and the possibility of involuntary manslaughter is excluded. The next step is to determine precisely what type of murder. If the actor killed with premeditation and deliberation, then the actor is eligible for first-degree murder liability in a majority of jurisdictions. If the actor killed under specified special circumstances, then he is eligible for first-degree murder liability in a minority of jurisdictions. If neither premeditation nor special circumstances exist, then the actor will be eligible for second-degree murder liability in a majority of jurisdictions. If the actor killed intentionally but under provocation or extreme mental or emotional disturbance (EMED), the actor may be liable for voluntary manslaughter or manslaughter. (This special form of intentional homicide that does not constitute murder is the focus of a separate chapter. See Ch. 7.)

If the actor killed unintentionally, he is still eligible for murder liability. There are two forms of unintentional murder—felony murder (see Ch. 8) and depraved heart murder. If the actor killed with an aggravated or gross form of recklessness, then he is eligible for depraved heart murder. Intentional murder may be simply distinguished from unintentional or gross reckless murder as follows: intentional murder requires the actor to intend the result of death, but gross reckless murder only requires depraved or extreme indifference toward the resulting death under circumstances where death is likely.

8.   If the actor kills unintentionally and does not qualify for gross reckless murder, then the next step is to assess whether the actor had conscious awareness that his or her conduct posed a risk of death. If the actor did have conscious awareness, then she is eligible for the recklessness variant of involuntary manslaughter. There are two principal differences between gross reckless murder and a reckless form of manslaughter: (i) the degree of recklessness and (ii) the likelihood of death resulting. Gross reckless murder requires a depraved or extreme indifference and that death is likely to result. The recklessness variant of manslaughter merely requires ordinary recklessness and a substantial risk of death.

If the actor kills without a conscious awareness of risk, then she is eligible for liability for the negligence variant of involuntary manslaughter. The simple difference between the recklessness and negligence variants of involuntary manslaughter is that the recklessness variant requires conscious awareness of the risk, but the negligence variant does not.

9.   Under the MPC, if an actor kills with purpose or knowledge, then he is eligible for murder liability. If the actor kills with recklessness, then he is eligible for liability for either murder or manslaughter, depending on the type of recklessness. If the actor kills with recklessness under circumstances manifesting extreme indifference to the value of human life (i.e., a gross form of recklessness), then he is eligible for murder liability. If the actor kills with (simple) recklessness, then he is eligible for manslaughter liability. The simple difference between the gross form of recklessness required for murder and plain recklessness is a matter of degree based on the indifference and disregard toward human life. The gross form of

recklessness sufficient for murder requires an extreme indifference, whereas recklessness requires mere indifference or disregard.

If the actor kills negligently, then he is eligible for negligent homicide. The simple difference between a reckless and negligent homicide is based on awareness of the risk. If the actor is consciously aware of the risk, then he kills recklessly and is eligible for manslaughter liability. If the actor is unaware of the risk, he kills negligently and is eligible for liability for negligent homicide.

10. For a reckless homicide—involuntary manslaughter under the common law and manslaughter under the MPC—it is somewhat unclear as to the precise elements that must be satisfied. What follows is a maximal conception of the elements:

    i.   conscious awareness of a risk;
    ii.   the risk is substantial (objectively);
    iii. conscious awareness that the risk is substantial;
    iv. the risk is unjustified (objectively);
    v.   conscious awareness that the risk is unjustified;
    vi. the actor's conduct constitutes a gross deviation from that of a reasonable or law-abiding person in the actor's situation.

11. The precise elements of the gross reckless forms of murder under the common law and MPC are unclear. Does gross recklessness necessarily include all of the elements of (simple) recklessness? What follows is a maximal conception of the elements of gross reckless murder under the MPC:

    i.   conscious awareness of a risk;
    ii.   the risk is substantial (objectively);
    iii. conscious awareness that the risk is substantial;
    iv. the risk is unjustified (objectively);
    v.   conscious awareness that the risk is unjustified;
    vi. the actor's conduct constitutes a gross deviation from that of a reasonable or law abiding person in the actor's situation;
    vii. the actor manifests extreme indifference to the value of human life.

The maximal conception of the elements of gross reckless murder under the common law is as follows:

    i.   conscious awareness of a risk;
    ii.   the risk is substantial (objectively);
    iii. conscious awareness that the risk is substantial;
    iv. the risk is unjustified (objectively);
    v.   conscious awareness that the risk is unjustified;
    vi. the actor's conduct constitutes a gross deviation from that of a reasonable or law-abiding person in the actor's situation;
    vii. death is likely to result (objectively);
    viii. the actor is (subjectively) aware that death is likely to result;
    ix. the actor manifests a wicked, depraved, or malignant heart.

12. It is clear that the following elements comprise negligent homicide under the MPC:

   i.   the actor should have been aware of a risk;
   ii. that is substantial (objectively);
   iii. unjustified;
   iv. and the lack of awareness of the risk constitutes a gross deviation from that of a reasonable or law-abiding person in the actor's situation.

What is unclear is whether the fourth element is necessary or superfluous. That is, is it possible for an actor to satisfy the first three elements but not satisfy the fourth? As a practical matter, it is probably not.

13. The negligence variant of involuntary manslaughter under the common law largely follows the MPC conception of negligent homicide, as set in #12 above. What is unclear, however, is the extent to which the common law's conception differs from the MPC.

14. Be on the lookout for actors who kill through the use of special skills or a particular expertise—e.g., the expert ski racer and instructor in *Hall*, a martial arts expert, or a NASCAR driver like Ricky. The special skills of such actors complicate the analysis. The special skills and expertise of such actors may serve to both exculpate and inculpate. They may exculpate because conduct otherwise posing a substantial risk, when performed by the average person, might not when undertaken by the expert. Also, they may inculpate because the expert should have greater awareness of the risk. (Of course, the expert may have even less awareness of his or her imposition of risk because of the expert's exaggerated perception of his or her own expertise.)

15. Keep in mind that the requisite indifference to human life for gross reckless murder is not general but rather specific. Gross reckless murder is typically formulated as requiring that the actor had a depraved indifference to human life. Although this might seem to suggest that the actor's indifference be to human life in general, probably the better understanding is that the actor must have a depraved indifference to the particular victim's life.

16. It is unclear under the MPC what is and what is not to be included as part of the actor's "situation." The MPC commentary concedes this ambiguity and asserts that the ambiguity is by design so as to allow the fact-finder maximum flexibility. The Commentary does, however, give some examples of what should be included: blindness or recently sustaining a blow or heart attack. But heredity, intelligence, and temperament are excluded.

17. The common law is similarly ambiguous as to the appropriate degree of individualization of the reasonable person standard. For example, courts are in conflict as to whether a defendant's intelligence should be relevant at all under the standard. Some courts find the defendant's individual capabilities relevant in assessing recklessness, but the defendant's intelligence, experience, and physical capabilities are irrelevant in determining negligence.

18. Be wary of situations where even a nonreckless or nonnegligent actor would have caused the death. You might be tempted to regard this as a defense for the reckless or negligent actor, but resist this temptation. (See [21] in the above Essay.)

19. Remember that in gross reckless murder under the common law, the requirement that death be likely to result does not necessarily require a high level of probability. It need not be more likely than not. Particularly where the gravity of the harm is high, even a quite low probability of death may qualify as likely. (See [7] in the above Essay.)

20. Remember that, in analyzing recklessness and negligence, the assessment of the unjustifiability of the risk is a sliding scale. The greater the importance of the objective, the greater the magnitude of the risk that may be imposed without criminal liability. The lower the importance of the objective, the lower the magnitude of the risk that may be imposed without criminal liability. (See [9]–[10] in the above Essay.)

21. Remember that in criminal law, unlike in tort law, a victim's contributory negligence is not a defense per se. But do not fall into the trap of believing that because it is not a defense, it is irrelevant. It may well be entirely relevant as a factor in assessing the defendant's recklessness or negligence. (See [20]–[21] in the above Essay.)

VARIATIONS ON THE THEME

1. Rather than driving while intoxicated, Ricky drives with a broken arm.

2. Rather than speeding, Ricky weaves in and out of traffic, crosses double lines, and fails to stop at stop signs and red lights.

3. Rather than being intoxicated, Ricky's father places a panther in the car, which distracts him.

4. Chip affirmatively opposes Walker and Texas Ranger's plan to kill him.

5. Chip is unaware of Walker and Texas Ranger's plan to kill him.

6. Rather than passing out in the road, Crêpe Boy decides to sit down in the middle of the road and enjoy a lunch of crêpes, croissants, Brie, and Perrier. After his lunch and while still in the road, Crêpe Boy enjoys a Galois while listening to discordant and cacophonous jazz.

7. Chip does not need to be rushed to the hospital. Rather than having to speed to save Chip's life, Ricky speeds because Ricky's father tells Ricky that there are drugs planted in his car and that the police are coming to arrest him.

8. Perhaps due to heredity or his father's influence on his temperament, Ricky feels the need to go fast while driving.

9. Last week, Ricky caused a near-fatal accident while speeding in town.

10. Rather than trying to ease Chip's pain, Walker killed Chip because he had thrown Chip's war medals off a bridge and was worried that he might find out.

11. Ricky feels the need to go fast, he does go fast, and he has never previously been in an accident.

ADDITIONAL READINGS

Joshua Dressler, Understanding Criminal Law 505–52 (5th ed. 2009)
George Fletcher, Rethinking Criminal Law 235–390 (1978)
Homicide Law in Comparative Perspective (Jeremy Horder ed. 2007)
Wayne R. LaFave, Criminal Law 764–857 (5th ed. 2010)
Jeff McMahon, The Ethics of Killing: Problems at the Margins of Life (2002)

SAMUEL H. PILLSBURY, JUDGING EVIL: RETHINKING THE LAW OF MURDER AND MANSLAUGHTER (1998)

PAUL H. ROBINSON, CRIMINAL LAW 707–25 (1997)

Lloyd Weinreb & Dan M. Kahan, *Homicide: Legal Aspects*, *in* 2 ENCYCLOPEDIA OF CRIME AND JUSTICE 790 (Joshua Dressler ed., 2d ed. 2002)

David Crump, *"Murder, Pennsylvania Style": Comparing Traditional American Homicide Law to the Statutes of Model Penal Code Jurisdictions*, 109 W. VA. L. REV. 257 (2007)

Stephen Garvey, *What's Wrong with Involuntary Manslaughter?*, 85 TEX. L. REV. 335 (2006)

7

HOMICIDE II:

PROVOCATION & EXTREME MENTAL
OR EMOTIONAL DISTURBANCE

INTRODUCTION

Under the common law, provocation or "heat of passion" is a mitigation defense reducing a defendant's liability from murder to the lesser homicide offense of voluntary manslaughter. Legally sufficient provocation inflames the passions such that even a reasonable man, under its influence, might temporarily act out of passion rather than reason. The precept underlying the mitigation is *not* that when provoked, it is reasonable to intentionally kill another. Rather, it is that when provoked, even a reasonable person might act unreasonably. Because provocation might influence even a reasonable man to unreasonably kill, one who kills under the influence of provocation lacks the vicious will or sufficient culpability required for murder. Despite killing intentionally, provocation negates the requisite mens rea, or malice aforethought, for murder.

The traditional common law approach to provocation imposed numerous rigid doctrinal requirements. Certain acts were deemed adequate provocation, and certain acts were not. The provocative acts might be required to be directly experienced or witnessed by the defendant rather than learned about indirectly. Words alone could not be adequate provocation. Between the time of the provocation and the killing, the defendant must not have "cooled off." The defense was inapplicable if the defendant killed an innocent nonprovoker.

The more modern approach to provocation has relaxed some of these requirements, making the analysis of provocation more flexible, fact-specific, and determinable by a jury. The analysis has been shorn of technical doctrinal requirements and reduced to a more holistic determination by a jury: whether the provocation claimed by the defendant was sufficient to make a reasonable person act unreasonably and intentionally kill another. What under the traditional approach was largely a matter of law has now become largely a question of fact.

The MPC approach similarly expands the scope of the defense, eliminating many of the traditional common law doctrinal requirements. The MPC correlate to the provocation defense applies when the actor kills because of an extreme mental or emotional disturbance (EMED) for which the defendant has a reasonable explanation or excuse. The successful assertion of the defense mitigates liability for murder to the lesser homicide charge of manslaughter.

Many of the debates over the preferable contours of the defense pivot on the dueling rationales for the defense. Some argue that provocation/EMED is best understood as a partial justification. By committing the wrongdoing that provokes the defendant, the victim, in some sense, partially deserves to be killed. The defendant did the "right thing" or was justified in giving the victim what he deserved. Others argue that the preferable rationale is as a partial excuse. The mitigation is a concession to human weakness and a recognition that even reasonable persons may kill under the compulsion of extreme emotions. The provoked killer acted wrongly but understandably and thus deserves lesser liability and punishment.

PROBLEM

In exchange for an apprehended serial killer (John Doe) agreeing not to plead the defense of insanity at trial, two police officers (Brad Pitstop and Morgan Freemason) agree to accompany Doe to a particular location seven miles out in the desert to await the delivery of a package. The package, sent by Doe, arrives by courier. Freemason gingerly opens it. He sees the severed head of Brad Pitstop's wife. Recoiling in horror, Freemason yells to Pitstop, "Don't look in the box." Curious, Pitstop demands to know the contents of the box. Freemason desperately repeats, "Don't look in the box." Given Freemason's look of horror and desperation, Pitstop insistently demands to know the box's contents. So as to prevent Pitstop from looking in the box, Freemason finally informs Pitstop: "It's your pregnant wife's head. It looks like she was killed about seven hours ago." Pitstop raises and points his gun at Doe. Freemason says, "Don't do it. If you kill him, he wins. He wants you to kill him." For the next seven minutes, Freemason continues to plead with Pitstop to put down his gun. Neither Doe nor the courier speaks. Overcome with grief and rage on receipt of the information that his wife and future child are dead, and without looking in the box, Pitstop kills both Doe and the courier. Pitstop is charged with two counts of murder.[1]

Analyze and discuss whether Brad Pitstop qualifies for the common law's provocation defense and the MPC's EMED defense for each count of murder.

LIST OF READINGS

OR. REV. STAT. § 163.135(1) (2010)

People v. Berry, 556 P.2d 777 (Cal. 1976)

People v. Casassa, 404 N.E.2d 1310 (N.Y. Ct. App. 1980)

Girouard v. State, 583 A.2d 718 (Md. Ct. App. 1991)

Maher v. People, 10 Mich. 212 (1862)

MODEL PENAL CODE § 210.3(1)(b) (Official Code and Revised Comments 1985)

ESSAY

Under the common law, Pitstop will likely obtain the provocation defense in some jurisdictions but not in others. Under the MPC, Pitstop will likely obtain the EMED defense.

Common Law

[1] The common law's general standard for sufficient provocation is that which would inflame the passions of a reasonable person so as to make him temporarily

---

[1] Aspects of the Problem were inspired by the film, SE7EN (New Line Cinema 1995).

act based on passion rather than reason. In general, the gruesome death of one's pregnant spouse could clearly suffice to inflame the passions of a reasonable person. Indeed, it is difficult to think of an event that is more provocative.

[2] Though Pitstop satisfies the general standard, there are further specific requirements. First, the defendant must actually act based on rage or passion. That is, even if a reasonable person would have acted out of passion under the circumstances, perhaps the defendant did not act out of passion. Under the facts here, Brad Pitstop was "[o]vercome with grief and rage," thus satisfying this requirement.

[3] Second, under the traditional common law rule, the source of the provocation must satisfy one of the traditionally accepted categories of adequate provocation. These categories of adequate provocation include aggravated assault or battery, mutual combat, illegal arrest, discovery of a spouse's adultery, and the commission of a serious crime or the infliction of a serious injury on a close relative. Here, Pitstop's provocation clearly satisfies the latter traditionally accepted category.

Under the modern rule, the source of the provocation need not fit into one of these rigid categories. The issue of whether the provocation is adequate is left for the jury to decide under the general standard above. As one court noted, "the law cannot . . . catalogue all the various facts and combination of facts which shall be held [as] adequate provocation." *Maher*, 10 Mich. at 222–23. As discussed above, presumably any jury would find the gruesome murder of a defendant's wife and future child as more than adequate provocation.

[4] Third, between the time of the provocation and the time of the killing, a reasonable person would not have "cooled off." While it may be understandable and deserving of mitigation if one kills in the immediate throes of passion or rage soon after the provocative incident, it is expected that a reasonable person will eventually cool off. While ordinarily the passage of time facilitates a cooling off, some cases have held that the passage of time may aggravate the provocation and further inflame even a reasonable person. Here, the facts state that Pitstop did not immediately kill but waited "seven minutes." Probably several minutes of time that elapsed between the provocation and the killing was not sufficient for a reasonable person to cool off.

[5] Fourth, the defendant must not have actually "cooled off." That is, even if a reasonable person would not have cooled off between the time of the provocation and the killing, it is possible that the particular defendant cooled off. Here, there is no evidence that Pitstop actually cooled off. Though Pitstop waited several minutes, the facts state that he kills while "[o]vercome with grief and rage."

[6] Fifth, there must be a causal link between the provocation and the killing. If a defendant would have killed the provoker anyway, even without the provocation, then the provocation was not the actual cause of the killing, and the defendant does not qualify for the mitigation. Here, there is no evidence that Pitstop would have killed absent the provocation. Again, the facts state that he kills while overcome with grief and rage upon learning that his wife and future child have been brutally killed.

[7] Sixth, some courts limit the provocation defense to killings of provokers. This rule may be understood as an aspect of the rationale of provocation being a partial justification. Only provokers partially deserve, in some sense, to be killed.

Thus, only the killing of a provoker is partially justified and worthy of mitigation. Under the instant facts, Doe was a provoker, but the courier was not. As a result, these courts would disallow the provocation defense to Pitstop's killing of the courier. Other courts allow the provocation defense even for the killing of a nonprovoker. Such courts may be utilizing the rationale of the provocation defense as a partial excuse. A provoked killing is mitigated not so much because the victim deserves it, but rather that the provocation reduced the capacity of the provoked to control her actions. The reduced capacity to control her actions applies to both types of victims—both provokers who may deserve to be killed as well as innocent, nonprovokers who do not. Such courts might allow the provocation defense not only for Pitstop's killing of Doe, but also for his killing of the courier.

[8] Seventh, some jurisdictions bar the provocation defense to defendants who provoked their victim into provoking the defendant into killing the victim. *E.g.*, Or. Rev. Stat. § 163.135(1). For example, *D* provokes *V* into provoking *D* who then kills *V*. Precluding the defense in this situation may be understood as an aspect of the partial justification rationale. If the defendant was the initial wrongdoer, then the victim is less deserving of being killed. Here, there are no facts supporting Pitstop as provoking Doe. As a result, this limitation would not preclude a provocation defense.

[9] Eighth, and related to our analysis of the traditional categories of adequate provocation in [3], the traditional common law rule is that words alone are not adequate provocation. It is helpful to distinguish between two different types of provocative words—insulting words and informational words. For example, a victim maligning the virtue of the defendant's mother is employing insulting words, but a victim stating that he has tortured and killed the defendant's mother is employing informational words. While some courts may bar both types of words as adequate provocation, and other courts may allow both as adequate provocation, comparatively more courts recognize the utterance of informational words to be adequate provocation. The rationale is that insulting words are often deemed too trivial to cause a reasonable person to kill, but informational words that describe the conduct that provokes may be as, or almost as, provocative as experiencing or witnessing the provocative conduct. Courts that bar even informational words as adequate provocation explain that in the absence of the defendant experiencing or witnessing the provocation, the risk is too great that the defendant will kill based on mistaken information.

[10] Whether the words alone rule applies here requires another inquiry: what exactly provoked Pitstop? Pitstop was not an eyewitness to his family's gruesome death. Rather, it was the informational words describing the contents of the box that allows Pitstop to infer the gruesome deaths of his family at the hands of Doe. On that basis, as the provocation is words alone, some courts would disallow provocation as a mitigation defense to Pitstop. However, one might argue that it was not mere words that provoked him. Rather, it was words *plus* seeing the box that contained his wife's head. There are two possible problems with this view. First, Pitstop never saw the contents of the box. Second, even if he did see the contents of the box, the rationale of the rule requiring more than words alone— preventing a person from killing by mistake under provocation—is not satisfied. There is still the possibility of mistake. Because Pitstop did not witness Doe killing his family, Pitstop does not know that Doe killed his family. It is possible,

though perhaps not likely, that someone else killed his family and then Doe arranged for the head to be delivered to Pitstop. As a result, the rationale of the words alone rule would militate against recognizing provocation here.

[11] The analysis above in [10] perhaps triggers another, more fundamental, issue. Who was the provocateur? The obvious and conventional answer is that it was Doe (assuming that he actually was the killer of Pitstop's family). But Doe did not speak any words. If the provocation was words alone, how can a nonspeaker be the provocateur? If the provocation was words alone, then one might argue that the provocateur was whoever uttered the provocative words—Morgan Freemason. If so, as discussed above in [7], some courts would refuse Pitstop a provocation defense for the killing of nonprovokers (the nonspeaking Doe and the courier). And if the provocation was not mere words but words plus the presence of the box, then one might argue that the provocateurs were the utterer of the words (Freemason) and the person responsible for the presence of the box (the courier). If so, then the courier was a provocateur, and courts that disallow the provocation defense for killings of nonprovokers would allow a provocation defense for Pitstop's killing of the courier.

Despite this analysis, however, courts would most likely identify only Doe as the provocateur.

Model Penal Code

[12] Under the MPC, a murder may be mitigated to manslaughter if the defendant killed while "under the influence of extreme mental or emotional disturbance [EMED] for which there is a reasonable explanation or excuse." MPC § 210.3(1)(b).

[13] There are two principal components of this standard: one subjective and the other partially objective and partially subjective. First, the subjective component is that the defendant must actually suffer from, and kill under the influence of, the EMED. The EMED is a mental or emotional trauma that is sufficiently substantial but need not arise to the level of insanity. Pitstop would presumably satisfy this component given that the facts state that he was "[o]vercome with grief and rage."

[14] Second, the defendant must have a "reasonable explanation or excuse" for the EMED. The assessment of the reasonableness of the explanation or excuse is partially objective in that it is considered from the viewpoint of a reasonable person. But the assessment is also partially subjective in that it is assessed from the viewpoint of a reasonable person "in the actor's situation under the circumstances as he believes them to be." MPC § 210.3(1)(b). Pitstop would also presumably satisfy this standard because being informed that one's family has been killed and one's wife's severed head is in a box supplies a reasonable explanation for EMED.

[15] Because EMED is much broader than provocation and lacks many of its rigid doctrinal requirements, the EMED mitigation is significantly more favorable to a defendant. For example, EMED need not fall within a certain category to be considered adequate, words alone may suffice, cooling off is not necessarily a bar, and the killing of a nonprovoker does not preclude the defense. MPC § 210.3, Comment at 61. As a result, many of the possible hurdles that Pitstop faced under the common law in obtaining a provocation defense would not preclude the EMED defense. The defense might even apply to the killing of the courier. And because the

reasonableness of the explanation for the EMED is considered "under the circumstances as he [Pitstop] believes them to be," MPC § 210.3(1)(b), the defense would apply even if Pitstop was mistaken, and Doe was not the killer of his family.

Conclusion

Pitstop satisfies most of the requirements for provocation, both under the traditional common law rules and the modern view. However, in jurisdictions which bar provocation for words alone, even informational words, he may lose the defense with respect to both Doe and the courier. In jurisdictions limiting the defense to the killing of a provoker, Pitstop may lose the defense with respect to the nonprovoker, the courier. Pitstop would likely obtain the EMED mitigation under the MPC.

TOOLS FOR SELF-ASSESSMENT

Go back to your written answer. Look for the issues identified in paragraphs [1]–[15] in the above Essay. Look also for the analysis that follows each issue, and mark your essay where you locate it. Do you fully describe the issue, identify the precise legal standard that applies, list the relevant facts, and show how the facts and law support a conclusion for each issue in a separate paragraph? Mark each conclusion in your essay. Are there sufficient reasons in the law and in the facts to support the conclusion?

1.   Do what you are told. In the Problem, you are asked to analyze and discuss whether Pitstop should receive the mitigation defenses of provocation and EMED. You should not analyze the criminal liability, if any, of Freemason, Doe, the courier, or Pitstop's wife.

2.   Do not analyze what is unnecessary. For example, it might be tempting to analyze whether Pitstop will ultimately be held criminally liable for the homicides of Doe and the courier. Do not do so. It is not necessary under the instructions following the Problem.

3.   Remember to include an analysis of the MPC's approach unless you are instructed otherwise.

4.   State the best possible arguments for alternative conclusions. Even as you reject possible conclusions as to why Pitstop should or should not obtain the mitigation defenses of provocation and EMED, make the best possible argument first, and only then explain why you are rejecting that conclusion.

5.   Be on the alert for red herrings. The Problem may include facts that are irrelevant or even designed to mislead you. For example, the fact pattern states that Pitstop's wife was killed seven hours before Pitstop kills Doe. This fact may mislead you into thinking that a reasonable person should have cooled off over the course of seven hours, the time period between the wrongdoing that provokes Pitstop and his killing of Doe. This is incorrect. The relevant time period is measured by the interval between when the defendant learns of the provoking incident and the time when the defendant kills the provoker. This time period is seven minutes.

6.   Be aware of the similarities and differences of the analysis of provocation under the common law and EMED under the MPC. Under the common law, provocation has numerous doctrinal requirements and comparatively rigid

classifications of what suffices as adequate provocation. In contrast, the MPC approach is much broader, includes fewer requirements, is easier to obtain, is more favorable to the defendant, and features a comparatively more holistic approach.

The following chart summarizes some of the key differences between the requirements of the common law and MPC approaches:

Common Law	MPC
External provoking event	No requirement
No cooling off	No requirement
Categories of Adequate Provocation	No requirement
Words alone insufficient	No requirement
Killing of actual provoker	No requirement
Defendant not initial provoker	No requirement

7.   The emotional effect of provocation elicited in the defendant is not limited to anger. Although it is the most typical emotion or passion that is the source of the common law "heat of passion" defense, the defense is not so limited. Any sufficiently intense passion or emotion—fear, fright, terror, jealousy or desperation—might be the basis for the defense.

8.   In your common law analysis, keep in mind the traditional categories of adequate and inadequate provocation. The categories of adequate provocation are listed in [3] of the above Essay. The traditional categories of inadequate provocation include the following: nonaggravated assault and battery, nonobserved adultery, infidelity of a nonspouse, words alone, and injuries to friends or distant relatives.

9.   Be alert to whether the defendant killed a provoker or nonprovoker. A provoked defendant killing a nonprovoker typically arises in three different situations. First, the defendant mistakenly believes that she is killing the provoker. Second, the defendant accidentally kills a nonprovoker in the attempt to kill the provoker. Third, the defendant kills a person that the defendant knows to be a nonprovoker. While some courts may allow the provocation defense to apply to all three situations or disallow the defense in all three, courts have been least likely to allow the defense in the third situation.

10. The following steps reveal the structure of the above Essay's analysis of the provocation defense under both the traditional common law as well as its modern application. These steps are somewhat oversimplified so as to afford a better view of the forest without the obstruction of the trees. But this should not be mistaken for, or taken as a substitute for, in-depth knowledge of the trees. While these steps are specifically suited to answer this particular Problem, the general structure of these steps with perhaps some modification might be useful to analyze any fact pattern involving provocation.

i.   Is the defendant charged with murder?

ii. If no, then no provocation defense.

iii. Does the source of the provocation qualify under one of the traditionally accepted categories?

iv. If no, then no provocation defense (under the traditional common law rule).

v. If yes, would a reasonable person have been unable to cool off before the killing?

vi. If no (a reasonable person would have cooled off), then no provocation defense.

vii. If yes, did the defendant actually fail to cool off?

viii. If no (the defendant did cool off), then no provocation defense.

ix. If yes (the defendant did not cool off), was there a causal link between the provocation and the killing?

x. If no, then no provocation defense.

xi. If yes, then did the defendant only kill the provoker?

xii. If no, then no provocation defense, in some jurisdictions, for killings of nonprovokers.

xiii. If yes, was the victim the initial provoker?

xiv. If no, then no provocation defense, in some jurisdictions, for defendants who are the initial provokers.

xv. If yes, was the provocation more than words alone?

xvi. If no, depending on whether the words are insulting or informational, and depending on the jurisdiction, then possibly no provocation defense.

xvii. If yes, then the defendant will likely obtain a provocation defense.

11. Remember to break down the MPC approach into its constituent parts. Even though the MPC approach is comparatively more holistic than the common law, it is nonetheless most easily applied by appreciating its constituent parts:

i. Is the defendant charged with murder?

ii. If no, then EMED mitigation is inapplicable.

iii. If yes, does the defendant have an EMED?

iv. If no, then EMED mitigation is inapplicable.

v. If yes, then did the defendant commit the murder under the EMED's influence?

vi. If no, then the EMED mitigation is inapplicable.

vii. If yes, then does the defendant have a reasonable explanation or excuse for the EMED?

viii. If no, then the EMED mitigation is inapplicable.

ix. If yes, then the defendant receives the EMED mitigation.

Steps i–ii reflect that the EMED mitigation is only available as a mitigation defense to a charge of murder. Steps iii–iv reveal that the defendant must actually have an EMED. That a reasonable person would have an EMED under the circumstances is neither necessary nor sufficient. As a result, this inquiry in step iii is referred to as a subjective inquiry—whether this particular defendant has an EMED. Steps v–vi illustrate that a defendant merely having an EMED is insufficient. The defendant must both have an EMED and kill under the EMED's influence. In a sense, there must be a causal link between the defendant's EMED and the defendant's commission of the homicide. Steps vii–ix reflect that the defendant must have a reasonable explanation or excuse for the EMED. Do not make the mistake of thinking that the defendant must proffer a reasonable explanation or excuse for the homicide. Rather, it is the existence of the defendant's EMED itself that requires a reasonable explanation or excuse. This level of the analysis is partially objective and partially subjective. It is partially objective because the explanation or excuse for the EMED must be (objectively) reasonable. But it is partially subjective because the reasonableness is to be assessed from a person in the defendant's situation. (Some but not all of the particular's defendant's traits, characteristics, and experiences may be a part of his "situation.") In addition, the reasonableness inquiry is partially subjective because it is assessed under the circumstances as the defendant believes them to be. That is, the reasonableness is NOT assessed under the (objectively) actual circumstances.

VARIATIONS ON THE THEME

For the following variations, assume all of the facts from the original hypothetical obtain unless otherwise noted.

1.   Pitstop also kills Morgan Freemason.
2.   Pitstop looks in the box and confirms that it is his wife's severed head before he shoots John Doe and the courier.
3.   Rather than Freemason informing Pitstop of the contents of the box, John Doe informs him.
4.   John Doe tells Pitstop, "I killed your wife."
5.   John Doe tells Pitstop that he did not kill his wife, but admits that he acquired it from the killer and arranged to have it sent to Pitstop.
6.   Pitstop's wife was not pregnant at the time of her death.
7.   Rather than Freemason informing Pitstop of the contents of the box, the courier informs him.
8.   Pitstop is an immigrant from a country and culture in which violence under such circumstances is quite common.
9.   Before Pitstop has shot John Doe and the courier, and while his gun is pointed at John Doe, the courier tells Pitstop, "If you don't kill Doe, you are a coward."
10. Before Pitstop has shot John Doe and the courier and while his gun is pointed at John Doe, Pitstop tells the courier, "You are a sleazy little pervball for doing business with John Doe." The courier replies to Pitstop, "If you don't kill Doe, you are a coward."
11. While investigating Doe's previous murders and trying to apprehend him, Pitstop often remarked to Freemason of his dislike of the murderer. Pitstop said, "I would love to torture and kill that S.O.B., just like he killed and tortured his victims."
12. Two years before apprehending Doe for his previous murders, Pitstop arrested Doe for larceny and failed to read Doe his *Miranda* rights (his rights to remain silent and obtain counsel).

ADDITIONAL READINGS

GEORGE P. FLETCHER, RETHINKING CRIMINAL LAW 242–50 (1978)

JEREMY HORDER, PROVOCATION AND RESPONSIBILITY (1992)

PAUL H. ROBINSON, CRIMINAL LAW 709–14 (1997)

Joshua Dressler, *Provocation: Explaining and Justifying the Defense in Partial Excuse, Loss of Self-Control Terms*, in CRIMINAL LAW CONVERSATIONS 319–41 (Paul H. Robinson, Stephen P. Garvey & Kimberly Kessler Ferzan eds., 2009) (with comments by Susan D. Rozelle, Vera Bergelson, Marcia Baron, Joan H. Krause, Kenneth Simons, Stephen P. Garvey, and Marianne Wesson)

Andrew J. Ashworth, *The Doctrine of Provocation*, 35 CAMB. L.J. 292 (1976)

Joshua Dressler, *Why Keep the Provocation Defense? Some Reflections on a Difficult Subject*, 86 MINN. L. REV. 959 (2002)

Stephen P. Garvey, *Passion's Puzzle*, 90 IOWA L. REV. 1677 (2005)

Victoria Nourse, *Passion's Progress: Modern Law Reform and the Provocation Defense*, 106 YALE L.J. 1331 (1997)

Susan D. Rozelle, *Controlling Passion: Adultery and the Provocation Defense*, 37 RUTGERS L.J. 197 (2005)

Richard Singer, *The Resurgence of Mens Rea: I—Provocation, Emotional Disturbance, and the Model Penal Code*, 27 B.C.L. REV. 243 (1986)

HOMICIDE III:

FELONY MURDER AND MISDEMEANOR MANSLAUGHTER

8

INTRODUCTION

Broadly stated, the felony murder doctrine imposes murder liability on a felon for a death, even if unintended, that results from the commission or attempted commission of a felony. Despite originating in early English common law, England abolished the felony murder doctrine, by statute, in 1957. But while the doctrine remains in the vast majority of states in America, it continues to be a source of fierce debate and controversy. Felony murder is best defended on the grounds of deterrence. First, because unintended deaths are a foreseeable result of committing felonies, the greater punishment for felony murder will deter actors from committing felonies. Second, even actors willing to commit felonies will be extra careful in the commission of such felonies so as to ensure that no one is killed. Skeptics reply that there is scant empirical evidence of such deterrence and also question how an unintended act can possibly be deterred.

The dilution of the element of mens rea as to the resulting death explains both felony murder's popularity among prosecutors as well as its severe criticism from judges and commentators. There are three rationales for this dilution. The traditional rationale is that the very commission of a felony, in which death results, itself constitutes the requisite mens rea for murder—malice aforethought. Alternatively, the mens rea required for the commission of the felony supplies the mens rea for or transfers to the resulting death. In contrast, the more modern rationale dispenses with this legal fiction, simply and baldly stating that the element of the resulting death in felony murder is strict liability. These three differing rationales have little practical difference, except in the case of a strict liability predicate felony. With such a felony, there is no mens rea to transfer to the resulting death.

Today, many jurisdictions impose three principal limitations on the scope of felony murder. First, the predicate felony must be inherently dangerous. Second, the felony must be independent from, and not merge into, the resulting death. Third, an act causing the death must be in furtherance of the felony. A death resulting from a felony that satisfies these requirements may be graded as high as first-degree murder.

The commission of felonies not sufficing for felony murder as well as the commission of some misdemeanors result in involuntary manslaughter liability under the correlate doctrine to felony murder—the misdemeanor manslaughter doctrine. While the MPC does not specifically recognize felony murder, it does have a correlate to the felony murder doctrine: an actor's commission of a specified felony that results in a death creates a nonconclusive presumption that the actor committed the homicide with a form of gross recklessness that suffices for murder. Like the felony murder doctrine, the MPC rule dilutes the element of mens rea as to the resulting death. But unlike the felony murder doctrine, the MPC rule mitigates this dilution by affording the defendant the opportunity to rebut this presumption of mens rea by supplying evidence that the defendant did not act with gross recklessness.

PROBLEM

Mr. Pink, Mr. White, Mr. Brown, and Mr. Blonde have just committed a burglary and are fleeing the scene of the crime in Mr. Pink's burnt umber MiniCooper with the police in pursuit. (In this jurisdiction, burglary is defined as the breaking and entering of the dwelling of another with the intent to commit a felony therein. The felony they intended to commit was assault with a deadly weapon.) After two hours of driving they reach their safe house. They hope that they have eluded the police but fear that the police will shortly find them. Sure enough, the police arrive a few minutes later and surround the house. A police officer, Griggs, shouts, "You are under arrest. Come out with your hands up." Mr. Blonde opens a window, points his gun at Griggs, shouts "Oh yeah? Now this is going to happen," and shoots and kills Griggs. The police return gunfire, and a shootout between the police and Mr. Blonde ensues. Mr. Blonde is the only felon that engages in the shootout. Believing that Mr. Brown is an undercover police officer who has tipped off the police to the location of their safe house, Mr. Pink shoots and kills Mr. Brown. Brandishing his gun, Mr. Blonde appears in front of the open window and shouts to the police, "Come get a taste." The police shoot and kill Mr. Blonde. During the shootout, Mr. Pink eyes Mr. White. Mr. Pink and Mr. White are stepbrothers. Mr. Pink hates Mr. White because he suspects that long ago, Mr. White touched his childhood drum set in an inappropriate manner. Mr. Pink shoots and kills Mr. White. Mr. Pink then surrenders to the police. Based on the predicate felony of burglary, the prosecutor charges Mr. Pink for the homicides of Griggs, Mr. Brown, Mr. Blonde, and Mr. White.[1]

Analyze and discuss Mr. Pink's felony murder liability, if any, under common law principles as well as the MPC's correlate principle. If you conclude that Mr. Pink may not have homicide liability based on the predicate felony, briefly discuss alternative bases for Mr. Pink's homicide liability.

LIST OF READINGS

People v. Hansen, 885 P.2d 1022 (Cal. 1994)
Commonwealth v. Claudio, 634 N.E.2d 902 (Mass. 1994)
State v. Sophophone, 19 P.3d 70 (Kan. 2001)
King v. Commonwealth, 368 S.E.2d 704 (Va. Ct. App. 1988)
State v. Canola, 374 A.2d 20 (N.J. 1977)

---

[1] Aspects of this Problem were inspired by the films RESERVOIR DOGS (Lions Gate 1992) and STEP BROTHERS (Columbia 2008).

MODEL PENAL CODE § 210.2(1)(b) (Official Code and Revised Comments 1985)
MPC Commentary § 2.03, at 263 & n.20

ESSAY

Mr. Pink is possibly liable for felony murder for the deaths of Griggs and Mr. Brown, probably not liable for felony murder for the death of Mr. Blonde, and not liable for felony murder for the death of Mr. White. Under the MPC's correlate doctrine to felony murder, Mr. Pink is possibly liable for the deaths of Mr. Brown and Mr. White, but not liable for the deaths of Griggs and Mr. Blonde.

Common Law

[1] Stated broadly, the felony murder doctrine holds a felon liable for murder for a death that occurs during or stems from the commission of a felony. Under this formulation, at least some of the homicides that occurred in relation to Mr. Pink's commission of the felony of burglary would render Mr. Pink eligible for felony murder liability. But perhaps no jurisdiction imposes felony murder so broadly. Most jurisdictions seek to limit such a broad scope of felony murder by imposing a number of requirements. There are three principal requirements.

INHERENTLY DANGEROUS FELONY

[2] First, the predicate felony must be inherently dangerous. There are two principal tests for determining whether a predicate felony is inherently dangerous. The "in the abstract" test considers whether the felony, apart from its commission in this particular case under these particular facts and circumstances, is inherently dangerous. Under the strict version of the test, a felony is only inherently dangerous if there is no possible way to commit the offense without endangering human life. It would seem quite possible to commit a burglary without endangering human life. As a result, applying this version of the test literally, burglary would not be inherently dangerous, and Mr. Pink would not be eligible for felony murder liability. Under a more relaxed version of the test, however, a felony is inherently dangerous if the felony's very elements establish the nature of the offense as dangerous. The elements of burglary include the forceful entry into the dwelling of another with the intent to commit a felony therein. Given the forcible nature of the entry and the foreseeable response of an occupant to such an invasion, burglary is most likely inherently dangerous.

[3] The other test, the "actual facts and circumstances" test, considers whether the felony was inherently dangerous as committed in this instance, given the particular facts and circumstances of the case. This test is much more likely to result in a determination of inherent danger. Under the circumstances here, not only was the intended felony inside the dwelling inherently dangerous—assault with a deadly weapon—but also the shootout with the police (while the burglary was arguably ongoing) was inherently dangerous.

[4] While some jurisdictions employ only one of the tests, other jurisdictions find a predicate felony inherently dangerous if either of the tests is satisfied. And still other jurisdictions allow the court to choose which test it shall employ. Regardless of the jurisdiction and the test employed, most courts would find Mr. Pink's predicate felony of burglary to be inherently dangerous.

INDEPENDENT FELONY—THE MERGER DOCTRINE

[5] The second requirement is that the predicate felony be independent from, and not mergeable with, the resulting death(s). The principal test employed to determine an actor's satisfaction of this requirement is the independent purpose test. While courts' employment of this test has been particularly controversial and problematic, the typical formulation of this test is as follows: If the defendant committed the predicate felony for a purpose independent from, or different than, the purpose for committing the conduct that caused the death, then the predicate felony is independent from, and does not merge with, the death, and the defendant is eligible for felony murder liability. But if the purpose for committing the predicate felony is not independent from, or is the same as, the purpose for committing the conduct that caused the death, then the predicate felony is not independent, it merges, and there is no felony murder liability.

[6] Application of this test to the predicate felony of burglary is particularly thorny because the purpose for committing burglary may vary depending on the type of felony that the perpetrator intends to commit inside the dwelling. Some courts have held that the type of intended felony determines whether the predicate felony of burglary satisfies the merger doctrine. Such courts have found that if the intended felony inside the dwelling is theft, then the purpose is to obtain property, which is different than the purpose for committing the conduct that causes the death. As such, the burglary is independent, does not merge, and the defendant is eligible for felony murder liability. But if the intended felony inside the dwelling is assault with a deadly weapon or assault with the intent to kill, then the purpose is to endanger human life, which is the same as the purpose for committing the act that causes the death. As such, the burglary is not independent, it merges, and the defendant is ineligible for felony murder liability. In these courts, Mr. Pink's predicate felony of burglary (with the intent to commit the felony of assault with a deadly weapon inside the dwelling) is not independent, it merges, and precludes felony murder liability.

[7] Perhaps most other courts analyze the predicate felony of burglary without considering the type of felony the defendant intended to commit inside the dwelling. They find that because the typical purpose of committing burglary is to obtain another's property, the purpose for committing it is independent from, and different than, the purpose of committing the conduct that causes the death. As such, burglary is independent, does not merge, and the defendant is eligible for felony murder liability. In these courts, Mr. Pink's predicate felony of burglary is independent, does not merge, and renders Mr. Pink eligible for felony murder.

ACT CAUSING DEATH IN FURTHERANCE OF THE FELONY

[8] The third requirement, in general, is that an act that causes the death must be in furtherance of the felony. But this "in furtherance" requirement is perhaps best understood as a constellation of three related requirements. The **first** aspect of this "in furtherance" requirement is that the death/act causing the death must be temporally, spatially, and causally linked to the predicate felony. An act causing the death that is not sufficiently linked to the predicate felony will generally not be in furtherance of the predicate felony.

[9] The spatial and temporal links are easily satisfied when the deaths occur during the course of the felony. If the act that causes the deaths occurs after the

felony is complete then the spatial and temporal links are not satisfied. In the instant facts, the deaths occur two hours and a considerable distance away from the site of the predicate felony. Seemingly, the acts causing the deaths do not occur "during" the commission of the felony. The burglary would seem to be complete and terminated some two hours before the deaths. However, most courts have held that a felony is not complete and is still ongoing and being perpetrated while felons are in flight from and escaping the scene of the felony. But once they reach a place of temporary safety, the felony is complete. Under the instant facts, it is not clear whether the felons have reached a place of temporary safety and thus it is not clear whether the predicate felony is complete prior to the deaths. The best argument in support of the felony not being complete is that the facts state that the felons reached their safe house fearing the police were in hot pursuit and their fears were confirmed when the police arrived at the safe house only a few minutes later. Because they only had a few minutes at the safe house before the police arrived, they did not reach a place of temporary safety. On this basis the temporal and spatial links are satisfied because the deaths occurred while the felony was ongoing. The best argument supporting the view that the felony had ended prior to the shootout is that by reaching the safe house before the police arrived (albeit only by a few minutes), the felons had reached a place of temporary safety thus ending the felony. On this basis the temporal and spatial links are not satisfied because the acts that caused the deaths occurred after the felony was completd.

It is unclear which is the better argument and thus it is unclear how any particular court would rule on this issue.

[10] To satisfy the causal link, both but-for causation and proximate causation must be established. The predicate felony must not only be the but-for cause of the deaths but also the proximate cause. The burglary is the but-for cause of all of the deaths. But for the burglary, the felons would not have been pursued by the police to their safe house, and the victims would not have died when and in the manner they did.

[11] Proximate causation is often analyzed differently with respect to felony murder. The typical standard of foreseeability (see the discussion in Ch. 5) is construed more narrowly in the context of felony murder. The requirement of foreseeability, as applied to felony murder, is variously understood as follows: (i) the death must be a natural and probable consequence of the felony, (ii) a logical nexus must exist between the felony and the death, or (iii) the felonious or wrongful nature of the conduct must have caused the death.

[12] As applied to the instant facts, the proximate causation analysis will vary depending on the particular understanding of the foreseeability requirement (as discussed above in [11]) and the particular victim. Let us first consider the deaths of Griggs and Mr. Blonde. While the deaths of Griggs and Mr. Blonde are not natural and probable consequences of the burglary, there is a logical nexus between the burglary and their deaths. Apart from the felonious or wrongful nature of the felons' conduct, Griggs would not have demanded their surrender, Griggs would not have been shot by Mr. Blonde, and Mr. Blonde would not have been shot by the police. Next let us consider Mr. Brown's death. Similarly, apart from the felonious nature of the felons' conduct, the police would not have pursued them to the safe house, Mr. Pink would have no reason to think that Mr. Brown was an undercover police officer who tipped off the police to the safe house's location,

and Mr. Brown would not have been shot and killed. Mr. Brown's death was perhaps not a probable consequence of the felony, but there was the requisite logical nexus. With respect to the deaths of Griggs, Mr. Blonde, and Mr. Brown, Mr. Pink satisfies two of the three constructions of the test for proximate causation.

[13] The casual link between the felony and Mr. Pink's killing of Mr. White is not as clear. True, under general rules of causation Mr. Pink is the direct cause of Mr. White's death—nothing intervenes between Mr. Pink's act and Mr. White's death. Direct causes are generally proximate causes. But this general rule of causation does not necessarily apply in felony murder. While Mr. Pink is most likely the proximate cause of Mr. White's death in a murder prosecution, he is perhaps not the proximate cause in a felony murder prosecution.

[14] The killing of Mr. White is neither a likely consequence nor is there a logical nexus between the burglary and Mr. White's death. Mr. Pink killing Mr. White seemed to have very little to do with the burglary. The felonious nature of the burglary is not itself the cause of Mr. White's death. Mr. White's death stems more from Mr. Pink's hatred of Mr. White. And this hatred was unrelated to the felonious nature of the burglary.

[15] As a result, the deaths of Griggs, Mr. Brown, and Mr. Blonde possibly satisfy the temporal, spatial, and causal aspects of the in furtherance requirement. Mr. Pink is possibly eligible for felony murder liability for their deaths. But by not satisfying the causal aspect of the in furtherance requirement regarding Mr. White, Mr. Pink is not eligible for the felony murder of Mr. White.

[16] The **second** aspect of the in furtherance requirement is that an act that causes the death must be in furtherance of the predicate felony. This second aspect only applies to a killing directly perpetrated by a felon. Thus it applies to the deaths of Griggs, Mr. Brown, and Mr. White—the killings directly perpetrated by a felon. It is inapplicable to the killing of Mr. Blonde (which was directly perpetrated by the police). The shootings of Griggs and Mr. Brown (perhaps assuming that he was an undercover police officer) were in furtherance of the felony in that they were killed so as to escape apprehension for the commission of the burglary. But the shooting of Mr. White was not in furtherance of the burglary. Moreover, it detracted from the burglary because it increased the chance of apprehension by the police by eliminating a source of resistance. As a result, the shootings of Griggs and Mr. Brown were in furtherance of the felony, and Mr. Pink is eligible for felony murder liability for their deaths, but the shooting of Mr. White was not in furtherance of the burglary and thus would preclude felony murder. Because this requirement is inapplicable to the death of Mr. Blonde, this requirement does not bar Mr. Pink's eligibility for felony murder liability for Mr. Blonde's death.

[17] The **third** aspect of the in furtherance requirement only pertains to a killing directly perpetrated by a nonfelon. There are two principal approaches to this type of killing: the agency view and the proximate cause view. Under the agency view, there is no felony murder liability for a killing directly perpetrated by a nonfelon. The rationale is that such a killing typically does not further or promote the predicate felony. Under these facts, the only killing directly perpetrated by a nonfelon is the killing of Mr. Blonde by the police. As a result, in an agency view jurisdiction Mr. Pink would have no felony murder liability for the death of Mr. Blonde.

[18] In contrast to the agency view, some courts adopt the proximate cause view. Under the proximate cause view, a felon can be held liable for felony murder,

even if a nonfelon directly perpetrated the killing, if the felon set into motion a chain of events in which death was foreseeable. By committing a burglary and fleeing from the police, Mr. Pink did set into motion a chain of events in which death was foreseeable. It is foreseeable that by committing a felony and fleeing from the police, force might be employed either by the police to secure the capture of the felons or by the felons to resist such capture. As a result, Mr. Pink is eligible for felony murder liability for the death of Mr. Blonde in jurisdictions following the proximate cause approach. But there are two possible exceptions recognized by some jurisdictions applying the proximate cause approach.

[19] One exception is for justified killings. A killing that is justified (for the distinction between justified and excused killings, see Ch. 11) is sometimes held not to be the basis for felony murder liability. The rationale is that a felon cannot be held criminally liable for the justified (and thus lawful) conduct of another. The police shooting and killing Mr. Blonde was most likely justified. It was a justified response to Mr. Blonde's shooting at the police. As a result, in a proximate cause approach jurisdiction that recognizes this exception, Mr. Pink would not be liable for felony murder for Mr. Blonde's death.

[20] Another exception that some proximate cause approach jurisdictions recognize is that felony murder does not apply to a nonfelon killing a co-felon. A surviving co-felon is sometimes found not liable for felony murder for the killing of a co-felon directly perpetrated by a nonfelon. Under the instant facts, a nonfelon killed Mr. Blonde who is a co-felon. As a result, in a proximate cause approach jurisdiction that recognizes this exception, Mr. Pink would not be liable for felony murder for Mr. Blonde's death.

[21] Apart from felony murder, there may be additional bases for Mr. Pink's homicide liability. With respect to all four counts of homicide, if a court found that the predicate felony of burglary did not suffice for felony murder then Mr. Pink may nonetheless be liable under the misdemeanor manslaughter doctrine. With respect to the deaths of Mr. Brown and Mr. White, Mr. Pink can be held liable for (non-felony) intentional murder. Whether Mr. Pink would have murder liability for Mr. Blonde's intentional murder of Griggs will depend on principles of accomplice liability. (See Ch. 17.)

Although Mr. Pink would not be liable for the felony murder of Mr. Blonde under either the agency view or under either exception to the proximate cause view, he might be liable for gross reckless/depraved heart murder. Some courts have held that when a felon shoots at the police, thereby provoking a return of gunfire by the police that kills another, the felon acts with gross recklessness toward human life. The death is attributable to the co-felons and the co-felons might be liable for gross reckless murder. Under the instant facts, however, Mr. Pink will not be liable for gross reckless murder of Mr. Blonde. Although Mr. Blonde did recklessly induce the police to return fire, that return fire did not kill *another*. Rather, he recklessly induced the police to kill *himself*. Because Mr. Blonde cannot commit a gross reckless murder of himself, there is no gross reckless murder that can be attributed to Mr. Pink.

Model Penal Code

[22] Although the MPC does not include the precise crime of felony murder, it does have a crime that is somewhat equivalent. Under § 210.2(1)(b), a homicide

committed in the commission of, or during flight after, a specified felony, including burglary, gives rise to a nonconclusive presumption that the actor acted with recklessness and extreme indifference, which suffices for murder. As discussed in [9], it is unclear whether the underlying felony was still ongoing. If the felony was ongoing, then the burglary would give rise to the nonconclusive presumption. If instead the felony was complete, then the nonconclusive presumption would not arise. Assuming the burglary was ongoing at the time of the killings and thus the nonconclusive presumption becomes operative, a jury could easily find that Mr. Pink acted with recklessness and extreme indifference with respect to both Mr. Brown and Mr. White. As a result, under the MPC correlate to felony murder, Mr. Pink would possibly be liable for the deaths of Mr. Brown and Mr. White. Because the MPC does not include the common law's felony murder doctrines, Mr. Pink would not have murder liability for the deaths of Griggs and Mr. Blonde via the predicate felony of burglary. Had Mr. Pink engaged in the shootout with the police, there is some authority that he could be liable for purposeful murder under § 210.2(1)(a) or extreme indifference murder, not relying on a predicate felony, under § 210.2(1)(b) for Mr. Blonde's death. MPC Comment § 2.03, at 263 & n.20. But because Mr. Pink did not actually engage in the shootout with the police, this possible basis for Mr. Pink's homicide liability for Mr. Blonde's death does not apply. Whether Mr. Pink would have any homicide liability for the death of Griggs would depend on the principles of accomplice liability. (See Ch. 17.)

Conclusion

Under the common law, Mr. Pink most likely satisfies the requirement that the predicate felony of burglary is inherently dangerous. In a majority of jurisdictions, Mr. Pink satisfies the independent felony requirement. But in a minority of jurisdictions, he would not satisfy the requirement and thus would have no felony murder liability for any of the four counts. With respect to the deaths of Griggs and Mr. Brown, Mr. Pink possibly satisfies the in furtherance requirement. With respect to the death of Mr. White, Mr. Pink does not satisfy the in furtherance requirement and would not have felony murder liability. With respect to the death of Mr. Blonde, Mr. Pink probably does not satisfy the in furtherance requirement.

Under the MPC's correlate doctrine to felony murder, Mr. Pink would possibly have murder liability for the deaths of Mr. Brown and Mr. White, but not for the deaths of Griggs and Mr. Blonde.

TOOLS FOR SELF-ASSESSMENT

Go back to your written answer. Look for the issues identified in paragraphs [1]–[22] in the above Essay. Look also for the analysis that follows each issue, and mark your essay where you locate it. Do you fully describe the issue, identify the precise legal standard that applies, list the relevant facts, and show how the facts and law support a conclusion for each issue in a separate paragraph? Mark each conclusion in your essay. Are there sufficient reasons in the law and in the facts to support the conclusion?

1. Do what you are told and do not analyze what is unnecessary. In the Problem, you are asked to analyze and discuss whether Mr. Pink is liable for felony murder. You need not analyze whether other persons committed felony murder.

2. Remember to include an analysis of the MPC's approach unless you are instructed otherwise.

3. State the best possible arguments for alternative conclusions. Even as you reject possible conclusions as to why Mr. Pink is or is not liable for felony murder of one of the victims, make the best possible argument first, and only then explain why you are rejecting that conclusion.

4. Be on the alert for red herrings. Some information in the fact pattern of a hypothetical may be irrelevant or even designed to mislead you. For example, the color and type of Mr. Pink's car is irrelevant. But sometimes relevant information is obscured by hiding in plain sight within obviously irrelevant information. That Mr. Pink's reason for killing Mr. White is personal animosity, rather than further-ance of the predicate felony, is relevant. But the particular reason for that personal animosity—inappropriate touching by Mr. White of Mr. Pink's childhood drum set—is irrelevant.

5. Remember that the MPC does not have a specific crime termed felony murder. However, the MPC does have a rough correlate to the felony murder doctrine. The commission of one of the specified felonies gives rise to a nonconclusive presumption that any resulting homicide was committed by the felon acting with recklessness manifesting extreme indifference to the value of human life. The effect of the nonconclusive presumption is that the jury should be instructed that it may, but need not, infer the requisite mens rea.

6. Keep in mind the key differences between the MPC and common law. First, under the common law, the predicate felonies rendering one eligible for felony murder are not always specified. Second, and as a result of the first difference, in some common law jurisdictions, the predicate felony must be analyzed to estab-lish it as inherently dangerous and nonmergeable. One need not undertake this analysis under the MPC.

7. Use the MPC-specified felonies as an aid to analyzing common law felony murder. The specified felonies in the MPC are very likely to satisfy the common law requirements of inherent dangerousness and nonmergeability. So, knowing the MPC-specified felonies provides a helpful check on your analysis of these two requirements under the common law.

8. Always be thinking felony murder. The hypothetical in this chapter pre-identifies the issue of felony murder. But in an actual law school or bar exam, the issue will probably not be pre-identified. Thus you must identify the issue in per-haps a dense set of facts with many other crimes being committed. Felony murder is often a favorite question on exams. Whenever a fact pattern includes the com-mission of a felony and a killing, which most criminal law exams will, always be thinking felony murder.

9. Perhaps the best way to approach a question involving felony murder is as the Essay does. The following steps illustrate, but somewhat oversimplify, the approach under the common law:

   i. Is there a death?
   ii. If no, FM is inapplicable.
   iii. If yes, was a felony committed?
   iv. If no, FM is inapplicable.
   v. If yes, consider whether the felony is **inherently dangerous**:

    vi.   Is the felony inherently dangerous under both the abstract test and the actual facts and circumstances test?

    vii.   If yes, go to step xi.

    viii.   If no, does the felony satisfy either test?

    ix.   If no, FM is inapplicable.

    x.   If yes, FM is possible depending on the test adopted by the jurisdiction.

    xi.   Consider whether the felony is **independent and nonmergeable**:

    xii.   Is the purpose of the felony different than the purpose of committing the conduct that causes the death (the independent purpose test)?

    xiii.   If no, then FM is inapplicable.

    xiv.   If yes, consider whether the act that caused the death was **"in furtherance"** of the felony:

    xv.   Are there sufficient temporal, spatial, and causal links between the felony and death?

    xvi.   If no, then FM inapplicable.

    xvii.   If yes, and a felon perpetrated the killing, is the act that caused the death in furtherance of the felony?

    xviii.   If not in furtherance, then no FM; if a nonfelon perpetrated the killing go to step xx.

    xix.   If yes, then FM liability.

    xx.   If a nonfelon perpetrated the killing, then no FM in an agency view jurisdiction.

    xxi.   If a proximate cause view jurisdiction, was the death foreseeable?

    xxii.   If no, then FM inapplicable.

    xxiii.   If yes, was the killing unjustified?

    xxiv.   Was the victim a nonfelon?

    xxv.   If yes to the questions in both xxiii and xxiv, then FM liability

    xxvi.   If no to either question, then FM liability is possible or not depending on the jurisdiction.

This oversimplified analysis may be simplified even further by thinking of felony murder as the broad principle of a death stemming from a felony subject to the three limitations of an inherently dangerous felony, a nonmergeable felony, and that the act causing death be in furtherance of the felony.

10. Consider alternatives to felony murder. Regardless of whether the requirements of felony murder are or are not satisfied, there may be additional bases for homicide liability. For example, if a death resulted from either a felony that was not inherently dangerous or from a misdemeanor, then the defendant may nonetheless be liable for the homicide under the related doctrine of misdemeanor manslaughter. And if a defendant is not liable for felony murder for a killing perpetrated by a nonfelon under the agency view or because of an exception to the proximate cause view, the defendant may nonetheless be liable for gross reckless murder.

11. In analyzing whether a predicate felony is inherently dangerous, remember that the in the abstract test is stricter and less likely to result in the conclusion of an inherently dangerous felony. If you conclude that under that test the felony is inherently dangerous, then it will most likely also be found as inherently dangerous under the actual facts and circumstances test. Under the latter test, a felony will almost always be found to be inherently dangerous. Why? Because any felony

murder prosecution will involve a dead body. And because a death did occur under the actual facts and circumstances, it is difficult to conclude that the felony was anything but inherently dangerous.

12. While the merger doctrine has given courts enormous difficulties, it need not be difficult for you. It is typically much, much more difficult to understand the wisdom of the doctrine than it is to apply it. Your principal task is not to understand its rationale but simply to apply it. The independent purpose test is fairly simple—if the purpose for committing the felony is the same as the purpose for committing the act that causes the death, then the felony merges, and there is no felony murder. If the purpose is different, the felony does not merge, and the defendant is eligible for felony murder liability.

But we can make this even simpler. Consider the following two columns of felonies, each of which result in a death:

Felony	Result	Felony
Arson →	Death	← Assault with a deadly weapon
Robbery →	Death	← Assault with the intent to kill
Kidnapping →	Death	

What is the typical reason for committing the felonies on the left? Obtaining $$$ or property.

Is obtaining $$$ or property a different reason than the reason for committing the conduct that causes the result of death? Yes. So, these felonies are independent, do not merge, and render the defendant eligible for FM.

What is the typical reason for committing the felonies on the right? Killing.

Is killing a different reason than the reason for committing the conduct that causes the result of death? No, the reasons are the same. So these felonies are not independent, they merge, and they bar FM liability.

If you can understand these clear cases, you are more than halfway toward being able to understand some of the more difficult cases like burglary, which is featured in the Problem. (Burglary is more difficult because the reason for committing it is sometimes $$$ and sometimes killing, depending on what felony is intended to be committed inside the dwelling.)

13. Note the "Goldilocks" effect of combining the first two limitations on the scope of felony murder. The inherent dangerous limitation requires the predicate felony to be sufficiently dangerous. But under the second limitation, the merger doctrine, compare the type of felonies generally included as supporting felony murder—armed robbery, arson, kidnapping, rape—with those generally excluded—assault with a dangerous weapon, assault with the intent to kill, and homicide itself. The merger doctrine includes less dangerous felonies as supporting felony murder and excludes more dangerous, indeed the most dangerous felonies. As a result, while the inherent dangerous limitation requires that predicate felonies be sufficiently dangerous, the merger doctrine requires felonies to be not too dangerous. The inherent dangerous limitation excludes the least dangerous felonies,

whereas the merger doctrine excludes the most dangerous felonies. The inherent dangerous limitation imposes a floor of dangerousness of the felony while the merger doctrine imposes a ceiling. The combined effect of the inherent dangerous limitation and the merger doctrine is that the felonies eligible for, or supporting, felony murder are the medium or moderately dangerous felonies. The felonies must be, as the porridge and bed preferred by Goldilocks, just right.

14. In analyzing killings directly perpetrated by a nonfelon, the following chart summarizes the two principal approaches along with one possible exception for a justified killing under the proximate cause view:

	Justified Killing	*Unjustified (or excused) Killing*
Agency	No FM	No FM
Proximate Cause (if death is foreseeable)	Possibly No FM	FM

15. In analyzing killings directly perpetrated by a nonfelon, the following chart summarizes the two principal approaches along with one possible exception under the proximate cause view where the victim is a co-felon:

	Co-Felon Victim	*Any Other Victim*
Agency	No FM	No FM
Proximate Cause (if death is foreseeable)	Possibly No FM	FM

VARIATIONS ON THE THEME

For the following variations, assume all of the facts from the original Problem obtain unless otherwise noted.

1. The felons commit burglary with the intent to commit the felony of larceny inside the dwelling.
2. The felons' predicate felony is armed robbery.
3. The felons' predicate felony is assault with the intent to kill.
4. The felons' predicate felony is larceny.
5. Rather than Mr. Blonde opening a window and shooting at the police and killing Griggs, Mr. Blonde merely appears in front of the window, and the police shoot and kill Mr. Blonde.
6. Rather than the felons committing a predicate felony, they instead commit a predicate misdemeanor.
7. Mr. Blonde shoots at Griggs and misses Griggs, but when the police return fire they accidentally shoot and kill Griggs.
8. The felons' predicate felony is a strict liability offense.

9. Rather than the felons fleeing from the scene of the crime with the police in pursuit, the police are already waiting for the felons at the safe house.

10. While the police are shooting at the felons, the police shoot and kill an innocent bystander.

ADDITIONAL READINGS

People v. Aaron, 299 N.W.2d 304 (Mich. 1980)

Regina v. Sterne, 16 Cox. Crim. Cas. 311 (1887)

GUYORA BINDER, FELONY MURDER (forthcoming 2011)

JOSHUA DRESSLER, UNDERSTANDING CRIMINAL LAW 521–35, 547–49 (5th ed. 2009)

GEORGE FLETCHER, RETHINKING CRIMINAL LAW 285–303, 307–19 (1978)

WAYNE LaFAVE, CRIMINAL LAW 785–807 (5th ed. 2010)

PAUL ROBINSON, CRIMINAL LAW 725–37 (1997)

Claire Finkelstein, *Merger and Felony Murder*, in DEFINING CRIMES 218 (R.A. Duff & Stuart P. Green eds., 2005)

Guyora Binder, *Making the Best of Felony Murder*, 91 B.U. L. REV. 403 (2011)

Guyora Binder, *The Origins of American Felony Murder Rules*, 57 STAN. L. REV. 59 (2004)

David Crump & Susan Waite Crump, *In Defense of the Felony Murder Doctrine*, 8 HARV. J.L. & PUB. POL'Y 359 (1985)

George P. Fletcher, *Reflections on Felony-Murder*, 12 SW. U.L. REV. 413 (1981)

James J. Tomkovicz, *The Endurance of the Felony-Murder Rule: A Study of the Forces That Shape Our Criminal Law*, 51 WASH. & LEE L. REV. 1429 (1994)

9

RAPE I:

RAPE BY FORCE OR THREAT OF FORCE

INTRODUCTION

The law of forcible rape continues to undergo rapid transformation. Traditionally, the paradigmatic example of forcible rape was a stranger jumping out of the bushes or lurking in a dark alley and violently forcing a victim to engage in intercourse. The most commonly litigated issue was whether the victim's resistance was sufficiently vigorous to establish that the intercourse was forced and against the victim's will. Forcible rape was considered to be a crime of violence and was established by proving violent acts of intercourse inflicted upon a resisting victim.

Resistance, while not a formal element of the offense, developed into a de facto element in the sense that courts would typically read a resistance requirement into rape statutes as a way of establishing force, nonconsent, or both. Even in jurisdictions that did not require victim resistance, its presence was considered highly probative of force, and its absence was considered highly probative of consent. Before rape reformists began to advocate for the elimination of the resistance requirement, victims were required to "resist to the utmost" in order to obtain a rape conviction. This standard has given way to less stringent resistance requirements including that a victim "resist in earnest" or merely that a victim's resistance be reasonable. And the degree of resistance sufficient to be reasonable may even be no resistance where resistance would be futile or foolhardy.

Rather than primarily a crime committed by a violent stranger, rape is increasingly typified by nonviolent, yet nonconsensual, intercourse committed by an acquaintance in a social setting. Under this view, rape is a violation of the victim's sexual autonomy. While the traditional conception of rape remains the majority view, the trend is to view nonconsent as the most important element in determining whether intercourse is rape. The difficulty lies in proving a victim's lack of consent to intercourse, especially where there is no extrinsic force or violence. Because the law is loathe to dispense with the force element, the modern trend is to establish force by proof of nonconsent. While the majority view requires that force be established by a showing of some extrinsic force, the trend is that force is established merely by proof of intercourse that is nonconsensual. That is, the amount of force that is inherent in an act of sexual intercourse suffices to satisfy the force element if the victim is not consenting.

Because this modern conception substantially dilutes force as an element, the principal issue becomes nonconsent. While nonconsent may be established by a showing of force or resistance (or the victim's objectively reasonable fear of substantial harm precluding resistance), there are also differing standards of nonconsent that require none of these. The modern, yet very much the minority, conception is that consent is performative. In other words, unless the victim affirmatively says or does something expressing consent, the victim has not consented. As a result, nonconsent is the default assumption; nonconsensual intercourse is rape.

(The next chapter will address rape committed by nonforcible means—rape by coercion and fraud.)

PROBLEM

THE ELEVATOR

Darcy, a 49-year-old woman, 5 feet tall and weighing 130 pounds, enters the elevator of her apartment building and pushes the button for the tenth floor. Doug, a 15-year-old boy, 5 feet 7 inches tall and weighing over 200 pounds, follows Darcy into the elevator. Doug and Darcy are complete strangers. Somewhere between the ninth and tenth floors, Darcy notices that the elevator has stopped. She looks up to see Doug manipulating the elevator controls and sees that the elevator doors are open to the elevator shaft. Doug tells Darcy to remove her clothing. Darcy does not respond. Doug tells her again. Darcy complies, and the two engage in intercourse.

THE HOT AIR BALLOON

Rex owns a hot air balloon and offers rides to tourists on weekends for extra income. Rex is 60 years old, 5 feet tall, and weighs 130 pounds. He sees Rhonda near his hot air balloon stand and approaches her to see if she would like to go for a ride. Rhonda, a 25-year-old woman who is 5 feet 7 inches tall and weighs 160 pounds, says no thanks. Rex pulls out his knife and, while pointing his knife at her, tells her that she will be going on a ride with him and motions toward the balloon. Rhonda climbs into the balloon's basket. Rex joins her inside. As the balloon ascends, Rhonda sees Rex drop the knife to the ground. Rhonda does not believe that Rex has any other knife or weapon in his possession. Sailing several hundred feet above the ground, Rex tells Rhonda to remove her clothing. Rhonda does not respond. Rex tells her again. Rhonda complies and requests that Rex use a condom. The two engage in intercourse.

Doug and Rex are each charged with rape by force or threat of force. Analyze and discuss each defendant's rape liability, if any, as well as any applicable defenses, under the common law and the MPC. In addition, determine which of the two scenarios presents the stronger case for rape liability.

LIST OF READINGS

People v. Williams, 841 P.2d 961 (Cal. 1992)
State v. Rusk, 424 A.2d 720 (Md. 1981)
State In the Interest of M.T.S., 609 A.2d 1266 (N.J. 1992)
MODEL PENAL CODE § 213.1 (Official Code and Revised Comments 1985)

ESSAY

Both Doug and Rex are most likely liable for rape by force or threat of force under both the traditional, majority view as well as the more modern but minority view. Both defendants are possibly liable under the MPC.

[1] Sexual intercourse is an element under any conception of rape. Here the element is uncontestably satisfied and thus will not be separately analyzed under each different conception of rape.

Common Law

[2] The traditional and majority conception of rape contains three elements: (i) intercourse, (ii) by force or threat of force, and (iii) without consent of the victim. This conception relies on the notion of rape as a crime of violence. The more modern and minority conception views rape as a violation of one's sexual autonomy, making nonconsensual intercourse rape regardless of the presence of extrinsic force or violence.

FORCE

[3] In the vast majority of jurisdictions, force is an element of rape. The element of force may be established directly—by the defendant's use of substantial force in obtaining intercourse—or indirectly. Force may be established indirectly by either the victim's sufficient physical resistance or the victim's objectively reasonable fear of substantial injury that precludes resistance. As a result, the nonelements of resistance or fear suffice to establish the required element of force.

[4] Neither Doug nor Rex employed substantial force to obtain intercourse with their victims. Substantial force is generally understood as that likely to cause death or serious bodily harm. Both Doug and Rex arguably did employ some force. Doug manipulated the elevator buttons so as to stop the elevator between floors with the doors open thus exposing the elevator shaft. Rex used a knife to force Rhonda into the balloon basket. Each use of force effected an imprisonment or felonious restraint. (In *Rusk*, the court found that the defendant similarly immobilized the victim by seizing her car keys and rendering her vulnerable.) On similar facts as the Elevator hypothetical, a court found that the defendant's advantages in size and strength also constituted the use of physical force.[1] But none of these uses of force rise to the requisite level of substantial force—force that is likely to cause death or serious injury.

One might argue that Rex's use of a knife clearly constitutes substantial physical force. However, this is not entirely clear. Rex's use of a knife, even if rising to the level of substantial force, did not compel the victim's submission to intercourse. The knife compelled Rhonda into the balloon basket, but once in the basket, the knife was no longer present and did not compel her submission to intercourse.

[5] Even if neither Doug nor Rex actually used substantial force to obtain intercourse, a threat of such force to obtain intercourse would suffice. There is no evidence in the facts that either Doug or Rex uttered any threat whatsoever to obtain intercourse. However, a threat of force need not be express; an implied threat may suffice. Arguably, the implied threat is that if the victims did not submit to

---

[1] The Elevator hypothetical is based on People v. Dorsey, 429 N.Y.S.2d 828 (1980). The court construed the defendant's act of manipulating the elevator to stop it between floors as a physical act directed against the victim. The court concluded that this act, plus the advantage in size the defendant enjoyed, constituted the use of physical force capable of overcoming resistance. Interestingly, the court did not analyze the stopping the elevator between floors as an effort to immobilize or unlawfully confine the victim.

intercourse, then they would be hurled down the elevator shaft and out of the balloon basket, respectively. These implied threats would clearly be threats of substantial harm—the victims would certainly die as a result of their falls. But there is not a clear basis to infer such implied threats.[2]

Perhaps the best argument to establish such implied threats is the prior wrongdoing of the defendants. Each defendant imprisoned or feloniously restrained each victim. Given their willingness to commit these criminal acts against their victims, the implied threat of hurling the victims to their deaths is made at least plausible. As a result, there is plausible but not clear support for the defendants' satisfaction of the force element through an implied threat. (Even if the evidence of an implied threat is insufficient, the same facts supporting an implied threat may be more persuasive in establishing the victims' objectively reasonable fear as discussed in [7] below.)

[6] In the absence of direct evidence of substantial physical force, the force element may be satisfied indirectly by a victim's physical resistance. There is no evidence in the facts suggesting that either victim physically resisted.

[7] The force element can also be established indirectly by an objectively reasonable fear of serious harm precluding resistance. There is no evidence in the facts as to whether the victims were in fear. However, there are ample facts to demonstrate that if they were in fear, that fear would be objectively reasonable. As discussed above in [5], the same facts that plausibly support the view that each victim was subjected to an implied threat of substantial bodily harm perhaps even more persuasively establish the objective reasonableness of the victims' fears that they would be hurled to their deaths. And, as discussed, the willingness of the defendants to imprison, restrain, and immobilize the victims further buttresses the reasonableness of the victims' fear. From the viewpoint of the victims, if the defendants are willing to criminally restrain them, then it is reasonable to infer that they might be willing to go further if the victims did not submit to intercourse.

The different facts of each case provide particular support that each victim had a reasonable fear of substantial harm. Rhonda could reasonably fear substantial harm from Rex given his previous use of a knife. Although Darcy was not subjected to the use of a deadly weapon as was Rhonda, arguably Doug's manipulation of the elevator controls made Darcy fear a willingness on Doug's part to cause serious bodily harm. Though this argument is not as strong in Darcy's case, because pushing elevator buttons does not quite rise to the level of assault with a deadly weapon, the argument is bolstered by Darcy's attacker being almost a foot taller than she, outweighing her by 70 pounds, and being nearly 35 years her junior. The combination of the defendant stopping the elevator and the defendant's physical advantages support the reasonableness of Darcy's fear of serious bodily harm.

[8] Although still a minority view, the more modern conception is that the element of force is satisfied by the force inherent in sexual intercourse that is nonconsensual. Extrinsic force is not required. Because the parties did engage in

[2] On similar facts, a court found that an implied threat was established under circumstances where the victim was stranded on a stalled elevator with a teenager who was significantly larger. The court stated that "[t]he law and common sense did not require that she ascertain what the defendant would do to her if she refused to remove her clothes." Dorsey.

intercourse, the force element would be satisfied if the intercourse was nonconsensual. (Whether the intercourse was nonconsensual will be discussed below in [9]–[13].)

NONCONSENT

[9] Under the traditional approach, nonconsent may be established directly by express verbal statements or physical conduct expressing nonconsent. The primary way for a victim to physically express nonconsent is physical resistance. Nonconsent may also be established indirectly by an objectively reasonable fear of serious harm that precludes resistance.

[10] There is no direct evidence of nonconsent. The victims neither expressly stated nonconsent nor physically resisted. Moreover, there is some direct evidence of consent. Doug and Rex would argue that Darcy and Rhonda's removal of their clothes constituted physical conduct expressing consent. Rex would have an additional argument that Rhonda expressed affirmative consent by requesting he use a condom. While such a request has occasionally been considered by a jury to be sufficient evidence of consent, most jurisdictions would not find this probative of consent. Therefore, this argument would likely fail.

[11] Despite the direct evidence of consent as discussed above in [10], the victims' nonconsent may be established indirectly because both victims most likely had an objectively reasonable fear of substantial harm that precluded resistance. The same facts discussed above in [5] that support an objectively reasonable fear establishing the force element equally serve to establish the nonconsent element.

[12] Under the minority/modern view, nonconsent may not be a formal element, but it is used to establish the formal element of force. Illustrative of the modern approach, *M.T.S.* conceives of consent as performative. It is not an internal attitude reflecting a state of desire or interest. Rather, consent is an external act akin to granting permission. According to this view, one must express permission either through words or actions. That is, if a victim says nothing and does nothing, then there is no consent. In addition, the express permission must be such that a reasonable person would conclude that it was affirmatively and freely granted. Applying this standard here, the victims failed to affirmatively consent through express words. Arguably, Darcy and Rhonda did express consent through actions— they removed their clothes. However, a reasonable person would probably conclude that the removal of clothing did not constitute affirmative and freely given permission under the circumstances. Given the criminal means by which the two defendants immobilized and restrained the victims, such permission as expressed by the removal of their clothes would most likely not be viewed as freely given.

MENS REA

[13] The primary mens rea issue in rape by force concerns the element or issue of the victim's nonconsent. Rather than affirmatively stating the requisite mens rea, the issue is more typically framed as whether a claim of mistake as to the victim's consent will be recognized. An overwhelming majority of jurisdictions allow a mistake of fact defense if the defendant honestly and reasonably believed the victim was consenting. Both defendants might raise this mistake of fact defense. Rex would argue that because Rhonda seemingly voluntarily removed her clothing and asked him to use a condom that he believed she was consenting. Doug would

similarly rely on Darcy's seemingly voluntary removal of her clothing as the basis of his mistaken belief that she was consenting. It is unlikely that either defendant would be successful in this defense. The facts of both cases establish that the defendants feloniously confined their victims in such a way that the victims were trapped and likely felt that they had no choice but to comply with the defendants' demands. Even if the defendants honestly believed their victims were consenting, their belief would probably be unreasonable.

[14] The trend, but still the minority view, is that the mens rea as to the element of the victim's nonconsent is either strict liability or quasi-strict liability. Under the strict liability view, a defendant's honest and reasonable belief that the victim was consenting is not a defense. Under one version of the quasi-strict liability view, a defendant is not entitled to an honest and reasonable mistake of fact defense if the defendant testifies that the encounter with the victim was clearly consensual. Jurisdictions adopting this view reason that if, under the defendant's own view, the encounter was clearly, unambiguously, and unequivocally consensual, then the defendant has no basis to be reasonably mistaken as to the victim's consent. See, e.g., *Williams*. If Doug and Rex were to argue that their encounters with the victims were unequivocally consensual, then they would be precluded from obtaining the reasonable mistake of fact defense in some jurisdictions.

Model Penal Code

[15] Under the MPC, rape is accomplished if the perpetrator compels a victim to submit to intercourse by force or by threat of imminent death, serious bodily injury, or extreme pain. As there is no mention of nonconsent, the MPC approach is entirely concerned with the conduct of the perpetrator rather than the victim's resistance or nonconsent. Doug and Rex could possibly be liable for compelling their victims to submit to intercourse by implied threats of death or serious bodily injury. As discussed above in [5], there is some, but not overwhelming, evidence to support an implied threat of death or serious harm. As a result, Doug and Rex would possibly be liable under the MPC.

Conclusion

[16] Under the traditional and majority view, both Doug and Rex most likely satisfy both the force and nonconsent elements because each of their victims probably submitted to intercourse based on an objectively reasonable fear of substantial bodily harm. Neither Doug nor Rex would likely prevail on a mistake of fact defense that their victim was consenting. Under the modern/minority view, both Doug and Rex probably satisfy the force element because probably neither victim expressed affirmative and freely given permission to engage in intercourse. Proof of extrinsic force is not required. Under the MPC, both Doug and Rex are possibly liable under the theory that they compelled their victims to submit to intercourse by an implied threat of death or serious bodily harm.

The Stronger Case for Rape Liability

[17] While the two scenarios have more in common than not, there are three arguably relevant differences. First, the means that each defendant employs to isolate and immobilize his victim differ. Whereas Doug manipulated elevator buttons, Rex used a knife. The use of the knife is obviously and superficially more egregious.

But arguably this obvious difference is not relevant because once Rex facilitated Rhonda's isolation in the balloon basket, he dropped the knife. As a result, at the time each defendant asked each victim to remove her clothing, the situations were largely parallel. In other words, the dropping of the knife makes the obviously more egregious initial use of the knife drop out as a relevant difference. On the other hand, Rex's use of a more harmful means to obtain his victim's isolation both enhances the credibility of any possible implied threat and bolsters the basis for Rhonda to fear him. That is, one who is willing to use the more harmful means of a knife to obtain his victim's isolation might well be more willing to hurl his victim to her demise. On balance, this factor supports The Hot Air Balloon as the stronger case for rape liability.

[18] The second arguably relevant difference is the disparity in height and weight between each defendant and victim. In The Elevator, the defendant enjoys a significant advantage in height, weight, and youth over the victim. In contrast, in The Hot Air Balloon, the defendant enjoys no such advantage. The physical disparity in The Elevator both enhances the credibility of any implied threat and elevates his victim's fear. This factor militates in favor of The Elevator as the stronger case for rape liability.

[19] Third, Rhonda's request that Rex use a condom slightly weakens the satisfaction of the element of nonconsent as well as slightly strengthening the basis for any mistake of fact defense as to the issue of consent. This factor favors The Elevator as the stronger case for rape liability.

[20] Although two out of the three differences favor The Elevator as the stronger case for rape liability, this numerical preponderance alone should not be dispositive because the relevance of the third difference—the requested use of a condom—is so slight. The ultimate issue may be which of the first two factors carries more weight.

[21] One might argue that The Elevator is the stronger case for rape liability. Although Doug uses less harmful means to secure the victim's isolation, once each victim is isolated, the means may no longer matter. The victim in The Elevator is facing a perpetrator who is 7 inches taller, 70 pounds heavier and 34 years younger. In contrast, though the perpetrator in The Hot Air Balloon used the more harmful means of isolation, thereby demonstrating a greater willingness to harm his victim, once he drops the knife, he is less capable of harming his victim than the perpetrator in The Elevator. In The Hot Air Balloon, the defendant is significantly shorter, lighter, and more elderly than the victim. On this basis—capacity to harm the victim—The Elevator is the stronger case for rape liability.

[22] On behalf of The Hot Air Balloon as the stronger case for rape liability, the equal and opposite argument might be made. Although Rex is less capable of harming his victim given his smaller stature, his use of the more harmful means of securing his victim's isolation—the knife—evidences a greater willingness to attempt to harm the victim.

[23] On balance, perhaps neither scenario creates a stronger case for rape liability.

TOOLS FOR SELF-ASSESSMENT

Go back to your written answer. Look for the issues identified in paragraphs numbered [1]–[23] above. Look also for the analysis that follows each issue, and mark your essay where you locate it. Do you fully describe the issue, identify the precise legal standard that applies, list the relevant facts, and show how the facts and law support a conclusion for each issue? Mark each conclusion in your essay. Are there sufficient reasons in the law and in the facts to support each conclusion?

1.   Do what you are told. Here, you are to analyze the defendants' rape liability, if any, as well as any applicable defenses, under both the common law and MPC. A complete answer would analyze their liability and any applicable defenses pursuant to the traditional conception of rape, the more modern rule, and the MPC. You are also asked to compare the scenarios and determine which presents a stronger case for rape liability and why.

2.   Do not analyze what is unnecessary. For example, do not analyze and discuss either defendant's possible criminal liability for false imprisonment, felonious restraint, or Rex's possible criminal liability for assault with a deadly weapon. The instructions direct you to only analyze the defendants' rape liability.

3.   Always analyze under the MPC as well as the common law unless you are instructed otherwise.

4.   State the best possible arguments for alternative conclusions. If, for example, you determine that either defendant has not satisfied an element of forcible rape, present the best possible argument that he has satisfied the element. It is possible that you will be unable to reach a conclusion if, for example, the issue presents a question of fact to be determined by a jury. If so, it becomes even more important that you clearly set out the possible opposing arguments.

5.   There are numerous ways to organize your essay. Set out below is the organizational structure of the above Essay as well as possible alternative organizational structures. There is no single organizational structure that is always preferable for all hypotheticals involving rape or any other type of law. But there are advantages and disadvantages depending on the hypothetical and the instructions as to how to analyze it. Appreciating the various possible organizational structures that you might employ for any given hypothetical or exam question will be of tremendous aid in selecting, if not the optimal organizational structure, then at least a preferable one. Having a good organizational structure will not only help clarify your analysis but also save you time. It is very important to have a sense of the possible organizational structures you might employ before you walk into an exam. Appreciating the possible ways of organizing your essay will also help prevent feeling overwhelmed and not knowing how to begin. You do not want to waste valuable time during the exam grappling with how to organize your essay.

Three outlines of possible organizational structures are set out on the next page. Structure #1 represents the organizational structure of the above Essay, and Structures #2 and #3 are possible alternatives.

The advantage of Structure #1 is that time is saved by analyzing both hypotheticals together. This can be done for this particular Problem only because the analysis of each hypothetical is largely similar. Structure #2 completes the analysis of each hypothetical separately. Structure #3 analyzes all of the elements under the traditional rule and only then analyzes the modern rule and then the MPC. Of course there are many different possible organizational structures, but the three above should give you a sense of the principal possibilities.

Structure #1	Structure #2	Structure #3
Introduction	Introduction	Introduction
Intercourse Element	Intercourse Element	Intercourse Element
Common Law	Hypothetical 1	Common Law
Force	Common Law	Traditional Rule
Traditional Rule	Force	Force
Hypos 1 & 2	Trad. Rule	Hypos 1 & 2
Modern Rule	Mod. Rule	Nonconsent
Hypos 1 & 2	Nonconsent	Hypos 1 & 2
Nonconsent	Trad. Rule	Mens Rea
Traditional Rule	Mod. Rule	Hypos 1 & 2
Hypos 1 & 2	Mens Rea	Modern Rule
Modern Rule	Trad. Rule	Force
Hypos 1 & 2	Mod. Rule	Hypos 1 & 2
Mens Rea	Model Penal Code	Nonconsent
Traditional Rule	Hypothetical 2	Hypos 1 & 2
Hypos 1 & 2	Common Law	Mens Rea
Modern Rule	Force	Hypos 1 & 2
Hypos 1 & 2	Trad. Rule	Model Penal Code
Model Penal Code	Mod. Rule	Hypos 1 & 2
Hypos 1 & 2	Nonconsent	Conclusion
Conclusion	Trad. Rule	Comparison of Hypos 1 & 2
Comparison of Hypos 1 & 2	Mod. Rule	
	Mens Rea	
	Trad. Rule	
	Mod. Rule	
	Model Penal Code	
	Conclusion	
	Comparison of Hypos 1 & 2	

6.   No matter how you organize your essay, consider the advantages of discussing the required element of intercourse first because it applies to any conception of rape, and because it is uncontestably satisfied under the facts. If you mention it at the outset before you address each of the different conceptions, you will avoid the waste of time involved in setting it out multiple times. (See [1].)

7.   One of the thorniest aspects of analyzing rape by force is that the elements of force and nonconsent can each be established by proving the existence of one of the following two nonelements: (i) physical resistance by the victim, or (ii) the victim's objectively reasonable fear of serious harm that precludes resistance. That is, the requisite, formal, statutory elements may be established indirectly by proof of nonelements. And most often, that is the way the formal elements are established. As a result, these nonelements become comparatively more important than the actual statutory formal elements.

8. Another thorny aspect of analyzing the elements of force and nonconsent is that each may be used to establish the other. Force can satisfy nonconsent. If the perpetrator employs or threatens sufficient force against the victim, and resistance by the victim would thus be futile or foolhardy, then the degree of reasonable resistance is no resistance. In turn, the victim's reasonable resistance suffices to establish nonconsent. As a result, through this circuitous path, the element of force satisfies the distinct element of nonconsent.

And nonconsent can satisfy the element of force, at least under the modern view. The element of force can be satisfied by that force inherent in an act of nonconsensual intercourse. As a result, once nonconsent is established, the intercourse is forcible.

9. Given that under the traditional/majority rule formal elements are most typically established by proof of nonelements, perhaps a particularly efficient and streamlined approach of analyzing forcible rape would be to focus on these nonelements. So you might choose to begin your analysis with the nonelements. If either the victim physically resisted or the victim had an objectively reasonable fear of serious harm that precluded resistance, the elements of both force and nonconsent are satisfied. If these nonelements cannot be established, only then would you analyze whether the elements of force and nonconsent can be established directly.

10. Do not make the mistake of construing the modern rule as eliminating entirely the force element. The modern rule does formally require the element of force to be proven. Rather than eliminating the requirement of force, the modern rule has diluted the degree of force that suffices. The degree of force need not be any more than that force inherent in an act of nonconsensual intercourse. It might be said that while the traditional rule requires a sufficient amount of force *extrinsic* from the act of intercourse, the modern rule only requires the amount of force *intrinsic* to the act of intercourse.

11. Keep in mind that the test for nonconsent under the modern view, at least as exemplified by the *M.T.S.* approach, is disjunctive. The victim does consent by *either* verbally expressing permission *or* by affirmative conduct expressing permission. That is, if either of the above disjuncts are satisfied, then the victim has consented, and the defendant cannot be liable for rape. This raises the possibility that if a victim clearly verbalizes a "no," but her conduct expresses a "yes" or vice versa, the victim has consented and the defendant cannot be liable for rape. However, such a "mixed message" scenario should be construed under the test of whether a reasonable person would conclude that the victim was consenting given all of the surrounding circumstances. And in such a "mixed message" scenario, a reasonable person might conclude that the victim was not consenting given the conflicting messages sent by the victim.

12. The following step-by-step analysis illustrates the reasoning followed in the above Essay:

Traditional/Majority Rule

    i. Did the defendant engage in intercourse with or effect penetration of the victim?

    ii. If no, then no rape liability.

    iii. If yes, did the defendant employ or threaten substantial force?

    iv. If yes, then go to step vii.

v. If no, did the victim either physically resist or have an objectively reasonable fear of serious harm?

vi. If no, then no rape liability.

vii. If yes, is there direct evidence of the victim's nonconsent?

viii. If yes, then go to step xi.

ix. If no, then did the victim either physically resist or have an objectively reasonable fear of serious harm?

x. If no, then no rape liability.

xi. If yes, is the element of consent a strict liability element in the jurisdiction?

xii. If yes, then the defendant is liable for rape.

xiii. If no, then was the defendant honestly and reasonably mistaken that the victim was consenting?

xiv. If no, then the defendant is liable for rape.

xv. If yes, then no rape liability.

Modern/Minority View

i. Did the defendant engage in intercourse with or effect penetration of the victim?

ii. If no, then no rape liability.

iii. If yes, did the defendant employ or threaten any amount of physical force?

iv. If yes, go to viii.

v. If no, did the victim affirmatively and freely express consent either through words or actions?

vi. If yes, then no rape liability.

vii. If no, go to viii.

viii. Does the jurisdiction recognize a defendant's honest and reasonable belief that the victim was consenting as a defense?

ix. If no, then the defendant is liable for rape.

x. If yes, is the defendant's mistake of fact claim barred by the equivocal conduct rule?

xi. If yes, then the defendant is liable for rape.

xii. If no, was the defendant honestly and reasonably mistaken that the victim was consenting?

xiii. If no, then the defendant is liable for rape.

xiv. If yes, then no rape liability.

VARIATIONS ON THE THEME

For the following variations, assume all of the facts from the original Problem obtain unless otherwise noted.

THE ELEVATOR

(1) When the elevator stops between floors, the doors remain closed.

(2) Instead of manipulating the elevator's buttons, Doug does nothing, and the elevator stops by itself and the doors open.

(3) Doug and Darcy are the same age and size.

(4) Doug and Darcy are not strangers.

(5) Instead of manipulating the elevator's buttons, Doug does nothing, and the elevator stops by itself and the doors remain closed.

(6)   Rhonda initiates a conversation with Rex. Rhonda requests that they go up in the balloon together. Rex neither possesses nor uses a knife.

(7)   Rhonda is a professional kickboxer.

(8)   Rex does not have a condom. Rhonda supplies him with one from her purse.

(9)   After the first time that Rex tells her to remove her clothing, she replies, "No, absolutely not."

(10) Rhonda and Rex were previously in a romantic relationship with each other. Rhonda requests that they go up in the balloon together. Rex neither possesses nor uses a knife.

ADDITIONAL READINGS

Susan Estrich, Real Rape (1987)

Joan McGregor, Is It Rape? On Acquaintance Rape and Taking Women's Consent Seriously 1–138, 195–248 (2005)

Stephen J. Schulhofer, Unwanted Sex: The Culture of Intimidation and the Failure of Law 1–113, 254–73 (1998)

Michelle J. Anderson, *Reviving Resistance in Rape Law*, 1998 U. Ill. L. Rev. 953

David P. Bryden, *Redefining Rape*, 3 Buff. Crim. L. Rev. 317 (2000)

Russell L. Christopher & Kathryn H. Christopher, *The Paradox of Statutory Rape*, __ Ind. L.J. __(forthcoming 2012)

Michelle Madden Dempsey & Jonathan Herring, *Why Sexual Penetration Requires Justification*, 27 Oxf. J. Leg. Stud. 467 (2007)

Deborah W. Denno, *Why the Model Penal Code's Sexual Offense Provisions Should be Pulled and Replaced*, 1 Ohio St. J. Crim. L. 207 (2003)

Donald Dripps, *Beyond Rape: An Essay on the Difference between the Presence of Force and the Absence of Consent*, 92 Colum. L. Rev. 7 (1992)

Douglas N. Husak & George C. Thomas III., *Date Rape, Social Convention, and Reasonable Mistakes*, 11 Law & Phil. 95 (1992)

Peter Westen, *Some Common Confusions about Consent in Rape Cases*, 2 Ohio St. J. Crim. L. 333 (2004)

RAPE II:

RAPE BY COERCION AND FRAUD

10

INTRODUCTION

In addition to the use or threat of physical force, the principal means used to obtain intercourse that the law of rape prohibits are coercion and fraud. While the criminalization of the use or threat of physical force protects the victim from physical violation, criminalizing the use of coercion and fraud affords protection from the violation of a victim's sexual autonomy. Some jurisdictions and the MPC treat rape by coercion or fraud as lesser forms of rape; the MPC terms it "gross sexual imposition." But obtaining intercourse by any of these means (force or threat of force, coercion, or fraud) is criminalized because they undermine and negate a victim's meaningful consent.

While rape by physical force triggers the issue of whether "No means no," rape by coercion and rape by fraud raise the issue of whether "Yes means yes." That is, the issue in rape by physical force often is whether the victim's claim of nonconsent, or "No," may be disregarded and interpreted as a "Yes" (perhaps because the victim did not sufficiently resist). In contrast, in both rape by coercion and rape by fraud, the issue is whether the victim's nominal consent should be treated as true, valid and legal consent. To put it simply, the law of rape by physical force must determine whether a victim's factual "No" should be construed as a legal "No." The law of both rape by coercion and rape by fraud must determine whether a victim's factual "Yes" should be construed as a legal "Yes."

Rape by coercion consists of obtaining intercourse by proposals involving nonphysical force or harm. Not all proposals of nonphysical force or harm suffice. While there is considerable diversity in approaches, the MPC standard has been influential. The MPC criminalizes rape by coercion where the perpetrator "compels . . . [the victim] to submit by any threat that would prevent resistance by a . . . [person] of ordinary resolution." MPC § 213.1(2)(a). Essentially, if a reasonable person would succumb to the threat and engage in intercourse, then it is rape; if a reasonable person would not, then it is not rape. While jurisdictions typically require (i) the coercive proposal be a threat (rather than an offer), and (ii) the gravity of the threat is such that a reasonable person would be unable to resist, some jurisdictions require only one or the other, or even neither. For example, Pennsylvania prohibits obtaining intercourse by "forcible compulsion"—expansively defined as "intellectual, moral, emotional, or psychological force." Seemingly, any coercive proposal might qualify.

Rape by fraud consists of obtaining intercourse by the use of fraudulent statements or conduct. There are three main approaches. First, any fraud suffices. Second, only fraud in specified contexts suffices. The two principal contexts are fraudulent medical treatment (e.g., in the gynecological or proctological setting) and spousal impersonation. The MPC follows this second approach by criminalizing fraud rendering the victim unaware that a sexual act has occurred or where the perpetrator impersonates the victim's husband. The third approach, which only the common law utilizes, is the fraud in the factum/fraud in the inducement distinction. Fraud in the factum renders the victim unaware of the nature of the act. Fraud in the inducement renders the victim aware of the nature of, but unaware of the true reason for, the act. Only fraud in the factum negates the victim's consent and constitutes rape. Considerable controversy and confusion persist in applying the distinction. This chapter will clarify both how the law has traditionally drawn the distinction narrowly and how more modern courts have drawn the distinction more expansively.

PROBLEM

D and V are in love and plan to wed. D drives V to the office of Dr. D, a renowned gynecologist, with whom V has an appointment for a gynecological examination. Dr. D's office is far, maybe three hours away. After Dr. D has begun the examination and V is lying on the examination table, Dr. D tells V that unless V has intercourse with him (Dr. D), he will tell D that she has syphilis and that she is unfit to marry. Fearful of losing the love of her life, V reluctantly agrees. After Dr. D and V engage in intercourse for a few minutes, a nurse informs Dr. D over the office intercom that he is needed to attend to a medical emergency regarding another patient in another examination room. Dr. D tells V to stay exactly where she is, not to move, and he will be back in ten minutes. While Dr. D is away, D, unaware of what has transpired between Dr. D and his beloved, sneaks into the room. Because of V's position on the examination table and the sheet covering her, she is unable to see that it is D. D rattles a few medical instruments so as to lead V to believe that the gynecological examination by Dr. D is about to resume. But V believes that Dr. D will resume engaging in intercourse with her. Seeing V tense up, D says to V in a whisper, so that his voice will plausibly sound like it could be that of Dr. D, "Relax, if you do not let me finish my examination I will not be able to diagnose any serious problem or disease that you might have which, if left untreated, might kill you." V responds, "OK, just get it over with Dr. D." D then engages in intercourse with V.

Analyze and discuss the criminal liability for rape, if any, of Dr. D and D. Make sure to specify the particular type of rape (or types of rape), if any, that Dr. D and D have each committed. Also, make sure to include in your analysis and discussion any applicable defenses.

LIST OF READINGS

Pa. Cons. Stat. Ann. § 3101 (West 2006)
Boro v. Superior Court, 163 Cal. App. 3d 1224 (1985)
State v. Lovely, 480 A.2d 847 (N.H. 1984)
Model Penal Code § 213.1(2)(a), (c); Comment to § 213.1, at 312–15 (Official Code and Revised Comments 1985)

ESSAY

Dr. D is most likely not liable for rape by coercion under the MPC but most likely is liable in some, but not all, states. Dr. D is not liable for rape by fraud.

D is liable in most jurisdictions for attempted rape by fraud and probably is liable for completed rape by fraud in some jurisdictions. Under the MPC, D is most likely liable for attempted rape by fraud. D probably is liable for rape by coercion in some jurisdictions, but not under the MPC.

Dr. D's Liability

Dr. D has neither used physical force nor fraud but has possibly obtained intercourse with V by use of a proposal involving nonphysical harm. The principal issue is whether Dr. D is liable for rape by coercion.

RAPE BY COERCION

Model Penal Code

[1] The MPC criminalizes rape by coercion under the crime of gross sexual imposition (GSI), a lesser degree of liability than rape. The standard for the rape by coercion form of GSI is if the perpetrator "compels" the victim to submit to intercourse by any "threat" that would prevent resistance by a person of "ordinary resolution." MPC § 213.1(2).

This standard encompasses three principal elements. First, the perpetrator's threat "compels" the victim to submit. The "compels" element requires that the victim submit from "coercion rather than bargain." MPC Comment to § 213.1 at 313–15. Second, the form or nature of the proposal is a threat rather than an offer. A threat proposes to make the recipient of the proposal worse off than the recipient was prior to the proposal. In contrast, an offer proposes to make the recipient of the proposal better off than the recipient was prior to the proposal. Third, the degree or gravity of the threatened harm is such that it prevents resistance by a person of "ordinary resolution." That is, if a reasonable person would succumb to the threat and engage in intercourse with the perpetrator, then it is GSI. If a reasonable person would not do so, then it is not GSI.

As a result, to be liable for rape by coercion under the MPC's GSI standard, a perpetrator must (i) compel a victim to submit to intercourse by a nonbargain, (ii) threat, (iii) of sufficient gravity that a reasonable person would be unable to resist.

[2] As to the first element, the distinction between bargain and coercion is not entirely clear. The MPC explains a bargain as offering "an unattractive choice to avoid some unwanted alternative." MPC Comment to § 213.1 at 314. But this explanation equally applies to a clearly coercive proposal such as "Your money or your life." The MPC supplies a better clue in its following example of a bargain: "If a wealthy man were to threaten to withdraw financial support from his unemployed girlfriend" unless she has intercourse with him. MPC Comment § 213.1 at 314. From that example, we might infer that a necessary condition for a bargain is the negotiated exchange of intercourse for money or some material good.

Because no money or material good is exchanged, Dr. D's proposal does not constitute a bargain. As a result, to the extent that Dr. D has compelled V's submission to intercourse, Dr. D satisfies the first element.

[3] As to the second element, that the proposal is a threat, Dr. D does propose to make V worse off than she was prior to the proposal. That is, Dr. D is proposing to make V worse off (by telling D bad things about her) than V was prior to Dr. D's utterance of the proposal (when Dr. D was not going to tell D anything bad about her). As a result, Dr. D satisfies the second element.

[4] As to the third element, the MPC does not provide explicit guidance as to the requisite degree or gravity of threatened harm. Although the prospect of losing the love of one's life is a significantly grave harm, a reasonable person perhaps would still not succumb because of the unlikelihood of the threatened harm actually occurring for two reasons. First, Dr. D might not carry out this threat because it could be easily refuted by V independently getting tested for syphilis. Second, even if Dr. D did follow through on the threat, it is unlikely that V would lose D due to a claim that she has syphilis because V can obtain independent confirmation that she does not have it. As a result, Dr. D probably fails to satisfy the third element.

Common Law

[5] Although the MPC approach has been influential, jurisdictions criminalize obtaining intercourse by coercion under a variety of standards.

[6] Pennsylvania criminalizes intercourse obtained by "forcible compulsion," which it defines as including "intellectual, moral, emotional, or psychological force." PA. CONS. STAT. ANN. §3101. Dr. D's threat, as would almost any threat, would presumably qualify as the requisite forcible compulsion. As a result, Dr. D would be liable for rape by coercion. (Note that Pennsylvania's standard does not require that the coercive proposal take the form of a threat.)

[7] New Hampshire criminalizes obtaining intercourse "by threatening to retaliate against the victim." *State v. Lovely*. Dr. D's threat would easily qualify as retaliation, and thus Dr. D would be liable for rape by coercion.

[8] In jurisdictions adopting some form of the MPC's reasonable person standard, Dr. D would probably not be liable for rape by coercion. A reasonable person would likely be able to resist the threat because, as discussed above in [4], it is unlikely that the threatened harm—V losing the love of her life, D—would actually occur.

RAPE BY FRAUD

[9] There are three principal approaches to determining what types of fraud suffice for rape by fraud liability. First, any fraud, without apparent limitation, suffices. Second, only specified types of fraud in particular contexts or as to particular matters suffice. And third is the application of the fraud in the factum/fraud in the inducement distinction. The MPC applies the second approach by criminalizing, as the crime of GSI, obtaining intercourse by defrauding the victim either as to the sexual nature of the act or by impersonating the victim's husband. Although different jurisdictions use one (or more) of the three approaches, only a small minority of jurisdictions use the first approach.

Did Dr. D commit rape by fraud? True, Dr. D did obtain intercourse by the threat to use a (presumably) material misrepresentation that V had syphilis. But the victim, V, was not defrauded into engaging in intercourse. As a result, there is no rape by fraud perpetrated by Dr. D. To the extent that Dr. D coerced V into submitting to intercourse, Dr. D did so through a threat to defraud not the victim, V, but rather, her lover, D. That is, Dr. D obtained intercourse through the coercive effect of a threatened fraudulent statement to be made to a third party. (In contrast, in *Boro*, the perpetrator obtained intercourse with the victim through the coercive effect of a statement defrauding the victim herself.)

CONCLUSION

Dr. D is most likely not liable for rape by coercion under the MPC but most likely is liable in some, but not all, states. Dr. D is not liable for rape by fraud.

D's Liability

There are four bases in the facts supporting D's possible liability for rape: (A) by rattling the medical instruments so as to suggest the commencement or continuation of a medical exam, (B) by whispering in a tone of voice suggestive of Dr. D, (C) by the content of his statement to V, and (D) by simply engaging in intercourse with V under circumstances where she is not consenting due to Dr. D's possible coercion. The first two bases involve possible rape by fraud, the third involves both rape by fraud and rape by coercion, and the last involves rape by coercion.

A. RATTLING THE MEDICAL INSTRUMENTS

Model Penal Code

[10] The MPC prohibits obtaining intercourse where the perpetrator defrauds the victim into being unaware of the sexual nature of the act. By seeking to defraud V into believing that the intercourse was penetration by a medical instrument (by rattling the medical instruments), D sought to make V unaware of the sexual nature of the act. But V was not defrauded into believing that the penetration was nonsexual. She believed that she would be engaging in intercourse (with Dr. D), and she actually did engage in intercourse (albeit with D). As a result, D did not commit rape by fraud.

[11] Though not rape by fraud, D has possibly committed *attempted* rape by fraud. D purposely defrauded V by trying to lead her to believe that penetration would be by medical instrument and not by a human organ. His rattling of the medical instruments probably constitutes a substantial step that strongly corroborates his purpose. MPC §5.01(2). Despite the fact that there was actual intercourse, D still only attempted rape by fraud because V was not defrauded—she was very much aware that a sexual act was being committed upon her. As a result, D probably committed attempted rape by fraud.

Common Law

[12] For the same reason as discussed above in [10], this is most likely not rape by fraud under the common law.

[13] D has probably committed attempted rape by fraud (see [11], above) in jurisdictions purporting to prohibit any fraud, without limitation, as well as in jurisdictions using a context-specific approach. He has also most likely committed attempted rape by fraud in jurisdictions applying the fraud in the factum/fraud in the inducement distinction. D is attempting to defraud V as to the very nature of the act (fraud in the factum). D is attempting to defraud V into believing penetration will be by medical instrument rather than by a human organ. Obtaining intercourse by this sort of fraudulent medical treatment is a paradigmatic type of fraud in the factum. Fraud in the factum is always viewed as vitiating consent and thus is always considered rape by fraud (in this case, attempted rape by fraud).

D's whispering in a tone of voice suggestive of Dr. D raises the possibility of rape by fraud via impersonation and/or fraudulent medical treatment.

Model Penal Code

[14] The only type of rape by fraud via impersonation that the MPC recognizes is spousal impersonation. Because Dr. D is not V's spouse, D's apparent impersonation of Dr. D would not suffice.

[15] But perhaps the better view is that D is committing a different type of rape by fraud than by impersonation. D is not trying to obtain V's submission to intercourse simply by impersonating someone with whom D believes V would consent to engaging in intercourse. Rather, by the *means* of impersonating Dr. D, D is trying to defraud V into believing that penetration will be by medical instrument. This is rape by fraud of the fraudulent medical treatment type that renders the victim unaware of the sexual nature of the act. And this type of rape by fraud is recognized under the MPC. But because V is not actually defrauded into believing penetration will be by medical instrument, D has only committed an attempt. By the means of impersonating Dr. D, D has committed an attempted rape by fraud of the fraudulent medical treatment type. As a result, by attempting to obtain intercourse with V by making her unaware of the sexual act, D has most likely committed attempted GSI (of the rape by fraud type).

Common Law

[16] Under the common law, whether D has committed rape by fraud depends on the particular approach to rape by fraud adopted by a jurisdiction. In those jurisdictions prohibiting fraud without limitation, D has committed rape by fraud.

In jurisdictions applying the context-specific approach, whether D has committed rape by fraud depends on the particular types of contexts recognized. Generally the only type of rape by fraud via impersonation that is recognized is spousal impersonation. This is obviously not spousal impersonation. A small number of jurisdictions, however, recognize rape by fraud by impersonation of a lover or an intimate. But this is not impersonation of a lover or an intimate. Rather, in this case, it is impersonation *by* an intimate *of* a nonintimate. An even smaller number of jurisdictions recognize impersonation of any type. D's impersonation of Dr. D would seem to constitute rape by fraud under that approach.

In jurisdictions applying the factum/inducement distinction, whether D has committed rape by fraud depends on whether the distinction is drawn narrowly, as courts traditionally have, or more broadly, as more modern courts do. Under the traditional, narrow construction of the distinction, intercourse obtained by impersonation is fraud in the inducement because the victim is aware of the nature of the act but defrauded as to the reason for the act. V was aware of the nature of the act—sexual intercourse—but was defrauded as to the reason for engaging in sexual intercourse—she believed that she was engaging in intercourse with Dr. D because of his threat. Under this traditional, narrow construction of the distinction, the "nature" of the act is limited to the sexual nature of the act. Awareness of intercourse is thus construed as awareness of the nature of the act. But more modern courts tend to apply the distinction more broadly. The "nature" of the act is construed more broadly than merely the sexual nature of the act; awareness of the nature of the act may include some awareness about the identity of one's partner. Under this broader interpretation, V is arguably unaware of the nature of the act—unaware of engaging in intercourse with D. And thus D's impersonation of Dr. D is fraud in the factum and thus rape by fraud.

[17] But as discussed in [15] above, this is not merely rape by fraud via impersonation. It really is, or also is, attempted rape by fraud via fraudulent medical treatment by the *means* of an impersonation. And, as discussed in [13] above, this type of (attempted) rape by fraud is recognized in most jurisdictions.

[18] In conclusion, by whispering in a tone of voice suggestive of Dr. D, D has probably committed a completed rape by fraud of the impersonation type in some jurisdictions and an attempted rape by fraud of the fraudulent medical treatment type in most jurisdictions.

The particular type of rape by fraud that D commits has considerable practical significance. The fraudulent medical treatment type of rape by fraud is recognized under the MPC and in most jurisdictions. In contrast, impersonation of one who is neither a spouse nor an intimate is only recognized as rape by fraud in a small minority of jurisdictions.

C. THE CONTENT OF D'S STATEMENT TO V

The content of D's statement, apart from the whispering tone used in making the statement, possibly supplies the basis for rape liability as rape by threat of physical force, rape by coercion, and rape by fraud.

Rape by Threat of Physical Force

[19] D has possibly committed rape by threat of physical force. D's statement is threatening, in some sense, death unless V complies. But there are a number of factors that would not support rape by threat of physical force. First, the threatened death or serious bodily harm via an untreated disease or medical problem is not imminent. Second, the disease or medical problem is not clearly physical force. And third, the threatened harm is neither being *inflicted* by D nor anyone else. As a result, D is most likely not committing rape by threat of physical force under either the MPC or common law.

Rape by Coercion—Model Penal Code

[20] Because D's statement is most likely not a bargain, the first element of rape by coercion under the MPC—compulsion—is satisfied. (See [2], above.)

[21] The threat element is most likely not satisfied. The statement does not seem to propose to make V worse off than she was prior to the proposal. Prior to the proposal, she was neither receiving a medical examination nor expecting to receive a medical examination. Proposing to not give V what she neither has nor expects to have is not proposing to make her worse off. On this basis, the statement would not qualify as a threat and would disqualify it as rape by coercion under the MPC.

[22] Even assuming that D's statement does qualify as a threat, a reasonable person would probably be able to resist the threat. A reasonable person would not succumb for the following two reasons. First, any reasonable person would realize that there are alternative doctors from which to obtain an independent diagnosis of whatever might be the medical problem. Second, V does not believe that she is getting a medical examination anyway.

As a result, D has probably not committed rape by coercion under the MPC because D has neither uttered a threat nor is the proposal one which a reasonable person would be unable to resist.

Rape by Coercion—Common Law

[23] In jurisdictions requiring a threat and/or utilizing the reasonable person standard, D's conduct would probably not qualify as rape by coercion. See [21] and [22], above.

In other jurisdictions, like Pennsylvania, it could easily qualify as rape by coercion. In his defense, D could make the following arguments. First, V would not be significantly coerced by the prospect of not being diagnosed if she does not comply when she knows that even if she does comply, she will not be properly diagnosed. This is because she knows that she is not receiving a medical exam but, rather, sexual intercourse. Second, the statement was not uttered to obtain intercourse. It is literally being used to obtain V's compliance with the purported medical procedure. (But, of course, the statement is being used indirectly to obtain intercourse.) Whether either of these defenses would be successful in a jurisdiction like Pennsylvania, which defines the requisite coercion broadly, is unclear.

Rape by Fraud

[24] In considering an actor's liability for rape by fraud, a fundamental threshold issue to address is whether the actor's statement is false. D's statement is not clearly false. It is true that an undiagnosed and untreated disease or medical problem may cause death. And it is true that if V does not comply, V will not receive a medical examination. (Of course, even if V does comply she will also not receive a medical examination.)

[25] But a statement need not be false in order for it to be the basis for rape by fraud liability. There need not be express fraud; implied fraud may suffice. D's statement is intentionally misleading. It implies that if V does comply, she will receive a medical examination. But this implication is untrue—no matter what, D will not be able to make an informed medical diagnosis of any medical problem that V might have.

[26] If this implied fraud suffices, it would support D committing attempted rape by fraud of the fraudulent medical treatment type under both the MPC and common law. (It is only an attempt because V is not defrauded into believing she is receiving medical treatment. See [10]–[11], above.)

[27] D's statement is also a basis for completed rape by fraud of the impersonation type under a few common law jurisdictions because the content of the statement misleads V into believing that D is Dr. D, and V is actually defrauded as to the identity of the person with whom she is engaging in intercourse. (See [16], above.)

D. ENGAGING IN INTERCOURSE WITH V WHEN SHE WAS NOT CONSENTING DUE TO DR. D'S COERCION

[28] Even apart from whether D actually coerced or defrauded V, D may be criminally liable for rape for engaging in intercourse with V when she was not consenting due to coercion by Dr. D. In general, if person X engages in intercourse with a victim, Y, whose consent has been negated by another, Z, then person X may be criminally liable for rape of Y.

[29] One possible obstacle to D committing rape in this way is whether he had sufficient mens rea that V was not consenting. D would argue that he was neither aware nor should have been aware that Dr. D had coerced V and that V was submitting to intercourse only because of Dr. D's coercion. D would argue that he was mistaken that V was already not consenting (due to Dr. D's coercion) before he employed any means (fraud or coercion) to negate her consent.

[30] Will D's exculpatory mistake of fact defense succeed under the common law? While the mens rea of rape is notoriously elusive and often unspecified, presumably it is only general intent. For a mistake to even possibly be a defense to a general intent offense, the mistake must be honest and reasonable. D's mistake is honest and presumably reasonable—he had no basis for believing that Dr. D had coerced V and thus no basis for believing that her consent was negated by Dr. D or anyone else (other than himself). The common law takes three possible approaches (see Ch. 3, "Mistake of Fact"):

1. Honest and Reasonable Mistake Is a Defense
2. Moral Wrong Doctrine
3. Legal Wrong Doctrine

Under approach 1, D would have a defense. Under approaches 2 and 3, he would not. Even under the facts as he believes them to be V is not consenting due to his fraud and possible coercion. As a result, the mistake would be disregarded, and D would be liable for rape by coercion (to the extent that Dr. D's coercion negated V's consent).

[31] Under the MPC, D would be liable for whatever crime that he would be committing under the facts as he believes them to be—rape by fraud and rape by coercion. MPC § 2.04(2).

D's Defenses to All Charges

D might raise the following three defenses that would apply to all of the possible rape charges against him.

[32] First, an actor cannot commit rape against a person who would have consented had he or she known of the true circumstances. That is, had V known that she was actually engaging in intercourse with D, V would have consented because she loves D.

There are three possible problems with this defense:

1. The premise of the argument is false—maybe she would not have consented. Despite loving D, perhaps V would not wish to have intercourse with him in Dr. D's office. Moreover, V might not wish to have intercourse with D immediately following her intercourse with, and possible rape perpetrated by, Dr. D.
2. Even if the premise of the argument is true, it may be irrelevant because she did not know it was D and thus was not consenting to the intercourse as she was experiencing it.
3. It is still not a defense to attempt liability even if it is a defense to the completed crime. To understand this, suppose that V not only would have consented had she known, but suppose that she actually did consent

because she knew it was D. He would still be liable for attempting to commit rape by fraud and/or coercion because he would not have believed that V was consenting.

D will probably not prevail under this defense.

[33] Second, V retrospectively consented. But even if V did attempt to retrospectively consent, the law of rape has not widely recognized a victim's ability to do this. Moreover, even retrospective consent would not be a defense to charges of attempted rape.

[34] Third, not only was V consenting all along but that D knew that she was consenting all along—perhaps they were both role playing. If true, this would be a good defense. But there is no evidence in the facts to support this conjecture. Moreover, one fact in the Problem may oppose the conjecture: V "tensed" when D entered the room.

Conclusion

Dr. D is most likely not liable for rape by coercion under the MPC but most likely is liable in some, but not all, states. Dr. D is not liable for rape by fraud. D is liable in most jurisdictions for attempted rape by fraud and probably is liable for completed rape by fraud in some jurisdictions. Under the MPC, D is most likely liable for attempted rape by fraud. D probably is liable for rape by coercion in some jurisdictions but not under the MPC. D's defenses will probably be unsuccessful.

TOOLS FOR SELF-ASSESSMENT

Go back to your written answer. Look for the issues identified in paragraphs [1]–[34] above. Look also for the analysis that follows each issue, and mark your essay where you locate it. Do you fully describe the issue, identify the precise legal standard that applies, list the relevant facts, and show how the facts and law support a conclusion for each issue in a separate paragraph? Mark each conclusion in your essay. Are there sufficient reasons in the law and in the facts to support the conclusion?

1. Do what you are told. In the Problem, you are asked to analyze and discuss the criminal liability of Dr. D and D for rape. You are to identify which type or types of rape each actor commits as well as any applicable defenses.
2. Do not analyze what is unnecessary. For example, it might be tempting to analyze evidentiary problems that the prosecution might face. Resist that temptation.
3. Always remember to analyze under the MPC unless you are instructed otherwise.
4. State the best possible arguments for alternative conclusions. Even as you reject possible conclusions as to whether an actor may have satisfied an element or may have a defense, make the best possible argument first, and only then explain why you are rejecting that conclusion.
5. Be on the alert for red herrings. Some information in the fact pattern of a hypothetical may be irrelevant or even designed to mislead you. Pay particular attention to detail, and do not assume that the same element that is required in

more than one jurisdiction will be treated the same in each jurisdiction. Take your time, and go through the entire analysis before drawing conclusions. For example, the fact that Dr. D's potential rape liability arose in a gynecological setting does not necessarily mean that a typical rape by fraud in the course of medical treatment analysis applies. You might be tempted to think that because the victim initially believed she was going to receive a gynecological exam that the resulting intercourse fits into the traditionally recognized category of rape by fraud in the medical treatment context. However, here V was aware that she was having intercourse with Dr. D.

6. What follows is a step-by-step process by which the Problem and, in fact, any rape by means of coercion or fraud problem may be analyzed. This approach transparently reveals each step in the chain of reasoning in analyzing what type of rape, if any, has been committed.

RAPE BY COERCION—MPC

The rape by coercion form of GSI is best understood as consisting of the following three elements:

1. The actor "compels" the victim,
2. to submit to intercourse by any "threat,"
3. that would prevent resistance by a person of "ordinary resolution."

1) Did the actor compel the victim?

    i.   Was the actor's proposal such that submission by the victim resulted from coercion rather than bargain?
    ii.   If no, then the actor has not committed GSI.
    iii.   If yes, then the actor has satisfied the first element of GSI.

2) Did the actor compel the victim to submit to intercourse by a threat?

    iv.   Did the actor's proposal propose to make the victim worse off than he or she was prior to the proposal?
    v.   If no, then the proposal is not a threat.
    vi.   If yes, then it is a threat, and the actor has satisfied the second element of GSI.

3) Would the actor's threat have prevented resistance by a person of ordinary resolution?

    vii.   Does the proposal threaten a sufficiently substantial harm (on its face) such that a reasonable person would submit?
    viii.   If no, then the threat does not qualify as GSI.
    ix.   If yes, then what is the likelihood that the threatened harm will occur?
    x.   If unlikely, then the threat may not qualify as GSI.
    xi.   If it is sufficiently likely, then the actor has satisfied the third element and is eligible for liability for GSI.

    i.   Despite the actor's fraud, was the victim aware of the sexual intercourse?

    ii.   If yes, then was the actor impersonating the victim's husband?

    iii. If yes, then the actor is eligible for liability for GSI.

    iv. If no, then the actor has not committed GSI.

    v.   If no (the victim was not aware of the sexual intercourse), then the actor is eligible for liability for GSI.

RAPE BY FRAUD—COMMON LAW

    i.   Due to the actor's fraud, was the victim unaware of the sexual intercourse?

    ii.   If yes, then the actor is eligible for liability for rape by fraud in most jurisdictions.

    iii. If no, then did the actor impersonate the victim's spouse?

    iv. If yes, then the actor is eligible for liability for rape by fraud in approximately half of the jurisdictions.

    v.   If no, then did the actor impersonate an intimate of the victim?

    vi. If yes, then the actor is eligible for rape by fraud liability in a small minority of jurisdictions.

    vii. If no, then it could still be rape by fraud in jurisdictions which either
        a.   purport to prohibit all fraud,
        b.   prohibit *any* impersonation, or
        c.   construe fraud in the factum expansively.

7.   Because Dr. D neither used physical force nor fraud to obtain intercourse with V, you must analyze whether he used coercion. Under the MPC, an actor commits the rape by coercion form of GSI if the actor obtains intercourse by compelling the victim to submit by any threat that would prevent resistance by a person of ordinary resolution. Breaking this offense into its three distinct elements makes the analysis much easier. The first element is that the actor must compel the victim. In order that the victim is compelled to submit, the submission must result from coercion rather than bargain. Here, you should probably consider whether there is any sort of exchange of intercourse for money or some material good. If yes, then it probably qualifies as a bargain and would not, therefore, satisfy the first element that the actor must compel the victim.

    The second element is that the victim is compelled to submit by a particular type of proposal—a "threat." A threat is best understood in opposition to an offer. The simple test for distinguishing whether a proposal is a threat or an offer is as follows: Does the proposal propose to make the victim worse off or better off than he or she was prior to the proposal? If worse off, then it qualifies as a threat; if better off, then it qualifies as an offer. The second element is only satisfied if the proposal is a threat.

    The third and final element is that the threat be of sufficient gravity to prevent resistance by a person of ordinary resolution. To determine whether this element is satisfied, you should first determine whether the threat is sufficiently grave or serious on its face. For example, if the threat is, "Have intercourse with me or I will take a penny from you," then the threat is not sufficiently grave to qualify as a threat to which a reasonable person would succumb. Second, assess the likelihood that the threatened harm will actually occur. A threatened harm may be sufficiently grave on its face yet unlikely to actually occur. For example, the threatened harm of losing the love of one's life with which Dr. D threatens V is sufficiently grave on its face, but the low probability of this result occurring (as explained in [4] in the above Essay) renders it easy to resist.

8.   There are several potential bases for criminal liability for D. Perhaps the clearest way to set up your analysis is to consider each aspect of his behavior and determine whether it satisfies the elements of any type or types of rape. Proceeding in chronological order, analyze each aspect of D's conduct that could support D's rape liability. Starting with the rattling of the medical instruments, you should analyze whether this behavior satisfies the elements of rape by fraud in the context of medical treatment. Next, continue this method of analysis with each subsequent form of D's conduct—the whispering impersonation of Dr. D, etc.

9.   Your strategy for analyzing rape by fraud under the MPC and the common law differs. Under the MPC you almost need no strategy—it is very straightforward. The MPC recognizes only two categories of rape by fraud. If the victim is unaware of the sexual act (due to the perpetrator's fraud) or the perpetrator impersonates her husband, then it is GSI. Unfortunately, the analysis under the common law is more complicated because of the differing approaches used by different jurisdictions as well as the ambiguity within each approach. As discussed in the above Essay, there are three principal approaches applied by the states. Each of these approaches will be separately discussed in the following three notes.

10. First, a small number of jurisdictions purport to broadly prohibit obtaining intercourse by fraud. Seemingly these jurisdictions criminalize intercourse obtained by *any* fraud without apparent limitation. While this makes your analysis under this approach quite easy—seemingly any fraud will qualify—your analysis should at least acknowledge the possibility that a court might exclude sufficiently trivial instances of fraud.

11. Second, some jurisdictions limit the type of fraud to specific categories (an approach much like the MPC). The principle categories of fraud recognized are where the victim is unaware of the sexual act and impersonation. Most jurisdictions prohibit fraud rendering the victim unaware of the sexual act. This most typically arises in a medical setting—specifically during a gynecological or proctological examination where the victim is expecting and is consenting to penetration by medical instrument and instead receives sexual intercourse (which they realize after the commencement of the intercourse). The most widely recognized form of impersonation, supporting rape by fraud liability, is spousal impersonation. While there is some authority that the majority rule is that spousal impersonation qualifies as rape by fraud (*Boro*), perhaps the better understanding is that jurisdictions are roughly split.

12. Third, some jurisdictions apply the fraud in the factum/fraud in the inducement distinction. Fraud in the factum consists of the perpetrator defrauding the victim as to the very nature of the act. Fraud in the inducement consists of the perpetrator defrauding the victim as to the reason for the act. Courts consider fraud in the factum as negating the victim's consent and constituting rape by fraud.

Fraud in the inducement, however, does not negate the victim's consent and does not qualify as rape by fraud. While the treatment of each type of fraud is clear, what is less clear is whether a particular instance of fraud is in the factum or in the inducement. Traditionally, courts have construed fraud in the factum narrowly by limiting what constitutes the "nature" of the act to the sexual nature of the act. That is, if the defrauded victim is unaware of the sexual nature of the act, then this is fraud in the factum. However, if the defrauded victim is aware of the sexual nature of the act, then it is fraud in the inducement. Courts today, however, may construe fraud in the factum more broadly by expanding the scope of the nature of the act. And by expanding the scope of the nature of the act to which the victim is unaware, more types of fraud qualify as fraud in the factum and thus as rape by fraud.

Boro aptly illustrates the ambiguity and confusion surrounding the factum/inducement distinction. *Boro* applies both the traditional narrow construction of fraud in the factum to the facts of the case as well as applies the more modern, broader construction of fraud in the factum to the category of spousal impersonation.

Under the facts of the case, the defendant defrauded the victim into believing that she had a life-threatening illness that could be best cured by engaging in intercourse with the defendant. Applying the traditional, narrow construction of fraud in the factum, the court held that because the victim was aware that she was engaging in intercourse, then she was aware of the (sexual) nature of the act. She was defrauded not as to the nature of the act but rather as to the reason for the act— that intercourse would have a medical benefit. Thus, it was fraud in the inducement and not rape by fraud.

After this narrow construction of fraud in the factum, however, the court construed fraud in the factum much more broadly to explain how spousal impersonation does constitute rape by fraud. Despite the fact that a victim of spousal impersonation is entirely aware of the sexual nature of the act, the court nonetheless found it to be fraud in the factum because the victim consents to an innocent act of marital intercourse while what the victim receives is an act of adultery. In finding spousal impersonation to be fraud in the factum, the court is expanding the concept of nature of the act beyond the merely sexual nature of the act. It is expanding nature of the act to include the marital versus adulterous nature of the act.

So, on an exam, as a matter of strategy, you could make an argument that any fraud might plausibly qualify as fraud in the factum simply by expanding the scope of what constitutes the nature of the act.

13. In applying the factum/inducement distinction, you should know the paradigmatic instances of each type as well as the close calls. Furthermore, you should be able to manipulate the distinction to make a plausible argument that any given instance of fraud is fraud in the factum and to make a plausible argument that it is fraud in the inducement. And, as discussed above in Tool #12, the way to manipulate the distinction so as to make plausible arguments either way is by defining (or redefining) the nature of the act.

The paradigmatic instance of fraud in the factum is where the victim has been defrauded into believing that penetration will be by medical instrument, but instead the victim receives penetration by a human organ. The paradigmatic examples of fraud in the inducement are fraud as to the degree of the perpetrator's affection for, or romantic commitment to, the victim as well as the perpetrator's societal status, wealth, or physical appeal. Examples of the close calls that have bedeviled courts include impersonation, *Boro*-type facts, false claims of sterility, and false claims of being disease free. So, the best strategy is to know these examples and be able to manipulate the factum/inducement distinction to make plausible arguments either way.

14. The Problem, as well as others you may face, poses a challenge because it does not fit neatly within any of the recognized categories of rape. The Problem conflates two categories of rape by fraud—fraudulent medical treatment and impersonation—that the law often treats differently. In analyzing a hypothetical of this type, do not merely rely on the law's treatment of particular categories because such a hypothetical straddles more than one category. Second, look carefully and closely at precisely how the perpetrator is defrauding the victim. For example, in the Problem, even though D is impersonating Dr. D, he is not attempting to obtain V's consent by impersonation per se. Rather, D is attempting rape by fraud of the fraudulent medical treatment type by the means of impersonation.

VARIATIONS ON THE THEME

For the following variations, assume all of the facts from the original Problem obtain unless otherwise noted.

1. Rather than Dr. D's original proposal, Dr. D proposes to V that if she does not have intercourse with him, he will charge her more for the gynecological examination. V has intercourse with Dr. D.

2. Rather than Dr. D's original proposal, Dr. D proposes to V that if she does have intercourse with him, he will charge her less for the gynecological examination. V has intercourse with Dr. D.

3. Rather than Dr. D's original proposal, Dr. D (falsely) tells V that she does have syphilis and that the most effective treatment is to engage in intercourse with someone who has been injected with an anti-syphilis serum. Dr. D (falsely) tells V that he has injected himself with the serum. V has intercourse with Dr. D.

4. All the facts are the same except that V and D are married.

5. Rather than Dr. D's original proposal, Dr. D proposes to V that if she does not have intercourse with him, he will infect her with syphilis with an infected instrument. V has intercourse with Dr. D.

6. Dr. D makes no proposals to V. Believing that any penetration will be by medical instrument for an appropriate medical reason, V consents to penetration. But Dr. D instead has intercourse with her.

7. In addition to all of the original facts, Dr. D (falsely) tells V that he is not HIV positive. V has intercourse with Dr. D.

8. Dr. D neither makes proposals to nor has intercourse with V. D and V are role playing. Both have consented to have intercourse with each other when D comes into the examination room and pretends to be a doctor (according to their agreement). But rather than having intercourse with V (as per their agreement), D penetrates her by medical instrument. V only finds out what D has actually done the next day, when he tells her.

9. Dr. D makes no proposals to V. Dr. D is not a renowned gynecologist, but he tells V that he is one. Based on Dr. D's claim, V has intercourse with Dr. D.

10. Dr. D makes no proposals to V. Dr. D (falsely) tells V that he is a gynecologist to the stars and that his patients include Paris Hilton and Angelina Jolie. Based on Dr. D's claim, V has intercourse with Dr. D.

11. Rather than Dr. D's original proposal, Dr. D proposes to V that if she does not have intercourse with him, he will (falsely) tell D that V did have intercourse with him (Dr. D). V has intercourse with Dr. D.

ADDITIONAL READINGS

Linda R. Hirshman & Jane E. Larson, Hard Bargains: The Politics of Sex (1998)

Stephen Schulhofer, Unwanted Sex: The Culture of Intimidation and the Failure of Law 114–253 (1998)

Alan Wertheimer, Consent to Sexual Relations 163–214 (2003)

Peter Westen, The Logic of Consent: The Diversity and Deceptiveness of Consent as a Defense to Criminal Conduct (2004)

Jeffrie G. Murphy, *Some Ruminations on Women, Violence, and the Criminal Law, in* In Harm's Way: Essays in Honor of Joel Feinberg 209 (Jules Coleman & Allen Buchanan eds., 1994)

Russell L. Christopher & Kathryn H. Christopher, *Adult Impersonation: Rape by Fraud as a Defense to Statutory Rape*, 101 Nw. U. L. Rev. 75 (2007)

Anne Coughlin, *Sex and Guilt*, 84 Va. L. Rev. 1 (1998)

Patricia J. Falk, *Rape by Fraud and Rape by Coercion*, 64 Brooklyn L. Rev. 39 (1998)

John Gardner and Stephen Shute, *The Wrongness of Rape, in* Oxford Essays in Jurisprudence 194 (Jeremy Horder ed., 2000)

Heidi Hurd, *Was the Frog Prince Sexually Molested?: A Review of Peter Westen's* The Logic of Consent, 103 Mich. L. Rev. 1329 (2005)

11

SELF-DEFENSE AND DEFENSE OF OTHERS

INTRODUCTION

Unlike most of the claims of exculpation addressed so far, self-defense and defense of others are neither failure of proof defenses nor mitigation defenses. That is, self-defense does not negate an element of the offense, nor does it generally mitigate a defendant's liability from a greater to a lesser crime. As justification defenses, self-defense and defense of others concede that all of the elements of the offense are satisfied but assert that under the circumstances, the defendant's conduct was permissible and lawful.

Although subject to numerous requirements and exceptions, the general principal of self-defense is that a nonaggressor is justified in the use of force when she reasonably believes that force is necessary against an aggressor posing an unlawful and imminent threat of harm. In addition to force being necessary, it must also be proportional. That is, an actor is limited to the use of nondeadly force to prevent a nondeadly attack but may use both deadly and nondeadly force to prevent a deadly attack. While there is no duty to retreat before using nondeadly force, many states impose a duty to retreat before using deadly force. This duty of retreat only applies if it can be done in complete safety. There are also numerous exceptions to this duty based on an actor being in her home or place of business.

The distinct defense of defense of others is, in some sense, derivative of the self-defense justification. Under the traditional but now minority rule, an actor employing force in protection of another is justified to the extent that the party defended would have been justified in self-defense. The party asserting the defense of others justification is said to "stand in the shoes" of the party being defended. In contrast, the modern and majority rule views the party using force in protection of another independently, based on what he or she reasonably believes. That is, the modern approach views the party asserting the defense of others justification as standing in her own shoes.

Not surprisingly, almost every aspect of the law of self-defense has proven controversial. The general criticism is that some legitimate and morally permissible instances of self-defense fall through the cracks and fail to satisfy the myriad of rigid doctrinal requirements. The inexorable trend has been toward the expansion of the scope of the law of self-defense. For example, many chafe at the requirement of retreat before using deadly force. Such critics argue that retreat is cowardly and law-abiding citizens should never cede ground to unlawful aggressors. The recent proliferation of "Make My Day" laws is illustrative of the trend. Perhaps the greatest battleground has been the element of imminence—requiring an actor to wait until the very last moment prior to an aggressor's attack before employing defensive force. Critics of the imminence requirement argue that it excludes many legitimate instances of self-defense and unnecessarily endangers the lives of victims of aggression. This issue has particularly come to the fore in the context of spousal abuse where the abuse victim opts to kill her abuser in a nonconfrontational context—while the abuser is sleeping. Another contested element, especially in this context, is proportionality. Some argue that this element unfairly disadvantages smaller and weaker self-defenders who are limited to nonlethal force that proves ineffective against the nonlethal force of a larger and stronger aggressor.

PROBLEM

Samantha is in the first trimester of her pregnancy and, because of health issues, cannot get out of bed. Samantha lives alone in a farmhouse out in the country with the nearest neighbor miles away. The nearest neighbor, Mrs. Kravitz, stops by every morning, every night, and occasionally other times during the day. One day after Mrs. Kravitz leaves in the morning, Sabrina, Samantha's evil twin sister, unexpectedly arrives. Sabrina credibly and truthfully tells Samantha that she will administer to Samantha ten doses of poison, one per hour for ten hours. No individual dose is lethal, but the cumulative effect of ten individually nonlethal doses will be. The poison and dosage is such that even as many as nine doses will not produce substantial bodily harm. But nine doses will significantly weaken Samantha to the point where she would be unable to even lift her arms. Samantha's fetus, however, will die upon receipt of the third dose but will not suffer substantial bodily harm from the first or second doses. Samantha's nondeadly force is ineffective. The only effective force she has at her disposal is the use of a gun. She has no means to call for help because she forgot to charge her cell phone battery. Samantha takes out her gun and points it at Sabrina. Undeterred, Sabrina just laughs and says, "You can't shoot me because I am not posing an imminent threat of deadly force." (In this jurisdiction, firing a weapon in the direction of another person constitutes deadly force. Although deadly force is permissible to protect against a kidnapping, kidnapping requires an unlawful confinement. Sabrina has not kidnapped Samantha because Samantha would not be able to leave, regardless of Sabrina's presence.)

Analyze and discuss the earliest point in time when Samantha would be justified, if at all, in using lethal force against Sabrina. If Mrs. Kravitz were to pay Samantha a visit at some point during the course of this slow poisoning, analyze and discuss the earliest point in time when Mrs. Kravitz would be justified, if at all, under the defense of others defense, in using lethal force against Sabrina.

LIST OF READINGS

Ha v. State, 892 P.2d 184 (Alaska Ct. App. 1995)
People v. Kurr, 654 N.W.2d 651 (Mich. Ct. App. 2002)
State v. Norman, 378 S.E.2d 8 (N.C. 1989)
MODEL PENAL CODE §§ 3.04, 3.05, 3.09 (Official Code and Revised Comments 1985)

ESSAY

In self-defense, Samantha would probably not be justified in using deadly force until just prior to the tenth dose under the common law and just prior to the ninth dose under the MPC. In defense of others, under both the common law and the MPC, both Samantha and Mrs. Kravitz would possibly be justified in using deadly force in protection of the fetus just prior to the third dose. Mrs. Kravitz would possibly be justified in using deadly force in protection of Samantha just prior to the tenth dose.

Self-Defense

COMMON LAW

[1] In order to be justified in the use of deadly self-defense force, (i) the actor must honestly and reasonably believe, (ii) that such force is necessary, (iii) against an imminent, (iv) and unlawful, (v) deadly threat posed by the aggressor, (vi) from which the actor cannot safely retreat, and (vii) the actor is not the initial aggressor.

[2] Samantha could easily satisfy all of the elements except imminence. She could reasonably believe that force was necessary to prevent the unlawful and deadly threat posed by Sabrina. Because she is bedridden, she would clearly be unable to retreat, and she clearly is not the initial aggressor.

[3] The only significant issue centers on the imminence requirement, and even that element can be easily satisfied if she waits long enough. If she waits until just prior to the tenth dose—the lethal dose—Sabrina would pose an imminent deadly threat. But because the facts suggest that Samantha would be physically unable to raise her arms after the ninth dose, she will be unable to employ force at the point when Sabrina's deadly force is clearly and uncontestably imminent. As a result, because Samantha cannot afford to wait until Sabrina's threat is clearly and uncontestably imminent, the issue then becomes whether there is an earlier point in time when Samantha could reasonably believe that Sabrina poses an imminent and deadly threat.

[4] One might argue that the earliest point in time in which Samantha could reasonably believe that Sabrina poses an imminent deadly threat is just prior to the administration of the first dose of poison. The argument would be that at that moment, Sabrina is embarking on the first step in a series of actions that will culminate in Samantha's death. Because the administration of the first dose constitutes deadly force, just prior to that first dose Sabrina's deadly threat is imminent. The difficulty with this argument, however, is that it denies a stated fact in the Problem that the first administration of the poison is nonlethal. Because it is nonlethal, at the point in time just prior to the first dose, Sabrina neither poses a deadly threat nor can Samantha reasonably believe that she does.

[5] Another argument in support of Sabrina posing an imminent deadly threat just prior to the first dose is based on inevitability. Even if not presently an imminent deadly threat, it is inevitable that Sabrina will pose an imminent deadly threat. The facts establish and Samantha could reasonably believe that it is inevitable that Sabrina will attempt to administer the tenth dose, thereby posing a deadly threat. That is, the inevitability of Sabrina posing a deadly threat in the future renders her an imminent deadly threat in the present. In short, inevitability equals imminence. However, courts have consistently held that inevitability does not equal imminence. Thus, the inevitability of a deadly threat does not suffice to establish the imminence of a deadly threat.

[6] All of the above arguments in [4]–[5] in support of Sabrina posing an imminent deadly threat just before the first dose equally apply to the time periods just before the administration of the second dose and the third dose, etc. However, the same reasons why Sabrina fails to pose an imminent deadly threat just prior to the first dose equally apply to these other time periods. For doses one through eight, each dose is neither independently deadly nor cumulatively deadly. As a result, just prior to each of the first eight doses, Sabrina neither poses an imminent deadly threat, nor can Samantha reasonably believe that Sabrina she does. And the inevitability of Sabrina posing an imminent deadly threat in the future does not qualify as an imminent deadly threat in the present.

[7] The time period just prior to the ninth dose is arguably different. This is the last opportunity Samantha has in which she will be physically able to defend herself. If she does not act now, she will be too weak to defend herself and prevent administration of the tenth dose. On this basis, one might argue, Sabrina poses an imminent deadly threat just prior to the ninth dose because if Samantha waits any longer to act, she will be dead.

[8] This argument, however, is not entirely persuasive for three reasons. First, one's inability to use force at a later time does not make a threat of deadly force imminent. Nor does the present ability to use force make a threat imminent or nonimminent. The ability or inability of an actor to use force has nothing to do with whether an aggressor poses an imminent or nonimminent threat. Second, the ninth dose is neither independently nor cumulatively lethal. Third, just prior to the ninth dose is not temporally imminent given that Sabrina will not use clearly lethal force—the tenth dose—for over an hour. Typically we think of imminence as meaning temporally about to happen, and we measure what is about to happen in terms of seconds away from happening, not hours.

[9] In conclusion, just prior to the tenth dose, Sabrina clearly poses an imminent deadly threat, and just prior to each of the first eight doses she does not. While just prior to the ninth dose is plausibly imminent, a literal and technical analysis of the imminence requirement probably establishes that Sabrina neither poses an imminent deadly threat nor could Samantha reasonably believe that Sabrina poses such a threat.

MODEL PENAL CODE

[10] The MPC provision on the use of deadly force in self-defense includes the following elements: (i) the actor believes that deadly force is necessary, (ii) for the purpose of self-protection, (iii) against the use of unlawful force, (iv) that is deadly; (v) the actor's force is immediately necessary on the present occasion; (vi) the actor did not provoke the use of force against herself; (vii) the actor is not under a duty to retreat; and (viii) depending on the mens rea of the offense with which the actor is charged, the actor is neither reckless nor negligent in believing that force is necessary.

[11] Just prior to the administration of the first dose, Samantha could clearly satisfy all elements except (iv) and (v). She could easily believe (neither recklessly nor negligently) that her force was necessary for the purpose of self-protection and that Sabrina's force was unlawful. In addition, Samantha neither provoked Sabrina nor violated a duty to retreat.

[12] The principle issue is the earliest point in time at which Samantha's deadly force would satisfy the requirement of being immediately necessary on the

present occasion against Sabrina's use of deadly force. This requirement is the MPC's alternative formulation of the common law's imminence requirement. But it is designed to be broader and more generous to the defendant in expanding the scope of self-defense. So, even if an aggressor's threat of deadly force is not imminent, it may nonetheless be immediately necessary on the present occasion for the actor to use deadly force. Typically, the common law imminence requirement and the MPC alternative standard will produce the same results. That is, there are few cases in which a threat is nonimminent, but the use of defensive force is nonetheless immediately necessary. The temporal aspect of the requirement that the force be *immediately* necessary essentially reduces to the common law imminence requirement. However, as applied to this Problem, the standards may actually produce different results.

[13] For the same reasons as discussed above in [3]–[8], it is not immediately necessary to use deadly force prior to the administration of each of the first eight doses. And also for the same reasons as discussed above in [3], it clearly would be necessary on the present occasion for Samantha to use deadly force just prior to the tenth dose. Again, the difficult issue is whether the element is satisfied prior to the ninth dose. Though prior to the ninth dose is probably not imminent, it probably is a point in time when Samantha's deadly force is immediately necessary. It is necessary because this is the last point in time in which Samantha will be physically able to prevent her death. And it is immediately necessary because if she waits until while the ninth dose is being administered or until just after it is being administered, she may be physically unable to use force.

[14] In conclusion, prior to each of the first eight doses, Samantha would clearly not be justified in employing deadly force. Just prior to the tenth dose, she clearly would be. Most likely, she would also be justified prior to the ninth dose.

Defense of Others

COMMON LAW

[15] The traditional/minority rule regarding the defense of defense of others is that the actor is justified only if and to the extent that the person being defended would have been justified in using such force in self-defense. That is, the party asserting a defense of others justification stands in the shoes of the person being defended. If the party being defended would have been justified in using self-defense force, then the person using defense of others force is also justified. But if the party being defended would not have been justified in self-defense in using such force, then neither would the defense of others party be justified. In addition, the traditional rule limits the scope of persons who can be protected to relatives, spouses, and those in an employment relation. Under the modern/majority rule, the defense of others party is justified regardless of whether the party being defended would be justified. Rather than standing in the shoes of the party being defended, the defense of others party is justified based on his or her reasonable beliefs.

[16] Some jurisdictions include fetuses within the scope of parties who may be defended under a defense of others justification. But others disallow a defense of others justification for protection of a fetus. Still other jurisdictions include fetuses but limit who may protect the fetus to the mother.

Samantha's Protection of the Fetus

[17] Under both the traditional/minority rule and the modern/majority rule, Samantha's deadly force against Sabrina might be eligible to be justified under a defense of others justification in protection of the fetus. While Sabrina did not clearly pose an imminent threat of deadly force to Samantha until just prior to the tenth dose, Sabrina does pose an imminent threat of deadly force to the fetus just prior to the third dose. As a result, Samantha could reasonably believe that Sabrina poses an imminent deadly threat just prior to administration of the third dose and would be eligible to be justified in using deadly force under the defense of defense of others in protection of the fetus.

[18] There is a possible difficulty under the traditional/minority rule. Under the rule, Samantha is only justified in the defense of others to the extent that the fetus would be justified in self-defense. But the fetus might not be able to satisfy one of the elements of justified self-defense—the fetus cannot form a belief or a reasonable belief that Sabrina poses a threat. As a result, the fetus would not be justified in using force against Sabrina, and thereby Samantha would not be justified under defense of others. But most likely this application of the traditional rule is too literal and too technical. As a result, this possible difficulty would probably not preclude Samantha's eligibility for a defense of others justification for using deadly force against Sabrina just prior to the third dose.

[19] This possible difficulty, discussed above in [18], does not pose a difficulty for Samantha under the modern/majority rule. Rather than standing in the shoes of the fetus, Samantha's eligibility for the defense is assessed by her reasonable beliefs. As discussed above in [17], Samantha could reasonably believe that Sabrina poses an imminent deadly threat just prior to administration of the third dose and would be eligible to be justified in using deadly force under the defense of defense of others in protection of the fetus.

[20] Some jurisdictions disallow a defense of others justification for the use of force in the protection of a fetus. In such a jurisdiction, Samantha would not be justified.

[21] In conclusion, in jurisdictions allowing a defense of others justification for the protection of a fetus, Samantha would most likely be justified in using deadly force against Sabrina just prior to the third dose.

Mrs. Kravitz's Protection of Samantha and the Fetus

[22] Under the traditional/minority rule, in defense of Samantha, Mrs. Kravitz would be unable, under a defense of others justification, to use deadly force against Sabrina any earlier than Samantha could in self-defense. As a result, Mrs. Kravitz could possibly, but probably not, be justified in using deadly force just prior to the ninth dose. She clearly would be eligible to be justified in using deadly force just prior to the tenth dose. An additional problem is that Mrs. Kravitz is neither a relative of, spouse of, or in an employment relation with Samantha.

[23] Under the modern/majority rule, in defense of Samantha, Mrs. Kravitz could only use deadly force against Sabrina when she reasonably believed that Sabrina posed an imminent deadly threat. The possible basis for Samantha to use force just prior to the ninth dose—she would be physically unable to use any force after the ninth dose—does not apply to Mrs. Kravitz. As a result, Mrs. Kravitz

would not be justified in using deadly force against Sabrina in defense of Samantha until just prior to the tenth dose.

[23] Even if Mrs. Kravitz could not use defense of others force in protection of Samantha any earlier than Samantha could use self-defense force, Mrs. Kravitz might be able to use deadly force against Sabrina just prior to the third dose under a defense of others justification in protection of the fetus. Apart from two obstacles discussed below in [24], Mrs. Kravitz would be justified in using force at the same time and to the same extent that Samantha herself would under a defense of others defense in protection of the fetus. As discussed above in [17]–[20], any defender of the fetus could reasonably believe that Sabrina poses an imminent, deadly threat just prior to the third dose. Thus, Mrs. Kravitz could be eligible to be justified under a defense of others defense in using deadly force against Sabrina at that time.

[24] There are two obstacles to Mrs. Kravitz being justified in defense of the fetus that did not apply to Samantha. First, some jurisdictions limit the defense of others justification in protection of a fetus to the mother of the fetus. Because Mrs. Kravitz is not the mother of the fetus, she would be ineligible for the defense in such jurisdictions. Second, under the traditional/minority defense of others rule, Mrs. Kravitz would be ineligible for the defense because she is neither a spouse of, a relative of, nor in an employment relationship with, the fetus.

[25] In conclusion, in protection of Samantha, under both the traditional/minority rule and the modern/majority rule, Mrs. Kravitz would probably not be eligible to use deadly force until just prior to the tenth dose. That Mrs. Kravitz lacked the requisite nexus to Samantha might bar her defense under the traditional/minority rule. In protection of the fetus, Mrs. Kravitz would be eligible to be justified in using deadly force just prior to the third dose to the same extent that Samantha would be eligible, subject to two additional obstacles.

MODEL PENAL CODE

[26] Though the MPC provision on the defense of others justification is considerably more complicated, essentially the MPC is consistent with the modern/majority view. The MPC justifies defense of others force based on the beliefs of the party employing defense of others force rather than requiring the actor to stand in the shoes of the party being defended. It is unclear whether the MPC extends the defense of others justification to the protection of fetuses. The following analysis assumes that the MPC does extend the defense to include the protection of fetuses.

Samantha's Protection of the Fetus

[27] For the same reasons as discussed above in [17], Samantha would probably be justified in using deadly force against Sabrina just prior to the administration of the third dose under the defense of others justification.

Mrs. Kravitz's Protection of Samantha and the Fetus

[28] With respect to the use of force in the protection of Samantha, Mrs. Kravitz might not be justified in using force as early as Samantha would be justified in self-defense. As discussed above in [13], it is immediately necessary for Samantha to

use deadly force in self-defense just prior to the ninth dose of poison because she would be physically unable to use any force after that dose. But Mrs. Kravitz would be physically able to employ force after the administration of the ninth dose to Samantha. Because Mrs. Kravitz would be physically able to employ deadly force against Sabrina just prior to the tenth dose of poison to Samantha, it is not until just prior to the tenth dose of poison that it is immediately necessary for Mrs. Kravitz to use deadly force against Sabrina.

[29] With respect to the protection of the fetus, for the same reasons as discussed above in [17], Mrs. Kravitz would be justified under a defense of others defense in using deadly force against Sabrina just prior to the third dose.

Conclusion

Self-defense: Under the common law, Samantha would probably not be justified in using deadly force until just prior to the tenth dose. Under the MPC, Samantha would most likely be justified just prior to the ninth dose.

Defense of Others: Under the common law, in jurisdictions allowing a defense of others justification for the protection of a fetus, Samantha would most likely be justified in using deadly force against Sabrina just prior to the third dose. Under the modern/majority rule, but not the traditional/minority rule, Mrs. Kravitz would probably be eligible to use deadly force just prior to the tenth dose in protection of Samantha. In protection of the fetus, Mrs. Kravitz would be eligible to be justified in using deadly force just prior to the third dose to the same extent that Samantha would be eligible, subject to two possible additional obstacles. Under the MPC, Samantha would probably be justified in using deadly force against Sabrina just prior to the administration of the third dose in protection of the fetus. Mrs. Kravitz would probably not be justified in using deadly force in protection of Samantha until just prior to the tenth dose. In protection of the fetus, Mrs. Kravitz would probably be justified in using deadly force against Sabrina just prior to the third dose.

TOOLS FOR SELF-ASSESSMENT

Go back to your written answer. Look for the issues identified in paragraphs numbered [1]–[29] above. Look also for the analysis that follows each issue, and mark your essay where you locate it. Do you fully describe the issue, identify the precise legal standard that applies, list the relevant facts, and show how the facts and law support a conclusion for each issue? Mark each conclusion in your essay. Are there sufficient reasons in the law and in the facts to support each conclusion?

1.   Do what you are told. Here, you are to analyze the earliest point in time when Samantha and Mrs. Kravitz's use of lethal force would satisfy the elements of the defenses of self-defense and defense of others.
2.   Do not analyze what is unnecessary. You need not analyze Sabrina's liability or any other defenses that Samantha and Mrs. Kravitz might satisfy.
3.   Always analyze under the MPC as well as the common law unless you are instructed otherwise.
4.   State the best possible arguments for alternative conclusions. For example, if you conclude that Samantha has not satisfied a particular requirement for the defense of others justification under the MPC, consider whether one might

reasonably disagree with your conclusion. If so, state the best possible argument opposing your analysis, and explain why it is wrong.

5. There are numerous ways to organize your answer. Set out below is the organizational structure of the above Essay as well an alternative organizational structure. There is no single organizational structure that is always preferable for all hypotheticals involving the defenses of self-defense or defense of others. But there are advantages and disadvantages depending on the hypothetical and the instructions as to how to analyze it. Appreciating the various possible organizational structures that you might employ for any given hypothetical or exam question will be of tremendous aid in selecting, if not the optimal organizational structure, then at least a preferable one. Having a good organizational structure will not only help clarify your analysis but also save you time. It is very important to have a sense of the possible organizational structures you might employ before you walk into an exam. You do not want to waste valuable time during the exam grappling with how to organize it.

Structure #1 below depicts the organizational structure of the above Essay, and Structure #2 depicts an alternative. Structure #1 is primarily organized by the type of defense. Then each defense is analyzed under the common law followed by its analysis under the MPC. Structure #2 utilizes the distinction between the common law and the MPC as the primary organizational feature. This approach would take advantage of similarities within the common law's treatment of both self-defense and defense of others as well as similarities within the MPC's treatment.

Structure #1	Structure #2
Introduction	Introduction
Self-defense	Common Law
Common Law	Self-defense
Model Penal Code	Defense of others
Defense of others	Samantha
Common Law	Mrs. Kravitz
Samantha	Model Penal Code
Mrs. Kravitz	Self-defense
Model Penal Code	Defense of others
Samantha	Samantha
Mrs. Kravitz	Mrs. Kravitz
Conclusion	Conclusion

6. Unlike topics in other chapters, the analysis of the defenses of self-defense and defense of others are not further illuminated by a flowchart or series of logical steps laying bare the analysis. There are no preferable sequential reasoning steps to be undertaken. Rather, the preferable approach is the laundry list of requirements that are set out in paragraphs [1] and [10]. There is not a particularly helpful way of sequencing the analysis of these requirements. As a result, the best view

of the forest without the obstruction of the trees is the "laundry list" of possible requirements under the common law and definite requirements under the MPC for each defense.

7. For the MPC, in particular, understand the relationship between the mens rea of the offense charged and the defenses of self-defense and defense of others. Section 3.04(1) merely requires that the actor believe that force is necessary, but § 3.09(2) modifies that view. If the actor's belief in the necessity of force is either reckless or negligent, the actor may lose the self-defense justification depending on the mens rea of the offense charged. The following charts depict this relationship between the nature of the belief and the type of requisite mens rea:

SELF-DEFENSE

Example 1: The actor correctly believes that defensive force is necessary.

Mens Rea of Offense Charged	Self-Defense Justification Status
Purpose	Justified
Knowledge	Justified
Recklessness	Justified
Negligence	Justified

Example 2: The actor incorrectly, but neither recklessly nor negligently, believes that defensive force is necessary.

Mens Rea of Offense Charged	Self-Defense Justification Status
Purpose	Justified
Knowledge	Justified
Recklessness	Justified
Negligence	Justified

Example 3: The actor incorrectly, but **recklessly**, believes that defensive force is necessary.

Mens Rea of Offense Charged	Self-Defense Justification Status
Purpose	Justified
Knowledge	Justified
Recklessness	**Unjustified**
Negligence	**Unjustified**

Example 4: The actor incorrectly, but **negligently**, believes that defensive force is necessary.

Mens Rea of Offense Charged	Self-Defense Justification Status
Purpose	Justified
Knowledge	Justified
Recklessness	Justified
Negligence	**Unjustified**

The quite detailed information contained in the above charts may be reduced to the following rule: *The defendant is eligible to be justified in self-defense if the requisite mens rea of the offense charged is greater than the "mental state" of the defendant's incorrect belief.* (For example, if the mens rea of the offense charged is purpose, knowledge, or recklessness, and the "mental state" of the defendant's incorrect belief is negligence, then the defendant is eligible for the self-defense justification because the mens rea of the offense is greater than the negligent "mental state" of the defendant's incorrect belief.)

8. Understand the different types of mistakes under the common law and MPC. The common law, but not the MPC, distinguishes between reasonable and unreasonable mistakes as to the necessity of using force. A reasonable belief renders one eligible for self-defense, and an unreasonable belief precludes a self-defense justification. The MPC, however, distinguishes between three types of beliefs: (i) beliefs that are neither reckless nor negligent, (ii) reckless beliefs, and (iii) negligent beliefs. Under the MPC as the charts in Tool #7 suggest, a belief that is neither reckless nor negligent always renders the actor eligible for a justification. Whether a reckless or negligent belief precludes eligibility for the justification defense depends on the mens rea of the offense charged. While we have become accustomed both within and without the criminal law to distinguishing between reasonable and unreasonable mistakes, distinguishing between reckless and negligent mistakes, as is required under the MPC analysis, does not come to us so easily. A mistake that is neither reckless nor negligent would be, in common law terms, a reasonable belief. A reckless belief that defensive force was necessary would be one in which the actor was consciously aware of a substantial risk that defensive force was unnecessary. A negligent belief that defensive force was necessary would be one in which the actor was *not* consciously aware of a substantial risk that defensive force was unnecessary but should have been aware.

For example, suppose it is late at night, and you are in a dangerous and deserted part of town and suddenly see your hated enemy walking toward you, and you see something shiny and metallic in his hand. Believing that your hated enemy is about to shoot you, you shoot and kill him. In fact, your hated enemy was only holding a cell phone. The following illustrate the three types of beliefs under the MPC:

Neither reckless nor negligent belief: if your belief that the shiny, metallic object is a gun is deemed, in common law terms, reasonable

Reckless belief: if you were consciously aware of a substantial risk that the shiny metallic object in your hated enemy's hand was not a weapon
Negligent belief: if you were not so consciously aware, but should have been aware

9. The following examples summarize the relationship between the actor's belief in the necessity of using defensive force, the significance of a mistake, the type of mistaken belief, and the justification status under the common law:

Example 1: The actor correctly believes that defensive force is necessary.
Outcome: Eligible for self-defense justification.

Example 2: The actor incorrectly, but reasonably, believes that defensive force is necessary.
Outcome: Eligible for self-defense justification.

Example 3: The actor incorrectly and unreasonably believes that defensive force is necessary.
Outcome: Not eligible for self-defense justification.
Minority
rule: If the defendant is charged with murder, even an unreasonable belief in the necessity of defensive force may provide a mitigation defense, reducing the defendant's liability from murder to manslaughter. This is sometimes termed imperfect self-defense. (That is, if an actor unreasonably believes in the necessity of defensive force, no state will grant the actor the full justification defense of self-defense. However, in some states, if the actor is charged with murder, the doctrine of imperfect self-defense will mitigate the actor's liability from murder to manslaughter. The defense of imperfect self-defense is not a full justification defense but rather only a mitigation defense.)

10. The following examples illustrate and compare the traditional/minority view and the modern/majority view of the defense of others justification:

Example 1: D and X reasonably believe that V is unlawfully using force against X. D uses force against V in defense of X. In fact, V unlawfully used force against X.

Outcome:	Traditional/minority view	Modern/majority view
	Eligible to be justified.	Eligible to be justified.

Example 2: D, but not X, reasonably believes that V is unlawfully using force against X. D uses force against V in defense of X. In fact, V lawfully used force against X.

Outcome:	Traditional/minority view	Modern/majority view
	Unjustified.	Eligible to be justified.

Example 3: D does not reasonably believe that V is unlawfully using force against X. D uses force against V in defense of X. In fact, V lawfully used force against X.

Outcome:	Traditional/minority view	Modern/majority view
	Unjustified.	Unjustified.

Note: If *D* unreasonably believes that *X* needs protection from *V*'s unlawful attack, *D* would not be justified in defense of others. But, in a minority of jurisdictions, *D* would be eligible for the mitigation defense of imperfect defense of others. Imperfect defense of others, similar to imperfect self-defense as discussed in Tool #9 above, mitigates a murder charge to manslaughter.

11. Did you confuse necessary force with proportional force in your answer to the Problem? In the Problem, that Samantha's use of deadly force prior to administration of the first dose would be *necessary* to prevent the administration of the first dose does not mean that it is *proportional* force. Carefully distinguish between proportional force and necessary force. In order to be eligible to be justified in self-defense, force must be both necessary and proportional. But the two elements do not always coincide. Sometimes force can be necessary but not proportional. And sometimes force can be proportional but not necessary.

Force that is necessary but not proportional: Martial Arts Champion elbows Little Granny in the ribs. Little Granny has a gun. The only way Little Granny can prevent the mild battery is to shoot Martial Arts Champion. Thus, Little Granny's shooting Martial Arts Champion would be necessary to prevent the battery. But doing so would constitute disproportional force because Little Granny would be using lethal force to prevent nonlethal aggression.

Force that is proportional but not necessary: Little Granny comes at Martial Arts Champion with a knife. Martial Arts Champion has a gun. Because Little Granny is employing deadly force, it would be proportional for Martial Arts Champion to also use lethal force and shoot her with his gun. But such deadly force would be unnecessary if Martial Arts Champion could easily take the knife from her or kick it out of her hand.

VARIATIONS ON THE THEME

For the following variations, assume that all of the facts from the original Problem apply except as noted.

1.   Rather than walking in and announcing her plan of poisoning Samantha, Sabrina walks in holding a shiny metallic object and announces, "I am going to kill you." Samantha believes that the shiny metallic object in Sabrina's hand is a gun. Samantha shoots and kills Sabrina.

2.   Rather than walking in and announcing her plan of poisoning Samantha, Sabrina walks in holding a shiny metallic object and announces, "I am going to kill you *today*." Samantha believes that the shiny metallic object in Sabrina's hand is a gun. Samantha shoots and kills Sabrina.

3.   Samantha is not bedridden, and Sabrina unlawfully confines her.

4.   Rather than walking in and announcing her plan of poisoning Samantha, Sabrina says, "You don't deserve to have a baby." Sabrina then picks up a baseball bat and starts to swing it toward Samantha's abdomen. Samantha shoots and kills Sabrina.

5.   Rather than walking in and announcing her plan of poisoning Samantha, Sabrina says, "I'm going to kill you with your own kitchen knife." Sabrina walks into the kitchen, but once in the kitchen she changes her mind. She walks back toward Samantha without a knife in her hand. As soon as Samantha sees Sabrina,

she shoots and kills her not realizing that Sabrina did not have a knife in her hand.

6.   Just as Samantha is in the process of shooting at Sabrina, Mrs. Kravitz walks into the room directly behind Sabrina. Samantha's shot misses Sabrina and hits and kills Mrs. Kravitz.

7.   Just as Samantha is about to justifiably shoot Sabrina, Mrs. Kravitz walks into the room. Believing that Samantha is unjustifiably aggressing against Sabrina, Mrs. Kravitz shoots and kills Samantha.

8.   Just as Samantha is about to justifiably shoot Sabrina, Mrs. Kravitz walks into the room and without any understanding of the situation, shoots and kills Sabrina.

9.   Just prior to the administration of the first dose, Samantha takes out her gun, points it at Sabrina and starts to pull the trigger. Sabrina, however, is quicker and kills Samantha with her own gun.

10. Samantha mistakenly believes that Sabrina is lying and is only injecting her with harmless water. Just before administration of the ninth dose, Samantha shoots and kills Sabrina.

ADDITIONAL READINGS

George P. Fletcher, A Crime of Self-Defense: Bernhard Goetz and the Law on Trial (1988)

George P. Fletcher & Luis E. Chiesa, *Self-Defense and the Psychotic Aggressor, in* Criminal Law Conversations 365–83 (Paul H. Robinson, Stephen P. Garvey & Kimberly Kessler Ferzan eds., 2009)

Larry Alexander, *A Unified Excuse of Preemptive Self-Protection*, 74 Notre Dame L. Rev. 1475 (1999)

Catherine L. Carpenter, *Of the Enemy Within, the Castle Doctrine, and Self-Defense*, 86 Marq. L. Rev. 653 (2003)

Russell Christopher, *Self-Defense and Defense of Others*, 27 Phil. & Pub. Aff. 123 (1998)

Anne M. Coughlin, *Excusing Women*, 82 Cal. L. Rev. 1 (1994)

Kimberly Kessler Ferzan, *Defending Imminence: From Battered Women to Iraq*, 46 Ariz. L. Rev. 213 (2004)

Claire Oakes Finkelstein, *On the Obligation of the State to Extend a Right of Self-Defense to its Citizens*, 147 U. Pa. L. Rev. 1361 (1999)

Victoria F. Nourse, *Self-Defense and Subjectivity*, 68 U. Chi. L. Rev. 1235 (2001)

Richard Singer, *The Resurgence of Mens Rea: II—Honest but Unreasonable Mistake of Fact in Self-Defense*, 28 B.C. L. Rev. 459 (1987)

12

NECESSITY AND DURESS

INTRODUCTION

Self-defense and defense of others are defenses to crimes committed against unlawful aggressors. In contrast, the offenses for which one asserts the defenses of necessity and duress are rarely committed against unlawful aggressors. While duress is a defense due to the unlawful aggression of a duressor, it is a defense to a crime committed against an innocent person. And unlike self-defense, defense of others, and duress, necessity typically lacks the involvement of an unlawful aggressor entirely. And unlike those defenses, necessity is a defense to crimes typically not even directed against a human being at all. Necessity, also termed choice-of-evils or lesser evils, is a defense for either crimes against persons or property. Also unlike self-defense and defense of others, necessity and duress are generally inapplicable as a defense to intentional homicides.

Though the contours of necessity and duress are overlapping and complementary, there are also significant differences. These differences stem from necessity being a justification defense and duress being an excuse defense. As a justification defense, like self-defense and defense of others, an actor pleading necessity concedes that all of the elements of the offense are satisfied but nonetheless asserts that under the circumstances, his conduct is entirely permissible and lawful. As an excuse defense, an actor pleading duress concedes both that all of the elements of the offense are satisfied and that his conduct is wrongful and unlawful. But despite the actor's conduct being wrongful and unlawful, an excuse defense asserts that it is unfair to hold the actor liable. In short, when asserting a justification defense, the defendant accepts responsibility for his conduct but denies that it was wrongful or unlawful. When asserting an excuse defense, the defendant concedes that his conduct was wrongful and unlawful but denies responsibility. As a justification defense, necessity involves an actor choosing the lesser evil. Despite committing the lesser evil—a criminal offense—the actor's conduct supplies a net benefit in avoiding an even greater evil. In contrast, as an excuse, the actor pleading duress typically has chosen the greater evil. So while necessity exculpates because the actor has done the right thing, duress exculpates despite the actor doing the wrong thing. An increasing number of commentators argue that duress should be a justification because the actor under duress typically commits the lesser evil. But because duress may apply even if the actor chooses the greater evil, most courts, commentators, and codes treat duress as an excuse.

Another important difference between duress and necessity is the nature of the source of the emergency giving rise to the defense. Duress is limited to human threats; natural sources of peril are excluded. Although this limitation is controversial, its rationale is clear. The criminal law can afford to be generous and exculpate the duressee only if there is someone to hold responsible for the crime committed by the duressee against the innocent third party. Limiting duress to human threats assures that the source of the duress—the duressor—can be prosecuted for the crime committed by the duressee. Traditionally, necessity was limited to natural sources of peril. There is little rationale for this traditional limitation, and it may stem simply from necessity cases typically involving natural perils. What typically was the case gradually evolved into a rule that it must be the case. Today, however, both the MPC and most jurisdictions have rejected this limitation and allow necessity to apply to both natural and human sources of emergency.

PROBLEM

Driving down a highway, Reese Robbie passes a prison and sees a sign warning drivers against picking up hitchhikers in this area. Shortly after passing the prison, Reese picks one up anyway. After some small talk, the hitchhiker says, "You don't recognize me, do you? You skipped out on Momma and me when I was little. You're my daddy, Reese Robbie." Reese says, "Ricky, is that you? How long has it been, a few years?" Ricky replies, "No, Dad, it's been twenty years." Reese responds, "I guess I should lay off the peyote."

Noticing that Ricky is bleeding, Reese asks, "What happened to you?" Ricky says, "I was shot by the police after I escaped from prison. I shot and seriously wounded three of them." While Reese is digesting Ricky's startling story, he sees three people lying in the road off in the distance. Ricky sees them too and says, "Those are the three cops I shot." Reese starts to slow down so that he can help them. Ricky yells out, "What are you doing? Keep driving! We can't stop and help them. I'm seriously injured; you've got to get me to a hospital!" Reese responds, "But they'll die out here within minutes if we don't stop and help them." Ricky takes out his gun, points it at his father's head and says, "Keep driving, run right over them or I'll kill you."

Reese quickly considers his options. He is driving on a steep narrow mountain road and if he does not stop, the only way to avoid hitting the three police officers who are stretched across the road is to drive off the cliff resulting in his and Ricky's certain death. If he does drive over the three in the road, he will certainly kill them all. And if he stops the car, Ricky will likely kill him and run over the three police officers himself.

Reese decides to run over the three police officers and takes Ricky to a hospital. Reese is arrested shortly thereafter and charged with the murder of the three police officers.[1]

Analyze and discuss whether Reese may successfully assert necessity and duress defenses to the murder charges under both the common law and the MPC.

LIST OF READINGS
Necessity
Commonwealth v. Leno, 616 N.E.2d 453 (Mass. 1993)
Regina v. Dudley & Stephens, 14 Q.D.B. 273 (1884)
MODEL PENAL CODE § 3.02 (Official Code and Revised Comments 1985)

---

[1] The Problem is based, in part, on a hypothetical in SANFORD H. KADISH, STEPHEN J. SCHULHOFER & CAROL S. STEIKER, CRIMINAL LAW AND ITS PROCESSES: CASES AND MATERIALS (8th ed. 2007) and discussed in MODEL PENAL CODE § 2.09, Comment at 378–79 (Official Code and Revised Comments 1985).

Duress

United States v. LaFleur, 971 F.2d 200 (9th Cir. 1991)

United States v. Contento-Pachon, 723 F.2d 200 (9th Cir. 1984)

Model Penal Code § 2.09 (Official Code and Revised Comments 1985)

ESSAY

Under the common law, Reese would neither obtain the necessity defense nor the duress defense in some jurisdictions but would possibly obtain the defenses in other jurisdictions. Under the MPC, Reese would most likely obtain both defenses.

Necessity

COMMON LAW

[1] In general, necessity justifies the commission of a criminal act if it avoids more harm than it causes. The following are possible requirements to obtain a necessity defense: (i) the actor faces an imminent emergency situation, (ii) the emergency stems from natural forces, (iii) the harm avoided is to persons or property, (iv) the harm committed is not homicide, (v) there is a reasonable causal link between the action taken and the harm avoided, (vi) the actor believes that her conduct will avoid the greater harm, (vii) either this belief is reasonable or it is objectively correct, (viii) the harm cannot be avoided by lawful means, (ix) the actor's choice of the lesser evil has not previously been foreclosed by legislative decision, (x) the actor neither caused nor contributed to the emergency, and (xi) the actor did not wrongfully place herself in a situation in which she would have to choose the lesser evil.

[2] As to the first requirement, Reese clearly faced an imminent emergency situation in which he had to choose between his own death and the deaths of the three police officers in the road.

[3] As to the second requirement, Reese is not facing an emergency created by a natural force. The emergency stems from a human source: Ricky threatening to kill him. As a result, Reese fails to satisfy this requirement. But most states no longer impose this requirement. As a result, Ricky would not obtain the necessity defense under the minority rule but would remain eligible for the defense under the majority rule.

[4] As to the third requirement, the harm Reese seeks to avoid is harm to persons—harm to himself and possibly Ricky.

[5] As to the fourth requirement, because Reese is asserting the necessity defense to homicide charges, Reese would clearly fail to satisfy it. But this is not a requirement in all states. As a result, Reese would not obtain the necessity defense in some jurisdictions but would remain eligible in others.

[6] As to the fifth requirement, failing to stop and thereby complying with Ricky's demand is an efficacious way of avoiding the threatened harm from coming to fruition.

[7] As to the sixth requirement, the facts fail to explicitly state whether he believes he is choosing the lesser evil. If Reese did lack the belief that he was choosing the lesser evil, then he would not satisfy this requirement and would not obtain the necessity defense. But by piecing together some of Reese's beliefs, there is a fairly strong argument that he did believe that he was choosing the lesser evil. He believes that the three police officers would die within minutes if they did not

receive immediate aid. He also believes that if he drives over the cliff, he and Ricky will die, and thus there would be no one to render immediate aid to the police officers. As a result, we might infer that he believes that if he drives over the cliff, all five of them will die, which is the worst outcome. Any other outcome is preferable. As a result, when he drove over the police officers, Reese probably did believe that he was choosing the lesser evil. (Whether he reasonably could believe this or whether he actually did choose the lesser evil is discussed below in [8].)

[8] As to the seventh requirement, some jurisdictions seem to require that the harm avoided must actually outweigh or even clearly outweigh the harm committed. Other jurisdictions merely require that the actor reasonably believe that the harm avoided is greater than the harm committed. One might argue that Reese satisfies neither one of these standards because he is killing three to save fewer than three. On this basis, Reese is clearly not choosing the lesser evil. But perhaps the better analysis reveals that Reese may well be avoiding the greater harm.

Consider Reese's three options. If, to avoid running over and killing the three police officers, Reese were to drive over the cliff, he and Ricky would surely die. And by eliminating the only source of possible aid to the police officers—himself—the three police officers would also die. As a result, by driving off the cliff, five people die and no one is saved. Option two is to stop the car, thereby temporarily saving the three police officers. But Ricky would then kill Reese and drive over the three police officers himself. As a result, by stopping the car, four die and one survives. Pursuant to the third option, which Reese does in fact choose, three are killed and two survive—Reese and Ricky. Thus, the option that Ricky chooses involves the greatest number of lives saved. Rather than viewing it as Reese killing three to save two, arguably the better view is that he killed only three rather than killing five (option one) or killing four (option two).

One might argue that if Reese had driven over the cliff, the three police officers would not have died anyway but could have been saved by someone else. Rather than having merely minutes to live absent receipt of aid, they might have lived for hours, long enough for another driver to come along and render aid. Alternatively, one might argue that had Reese stopped the car, Ricky would not have run over the three police officers himself. From either of these alternative scenarios, two different arguments could be made. First, Reese's belief that the police officers would die anyway was unreasonable. Second, if the three police officers would not have died anyway, the harm Reese avoided does not actually outweigh the harm Reese committed.

This is ultimately less an issue of law than an issue of fact and is up to the jury or fact finder to determine. (This situation is somewhat analogous to that faced by the defendants in *Dudley & Stephens* in which they did not know how long they could survive without cannibalizing someone.)

[9] As to the eighth requirement, Reese has no lawful option to prevent the deaths of the three police officers lying in the road. His only alternative options are to drive off the cliff or to stop the car in the road. Neither of those alternatives avoids the deaths of the three police officers. As a result, Reese satisfies this requirement.

[10] As to the ninth requirement, no legislative decision has foreclosed Reese's course of conduct from being the lesser evil.

[11] As to the tenth requirement, Reese neither caused nor contributed to the emergency that Ricky caused entirely on his own.

[12] As to the eleventh requirement, by picking up a hitchhiker near a prison despite the posted warnings, Reese arguably did wrongfully place himself in a situation in which he might be forced to choose the lesser evil. However, it is not entirely clear that he *wrongfully* placed himself in the situation. If picking up a hitchhiker near a prison is not a criminal act, then perhaps Reese did not wrongfully place himself in the situation. As a result, Reese probably satisfies this requirement.

MODEL PENAL CODE

[13] In order to satisfy the necessity defense, termed choice-of-evils defense under the MPC, the following requirements must be satisfied: (i) the actor believes his conduct is necessary to avoid a harm or evil; (ii) the harm sought to be avoided is greater than that sought to be prevented by the law prohibiting his conduct; (iii) neither an exception to the offense charged nor another defense applies; (iv) there is no legislative purpose to exclude the justification for the actor's situation; and (v) if charged with an offense requiring a mens rea of recklessness or negligence, the actor was not reckless or negligent in either bringing about the situation or in appraising the necessity of his conduct.

[14] As to the first requirement, Reese believes driving over the three police officers is necessary to avoid a harm or evil—either his own death or the death of all five.

[15] As to the second requirement, as discussed above in [7]–[8], the harm Reese seeks to avoid is the death of five. The harm sought to be prevented by the jurisdiction's murder statute is the death of three. Based on a numerical comparison of deaths avoided versus lives saved, avoiding the death of five is greater than causing the death of three. As a result, Reese most likely satisfies this requirement.

[16] As to the third requirement, no exceptions to the offense apply and, with the possible exception of duress (see analysis of duress below), no other defense applies. As a result, Reese possibly satisfies the third requirement.

[17] As to the fourth requirement, no legislative purpose excludes Reese's choice-of-evils claim.

[18] As to the fifth requirement, Reese is not charged with an offense for which recklessness or negligence suffices. Rather, Reese is charged with murder requiring purpose, knowledge, or a gross form of recklessness. However, even if Reese was charged with a reckless or negligent homicide, this requirement would arguably not preclude Reese from obtaining the defense. There is no evidence in the facts that Reese was reckless or negligent in appraising the necessity of his conduct. And arguably he was not reckless or negligent in bringing about the situation. He did not wrongfully (in the sense of criminally) do anything to bring about the situation. Surely he was unwise and imprudent in picking up a hitchhiker near a prison but this presumably does not rise to the level of recklessly or negligently (in the sense of criminal culpability for) bringing about the situation.

Duress

COMMON LAW

[19] In order to satisfy the defense of duress, some if not all of the following requirements must be satisfied: (i) the coercion is based on a threat, not an offer

or inducement, (ii) the threat is of imminent harm, (iii) of death or serious bodily injury, (iv) that is unlawful, (v) the threat is from a human and not a natural source, (vi) the threatened harm is directed at the defendant or the defendant's relative, (vii) the defendant has no reasonable opportunity to avoid the threatened harm, (viii) the defendant did not culpably place herself in a situation in which she could expect to be subject to coercion, (ix) the defendant's criminal act is specifically commanded by the duressor, (x) the defense is not asserted to an intentional killing, and (xi) the defendant reasonably believes that the threat would be carried out if the defendant did not comply.

[20] As to the first requirement, Reese is clearly subjected to a threat—the threat of being killed.

[21] As to the second requirement, the threatened harm is clearly imminent.

[22] As to the third requirement, Reese is clearly subject to a threat of death.

[23] As to the fourth requirement, the threat of death to which Reese was subjected was clearly unlawful.

[24] As to the fifth requirement, Reese was clearly subjected to a threat from a human source—Ricky.

[25] As to the sixth requirement, the threat is clearly directed at Reese himself.

[26] As to the seventh requirement, Reese clearly had no opportunity to escape from the threatened harm.

[27] As to the eighth requirement, Reese clearly did place himself in a situation in which he might be subjected to coercion. Reese picked up a hitchhiker in an area near a prison despite signs warning him not to do so. However, it is unclear whether Reese culpably or wrongfully placed himself in the situation. The classic example of an actor who fails to satisfy this requirement and loses the duress defense is one who joins a criminal gang. Unlike an actor who joins a criminal gang, it is not clear that Reese's conduct was wrongful or culpable. His unwise and imprudent conduct does not rise to the level of wrongful or culpable. As a result, Reese probably satisfies this requirement.

[28] As to the ninth requirement, Reese running over the three police officers was specifically commanded by Ricky.

[29] As to the tenth requirement, Reese has been charged with three intentional killings, so he does not satisfy this requirement. However, in some jurisdictions, there is no express limitation on the offenses to which duress may be asserted. In jurisdictions not allowing the defense for intentional killings, some allow a defense of imperfect duress that reduces the defendant's liability from murder to manslaughter. As a result, in some jurisdictions, Reese will not obtain the defense to the murder charges. In other jurisdictions, the defense may mitigate his liability from murder to manslaughter. In still other jurisdictions, he would remain eligible for the duress defense.

[30] As to the eleventh requirement, Reese's belief that Ricky would carry out the threat if he did not comply is arguably reasonable. One might argue, however, that because Reese was Ricky's father, Ricky would not be able to shoot Reese if Reese did not comply, and thus Reese's belief was unreasonable. Given that son and father have been estranged for 20 years, Ricky has shot and seriously wounded three police officers, and is willing to point a gun at his father, Reese's belief that Ricky would carry out the threat is particularly reasonable.

[31] The MPC requires the following elements in order for a defendant to satisfy the duress defense: (i) the defendant was coerced by the use or threat of unlawful force, (ii) against himself or any other, (iii) which a person of reasonable firmness in his situation would have been unable to resist; (iv) the defendant did not recklessly place himself in a situation in which it was probable that he would be coerced; and (v) if the defendant is charged with an offense requiring a mens rea of negligence, the defendant did not negligently place himself in such a situation.

[32] As to the first and second requirements, Reese was clearly subjected to a threat of unlawful force against himself.

[33] As to the third requirement, there is no precise calculus for determining what sort of threats a reasonable person should or should not be able to resist. The MPC does not bar the duress defense to a charge of murder, but presumably a reasonable person would be able to resist committing murder to avoid a threat of comparatively minor harm. Conversely, if the defendant is threatened with being killed unless she commits a comparatively minor crime, almost any reasonable person would be unable to resist. Here, unlike the above two examples, we neither have a case in which almost any reasonable person would resist the threat nor a situation in which almost any reasonable person would not resist the threat. Rather, the defendant is threatened with the same crime he is coerced to commit. The offense threatened is proportional to the offense committed. Given that the MPC specifically allows duress as a defense to murder, and Reese has been subjected to the most coercive of all threats, most likely a person of reasonable firmness in Reese's situation would have been unable to resist. As a result, Reese probably satisfies this requirement.

[34] As to the fourth requirement, Reese clearly placed himself in a situation in which he had an increased chance of being subject to duress. However, it is unclear that he would *probably* be subjected to duress. It is also unclear that he recklessly did so. True, he was aware of the signs warning him not to pick up hitchhikers, and he was unwise and imprudent for doing so, but this may not rise to the level of the criminal and culpable state of being reckless. As a result, Reese probably satisfies this requirement (of not recklessly placing himself in such a situation).

[35] As to the fifth requirement, Reese is not charged with an offense for which negligence suffices as the mens rea. However, if he was charged with negligent homicide, he most likely did not negligently place himself in such a situation as discussed above in [34].

Conclusion

Necessity: Under the common law, Reese would obtain the defense neither in jurisdictions requiring the emergency situation to stem from a natural source nor in jurisdictions barring necessity as a defense to murder. Reese would also not prevail if he lacked a belief that he was choosing the lesser evil, if his belief that by driving over the cliff all five would die was unreasonable, or if by his noncriminal conduct he nonetheless wrongfully placed himself in the emergency situation. As a result, Reese would fail to obtain the defense in some jurisdictions and would possibly obtain the defense in other jurisdictions. Under the MPC, Reese would most likely obtain the defense.

Duress: Under the common law, Reese would not obtain the defense in jurisdictions barring duress as a defense to murder. Reese would also not prevail if by his noncriminal conduct, he nonetheless wrongfully placed himself in a situation in which he could be expected to be subjected to coercion. As a result, Reese would fail to obtain the defense in some jurisdictions and would possibly obtain the defense in others. Under the MPC, Reese would most likely obtain the defense.

TOOLS FOR SELF-ASSESSMENT

Go back to your written answer. Look for the issues identified in paragraphs numbered [1]–[35] above. Look also for the analysis that follows each issue, and mark your essay where you locate it. Do you fully describe the issue, identify the precise legal standard that applies, list the relevant facts, and show how the facts and law support a conclusion for each issue? Mark each conclusion in your essay. Are there sufficient reasons in the law and in the facts to support each conclusion?

1. Do what you are told. Here, you are to analyze whether Reese satisfies the requirements for the defenses of necessity and duress with respect to the three counts of murder.

2. Do not analyze what is unnecessary. You need not analyze any other crimes that Reese may have committed, defenses other than necessity and duress, nor offenses that may have been committed by Ricky.

3. Always analyze under the MPC as well as the common law unless you are instructed otherwise.

4. State the best possible arguments for alternative conclusions. For example, if you decide that Reese has not satisfied a particular requirement for the necessity defense, consider whether one might reasonably disagree with your conclusion. If so, state the best possible argument opposing your analysis, and explain why it is wrong.

5. There are numerous ways to organize your answer. Set out on the next page is the organizational structure of the above Essay as well an alternative organizational structure. There is no single organizational structure that is always preferable for all hypotheticals involving necessity or duress. But there are advantages and disadvantages depending on the hypothetical and the instructions as to how to analyze the hypothetical. Appreciating the various possible organizational structures that you might employ for any given hypothetical or exam question will be of tremendous aid in selecting, if not the optimal organizational structure, then at least a preferable one. Having a good organizational structure will not only help clarify your analysis but also save you time. It is very important to have a sense of the possible organizational structures you might employ before you walk into an exam. You do not want to waste valuable time during the exam grappling with how to organize it.

Structure #1 depicts the organizational structure of the above Essay, and Structure #2 depicts an alternative. Structure #1 is primarily organized by the particular defense. One defense is analyzed under the common law followed by its analysis under the MPC. Then the same process is repeated for the other defense. Structure #2 utilizes the distinction between the common law and the MPC as the primary organizational feature.

6. Unlike topics in other chapters, the analysis of the defenses of necessity and duress are not further illuminated by a flowchart or series of logical steps

Structure #1	Structure #2
Introduction	Introduction
Necessity	Common Law
Common Law	Necessity
Model Penal Code	Duress
Duress	Model Penal Code
Common Law	Necessity
Model Penal Code	Duress
Conclusion	Conclusion

laying bare the analysis. There are few sequential reasoning steps to be undertaken. Rather, the preferable approach is the laundry list of requirements that are set out in paragraphs [1], [13], [19], and [31]. There is not a particularly helpful way of sequencing the analysis of these requirements. As a result, the best view of the forest without the obstruction of the trees is the "laundry list" of possible requirements under the common law and definite requirements under the MPC for each defense.

7.   Did you fall for the red herring that Reese's duty to rush his wounded son to the hospital was somehow relevant in the analysis of Reese satisfying the necessity defense? You might have been tempted to argue that Reese running over the three police officers in the road was obligatory because of a duty to save his son. And if it is obligatory, then it must also be permissible under the necessity defense. Although Reese did have such a duty to his son, that duty is limited to the use of lawful means. It does not give Reese license to kill the three police officers or anyone else. That Reese was under a duty to his son is irrelevant in analyzing whether Reese satisfies the requirements of a necessity defense.

8.   Did you make the mistake of concluding that Reese did not choose the lesser evil with respect to the necessity defense? This is an easy mistake to make. The typical and shortcut method most commonly employed in situations requiring the counting of lives killed versus lives saved is simply to tally up the number of lives killed as compared to the lives saved. Utilizing this method yields the view that Reese killed three and saved two, the harm committed was greater than the harm avoided, and thus Reese chose the greater evil. But there are a number of situations in which this shortcut method will produce the wrong result.

There are two classic examples. First, consider an operation to sever endangered Siamese twins. If as a result of the operation, one twin is killed and one twin survives, the shortcut method would yield the result of killing one to save one, and thus the operation does not constitute choosing the lesser evil. But arguably the better approach is to view the operation as killing one so as to prevent the deaths of two. In this way, the operation does constitute choosing the lesser evil. Second, suppose there are two mountain climbers, D and V, attached by a rope and V falls off of the mountain but is still attached to D by the rope and will pull D down with him when D can no longer bear V's weight. Unable to hold on any longer, D cuts the rope, killing V. Under the shortcut method we might say that D kills one to save one and thus did not choose the lesser evil and thus is not eligible for the necessity defense.

But again, the better analysis is that *D* killed one to prevent the death of two and thus did choose the lesser evil and thus is eligible for the necessity defense.

In both of these examples as well as in the Problem, utilization of the shortcut method of counting lives killed versus lives saved, fails to reveal what is arguably the correct answer that the actor in each case did choose the lesser evil. How do we know for any given situation of necessity whether it is a type in which the shortcut method will produce the correct result or the incorrect result as in these three examples? Since there are a myriad of factual scenarios wherein the shortcut method might produce the incorrect result, it is too difficult to generalize about the type of scenarios in which the shortcut method will not work. The better approach, then, is to come up with an alternative test than the shortcut method. The preferable approach requires comparing the outcome of what the defendant did do versus the outcome of other possible courses of action that the defendant did not do. It is only through this method that we can see that an actor who killed a greater number than saved, nonetheless, chose the lesser evil. For example, in the Siamese twin case, compare the consequences of what the actor did do to the consequences of alternative courses of action that the actor did not take. The consequences of the course of action the actor did take was killing one and saving one. The consequences of the alternative course of action—doing nothing—would be the death of both twins. The comparison reveals that what the actor did do was preferable to the alternative course of action and that killing one prevented the death of two. Similarly, in the mountain climbing example, compare the consequences of what the actor did do to the alternative course of action—doing nothing. The consequences of what the actor did do—killing one to save one—are preferable to the consequences of doing nothing: both mountain climbers die. The comparison of the consequences of the various courses of action reveals that killing one prevented the death of two, which did constitute choosing the lesser evil.

In order to avoid the mistake of the shortcut method of simply comparing lives killed versus lives saved, supplement your analysis with a comparison of the outcome of what the actor did do versus alternative courses of action. For the Problem, the above Essay demonstrates the results of the comparison of the various courses of action. See [8] in the above Essay.

9.   For the MPC, in particular, understand the relationship between the mens rea of the offense charged and the defenses of duress and choice-of-evils. The following charts depict how an actor may or may not obtain the particular defense depending on the type of mens rea of the offense charged:

NECESSITY:

Example 1:   The actor is **reckless** in either bringing about the situation requiring a choice-of-evils or in appraising the necessity of his conduct.

Mens Rea of Offense Charged	Necessity Justification Status
Purpose	Justified
Knowledge	Justified
Recklessness	**Unjustified**
Negligence	**Unjustified**

Example 2: The actor is **negligent** in either bringing about the situation requiring a choice-of-evils or in appraising the necessity of his conduct.

Mens Rea of Offense Charged	Necessity Justification Status
Purpose	Justified
Knowledge	Justified
Recklessness	Justified
Negligence	**Unjustified**

DURESS:

Example 1: The actor **recklessly** places herself in a situation in which it was probable that she would be subjected to duress.

Mens Rea of Offense Charged	Duress Excuse Status
Purpose	No excuse
Knowledge	No excuse
Recklessness	No excuse
Negligence	No excuse

Example 2: The actor **negligently** places herself in a situation in which it was probable that she would be subjected to duress.

Mens Rea of Offense Charged	Duress Excuse Status
Purpose	Excused
Knowledge	Excused
Recklessness	Excused
Negligence	**No excuse**

10. Keep in mind that the MPC standard for duress may be understood as a sliding scale. The MPC requires that the threat be such that a person of reasonable firmness would be unable to resist. This language may be simplified to the following: if a reasonable person would succumb to the threat, then the actor is eligible for the duress defense; if a reasonable person would not succumb to the threat, the actor is not eligible for the duress defense. Under either articulation of the standard, this amounts to a sliding scale. The more serious or grave the threatened harm, the more serious the crime that may be excused by the duress defense. The less serious or grave the threatened harm, the less serious the offense that may be excused by the duress defense. So, a threat of minor harm is not sufficient

to excuse the commission of a serious offense. If the actor commits a particularly serious offense, the actor must have been subjected to a threat of fairly serious harm in order to obtain the defense. As the seriousness of the threat of harm increases, the seriousness of the type of offense that may be excused by the duress defense also increases. As a result, the seriousness of the threat and the seriousness of the offense that the threat may excuse slide together along a scale from less serious to more serious.

11. Perhaps the most difficult aspect of analyzing cases of necessity involve understanding the relationship between the actor's beliefs, the actor's mistakes, and whether her conduct actually constitutes the lesser evil. The following series of abstract examples explains this relationship and compares the outcomes under the common law and MPC:

Example 1: The actor's conduct does constitute the lesser evil, but the actor fails to believe the conduct is necessary to avoid the harm or evil.

Outcome:	Common Law	MPC
	Unjustified.	Unjustified.

Example 2: The actor's conduct does constitute the lesser evil, and the actor does believe the conduct is necessary to avoid the harm or evil.

Outcome:	Common Law	MPC
	Eligible to be justified.	Eligible to be justified.

Example 3: The actor's conduct does *not* constitute the lesser evil because the actor makes a *reasonable* factual mistake about the means to obtain the lesser evil.

Outcome:	Common Law	MPC
	Eligible to be justified.	Eligible to be justified.

Example 4: The actor's conduct does *not* constitute the lesser evil because the actor makes an *unreasonable* factual mistake about the means to obtain the lesser evil.

Outcome:	Common Law	MPC
	Unjustified.	Depends on mens rea, see Tool #9.

Example 5: The actor's conduct does *not* constitute the lesser evil because the actor (reasonably or unreasonably) incorrectly weighs the competing harms (in the view of the judge or jury).

Outcome:	Common Law	MPC
	Unjustified.	Unjustified.

To illustrate the analysis of these abstract examples, consider the following scenario. Suppose a raging forest fire is headed in the general direction of both Yellowstone National Park and the habitat of the nearly extinct Wyoming spotted owl. Ranger Roger causes another fire, under circumstances that vary in the five examples below, and is charged with the offense of destruction of forest lands. Ranger Roger pleads the necessity defense.

Example 1: Unaware of the raging fire, Ranger Roger carelessly fails to extinguish a campfire. The unextinguished campfire serves as a firebreak that diverts the raging forest fire away from both Yellowstone and the spotted owls.

Example 2: Aware of the raging fire, Ranger Roger intentionally sets a firebreak that successfully diverts the raging fire from both Yellowstone and the spotted owls.

Example 3: Despite setting a firebreak based on the best available information about the winds and in full compliance with the Forest Ranger Manual, the firebreak diverts the raging fire toward Yellowstone, causing immeasurable damage.

Example 4: Because Ranger Roger sets a firebreak based on the dated and unreliable information about the winds and not in compliance with the Forest Ranger Manual, the firebreak diverts the raging fire toward Yellowstone causing immeasurable damage.

Example 5: Believing that the burning of the spotted owls' habitat was the greater evil, and the burning of Yellowstone was the lesser evil, Ranger Roger intentionally sets a firebreak that successfully diverts the raging fire from the spotted owls' habitat and toward Yellowstone, thereby causing immeasurable damage to Yellowstone. While perhaps reasonable minds may differ as to which was the greater and lesser evil, the jury determines that Ranger Roger incorrectly weighed or balanced the evils—the burning of Yellowstone was the greater evil.

VARIATIONS ON THE THEME

For the following variations, assume that all of the facts from the original Problem obtain except as noted.

1. Ricky's gun was unloaded.
2. Ricky's gun was a toy water pistol.

3. Rather than threatening to shoot Reese, Ricky threatens to come at Reese like a spider monkey.

4. The three police officers were not minutes away from dying but would have lived for hours more if they were not run over.

5. Rather than all three police officers being minutes away from dying, only two were minutes away from dying. But one of the three would have lived for hours longer.

6. Reese and Ricky are not father and son; they are strangers.

7. Rather than Reese driving by a prison, Reese is driving by a law school when he picks up Ricky who is hitchhiking. Rather than having escaped from prison and having shot three police officers, Ricky has escaped from law school and has shot three law professors who are now lying in the road.

8. After Ricky threatens to kill Reese if Reese stops the car (so as not to run over the three police officers), Reese does try to stop the car by depressing the brake pedal, but the brakes do not work.

9. Rather than three police officers lying in the road, there are only two.

10. Rather than threatening to kill Reese, Ricky threatens to break Reese's arm.

ADDITIONAL READINGS

Joshua Dressler, Understanding Criminal Law 289–322 (5th ed. 2009)

Kent Greenawalt, Conflicts of Law and Morality 286–310 (1987)

Leo Katz, Bad Acts and Guilty Minds: Conundrums of the Criminal Law 8–81 (1987)

Paul H. Robinson, Criminal Law 407–18, 536–39 (1997)

Luis Ernesto Chiesa Aponte, *Normative Gaps in the Criminal Law: A Reasons Theory of Wrongdoing*, 10 New Crim. L. Rev. 102 (2007)

Kyron Huigens, *Duress Is Not a Justification*, 2 Ohio St. J. Crim. L. 303 (2004)

Claire O. Finkelstein, *Duress: A Philosophical Account of the Defense in Law*, 37 Ariz. L. Rev. 251 (1995)

George P. Fletcher, *Should Intolerable Prison Conditions Generate a Justification or an Excuse for Escape?* 26 U.C.L.A L. Rev. 1355 (1979)

Michael Hoffheimer, *Codifying Necessity: Legislative Resistance to Enacting Choice-of-Evil Defenses to Criminal Liability*, 82 Tulane L. Rev. 191 (2007)

Peter Westen & James Mangiafico, *The Criminal Defense of Duress: A Justification, Not an Excuse—And Why It Matters*, 6 Buff. Crim. L. Rev. 833 (2003)

MENTAL IMPAIRMENT DEFENSES:

13

DIMINISHED CAPACITY, INTOXICATION, AND INSANITY

INTRODUCTION

In contrast to the situational defenses in the previous chapters, the defenses in this chapter might be called defenses of mental impairment. Whereas self-defense, defense of others, necessity, and duress are all defenses arising from an external situation of emergency, the mental impairment defenses of intoxication, diminished capacity, and insanity involve an internal characteristic or feature of the actor. These internal characteristics or features make the actor's compliance with the law difficult, preclude the actor from having a fair opportunity to obey the law, and render the actor not culpable or not fully culpable.

While the situational defenses are exclusively affirmative defenses (applying even if all the elements of the offense have been satisfied), the mental impairment defenses exculpate in four different ways. First, like the situational defenses, each mental impairment defense may be an affirmative defense. Second, some may exculpate by negating the mens rea element of the offense. Third, one mental impairment defense may negate the voluntary act element. And fourth, some may be used as evidence to establish another defense.

Each of these mental impairment defenses differ as to which of these four exculpatory functions they serve. Insanity may serve to negate the requisite mens rea, provide an affirmative defense, or supply evidence used to establish another defense. Diminished capacity either negates the mens rea element or functions as a partial affirmative defense (in its latter form, the defense is sometimes termed "diminished responsibility" or "partial responsibility"). Intoxication can serve all four functions. These mental impairment defenses intertwine and interrelate to such an extent that evidence of insanity may be used to establish the distinct defense of intoxication; and conversely, evidence of intoxication may be used to establish the distinct defense of insanity.

The analysis of the intoxication defense often rests on the distinction between voluntary and involuntary intoxication. Involuntary, or not self-induced, intoxication has greater exculpatory power than voluntary or self-induced intoxication. Involuntary intoxication may be a defense to both specific and general intent offenses and supports both a "temporary" insanity and a "fixed" insanity defense. Nonetheless, even voluntary intoxication can be a defense under limited circumstances.

Diminished capacity is a defense based on an actor's mental abnormality not rising to the level of insanity. The requisite degree of mental abnormality is rarely specified. Its mens rea negating form is recognized in about half of the jurisdictions. Some jurisdictions recognize that it may negate both specific and general intent mens rea, while other jurisdictions limit it to negating specific intent mens rea. In its affirmative defense form, diminished capacity mitigates murder to manslaughter in a small number of jurisdictions.

The insanity defense is recognized in almost every state and is based on a mental disease that, generally speaking, causes the actor to either (i) not know or appreciate what she did, (ii) not know or appreciate that what she did was wrong, or (iii) not have the ability or capacity to control what she did. Although there is no single majority test for what suffices as insanity, there is considerable similarity and overlap among the differing tests. Jurisdictions split over the above three factors, leading to five different tests for the insanity defense. A principal feature underlying differences among the tests is the cognitive/volitional distinction. Cognitive-impairment-based tests involve (i) and/or (ii); volitional-impairment-based tests involve (iii). Tests are either cognitive-based, volitional-based, either cognitive or volitional-based, or neither.

PROBLEM

After a night of heavy drinking, Mick Memento decides to head home to his lovely wife, Velma. The door is unlocked and he walks in. Hearing the sound of Velma's voice and that of another man, he runs up the stairs, throws open the bedroom door, and sees his wife engaged in intercourse with another man. Unable to control his inflamed passion and rage, and believing that he is upholding his sacred moral obligation to defend his marriage, Mick shoots and kills Velma's lover, Brennan. (Although Mick personally believes that killing Brennan is morally right, he knows that society regards it as unlawful and immoral.) Velma screams out, "Oh my God, what have you done?" Mick replies, "What?! I'm defending our sacred marital bond, what are you doing with this guy?" Before Velma has a chance to answer, there is a loud noise downstairs as someone bursts through the door. Mick rushes downstairs, sees an unlawful intruder in his home and shoots and kills the intruder. The police arrive shortly thereafter and arrest Mick.

Before this night, Mick was diagnosed with Short Term Memory Loss disorder (STML). According to the diagnosis, his memory is completely intact regarding events that occurred prior to the last year. He has no memory, however, of events that have occurred within the last 12 months. Unfortunately for Mick, the last 12 months have been a period of significant change and upheaval. Nine months ago Velma filed for divorce, and three months ago Mick moved out of the house. Two months ago the divorce became final, and one month ago his ex-wife married Brennan.

On the night of the shootings, due to his STML, Mick had forgotten that he no longer was married and that he no longer lived with his wife in their home. As a result, on that night, he was suffering from the delusion that he was entering his own home, that Velma was still his wife, and that she was committing adultery in violation of their marital vows. He was further deluded that he was defending his home from an unlawful intruder. In fact, the apparent unlawful intruder was Ned, the next door neighbor who had heard the initial gunshot and had come over to render aid. During the period when they were neighbors, Mick and Ned had become very close, each proclaiming that they would be "BFF." Mick neither remembered nor recognized his best friend Ned, because Ned had moved in only 11 months ago.

Mick is charged with the murders of Brennan and Ned. In this jurisdiction, murder is a specific intent crime defined as intentionally causing the death of a human being. Also in this jurisdiction, only a lawful occupant, which Mick was not, may lawfully use deadly force against an unlawful intruder.

Analyze and discuss, under both the common law and MPC, what plausible mental impairment defenses Mick might raise to these charges and whether they will succeed.

LIST OF READINGS

Clark v. Arizona, 548 U.S. 735 (2006)
Montana v. Egelhoff, 518 U.S. 37 (1996)
People v. Wetmore, 583 P.2d 1308 (Cal. 1978)
State v. Johnson, 399 A.2d 469 (R.I. 1979)
State v. Sexton, 904 A.2d 1092 (Vt. 2006)
Model Penal Code §§ 2.08, 4.01 & Explanatory Note, 4.02 (Official Code and Revised Comments 1985)

ESSAY

Intoxication fails to provide a defense to either charge. Diminished capacity possibly mitigates Mick's liability for murder to manslaughter for both charges. Insanity possibly supplies a defense in some jurisdictions for Brennan's murder and possibly supplies a defense in all jurisdictions for Ned's murder.

Murder of Brennan

INTOXICATION

Common Law

[1] Under the common law, intoxication may provide a defense either by negating mens rea, negating the voluntary act element, or by providing evidence supporting insanity. There is no evidence in the facts that Mick's intoxication caused him to act involuntarily. There is also no evidence of insanity or mental disease brought on by long-term alcohol abuse.

[2] With respect to a specific intent offense, both voluntary and involuntary intoxication may negate the mens rea. Here, Mick's intoxication fails to negate the mens rea of the offense charged. Despite being intoxicated, Mick intentionally and knowingly killed a human being—Brennan.

Model Penal Code

[3] Under the MPC, intoxication may exculpate either by negating the mens rea, negating the voluntary act element, or serving as an affirmative defense. As discussed above in [1]–[2], Mick's intoxication neither negates the mens rea nor the voluntary act element. Intoxication is an affirmative defense when there is evidence of (i) either pathological intoxication or involuntary intoxication and (ii) the actor's insanity. That is, in order to satisfy the defense, both (i) and (ii) must be satisfied. Here, there is no evidence in the facts establishing element (i). As a result, Mick will not be able to successfully raise intoxication as a defense.

DIMINISHED CAPACITY

Common Law

[4] Diminished capacity is generally defined as a mental abnormality not rising to the level of insanity. Diminished capacity serves as a defense either by negating mens rea or by mitigating murder to manslaughter. As a mitigation, diminished capacity (more precisely termed "diminished responsibility" or "partial responsibility") is only recognized in a small number of states. The defense requires that the actor suffer from a mental abnormality that need not rise to the level of that which suffices for insanity. And this mental abnormality must cause the actor to be unaware that his conduct is unlawful or render him unable to conform his conduct to the law. In its mens rea negating form, some jurisdictions recognize it for all offenses, some jurisdictions limit it to specific intent offenses, and some jurisdictions decline to recognize it for any offense. Here, Mick's STML plausibly qualifies as the requisite "mental abnormality" sufficing for diminished capacity.

[5] Mick's diminished capacity, however, fails to negate the requisite mens rea. Despite the mental abnormality of his STML, he intentionally and knowingly killed a human being—Brennan. As a result, Mick's diminished capacity fails to provide a defense by negating the mens rea.

[6] Mick's STML might qualify him for the "partial responsibility" form of diminished capacity. Due to his STML, he was mistaken about his home and his wife which, in turn, caused him to act from uncontrollable rage. Therefore, Mick's STML caused him to be unable to conform his conduct to the law. Although only recognized in a few states, Mick would possibly satisfy this defense which would mitigate his liability for murder of Brennan to manslaughter.

Model Penal Code

[7] The MPC recognizes diminished capacity as a defense. It serves as a defense either by negating mens rea or by mitigating murder to manslaughter. In its mens rea negating form, an actor's mental disease or defect may negate the mens rea for any offense. Here, Mick's STML plausibly qualifies as the requisite "mental disease or defect." However, it fails to negate the requisite mens rea. Despite the mental disease or defect of his STML, he intentionally and knowingly killed a human being, Brennan. As a result, Mick's diminished capacity in the form of a mental disease or defect fails to negate the mens rea and thus fails to provide a defense.

In its capacity as a mitigation defense, diminished capacity serves to reduce an actor's liability from murder to manslaughter. The standard is whether the homicide was the result of an "extreme mental or emotional disturbance for which there is a reasonable explanation or excuse" (EMED). This is an expanded version of the common law's provocation defense. (For a discussion of provocation and EMED, see Ch. 7.) The requisite reasonable explanation or excuse is assessed by one in the actor's situation believing what the actor believes. Given that Mick believed (due to his medically diagnosed STML) that he was in his own home, and his wife was engaging in intercourse with another man, his emotional disturbance of extreme rage was reasonable. As a result, Mick would most likely obtain the EMED defense, reducing his liability from murder to manslaughter.

Common Law

[8] The vast majority of states recognize an insanity defense. Apart from the MPC test, there are four principal tests: the *M'Naghten* test, the Irresistible Impulse test (perhaps the test is better understood as a supplement to the *M'Naghten* test rather than as a standalone test), the Product test, and the Federal test (applicable in all federal jurisdictions). A slim majority of states apply the *M'Naghten* test either in full or in part. Only a few states apply the Irresistible Impulse test, and only one state applies the Product test.

Each test requires the actor to have a mental disease. This requirement is typically neither defined nor explained by courts. However, there have been a few attempts to explain the term. For example, any mental abnormality significantly affecting mental or emotional processes and significantly impairing volition; significant impairment of cognitive or volitional capacity; and, any mental abnormality that suffices to cause the requisite impairment of either cognitive or volitional capacity provided by the particular test for the insanity defense. Here, Mick arguably had a mental disease—the STML disorder. By not being able to remember anything that occurred within the last 12 months, his cognitive capacity is significantly impaired. His mental processing and perception of reality and the world around him is distorted by his inability to recall recent events.

[9] Under the **M'Naghten** test, an actor is insane if at the time of the crime the following elements are satisfied: (i) the actor has a mental disease, and either (ii) he did not know the nature and quality of his act, or (iii) he did not know that his conduct was wrong, and (iv) the mental disease caused either (ii) or (iii). *M'Naghten's Case*, 8 Eng. Rep. 718 (H.L. 1843). (That is, in order to obtain the insanity defense, an actor has to satisfy (i) and (iv) and either (ii) or (iii).) The *M'Naghten* test is understood as a cognitive-impairment-based test for insanity. It formally requires *total* cognitive incapacity rather than a sufficient *degree* of cognitive incapacity. This total incapacity requirement has been criticised as unrealistic because it would exclude many "truly" insane persons because they know what they are doing or they know right from wrong to some extent or degree.

[10] Element (ii) is best understood as the actor lacking knowledge of the physical nature and physical consequences of her conduct. For example, if an actor thinks that she is slicing a tomato with a knife but in fact is slashing a human being then she does not know the nature and quality of her act. But if she is aware that she is slashing a human being and aware that this will cause physical harm to the human being, then she does know the nature and quality of her act. Mick does not satisfy element (ii). He understood the physical nature, quality, and consequences of his action. He understood that he was killing a human being.

As to element (iii), courts are split as to whether to construe the term "wrong" to mean legally wrong or morally wrong. In jurisdictions construing the term to mean legally wrong, Mick would not satisfy the element. The facts state that he did know that his conduct constituted a crime. In jurisdictions construing the term to mean a moral wrong, Mick could argue that he did not know that what he was doing was morally wrong. Rather, as the facts state, Mick believed that what he was doing was morally right in defending what he believed to be his marriage. Mick's argument, however, would not succeed. The issue is not whether an actor personally knows that his conduct is morally right or wrong, but whether the actor knows that society finds his conduct morally right or wrong. Because the facts state that Mick knew that society would find his conduct morally wrong, he would fail to satisfy element (iii).

Satisfaction of element (iv)—that the mental disease caused (ii) or (iii)—necessarily requires satisfaction of either (ii) or (iii). Because Mick satisfied neither (ii) nor (iii), as discussed above in [9], Mick cannot satisfy the fourth element.

[11] Although Mick possibly satisfies element (i), he fails to satisfy (ii)–(iv). As a result, Mick fails to satisfy the *M'Naghten* test for the insanity defense.

[12] The **Irresistible Impulse test** adds an additional element to the *M'Naghten* test—if the actor acted from an irresistible and uncontrollable impulse. This supplements the *M'Naghten* cognitive-based-impairment test with a volitional-based-impairment element. This additional element need not be satisfied in order for an actor to obtain the insanity defense. It merely provides an additional basis to obtain the defense. Generally speaking, an actor satisfies this element if she is unable to control her conduct. As the element is sometimes explained, it is sufficient (but not necessary) to satisfy the element if the actor would have committed the crime even if a police officer was standing next to him. While total volitional incapacity suffices, as in the example above, and traditionally some courts required it, today most courts do not require total volitional incapacity. The elements of the Irresistible Impulse Test (when coupled with the *M'Naghten* test) are as follows: (i) the actor has a mental disease, and either (ii) he did not know the nature and quality of the act, or (iii) he did not know that his conduct was wrong, or (iv) he acted from an irresistible and uncontrollable impulse, and (v) the mental disease caused either (ii), (iii), or (iv). (That is, in order to obtain the insanity defense, the actor must satisfy (i) and (v) and either (ii), (iii), or (iv).)

As discussed above in [8]-[10], Mick's STML is arguably a mental disease or defect satisfying element (i), but Mick neither satisfies element (ii) nor (iii). However, Mick does arguably satisfy element (iv). As the facts state, he was "[u]nable to control his inflamed passion and rage." Unable to control his anger, he most likely killed Brennan under an irresistible and uncontrollable impulse.

It is less clear whether Mick satisfies element (v)—that his STML caused him to act from an irresistible and uncontrollable impulse. The STML is a but-for cause of his irresistible impulse. As a result of the STML, Mick believes that his wife is engaging in adulterous intercourse with another man in Mick's home, which gives rise to his uncontrollable urge to kill Brennan. But for the STML, he would not have believed that his wife's house was still his, he would not have been in his wife's house, he would not have seen his wife engaging in intercourse with another man, he would not have believed his wife was engaging in adultery, and he would not have been "unable to control his inflamed passion and rage," and he would not have killed Brennan.

It is unclear, however, whether but-for causation suffices. The precise nature of the causal link between the mental disease and the cognitive or volitional incapacity is rarely specified. As to this issue, authorities are sparse, ambiguous, and conflicted. Thus it is not entirely clear whether but-for causation suffices or whether some further causal relationship is required. And even if some further causation is required, whether it would be proximate causation and what the specific test would be remains unclear.

Assuming that proximate causation is required, Mick's STML may fail to qualify. Arguably, the provocation (of Mick seeing what he believed was his wife engaging in adultery) was an intervening event precluding the STML from being the proximate cause. The provocation is an intervening event because it occurs after Mick's mental disease and prior to his volitional incapacity. Although not all intervening events are proximate causes, even assuming that the provocation is a proximate cause of Mick's volitional incapacity does not preclude Mick's mental disease from also being a proximate cause. (One result may have multiple proximate causes. See Ch. 5.)

Depending on the nature of the requisite causal link between the mental disease and the volitional incapacity, and the precise test a court adopts to assess that causal link, Mick possibly satisfies the causal element. If but-for causation suffices, Mick clearly satisfies element (v). If some further causal link is required—for example, proximate causation—either the provocation is the proximate cause or, possibly, both the mental disease and the provocation are proximate causes.

[13] By possibly satisfying elements (i), (iv), and (v), Mick possibly satisfies the Irresistible Impulse test for the insanity defense.

[14] The **Product test** is recognized in only one state—New Hampshire. Under this test, an actor is insane if her criminal offense was the product of a mental disease or defect. The mental disease must be a but-for cause of the actor's commission of the crime. The test was designed to give the jury greater discretion in determining whether the mental disease caused the criminal conduct. The Product test differs from the other tests for insanity in three ways. First, the other tests require causation between the mental disease and a cognitive or volitional incapacity. In contrast, the Product test requires causation between the mental disease and the crime. Second, under the other tests, something more than but-for causation may be required (See [12]). In contrast, the Product test explicitly requires only but-for causation. Third, the other tests require either cognitive or volitional incapacity. In contrast, the Product test requires neither.

Arguably, a reasonable jury could find that Mick's STML caused him to kill Brennan. As discussed above in [12], Mick's STML is most likely a but-for cause of his killing Brennan. Therefore, Mick possibly satisfies the Product test.

[15] The **Federal test** for insanity requires the following elements: (i) the actor has a severe mental disease or defect, and either (ii) he was unable to appreciate the nature and quality of the act, or (iii) he was unable to appreciate that his conduct was wrong, and (iv) the mental disease caused either (ii) or (iii). (That is, in order to obtain the insanity defense, the actor must satisfy (i) and (iv) and either (ii) or (iii).) Like the *M'Naghten* test, the Federal test is a cognitive-impairment-based test. But there are two principal differences. First, whereas the *M'Naghten* test requires there be a mental disease or defect, the Federal test requires that the mental disease or defect be *severe*. Second, while the *M'Naghten* test requires *lack of knowledge*, the Federal test requires an *inability to appreciate*, which suggests a broader test than *M'Naghten*.

[16] Mick fails to satisfy the Federal test. True, his STML is arguably a mental disease or defect, and probably one that it is severe. But as discussed above in [10], Mick satisfies neither element (ii) nor (iii), and thereby fails to satisfy element (iv).

Model Penal Code

[17] A substantial minority of states follow the **MPC test**. Under this test, an actor obtains the insanity defense if, at the time of the commission of the offense, the actor: (i) has a mental disease or defect, and either (ii) lacks substantial capacity to appreciate the legal (or, at the legislature's discretion, moral) wrongfulness of the conduct, or (iii) lacks substantial capacity to conform her conduct to the requirements of the law, and (iv) the mental disease or defect causes (ii) or (iii). (That is, in order to obtain the insanity defense, an actor must satisfy (i) and (iv) and either (ii) or (iii).) There are a number of differences between the MPC test and the other tests. First, unlike the *M'Naghten* and Federal tests, the MPC test includes both cognitive and volitional impairment elements. Second, unlike the *M'Naghten* test, the requisite incapacity need not be total but merely substantial. Third, unlike the *M'Naghten* test (but like the Federal test), the MPC test merely requires that the actor not *appreciate* that her conduct was wrong rather than not *know* that her conduct was wrong. In each of these three respects, the MPC test is broader.

As discussed above in [8] and [10], Mick arguably satisfies element (i) but fails to satisfy (ii). Mick possibly satisfies element (iii) because, as the facts state, he was "[u]nable to control his inflamed passion and rage." This uncontrollable passion and rage arguably robbed Mick of the substantial capacity to conform his conduct to the law. And as discussed above in [12], the STML is a but-for cause of his inability to conform his conduct to the law. However, as discussed above in [12], it is unclear whether mere but-for causation is sufficient to satisfy element (iv).

[18] By possibly satisfying elements (i), (iii), and (iv), Mick possibly satisfies the MPC test for insanity.

Murder of Ned

INTOXICATION

[19] For the reasons discussed above in [1]–[3], Mick's intoxication will not provide a defense to the charge of murdering Ned under either the common law or the MPC.

DIMINISHED CAPACITY

Common Law

[20] As discussed above in [4], Mick's STML plausibly qualifies as the requisite "mental abnormality" for diminished capacity. However, as discussed above in [5], Mick's diminished capacity fails to negate the requisite mens rea. Despite the mental abnormality of his STML, he intentionally and knowingly killed Ned. As a result, Mick's diminished capacity fails to provide a defense by negating the mens rea. As discussed above in [6], in its mitigation form, Mick's diminished capacity may reduce his liability for murder to manslaughter.

Model Penal Code

[21] In its mens rea negating form, as discussed above in [7], Mick's STML fails to negate the requisite mens rea of the murder offense and thus fails to provide a defense. In its mitigation form, mitigating murder to manslaughter, the standard is whether the homicide was the result of an "extreme mental or emotional disturbance for which there is a reasonable explanation or excuse." It is not entirely

clear how this provision should be applied here because how EMED applies to non-emotional, purely mental disturbances is unclear. Most cases involving EMED are applied to non-mental, purely emotional disturbances involving extreme rage, fear, or grief. While Mick killed Brennan under the purely emotional, non-mental, disturbance of extreme rage (as discussed in [7]), Mick's killing of Ned occurs while he is under a non-emotional, purely mental disturbance.

One might argue that Mick should obtain the defense. His extreme mental disturbance was his delusion that he was protecting his own home from a strange and unlawful intruder whom he could lawfully kill. His STML disorder constitutes a reasonable explanation for his extreme mental disturbance of suffering delusions. On this basis, Mick would obtain the EMED defense, thereby reducing his liability from murder to manslaughter.

One might object, however, that Mick should not obtain the defense. Granted, his STML disorder could constitute a reasonable explanation for an extreme mental or emotional disturbance—if only he had one. But Mick does not. Mick's delusion does not constitute an extreme mental or emotional disturbance for two reasons. First, Mick's disturbance did not involve the sort of disturbances—rage, fear, grief, etc.—which are widely recognized as extreme mental or emotional disturbances. Second, "delusions" is nothing more than a fancy and vaguely medical-sounding term for a plain mistake of fact. Mistakes of fact are not extreme mental or emotional disturbances.

Because it is unclear whether Mick's delusion/mistake of fact qualifies as an extreme mental or emotional disturbance, Mick only possibly satisfies this defense.

INSANITY
Common Law
[22] Under the **M'Naghten** test, an actor is insane if at the time of the crime the following elements are satisfied: (i) the actor has a mental disease, and either (ii) he did not know the nature and quality of the act, or (iii) he did not know that his conduct was wrong, and (iv) the mental disease caused either (ii) or (iii). As discussed above in [8], Mick arguably satisfies element (i). As discussed above in [10], he fails to satisfy element (ii) because he understood that he was killing a human being. Mick arguably satisfies element (iii) because he neither knew that his conduct was wrong nor realized that society would find his conduct wrong. Mick believed that killing Ned was both morally and legally permissible.

One might argue, however, that the *M'Naghten* test formally and technically requires a total lack of cognition. Mick does not totally lack cognition. While he is out of touch with the reality of the last 12 months, he is not completely out of touch with reality. As a result, under this absolutist account Mick would not obtain the insanity defense.

As a practical matter, however, it is unlikely that such an absolutist account would be applied. As a result, Mick possibly satisfies element (iii).

Mick arguably satisfies the fourth element—that the mental disease caused (iii). As a result of his STML disorder, he was mistaken about his house and Ned. Due to those mistakes, he did not realize that it was wrong to shoot Ned. Therefore, as a result of his STML, he did not realize that it was wrong to shoot Ned. That is, the STML was a but-for cause of Mick's not knowing that shooting Ned was wrong.

However, as discussed in [12] above, it is not clear whether but-for causation suffices.

Assuming that proximate causation is required between the mental disease and the cognitive incapacity, Mick's STML is possibly the proximate cause of his cognitive incapacity. Mick's STML is comparatively more likely the proximate cause with respect to his killing of Ned than with respect to his killing of Brennan. As discussed above in [12], with respect to Mick's killing of Brennan, the provocation was an intervening event between the mental disease and the volitional incapacity and thus the provocation was an attractive candidate for the proximate cause of his volitional incapacity. In contrast, with respect to his killing of Ned, there is no intervening event between the mental disease and the cognitive incapacity. Without such an intervening event there is no other candidate to be the proximate cause of his cognitive incapacity. Therefore, the mental disease is possibly both the but-for cause and the proximate cause of the cognitive incapacity.

Depending on the requisite nature of the causal relationship between the mental disease and the cognitive incapacity, Mick either clearly or possibly satisfies element (iv). If the requisite causal link is but-for causation, Mick clearly satisfies element (iv), but if the requisite causal link is proximate causation, then Mick only possibly satisfies element (iv).

[23] By possibly satisfying elements (i), (iii), and (iv), Mick possibly satisfies the *M'Naghten* test for the insanity defense.

[24] The elements of the **Irresistible Impulse test** are as follows: (i) the actor has a mental disease, and either (ii) he did not know the nature and quality of the act, or (iii) he did not know that his conduct was wrong, or (iv) he acted from an irresistible and uncontrollable impulse, and (v) the mental disease caused either (ii), (iii), or (iv). The Irresistible Impulse test broadens the *M'Naghten* test by adding an additional element, but this element need not be satisfied. (In fact, Mick does not satisfy this added element. Mick lacks an irresistible and uncontrollable impulse.) Because of the relationship between the *M'Naghten* test and the Irresistible Impulse test, satisfaction of the *M'Naghten* test necessarily entails satisfaction of the Irresistible Impulse test. Because Mick possibly satisfies the *M'Naghten* test, he possibly satisfies elements (i), (iii), and (v), thereby possibly satisfying the Irresistible Impulse test for the insanity defense.

[25] As discussed above in [14], Mick possibly satisfies the **Product test**. His killing of Ned was the product of his STML mental disease; Mick's STML is the but-for cause of his killing Ned.

[26] The **Federal test** for insanity requires the following elements: (i) the actor has a severe mental disease, and either (ii) he was unable to appreciate the nature and quality of the act, or (iii) he was unable to appreciate that his conduct was wrong, and (iv) the mental disease caused either (ii) or (iii). As discussed above in [16], Mick possibly satisfies element (i). As discussed above in [22], Mick fails to satisfy element (ii), possibly satisfies element (iii), and possibly satisfies element (iv). As a result, he possibly satisfies the Federal test for the insanity defense.

Model Penal Code
[27] An actor obtains the insanity defense if, at the time of the commission of the offense, the actor: (i) has a mental disease, and either (ii) lacks substantial capacity

to appreciate the legal (or, at the discretion of the legislature, moral) wrongfulness of the conduct, or (iii) lacks substantial capacity to conform his or her conduct to the requirements of the law, and (iv) the mental disease causes (ii) or (iii). As discussed above in [8], Mick possibly satisfies element (i). He arguably satisfies element (ii) because he both believes his conduct to be morally and legally permissible and believes that society regards his conduct as morally and legally permissible. He fails to satisfy element (iii) because he was able to control his conduct. And as discussed above in [22], Mick possibly satisfies element (iv). An Explanatory Note to the MPC's insanity provision provides further support for Mick's satisfaction of the causal link in element (iv). It states that "[a]n individual's failure to appreciate the criminality of his conduct may consist in . . . a misapprehension of material circumstances." MPC § 4.01, Explanatory Note. Mick's failure to appreciate the criminality of his conduct consisted in his misapprehension of the following material circumstances: (i) he was not a lawful occupant and thus was ineligible to use deadly force against an unlawful intruder and (ii) Ned was not an unlawful intruder.

By possibly satisfying elements (i), (ii), and (iv), Mick possibly satisfies the MPC test for insanity.

Conclusion

Murder of Brennan: Under both the common law and the MPC, intoxication fails to provide a defense. Diminished capacity, in its mens rea negating form, fails to provide a defense under either the common law or the MPC. In its mitigation form, it possibly provides a defense under the common law and most likely provides a defense under the MPC. With respect to the insanity defense, Mick possibly satisfies the Irresistible Impulse test, the Product test, and the MPC test. He fails to satisfy the *M'Naghten* and Federal tests.

Murder of Ned: Under both the common law and the MPC, intoxication fails to provide a defense. Diminished capacity, in its mens rea negating form, fails to provide a defense under either the common law or the MPC. In its mitigation form, it possibly provides a defense under both the common law and the MPC. With respect to the insanity defense, Mick possibly satisfies all five tests.

TOOLS FOR SELF-ASSESSMENT

Go back to your written answer. Look for the issues identified in paragraphs numbered [1]–[27] above. Look also for the analysis that follows each issue, and mark your essay where you locate it. Do you fully describe the issue, identify the precise legal standard that applies, list the relevant facts, and show how the facts and law support a conclusion for each issue? Mark each conclusion in your essay. Are there sufficient reasons in the law and in the facts to support each conclusion?

1.   Do what you are told. Here, you are to analyze the possible mental impairment defenses of intoxication, diminished capacity, and insanity.

2.   Do not analyze what is unnecessary. You need not analyze any other crimes that Mick may have committed apart from the two murder charges. For example, do not analyze whether he committed breaking and entering or burglary or whether he illegally possessed a gun.

3. Always analyze under the MPC as well as the common law unless you are instructed otherwise.

4. State the best possible arguments for alternative conclusions. For example, if you determine that Mick does not satisfy the elements of the Irresistible Impulse test, make sure you make the best case for why he might satisfy the test.

5. There are numerous ways to organize your answer. Set out below is the organizational structure of the above Essay as well as possible alternative organizational structures. There is no single organizational structure that is always preferable for all hypotheticals involving mental impairment defenses. But there are advantages and disadvantages depending on the hypothetical and the instructions as to how to analyze the hypothetical. Appreciating the various possible organizational structures that you might employ for any given hypothetical or exam question will be of tremendous aid in selecting, if not the optimal organizational structure, then at least a preferable one. Having a good organizational structure will not only help clarify your analysis but will also save you time. It is very important to have a sense of the possible organizational structures that you might employ before you walk into an exam. You do not want to waste valuable time during the exam grappling with how to organize it.

Structure #1 depicts the organizational structure of the above Essay and Structures #2 and #3 depict alternatives:

Structure #1	Structure #2	Structure #3
Introduction	Introduction	Introduction
Murder of Brennan	Intoxication	Common Law
Intoxication	Common Law	Murder of Brennan
Common Law	Murder of Brennan	Intoxication
Model Penal Code	Murder of Ned	Diminished Capacity
Diminished Capacity	Model Penal Code	Insanity
Common Law	Murder of Brennan	Murder of Ned
Model Penal Code	Murder of Ned	Intoxication
Insanity	Diminished Capacity	Diminished Capacity
Common Law	Common Law	Insanity
Model Penal Code	Murder of Brennan	Model Penal Code
Murder of Ned	Murder of Ned	Murder of Brennan
Intoxication	Model Penal Code	Intoxication
Common Law	Murder of Brennan	Diminished Capacity
Model Penal Code	Murder of Ned	Insanity
Diminished Capacity	Insanity	Murder of Ned
Common Law	Common Law	Intoxication
Model Penal Code	Murder of Brennan	Diminished Capacity
Insanity	Murder of Ned	Insanity
Common Law	Model Penal Code	Conclusion
Model Penal Code	Murder of Brennan	
Conclusion	Murder of Ned	
	Conclusion	

Structure #1 (depicting the above Essay) is organized by the charged offense—the murder of Brennan and the murder of Ned. Within each charge, each possibly applicable defense is analyzed first under the common law and then under the MPC. This structure probably would be most effective for hypotheticals containing numerous offenses. Structure #2 is primarily organized by possibly applicable defenses. Each defense is then analyzed under the common law and the MPC. This structure may be the most efficient when faced with a large number of possibly applicable defenses and only a few offenses. Structure #3 is primarily organized by the distinction between the common law and the MPC. This structure is likely the most laborious and the least efficient. Of course, there are many possible organizational structures, but the three above should give you a sense of the possibilities.

6. Do not be confused by the causation element of the various insanity tests. In general, the insanity defense perhaps presupposes a causal link between the mental disease and the commission of the crime. But in all of the tests except the Product test, the requisite causal link is literally between the mental disease and one of the following elements: (i) not knowing or appreciating what was done, (ii) not knowing or appreciating that what was done was wrong, or (iii) not having the capacity to exercise control. That is, the requisite causal link is *not* between the mental disease and the crime. In the Product test, however, the requisite causal link is between the mental disease and the commission of the crime.

7. Do not be misled by the banality of the actor's mistakes. Intuitively you might find that Mick cannot possibly be insane because he is not under a delusion regarding God, devils, or space aliens. Instead, Mick's mistakes are less exotic. But because they are the result of his STML mental disease, they may still qualify as the basis for an insanity defense.

8. Keep in mind the various meanings of "wrong." For example, under the *M'Naghten* test, one of the elements is that the actor not know that her conduct is wrong. Jurisdictions are split as to whether this means legally wrong or morally wrong. Even in those jurisdictions interpreting it to mean morally wrong, an actor's personal belief that her conduct was not morally wrong does not suffice. If an actor personally believes that her conduct is morally permissible but is aware that society in general would regard her conduct as morally wrong, then she does not qualify as insane. An exception to this rule is recognized by some jurisdictions—the actor believed that God directly commanded her to commit the crime. This is sometimes referred to as the deific decree doctrine. However, if the actor believes that God merely approves of the conduct, then the exception is inapplicable.

9. Did you make the mistake of analyzing an exculpatory mistake of fact defense or a justification defense based on a mistake of fact? Although it may be tempting, the instructions clearly limit your analysis to the mental impairment defenses. In any event, neither a mistake of fact nor a justification defense entirely precludes Mick's liability. With respect to the charge of murdering Brennan, Mick has made two mistakes of fact—whether he is in his own house and whether he is still married to Velma. However, neither of these mistakes negates the requisite mens rea of murder. Despite his mistakes, he was entirely

aware that he was killing a human being. As a result, a simple mistake of fact defense will not succeed.

With respect to the charge of murdering Ned, Mick has made two relevant mistakes of fact: whether he is in his own house and whether Ned is an unlawful intruder who Mick may justifiably kill. However, neither of these mistakes negates the requisite mens rea of murder. Despite his mistakes, he was entirely aware that he was killing a human being. These mistakes also fail to support a full justification defense as the facts of the Problem state.

10. Do not be confused by the overlapping and intertwining relationship between intoxication and insanity. What makes this relationship confusing is that sometimes evidence of intoxication is used to prove the defense of insanity, and sometimes evidence of insanity is used to prove the defense of intoxication. For example, under the common law, evidence of long-term alcohol or drug abuse may be used to show that the defendant suffers from a substance-induced mental disorder and that this disorder persists even when the actor is not intoxicated. Evidence of this condition may be used to establish a traditional insanity defense. Conversely, evidence of insanity can be used to establish the defense of intoxication. For example, under the MPC, evidence that the actor qualifies under the MPC's test of insanity coupled with either evidence of involuntary intoxication or pathological intoxication establishes the affirmative defense of intoxication (*not insanity*). That is, evidence of insanity, in part, establishes the distinct affirmative defense of intoxication. (Why, you might ask yourself, if one has already established insanity, would an actor assert the seemingly superfluous defense of intoxication? While both defenses may result in an acquittal, the defense of intoxication avoids indefinite civil commitment.)

11. The following steps reveal the analysis of the applicability of each of the three defenses under the common law and the MPC to any offense. These steps are somewhat oversimplified so as to provide a better view of the forest without the obstruction of the trees. But this should neither be mistaken for nor taken as a substitute for in-depth knowledge of the trees. While these steps are specifically suited to answer this particular hypothetical, this general structure with perhaps some modification might be useful to analyze any fact pattern involving any of the three mental impairment defenses.

Intoxication–Common Law

    i.   Is the intoxication voluntary or involuntary?

    ii.   If involuntary, then go to xviii.

    iii.   If voluntary, was the actor unconscious?

    iv.   If no, then the intoxication does not negate the voluntary act requirement.

    v.   If yes, did the actor commit an act (voluntary or involuntary)?

    vi.   If no, the voluntary act requirement is negated.

    vii.   If yes, was the defendant charged with a specific intent offense?

    viii.   If no, then intoxication fails to negate the voluntary act element.

    ix.   If yes, then intoxication may negate the voluntary act element.

    x.   As to voluntary intoxication causing insanity, does the intoxication cause temporary or fixed insanity?

xi.   If temporary, there is no defense.

xii. If fixed, it may support an insanity defense.

xiii. As to voluntary intoxication possibly negating the mens rea, is the actor charged with a specific intent offense?

xiv. If no, the intoxication is no defense.

xv.   If yes, does the intoxication negate the requisite mens rea?

xvi. If no, then intoxication is no defense.

xvii. If yes, intoxication is a defense.

xviii. If the intoxication is involuntary, was the actor unconscious?

xix. If yes, then the intoxication negates the voluntary act requirement.

xx.   If no, did the intoxication negate the requisite mens rea?

xxi. If yes, then intoxication is a defense.

xxii. If no, does the intoxication establish either temporary or fixed insanity?

xxiii. If no, then intoxication is no defense.

xxiv. If yes, then it may support an insanity defense.

Intoxication–Model Penal Code

i.   Did the intoxication render the actor unconscious at the time of the crime?

ii.   If yes, the intoxication may negate the voluntary act element.

iii. If no, was the intoxication pathological, and did the actor's condition qualify under the test for insanity?

iv.   If yes, then the intoxication provides an affirmative defense.

v.   If no, was the intoxication self-induced or not self-induced?

vi.   If not self-induced, go to xii.

vii. If self-induced, then was the actor charged with an offense with a mens rea greater than recklessness?

viii. If no, then intoxication is not a defense.

ix.   If yes, does the intoxication negate the requisite mens rea?

x.   If yes, then intoxication provides a defense.

xi.   If no, then intoxication does not provide a defense.

xii. If the intoxication is not self-induced, does the intoxication negate the requisite mens rea?

xiii. If yes, then intoxication is a defense.

xiv. If no, does the actor's condition qualify under the test for insanity?

xv.   If no, then intoxication is not a defense.

xvi. If yes, then intoxication is an affirmative defense.

Diminished Capacity–Common Law

i.   Did the actor have an abnormal mental condition at the time of the commission of the offense?

ii.   If no, then no diminished capacity defense.

iii. If yes, is the actor charged with a specific intent offense?

iv.   If yes, is the actor in a jurisdiction that recognizes the defense to both specific and general intent offenses, or in a jurisdiction recognizing the defense only for specific intent offenses or in a jurisdiction that declines to recognize it as negating mens rea?

  v. If in a jurisdiction declining to recognize it as negating mens rea, go to xvi.

  vi. If in a jurisdiction recognizing it only for specific intent, then has the actor been charged with a specific intent offense?

  vii. If no, go to xvi.

  viii. If yes, does the diminished capacity negate the specific intent mens rea?

  ix. If no, go to xvi.

  x. If yes, then diminished capacity is a defense.

  xi. If the actor is in a jurisdiction recognizing the defense for both specific and general intent offenses, is the defendant charged with a strict liability offense?

  xii. If yes, go to xvi.

  xiii. If no, does the mistake negate the requisite mens rea?

  xiv. If yes, then diminished capacity is a defense.

  xv. If no, go to xvi.

  xvi. Is the actor both charged with murder and in a jurisdiction recognizing diminished capacity as a mitigation?

  xvii. If no, then diminished capacity is not a defense.

  xviii. If yes, diminished capacity may be a mitigation defense reducing the charge of murder to manslaughter.

Diminished Capacity–Model Penal Code

  i. Is the actor charged with murder?

  ii. If no, EMED is inapplicable.

  iii. If yes, did the actor commit the homicide due to EMED?

  iv. If no, then no EMED defense.

  v. If yes, from the viewpoint of a person in the actor's situation under the facts as the actor believes them to be, is there a reasonable explanation or excuse for the EMED?

  vi. If no, then no EMED defense.

  vii. If yes, the EMED defense will mitigate murder to manslaughter.

Insanity–Common Law

The following step-by-step analysis deviates from the particular ordering of the steps in the above Essay in an effort to lay bare the reasoning steps in the simplest and most concise form. With perhaps some modification, it is well suited to use for the analysis of any hypothetical. The somewhat different ordering of these steps in the above Essay reflects the particular facts of the Problem, especially the increased emphasis on the causal link between the mental disease and the actor's inability to know or control his conduct.

  i. Was the actor at the time of the offense unable to appreciate the nature and quality of her conduct?

  ii. If yes, go to v.

  iii. If no, was the actor unable to appreciate the wrongfulness of her conduct?

  iv. If no, go to viii.

v.   If yes, was the inability caused by a severe mental disease or defect?

vi.   If yes, then the actor satisfies the **Federal test** for the insanity defense. Continue on to viii to determine whether the actor satisfies any other tests for insanity.

vii.   If no, go to viii.

viii.   At the time of her act, did the actor not know the nature and quality of the act?

ix.   If yes, then go to xii.

x.   If no, did the actor not know that her conduct was wrong?

xi.   If no, then go to xv.

xii.   If yes, was the failure to know caused by a mental disease?

xiii.   If yes, the actor satisfies both the *M'Naghten* test and the **Irresistible Impulse test** for the insanity defense. Continue on to xv.

xiv.   If no, go to xv.

xv.   Did the actor act from an irresistible and uncontrollable impulse?

xvi.   If no, go to xx.

xvii.   If yes, was the actor's impulse caused by a mental disease?

xviii.   If yes, then the actor satisfies the **Irresistible Impulse test** for the insanity defense. Continue on to xx.

xix.   If no, go to xx.

xx.   Was the actor's crime the product of a mental disease or defect?

xxi.   If yes, then the actor satisfies the **Product test** for the insanity defense. Continue on to the MPC test below (applied by a substantial minority of states).

xxii.   If no, then go to MPC test below.

Insanity–Model Penal Code

i.   Did the actor, at the time of the conduct, lack the substantial capacity to appreciate that her conduct was either legally or morally wrong?

ii.   If yes, go to v.

iii.   If no, did the actor lack substantial capacity to conform her conduct to the law?

iv.   If no, then the actor does not satisfy the MPC test for the insanity defense.

v.   If yes, was the actor's incapacity caused by a mental disease or defect?

vi.   If no, then the actor fails to satisfy the MPC test for the insanity defense.

vii.   If yes, then the actor does satisfy the MPC test for the insanity defense.

12. To avoid feeling overwhelmed and confused by the five different tests of insanity, appreciating the similarity of the tests is helpful. Four of the five tests use one or more of the following three criteria: (i) the actor did not know what he was doing; (ii) the actor did not know what he was doing was wrong; or (iii) the actor could not control doing it. Seeing these substantial similarities along with the minimal differences between the tests is best seen in the form below.

M'Naghten Test	Irresistible Impulse Test
1. Due to a mental disease	1. Due to a mental disease
2. did not know nature and quality of act, **or**	2. did not know nature and quality of act, **or**
3. that act was wrong	3. that act was wrong, **or**
	4. acted from irresistible or uncontrollable impulse

MPC Test	Federal Test
1. Due to a mental disease	1. Due to a **severe** mental disease
2. lacks substantial capacity to appreciate legal or moral wrongfulness of act, **or**	2. unable to appreciate nature and quality of act, **or**
3. conform her conduct to the law	3. that act was wrong

Product Test
1. As the product of a mental disease, the actor commits the crime.

VARIATIONS ON THE THEME

For the following variations, assume that all of the facts from the original Problem obtain except as noted.

1.   After shooting Ned, Mick throws his gun under the bed and hides in the closet.

2.   After shooting Ned, Mick runs out of the house and throws different parts of his gun into different garbage receptacles.

3.   Mick was not drinking at all that night.

4.   Mick is 50 years old and has been drinking heavily almost every night for the past 35 years.

5.   Rather than having STML, Mick was smoking marijuana which, unbeknownst to him, was laced with PCP, which caused him to hallucinate. The hallucinations then caused all of his mistaken beliefs.

6.   Rather than believing his wife was consensually engaging in intercourse with Brennan, Mick believes that his wife is being raped by Brennan.

7.   While he was drinking at a bar that night, someone slipped PCP into one of his drinks, which caused Mick to become delusional, which caused all of his mistaken beliefs.

8.   Rather than STML, Mick was taking very powerful prescription medication in accordance with his doctor's instructions that produced an unexpected side effect leading to all of his mistaken beliefs.

9.   Same as in 8 except that Mick was taking triple the dose suggested by his doctor.

10. Rather than STML, his memory loss was due to Alzheimer's.

11. Mick does not suffer from STML. But Mick was laboring under the belief that the house was a haven for terrorists, Satanists, and space aliens, so he set the house on fire killing both Velma and Brennan.

12. Mick does not suffer from STML. Mick knew that killing Brennan and Ned was legally wrong and that society would regard it as legally and morally wrong, but that God approved. Mick believed that God spoke to him and said, "I'll throw a party for you up in heaven if you kill Brennan and Ned."

13. Same as in 12 except that rather than approving and throwing a party for Mick, God commanded that Mick kill Brennan and Ned.

14. Mick did not kill Brennan under the influence of "inflamed passion and rage."

ADDITIONAL READINGS

JOSHUA DRESSLER, UNDERSTANDING CRIMINAL LAW 323–77 (5th ed. 2009)

GEORGE P. FLETCHER, RETHINKING CRIMINAL LAW 835–46 (1978)

MICHAEL S. MOORE, LAW AND PSYCHIATRY: RETHINKING THE RELATIONSHIP (1984)

Ken Levy & Walter Sinnott-Armstrong, *Insanity Defenses, in* OXFORD HANDBOOK ON THE PHILOSOPHY OF THE CRIMINAL LAW (John Deigh & David Dolinko eds., 2011)

Stephen J. Morse, *Diminished Capacity, in* ACTION AND VALUE IN CRIMINAL LAW 239 (Steven Shute, John Gardner & Jeremy Horder eds., 1993)

Christopher Slobogin, *Abolition of the Insanity Defense, in* CRIMINAL LAW CONVERSATIONS 473–91 (Paul H. Robinson, Stephen P. Garvey & Kimberly Kessler Ferzan eds., 2009) (with comments by Susan D. Rozelle, Sherry F. Colb, Paul Litton & Matt Matravers)

Douglas N. Husak, *Addiction and Criminal Liability* 18 LAW & PHIL. 655 (1999)

Arnold Loewy, *The Two Faces of Insanity*, 42 TEXAS TECH. LAW REV. 513 (2009)

Stephen J. Morse & Morris B. Hoffman, *The Uneasy Entente Between Legal Insanity and Mens Rea: Beyond Clark v. Arizona*, 97 J. CRIMINAL LAW & CRIMINOLOGY 1071 (2007)

Christopher Slobogin, *The Integrationist Alternative to the Insanity Defense: Reflections on the Exculpatory Scope of Mental Illness in the Wake of the Andrea Yates Trial*, 30 AM. J. CRIM. L. 315 (2003)

Peter Westen, *The Supreme Court's Bout with Insanity: Clark v. Arizona*, 4 OHIO ST. J. CRIM. L. 143 (2006)

14

BURDEN OF PROOF

INTRODUCTION

Depending on the issue, the criminal law assigns the responsibility to either the prosecution or the defendant for establishing the relevant facts in a criminal trial with sufficient certainty and persuading the jury (or fact-finder) as to those facts. Whichever party bears this responsibility has the burden of proving the fact(s) or establishing the issue. The burden of proof consists of two components: the burden of production of evidence and the burden of persuasion.

Satisfaction of the burden of production on an issue triggers the allocation of the burden of persuasion; if the burden of production is not satisfied, there is no burden of persuasion. The trial judge determines, as a matter of law, whether a party has presented sufficient evidence to satisfy a burden of production of evidence. Failure to satisfy this burden will prevent the jury/fact-finder from being allowed to deliberate on that issue. Once the burden of production on an issue has been satisfied, the issue is considered properly before the jury/fact-finder. During deliberations, the jury/fact-finder will determine which party prevails on an issue by determining whether the party assigned the burden of persuasion has proved the facts with the requisite degree of certainty.

With respect to any given issue, a single party might incur both burdens, or each party might shoulder different burdens. Although the rules determining which party—the prosecution or the defendant—bears which burden concerning which issues varies by jurisdiction, the Due Process clause of the U.S. Constitution imposes some constraints on the nature, degree, and allocation of the burden. The Constitution merely provides a floor or minimum level of due process that a jurisdiction must afford to a defendant. But jurisdictions are free to, and many do, provide greater due process rights to defendants than the Constitution requires.

All jurisdictions, the MPC, and the Constitution clearly require the prosecution to prove the defendant's guilt. That is, the defendant is presumed innocent unless and until the prosecution proves the defendant's guilt beyond a reasonable doubt. But what constitutes the "guilt" that the prosecution must prove is less clear. At a minimum, the prosecution must bear the burdens of production and persuasion in proving every element of the offense. More complicated is the matter of defenses. The very standard for the burden of proof for a defense will generally vary depending on which party shoulders the burden. For example, if the prosecution bears the burden of persuasion on a defense, the prosecution must disprove it beyond a reasonable doubt. But if the defendant bears the burden of persuasion, generally the defendant only need prove it by the much lower evidentiary standard—by a preponderance of the evidence.

Which party bears the burden of proof on defenses is perhaps the most contentious and complicated issue. The answer may vary depending on the nature or type of defense, the relationship between the defense and the elements of the offense, the particular jury instructions, and the jurisdiction. The principal readings addressing this issue are four, sometimes conflicting and often confusing, Supreme Court opinions. But this chapter clarifies the confusing state of the law by breaking down the analysis of the burden of proof, particularly with respect to allocating the burden of persuasion for a wide variety of defenses, into a series of easy to understand steps. This step by step approach serves both as a chronological guide through the burden of proof issues as they arise in a criminal trial and a revealing view of the inner logic of the law of the burden of proof.

PROBLEM

Various defendants are charged with Murder in the following jurisdictions:

Jurisdiction A: Murder has the following elements:

1. Purposely, and with prior calculation and design
2. Causing the death of another

> In Jurisdiction A, the trial court specially instructs the jury that even if the defendant fails to satisfy the burden of persuasion on self-defense, the jury may still consider the defendant's evidence on self-defense in determining whether the prosecution has proved the defendant's guilt beyond a reasonable doubt.

Jurisdiction B: Murder has the following elements:

1. Purposely, and with prior calculation and design
2. Causing the death of another

Jurisdiction C: Murder has the following elements:

1. Unlawfully
2. Causing the death of another
3. With Intent to Kill

Jurisdiction D: Murder has the following elements:

1. With Purpose and Prior Calculation and Design
2. Causing the death of another
3. Unlawfully

Each defendant asserts the following defenses to their respective Murder charges:

1. Self-defense
2. Necessity
3. Duress
4. Provocation
5. Alibi
6. Statute of limitations

Analyze and discuss the application of the burden of proof to the prosecutions in each of these jurisdictions. In particular, analyze and discuss what the burden of proof entails with respect to each issue and which party—the prosecution or the defendant—bears the burden of proof on which issues. In addition, analyze and discuss whether it is constitutional or unconstitutional for each jurisdiction to allocate the burden of persuasion to the defendant for each defense. (Because no specific facts of the various defendants' conduct are specified, you should not address whether any of the parties can satisfy their respective burdens of proof.) You need not analyze under the MPC.

LIST OF READINGS

Martin v. Ohio, 480 U.S. 228 (1987)
Patterson v. New York, 432 U.S. 197 (1977)
Mullaney v. Wilbur, 421 U.S. 684 (1975)
In re Winship, 397 U.S. 358 (1970)

ESSAY

In each jurisdiction, the prosecution bears the burden of proof for proving each element of the offense and disproving some of the defenses, beyond a reasonable doubt. The defendant will bear the burden of proving at least one defense, probably by a preponderance of the evidence.

In all jurisdictions, the prosecution must bear the burden of persuasion for the defenses of necessity and alibi, but the defendant may bear it for statute of limitations. For the defenses of self-defense, duress, and provocation, the party bearing the burden of persuasion varies depending on the jurisdiction.

[1] In all four jurisdictions, the prosecution has the burden of proof in establishing the defendant's guilt beyond a reasonable doubt. According to *In re Winship*, a criminal defendant is presumed innocent under the Due Process clause of the U.S. Constitution unless and until the prosecution proves the defendant guilty beyond a reasonable doubt.

[2] The beyond a reasonable doubt standard is the highest standard of proof. It requires more proof than both the civil law standard of proof by a preponderance of the evidence and the heightened civil law standard of clear and convincing evidence. It requires a very high level of probability of guilt but somewhat less than 100 percent probability or absolute certainty of guilt. But exactly what numerical degree of probability is required is unclear.

In fact, the beyond a reasonable doubt standard is inherently nonquantitative. Courts' attempts to quantify the standard by assigning a specific level of probability—e.g., 80 percent or 90 percent—have been struck down as unconstitutionally diluting the standard. Rather, the standard is qualitative. While there have been various articulations of the standard, perhaps the clearest standard that passes constitutional muster is that a juror must have an abiding conviction or a settled and fixed conviction of the guilt of the defendant.

[3] Under *Winship*, in order to prove the defendant guilty beyond a reasonable doubt, the prosecution must prove "every fact necessary to constitute the crime charged." This means that the prosecution must prove, at the very least, each element of an offense charged. This burden of proof entails both the burden of

production and persuasion on proving each element of the offense. Though not addressed by *Winship*, the prosecution may also bear the burden of disproving a defense, as will be discussed below in [8]–[9].

[4] The prosecution has satisfied its burden of production of evidence if the trial judge rules, as a matter of law, that a rational juror could believe beyond a reasonable doubt that the defendant was guilty. If the judge rules that the prosecution has failed to satisfy this standard, the defendant is entitled to a directed verdict of acquittal. If the prosecution does satisfy the standard, the defendant is not entitled to a directed verdict, and the prosecution is entitled to have the jury (or fact-finder) deliberate on the case. During deliberations, the jury/fact-finder will determine if the prosecution has met its burden of persuasion in proving the elements of the offense. But before the case goes to the jury/fact-finder, the defendant is entitled to present a defense.

[5] Whether the prosecution or defendant bears the burden of proof regarding a defense depends on the type of defense and perhaps the particular elements of the offense and the particular jurisdiction.

[6] If the defendant has the burden of production on a defense, then the defendant must supply more than a mere scintilla of evidence but less than that which would make it more probable than not. Though the amount that suffices to satisfy the burden of production may vary by jurisdiction, it must be enough to make the defense claim just barely plausible. If the defendant fails to satisfy this burden, the defense will not be considered by the jury/fact-finder.

[7] The defendant's satisfaction of the burden of production on a defense will either result in the defendant also shouldering the burden of persuasion to prove the defense or the burden being allocated to the prosecution to disprove the defense.

[8] Of course, even if it is constitutionally permissible to allocate the burden of persuasion to a defendant for a particular defense, many states nonetheless allocate the burden of persuasion to the prosecution to disprove most affirmative defenses. For such states, the types of defenses for which the burden of persuasion is allocated to the prosecution are generally similar to the defenses on which *Mullaney* would bar allocating the burden of persuasion to the defendant. (See [10]–[11] below.) Other types of defenses include policy or extrinsic defenses such as Statute of Limitations. (Additional examples include diplomatic immunity, competency to stand trial, and, perhaps, entrapment.) The burden of persuasion for these policy defenses is generally borne by the defendant.

[9] If the defendant bears the burden of persuasion, it is constitutionally permissible for a jurisdiction to require that the defendant prove the defense beyond a reasonable doubt. But most jurisdictions only require a defendant to prove a defense by a preponderance of the evidence. If the prosecution bears the burden of persuasion on a defense, the prosecution must disprove it beyond a reasonable doubt.

Jurisdiction A

[10] In this jurisdiction, the burden of persuasion can be constitutionally allocated to the defendant for only some of the defenses.

[11] Under *Mullaney*, allocating the burden of persuasion to the defendant for the defenses of self-defense, necessity, duress, and provocation would be

unconstitutional. *Mullaney* held that it was unconstitutional to allocate the burden of persuasion to a defendant for a defense that satisfies the following criteria: (i) relates to the defendant's blameworthiness, (ii) affects the degree of punishment, and (iii) enjoys historical recognition in the Anglo-American legal tradition. The above four defenses satisfy the *Mullaney* criteria. Though not overruled, *Mullaney* has been largely supplanted by *Patterson*.

[12] Under *Patterson*, allocating the burden of persuasion to the defendant on these four defenses would probably also be unconstitutional. *Patterson* held that it is unconstitutional to allocate the burden of persuasion to a defendant for a defense that negates an element of the offense. Each of these defenses involves imminent threats and sudden situations that probably negate the element of prior calculation and design.

[13] *Martin v. Ohio* applies and extends the *Patterson* rule to a special situation. Under *Martin*, allocating the burden of persuasion to the defendant for the defense of self-defense where the defendant was charged with an offense containing the same elements as the offense in Jurisdiction A was upheld as constitutional. The constitutionality of the allocation hinged on the trial court's special instruction to the jury that it could consider the self-defense evidence even if the defendant failed to establish self-defense by a preponderance of the evidence. This special instruction effected only a partial, not a full, allocation of the burden of persuasion to the defendant. Because the trial court in Jurisdiction A gives the same jury instruction as in *Martin*, allocating the burden of persuasion on the defense of self-defense to the defendant would be constitutional under *Martin*.

[14] The burden of persuasion on the defense of alibi cannot be constitutionally allocated to the defendant. *Winship* and *Patterson* would bar the allocation because an alibi necessarily seeks to negate the elements of the offense by claiming the defendant did not commit the offense.

[15] The burden of persuasion on the defense of statute of limitations can be constitutionally allocated to the defendant. *Mullaney* would not bar the allocation because the defense fails to bear on blameworthiness. *Patterson* would not bar the allocation because the defense fails to negate an element of the offense.

[16] In conclusion, the burden of persuasion on the defenses of necessity, duress, provocation, and alibi probably cannot be constitutionally allocated to the defendant. It can be constitutionally allocated to the defendant for the defenses of self-defense and statute of limitations.

Jurisdiction B

[17] In this jurisdiction, the same analysis applies with respect to all the defenses except self-defense. Here, it would be unconstitutional to allocate the burden of persuasion to the defendant for the defense of self-defense.

[18] Unlike in Jurisdiction A, in Jurisdiction B there is no special jury instruction. Thus, *Martin* is inapplicable. Because self-defense would probably negate the element of prior calculation and design, *Patterson* would probably bar the allocation of the burden of persuasion to the defendant on the defense of self-defense.

[19] In conclusion, the burden of persuasion on the defenses of self-defense, necessity, duress, provocation, and alibi cannot be constitutionally allocated to the defendant. It can be constitutionally allocated to the defendant for the defense of statute of limitations.

Jurisdiction C

[20] As discussed above in [11] with respect to Jurisdiction A, under *Mullaney*, it would be unconstitutional to allocate the burden of persuasion to the defendant for the defenses of self-defense, necessity, duress, and provocation.

[21] Under *Patterson* as well, the defenses of self-defense and necessity cannot be constitutionally allocated to the defendant. Both are justification defenses. Justified conduct is lawful conduct. As a result, both self-defense and necessity would negate the element of the offense of unlawfulness, and thus the burden of persuasion on these defenses cannot be constitutionally allocated to the defendant (absent some special instruction to the jury as in *Martin*).

[22] But *Patterson* changes the analysis under *Mullaney* for the defenses of duress and provocation. Under *Patterson*, the burden of persuasion for these defenses can be constitutionally allocated to the defendant. Duress is an excuse defense. Though not subject to conviction and punishment, excused conduct is nonetheless unlawful conduct. Likewise, provoked conduct is unlawful conduct. Provocation is only a mitigation defense, mitigating murder to the lesser crime of voluntary manslaughter. As a result, neither duress nor provocation would negate the element of unlawfulness. Nor do they negate any other element of the offense. Because they fail to negate an element of the offense, the burden of persuasion on the defenses of duress and provocation can constitutionally be allocated to the defendant.

[23] The burden of persuasion on the defense of alibi cannot be constitutionally allocated to the defendant for the same reason as discussed above in [14].

[24] The burden of persuasion on the defense of statute of limitations can be constitutionally allocated to the defendant for the same reason as discussed above in [15].

[25] In conclusion, the burden of persuasion on the defenses of self-defense, necessity, and alibi cannot be constitutionally allocated to the defendant. It can be constitutionally allocated to the defendant for the defenses of duress, provocation, and statute of limitations.

Jurisdiction D

[26] Jurisdiction D's murder statute shares elements with the murder statutes in the other jurisdictions. It shares the "prior calculation and design" element with Jurisdictions A and B and the "unlawful" element of Jurisdiction C.

[27] As discussed above in [12] with respect to Jurisdiction A, the defenses of self-defense, necessity, duress, and provocation each probably negates the element of prior calculation and design. As a result, it is probably unconstitutional to allocate the burden of persuasion on these defenses to a defendant under *Patterson* (absent any special jury instructions as were given in, for example, *Martin*).

[28] There is an additional ground for the unconstitutionality of allocating the burden of persuasion to the defendant on the defenses of self-defense and necessity. As discussed above in [21] with respect to Jurisdiction C, the justification defenses of self-defense and necessity negate the element of unlawfulness. As a result, the burden of persuasion for neither self-defense nor necessity can be constitutionally allocated to the defendant under *Patterson* (absent some special instruction to the jury, as in *Martin*).

[29] As discussed above in [22] with respect to Jurisdiction C, duress and provocation fail to negate the element of unlawfulness. On that basis alone,

it would be constitutional to allocate the burden of persuasion to the defendant for these defenses. But despite not negating the unlawfulness element, these defenses may negate the "prior calculation and design" element as discussed above in [12]. As a result, to the extent that duress and provocation negate the "prior calculation and design" element, allocating the burden of persuasion to the defendant for those defenses is unconstitutional (absent any special instruction as in *Martin*).

[30] The burden of persuasion on the defense of alibi cannot be constitutionally allocated to the defendant for the same reason as discussed above in [14].

[31] The burden of persuasion on the defense of statute of limitations can be constitutionally allocated to the defendant for the same reason as discussed above in [15].

[32] In conclusion, the burden of persuasion on the defenses of self-defense, necessity, duress, provocation, and alibi cannot be constitutionally allocated to the defendant. It can be constitutionally allocated to the defendant for the defense of statute of limitations.

Conclusion

Jurisdiction A: The burden of persuasion on the defenses of necessity, duress, provocation, and alibi probably cannot be constitutionally allocated to the defendant. It can be constitutionally allocated to the defendant for the defenses of self-defense and statute of limitations.

Jurisdiction B: The burden of persuasion on the defenses of self-defense, necessity, duress, provocation, and alibi cannot be constitutionally allocated to the defendant. It can be constitutionally allocated to the defendant for the defense of statute of limitations.

Jurisdiction C: The burden of persuasion on the defenses of self-defense, necessity, and alibi cannot be constitutionally allocated to the defendant. It can be constitutionally allocated to the defendant for the defenses of duress, provocation, and statute of limitations.

Jurisdiction D: The burden of persuasion on the defenses of self-defense, necessity, duress, provocation, and alibi cannot be constitutionally allocated to the defendant. It can be constitutionally allocated to the defendant for the defense of statute of limitations.

TOOLS FOR SELF-ASSESSMENT

Go back to your written answer. Look for the issues identified in paragraphs [1]–[32] above. Look also for the analysis that follows each issue, and mark your essay where you locate it. Do you fully describe the issue, identify the precise legal standard that applies, list the relevant facts, and show how the facts and law support a conclusion for each issue in a separate paragraph? Mark each conclusion in your essay. Are there sufficient reasons in the law and in the facts to support the conclusion?

1. Do what you are told. In the instructions to the Problem, you are asked to analyze and discuss the application of the burden of proof in each of the four jurisdictions. You are to identify which party bears the burden of proof on which issues

and, specifically, you are to discuss the constitutionality of allocating the burden of persuasion to the defendant for each specified defense.

2. Do not analyze what is unnecessary. Because no facts of the various defendants' conduct are specified, you should not address whether any of the parties can, in fact, satisfy their respective burdens.

3. Always analyze under the MPC unless you are instructed otherwise. Here, the instructions specifically state that you need not do so.

4. State the best possible arguments for alternative conclusions. Even as you reject possible conclusions as to which party bears the burden of production or persuasion on a given issue, make the best possible argument first, and only then explain why you are rejecting that conclusion.

5. Be on the alert for red herrings. Some information in the fact pattern of a hypothetical may be irrelevant or even designed to mislead you. Pay particular attention to detail, and do not assume that an element that appears in more than one jurisdiction will be treated the same in your analysis. Take your time, and go through the entire analysis before drawing conclusions. For example, note that the element "unlawfully" appears in both Jurisdictions C and D. Do not assume that because duress and provocation fail to negate the element of unlawfulness in Jurisdiction C—and so the burdens of persuasion therefore can be allocated to the defendant—they can automatically be allocated to the defendant in Jurisdiction D. Because Jurisdiction D contains the additional element, "With Purpose and Prior Calculation and Design," which is arguably negated by duress and provocation, allocating the burdens of persuasion to the defendant would be unconstitutional.

6. What follows is a step-by-step guide that proceeds chronologically through the burden of proof issues as they arise in a criminal trial and reveals the inner logic of the law of the burden of proof. This approach transparently reveals each step in the chain of reasoning as to determining the burden of proof. It can be used not merely for the specific hypothetical in this chapter but for any burden of proof problem.

    i.   *What is the burden of proof?* It consists of two components: the burden of production of evidence and the burden of persuasion. The prosecution bears both burdens as to every fact necessary to constitute the crime charged. The defendant bears the burden of production as to defenses. Either the prosecution or the defendant will bear the burden of persuasion on defenses.

    ii. *Who bears the burden of proof regarding the defendant's guilt?* The prosecution. That is, the defendant is presumed innocent unless and until the prosecution meets its burden.

    iii. *What is the standard of proof?* The prosecution must prove the defendant's guilt beyond a reasonable doubt.

    iv. *How much proof satisfies the beyond a reasonable doubt standard?* It is more than a preponderance of the evidence and more than clear and convincing evidence but less than absolute certainty. It is nonquantifiable; the jury must have an "abiding conviction" or a "firm and fixed" conviction of the defendant's guilt.

v. *What specifically must the prosecution prove?* Each element of the offense charged (and possibly disproving some defenses as will be discussed below in xxvi).

vi. *How much evidence suffices to satisfy the prosecution's burden of production?* Sufficient evidence such that a rational jury could find the defendant guilty beyond a reasonable doubt.

vii. *What is the consequence of the prosecution's failure to satisfy this burden?* The defendant is entitled to a directed verdict of acquittal if a judge determines as a matter of law that no rational jury could find the defendant guilty beyond a reasonable doubt.

viii. *What is the consequence of the prosecution's satisfaction of this burden?* The defendant is not entitled to a directed verdict of acquittal, and the prosecution is entitled to have the jury (or fact-finder) deliberate on the case. During deliberations, the jury/fact-finder will determine if the prosecution has met its burden of persuasion in proving the elements of the offense. But before the case goes to the jury/fact-finder, the defendant is entitled to present a defense.

ix. *Who bears the burden of proof on a defense?* It depends on the type of defense and perhaps on the particular elements of the offense and the particular jurisdiction.

x. *With respect to the type of defense, is the defense an alibi/failure of proof defense or an affirmative defense?* The defense is an alibi/failure of proof defense if it exculpates exclusively by negating an element. The defense is an affirmative defense if it may exculpate even if the elements of the offense are satisfied.

xi. *Who bears the burden of persuasion on an alibi/failure of proof defense?* The prosecution always bears the burden of persuasion on disproving it beyond a reasonable doubt.

xii. *Who bears the burden of production on an affirmative defense?* The defendant bears the burden of production.

xiii. *How much evidence is required to satisfy the burden of production regarding a defense?* A scintilla of evidence or just enough evidence to make the defense barely plausible.

xiv. *What is the consequence of the defendant failing to satisfy the burden?* The defendant is not entitled to argue the defense to the jury, and the court will not instruct the jury on it.

xv. *What is the consequence of the defendant satisfying the burden?* Satisfaction of the burden triggers the issue of which party shall bear the burden of persuasion on the defense.

xvi. *Who bears the burden of persuasion?* Many states allocate the burden of persuasion on specified defenses—most affirmative defenses—to the prosecution. Other states allocate it to the defendant when it is constitutionally permissible.

xvii. *When is it constitutionally permissible to allocate it to the defendant?* It depends on the relationship between the particular defense, the offense, and the jury instructions. Absent special jury instructions, it is constitutionally permissible (to allocate the burden of persuasion on affirmative defenses to the defendant) unless the defense negates an element of the offense.

xviii. *Does the defendant's particular defense negate an element of the offense?*

xix. If no, then it *is* constitutional to allocate the burden of persuasion to the defendant.

xx. *If yes, is there a special instruction, like in* Martin, *allowing the jury to consider the defense even if the defendant does not satisfy the burden of persuasion on the defense?*

xxi. If no, then it is unconstitutional.

xxii. If yes, then it is constitutional.

xxiii. *If the defendant does have the burden of persuasion for a defense, what is the standard of proof that the defendant must satisfy?* It is constitutionally permissible to require the defendant to prove the defense beyond a reasonable doubt. However, most states only require the defendant to prove a defense by a preponderance of the evidence.

xxiv. *What is the consequence of the defendant failing to satisfy the burden of persuasion on a defense?* The jury/fact-finder will neither acquit nor mitigate the charge based on that defense.

xxv. *What is the consequence of the defendant satisfying the burden of persuasion on a defense? Depending on the defense, the jury/fact-finder will either acquit the defendant or mitigate the charge.*

xxvi. *If the prosecution bears the burden of persuasion on a defense, what is the standard of proof?* The prosecution must disprove the defense beyond a reasonable doubt.

xxvii. *What is the consequence of the prosecution failing to satisfy the burden of persuasion on a defense?* See the answer to xxv.

xxviii. *What is the consequence of the prosecution failing to satisfy the burden of persuasion on proving each element of the offense beyond a reasonable doubt?* The jury/fact-finder will acquit on that offense.

7. Know how to distinguish alibi/failure of proof defenses from affirmative defenses. Affirmative defenses may exculpate even if they do not negate an element of the offense; but, alibi/failure of proof defenses exculpate only if they negate an element of the offense. Alibi/failure of proof defenses assert only that an element of the offense is not satisfied. For example, a defendant might assert that she lacked the requisite mens rea or intent, or was not at the scene of the crime, or was not the one who committed the deed. In all of these examples, the defendant is seeking to negate an element of the offense. The prosecution retains the burden of persuasion on disproving these defenses because proving the elements of the offense necessarily entails disproving these defenses. For example, if the defendant's intent is an element, then the prosecution bears the burden of persuasion on this intent. And proving the defendant's intent necessarily entails disproving the defendant's assertion that she lacked intent. That is, proving the presence of intent also disproves the absence of intent. (Proving *x* disproves *not-x*.)

Affirmative defenses may or may not negate an element of the offense. For example, the defense of self-defense may sometimes exculpate by negating an element of the offense—for example, unlawfulness—and sometimes exculpate even without negating an element. Unlike who bears the burden of persuasion for alibi/failure of proof defenses, the prosecution does not necessarily retain the burden of persuasion on disproving affirmative defenses because proving the elements of the offense does not necessarily entail disproving these defenses.

Only the prosecution has the burden of persuasion on failure of proof defenses because failure of proof defenses only exculpate by negating an element of the offense. In contrast, sometimes the prosecution and sometimes the defendant has the burden of persuasion on affirmative defenses because affirmative defenses sometimes exculpate by negating an element and sometimes exculpate even without negating an element. When an affirmative defense does negate an element, the Constitution assigns the burden of persuasion to the prosecution.

8.   The key to understanding the issue of allocation of the burden of persuasion on a defense is the concept of negation. The simple rule that if a defense negates an element of the offense, the prosecution must bear the burden of persuasion on that defense is clear. What is less clear is precisely when or under what conditions a defense does negate an element of an offense. To help clarify, consider the following examples. An alibi defense of "I was out of town at the time of the crime" seeks to negate the actus reus element of commission of the crime. A failure of proof defense claiming absence of intent seeks to negate a mens rea element requiring the presence of intent. The *Mullaney* defendant's defense of provocation seeks to negate the offense element of malice, defined as without provocation. (That is, the presence of provocation negates the element of acting without provocation.) The defense of self-defense seeks to negate an offense element of "unlawful." (Self-defense is a justification defense; justified conduct is lawful conduct. Therefore, the defendant's defense of lawful, justified, self-defense conduct seeks to negate the element of "unlawful.") The general rule is that if a defense is the converse of an element of an offense, then the defense "negates" that element (for the purpose of allocating the burden of persuasion). To put it abstractly, if an element of the offense is x, and the defendant asserts the defense of *not-x*, the relationship between the offense element and the defense is such that the defense "negates" the offense element. The significance of this concept of negation is, of course, that if a defense negates an offense element the prosecution bears the burden of persuasion on disproving that defense.

9.   In order to avoid being confused by the quartet of seemingly conflicting Supreme Court cases, try to understand them in relation to each other. *Winship* held that the prosecution bears the burden of proof (thus both the burdens of production and persuasion) on proving the defendant's guilt beyond a reasonable doubt. What constitutes proving the defendant's "guilt?" According to *Winship*, the prosecution at least has to prove "every fact necessary to constitute the crime charged." This clearly includes proving every element of the offense. But unclear is whether proving the defendant's "guilt" also includes disproving any defenses. *Winship* is silent on defenses. The next Supreme Court decision on burden of proof, *Mullaney*, does address defenses. It is unconstitutional for the defendant to bear the burden of persuasion on certain defenses—those that (i) bear on the degree of blameworthiness or culpability, (ii) affect the degree of punishment, and (iii) have traditionally or historically been recognized as a defense. Once the defendant has satisfied the burden of production, the prosecution must bear the burden of persuasion on these defenses. Though technically not overruled, *Mullaney* has been supplanted by *Patterson*. Under *Patterson*, a jurisdiction may constitutionally allocate the burden of persuasion to the defendant for any defense unless the

defense negates an element of the offense. So, under *Patterson*, it is constitutional to allocate the burden of persuasion to the defendant even for defenses that satisfy the three-part *Mullaney* test. It is only unconstitutional to allocate the burden of persuasion to the defendant for defenses that negate an element of the offense.

A fundamental difference separates the *Mullaney* and *Patterson* approaches to allocating the burden of persuasion on defenses. *Mullaney* focuses solely on the type of defense; *Patterson* focuses on the relationship between the defense and the elements of the offense. Under *Mullaney*, if a defense must constitutionally be allocated to the prosecution with respect to one offense, it must also be so allocated with respect to all offenses. In contrast, under *Patterson*, whether a defense must constitutionally be allocated to the prosecution with respect to one offense will not determine whether it must also be so allocated with respect to all offenses. The same defense might constitutionally be allocated to the prosecution with respect to one offense and to the defendant with respect to another offense.

Martin appears to be an exception to *Patterson*'s rule. Applying the rule of *Patterson* to the facts of *Martin*, the defendant's defense of self-defense (requiring force used against only an imminent threat) seemingly negates the offense element of "prior calculation and design." As a result, the *Patterson* rule would seemingly find it unconstitutional to allocate the burden of persuasion to the defendant for that defense. But *Martin* ruled that it was constitutional to allocate the burden of persuasion for the defense to the defendant. How does *Martin* not violate the *Patterson* rule? Typically, a trial court judge instructs the jury that if it determines that a defendant did not satisfy its burden of persuasion on proving a defense, the defendant cannot prevail on that defense. But the *Martin* trial court gave a special instruction to the jury that it could consider the defendant's evidence of self-defense in determining whether the defendant was guilty, even if the jury found that the defendant did not satisfy his burden of persuasion. This had the effect of making a partial, not a full, allocation of the burden of persuasion to the defendant. In effect, the prosecution at least partially had to disprove self-defense. As a result, *Patterson* was not (fully) violated by *Martin*.

10. Consider applying only *Winship* without considering *Patterson* or *Mullaney* in determining burden of proof issues. The rule in *Winship* is that a criminal defendant is presumed innocent unless and until the prosecution proves beyond a reasonable doubt every element of the crime charged. Because we know that a defendant never has to disprove an element of the offense, anytime a defense relates to or negates an element of the offense, the prosecution will always bear the burden of persuasion. While it is a good idea to have a solid handle on the holdings and reasoning of the other three major cases in this area, simply conducting a proper analysis under *Winship* of the elements/defenses in any case or hypothetical should lead one to the correct result (apart from the special *Martin*-type situations).

11. Keep in mind that the burden of production of evidence is separate and distinct from the burden of persuasion. It is the judge who determines whether a party has satisfied the burden of production of evidence. The jury/fact-finder, whose responsibility it is to make a decision on satisfaction of the burden of persuasion, will not even have the opportunity to consider the evidence until the judge has determined that the burden-holding party has presented adequate evidence and satisfied the burden of production. It is only after the requisite evidence

has been presented that the jury/fact-finder begins its process of determining whether either party has satisfied its burden of persuasion.

12. Keep in mind the difference between what the Constitution requires, with respect to the allocation of the burden of persuasion on a defense, and what jurisdictions actually do. For example, many jurisdictions allocate the burden of persuasion to the prosecution for defenses that do not negate an element of the offense (and for which the burden of persuasion could constitutionally be allocated to the defendant).

VARIATIONS ON THE THEME

For the following variations, analyze the burden of proof. For each of the following variations, the defendant asserts the following defenses:

    i.   Self-defense
   ii.   Necessity
  iii.   Duress
  iv.   Provocation
   v.   Alibi
  vi.   Statute of Limitations

1. Murder has the following elements:

    i.   Causing the death of another
   ii.   With malice (defined to be the absence of provocation)

The trial court specially instructs the jury that even if the defendant fails to satisfy the burden of persuasion on self-defense, the jury may still consider the defendant's evidence on self-defense in determining whether the prosecution has proved the defendant's guilt beyond a reasonable doubt.

2. Murder has the following elements:

    i.   Causing the death of another
   ii.   With malice (defined to be the absence of provocation)

3. Murder has the following elements:

    i.   With intent to kill
   ii.   Causing the death of another

4. Murder has the following elements:

    i.   With intent to kill
   ii.   Causing the death of another

With respect to this offense, the trial court specially instructs the jury that even if the defendant fails to satisfy the burden of persuasion on self-defense, the jury may still consider the defendant's evidence on self-defense in determining whether the prosecution has proved the defendant's guilt beyond a reasonable doubt.

5. Murder has the following elements:

    i.   Unlawfully
    ii. Causing the death of another
    iii. With Intent to kill

In this jurisdiction, the following defenses are designated as affirmative defenses on which the defendant bears the burden of persuasion: Self-Defense, Necessity, and Duress.

6. Murder has the following elements:

    i.   Unlawfully
    ii. Causing the death of another
    iii. With Intent to kill

In this jurisdiction, the following defenses are designated as affirmative defenses on which the defendant bears the burden of persuasion: Provocation, Alibi, and Statute of Limitations.

ADDITIONAL READINGS

MODEL PENAL CODE § 1.12, 1.13(9) (Official Draft and Revised Comments 1985)

GEORGE FLETCHER, BASIC CONCEPTS OF CRIMINAL LAW 14–19, 93–100 (1998)

Larry Alexander, *The Supreme Court, Dr. Jekyll, and the Due Process of Proof*, 1996 SUP. CT. REV. 191

Ronald J. Allen, *More on Constitutional Process of Proof Problems in Criminal Cases*, 94 HARV. L. REV. 1795 (1981)

Donald A. Dripps, *The Constitutional Status of the Reasonable Doubt Rule*, 75 CAL. L. REV. 1665 (1987)

George Fletcher, *Two Kinds of Legal Rules: A Comparative Study of Burden-of-Persuasion Practices in Criminal Cases*, 77 YALE L.J. 880 (1968)

John C. Jeffries Jr. & Paul B. Stephan, *Defenses, Presumptions, and Burdens of Proof in the Criminal Law*, 88 YALE L.J. 1325 (1979)

Scott E. Sundby, *The Reasonable Doubt Rule and the Meaning of Innocence*, 40 HASTINGS L.J. 457 (1989)

Barbara D. Underwood, *The Thumb on the Scales of Justice: Burdens of Persuasion in Criminal Cases*, 86 YALE L.J. 1299 (1977)

Peter Westen, *Egelhoff Again*, 36 AM. CRIM. L. REV. 1203 (1999)

ATTEMPT

15

INTRODUCTION

The criminal offense of attempt is of relatively recent origin. Although roots of the offense date back to fourteenth-century English common law, the offense did not fully become a fixture in the criminal law until the late eighteenth century. Attempt was criminalized under the doctrine that the intention (to commit a crime) was to be taken for the deed. But even then, an intention alone did not suffice. Some overt act manifesting the intent was required, even if the act itself was innocent. As one court explained, "The intent may make an act, innocent in itself, criminal; nor is the completion of an act, criminal in itself, necessary to constitute the criminality."[1]

The elements of the modern crime of attempt are similar. Under the majority rule, the requisite mens rea is the purpose or specific intent to commit the substantive or target offense. This is true even if the mens rea of the target offense is general intent, a lesser mens rea. The rationale for the higher level of mens rea for attempt is that without the presence of wrongful conduct or harmful results, we are less confident that the offender is truly culpable. A higher level of mens rea for attempt serves, in effect, as a substitute guarantor of culpability in the absence of harmful results or conduct. Under the minority rule, however, the mens rea for attempt is not higher—whatever mens rea suffices for the target offense suffices for the attempt.

Much of attempt law is devoted to divining the threshold separating lawful conduct preparatory to an attempt from conduct constituting a criminal attempt. Courts have developed a bewildering variety of tests to draw that line. The most commonly used test is from the MPC. An actor must commit a substantial step toward the target offense that strongly corroborates the actor's intent. This test not only specifies how close the actor must come to committing the target offense but also requires the conduct to evidence the actor's mens rea. Other tests simply specify that the actor take the first step toward, the last step toward, or come dangerously close to, completing the target offense. The dilemma is that locating the threshold too far away from the target offense results in ensnaring too many innocents who never would have committed the target offense; and, locating the threshold too close to the target offense precludes an opportunity for the police to intervene and prevent the substantive offense.

Rationales for why the law should bother with punishing conduct that produces no harm—attempts—abound. First, such conduct does produce harm, if not the concrete harm of substantive offenses, then at least a psychological harm. Second, even apart from any harm, the conduct is simply wrong and deserving of

---

[1] R v. Scofield, Cald. 397 (1784).

punishment. Third, punishing attempts serves to deter actors from committing the substantive offense. And fourth, criminalizing an actor's conduct before it has reached the stage of causing concrete harm affords the police a lawful basis to intervene in the actor's course of conduct and prevent the completion of the substantive offense, thereby preventing the concrete harm from occurring.

PROBLEM

Lilli Lifeguard is on duty as a lifeguard at a beach on the ocean. Sitting on her observation platform, Lilli scans the water for swimmers in need of aid. It is early in the morning, and typically at this hour people just sit on the beach. However, she spies one lone swimmer. It is her hated enemy, Clem Nemesis. He is thrashing and flailing about and yelling, "Help! Help! I'm drowning." Lilli's first thought is that she must save Clem. But then she thinks how sweet her life would be if Clem were dispatched from this world. She quickly realizes that letting Clem die is wrong and cruel and terrible. For Lilli, the thought of not saving Clem and letting him die is sweet sweetness but is also so, so wrong. Lilli is torn as to what to do and wracked with indecision. Two seconds have now passed since Lilli began to decide what she should do. Lilli continues to vacillate. Five seconds have now passed. Lilli continues to mentally weigh the pros and cons. After eight seconds have passed, Lilli finally decides that she must save Clem. Lilli jumps down to the sand, runs to the water, swims to Clem, and brings him ashore. Clem has lost consciousness but soon regains it and walks away apparently unharmed.[2] (Assume for purposes of your analysis that Lilli has a contractual duty to rescue drowning swimmers. The breach of this duty could support criminal liability for an omission.)

Analyze and discuss whether Lilli is liable for the attempted murder of Clem under both common law and MPC principles. If you determine that Lilli satisfies the elements of attempted murder, analyze and discuss the earliest point attempt liability attached.

(This Problem is in two parts. The first part is above. The second part follows the Essay to the first part. Analyze and discuss the first part, above, before reading the second part.)

LIST OF READINGS

United States v. Mandujano, 499 F.2d 370 (5th Cir. 1974)

People v. Staples, 85 Cal. Rptr. 589 (Cal. Ct. App. 1970)

Smallwood v. State, 680 A.2d 512 (Md. 1996)

People v. Rizzo, 158 N.E. 888 (N.Y. 1927)

King v. Barker, [1924] N.Z.L.R. 865

MODEL PENAL CODE § 5.01 (Official Code and Revised Comments 1985)

JOSHUA DRESSLER, UNDERSTANDING CRIMINAL LAW 379–402, 411–15, 418–19 (5th ed. 2009)

ESSAY

In many jurisdictions, as well as the MPC, committing an attempt by omission, though unusual, is explicitly recognized as a form of attempt liability. The challenges

---

[2] Aspects of this Problem were inspired by an example from GEORGE FLETCHER, BASIC CONCEPTS OF CRIMINAL LAW 179 (1998).

of analyzing attempt liability, already substantial, are heightened and compounded by analyzing attempt by omission.

Under the common law, whether Lilli Lifeguard is liable for the attempted murder of Clem Nemesis will vary depending on the jurisdiction. Under the MPC, Lilli would most likely not be liable.

[1] Under the common law, the principal elements of an attempt offense are the mens rea of specific intent (under the majority rule) and the actus reus of conduct that is sufficient to cross over the threshold from mere lawful preparation to the early stages of commencement of the target offense. The principal possible defenses to an attempt offense are impossibility and abandonment.

[2] Under the MPC, the principal elements of an attempt offense are the mens rea, which varies depending on the nature of the target offense and the type of element of the offense to which it pertains, and the actus reus of conduct constituting a substantial step toward the target offense that strongly corroborates the requisite mens rea. The principal possible defenses are the same as under the common law.

Mens Rea

COMMON LAW

[3] Under the majority rule, the requisite mens rea for attempt is specific intent. The precise nature of specific intent is somewhat ambiguous. Specific intent may vary depending on the type of target offense and the type of element of the offense to which it pertains. Lilli's target offense is a result crime—murder. Most simply, for a result element or crime, specific intent is purpose. That is, the actor, by intentionally engaging in conduct toward the commission of the target offense, must have the purpose of causing the prohibited result. Specific intent may also be explained, for a result element or crime, as comprising two intents: (i) the intent to engage in conduct and (ii) the intent that the conduct causes the prohibited result. DRESSLER, at 391–92. The actor must satisfy both types of intent in order to satisfy the requisite mens rea of specific intent.

[4] It is not entirely clear whether Lilli has the requisite mens rea of specific intent during the eight-second period in which she fails to act. True, she does intentionally and purposefully engage in the conduct that could cause the prohibited result. Lilli intentionally and purposefully fails to act—the conduct that could cause the death of Clem. Lilli thereby clearly satisfies the first type of requisite intent. But her satisfaction of the second type of intent—intending that her failure to act cause Clem's death—is unclear.

[5] Whether Lilli satisfies that second type of intent may depend on how her mental process during the eight-second interval is characterized. Two different characterizations are plausible. One characterization views the interval as a period of evaluation and indecision. Under this characterization, Lilli weighed and evaluated the different options without ever forming the intent or purpose to kill Clem. She considered, weighed, and evaluated the option of killing Clem, but she never actually reached the stage of having the intent or purpose of killing him. That is, she never crossed the threshold from indecision to decision (to kill Clem). As a result, under the evaluation/indecision characterization, Lilli lacks the requisite specific intent for attempted murder.

[6] The other characterization views the interval as a vacillation between intending to save Clem and intending to kill him. The vacillation characterization is not so much a period of indecision but rather a period of rapidly changing decisions. Rather than viewing Lilli as undecided, she decided to save, then decided to kill, then decided to save, and so on and so on. She vacillated between intending to kill and intending not to kill. Because she did reach a stage (however temporary) of having the intention and purpose that her inaction kill Clem, she arguably satisfies the requite mens rea of specific intent. (Of course, the argument may still be made that she subsequently abandoned her specific intent. The abandonment defense will be discussed in [23]–[27] below.)

[7] Which is the more plausible characterization of the facts? There is evidence of both characterizations in the facts. The facts depict Lilli's mental process both as a period of indecision in which she never formed the intent or purpose to kill Clem as well as a period of vacillation in which she first intended to save, then she intended to kill, and then repeatedly changed her mind back and forth.

[8] Even if it is indeterminate as to which is the more plausible characterization of the facts, perhaps there is still more support for concluding that Lilli lacked the requisite intent to kill Clem. If the indecision characterization is correct, then she never had the requisite intent. And even if the vacillation characterization approach is correct, it is still plausible that Lilli lacked the requisite intent. Even under the vacillation characterization, it is not clear that her transient formation of the intent to kill Clem was sufficiently fixed and firm.

[9] How firm and fixed must an intention be to qualify as a sufficiently formed intention? Ordinarily, we might think that holding an intention for less than eight seconds is insufficient. But there are three reasons why such a short period of time might well suffice here. First, in this case, seconds make the difference between the life and death of the swimmer. This perhaps militates toward a comparatively short time frame for what qualifies as a firm and fixed intention. Second, our conventional yardstick for assessing a firm and fixed intention may be based on affirmative conduct rather than the comparatively infrequent cases of failures to act. In the context of affirmative conduct, the actor's period of indecision or vacillation may be as long or short as the actor wishes because the actor's commission of an act that could cause the death of the victim comes only *after* the actor reaches a firm and fixed intention to kill. In contrast, in a failure to act case, as here, the actor's conduct that could cause the death of the victim is occurring *while* the actor is evaluating or vacillating. The entire time while Lilli is evaluating/vacillating as to whether she should fail to save Clem, she is failing to save him. That is, while she is thinking about whether she should do it, she already is doing it. Third, analogizing to the law of premeditated and deliberated killing may support a brief time frame. Many courts find that premeditation and deliberation can occur in a very short time period. For example, it can occur as late as while the actor is pulling the trigger. If a mental state such as premeditation and deliberation—which inherently would seem to require some considerable time—can be formed that quickly, then surely the mental state of intention—which does not inherently take a considerable amount of time to form—can also become sufficiently firm and fixed in less than eight seconds.

[10] While unclear, there is probably more support for the conclusion that Lilli lacks the requisite specific intent. This is because the indecision characterization

clearly supports the conclusion of no intent, and the vacillation characterization supports either a conclusion of no intent or a conclusion of intent. Thus, there is slightly more support for Lilli lacking the requisite mens rea under the majority rule requiring specific intent.

[11] Under the minority rule, the requisite intent for attempt is whatever mens rea would suffice for the target offense. Given her target offense of murder, the mens rea of gross recklessness or depraved indifference would suffice for the mens rea of attempt. In waiting eight seconds before undertaking a rescue when seconds could mean the difference between life and death, Lilli's failure to rescue would most likely qualify as gross recklessness and depraved indifference. As a result, Lilli would most likely satisfy the requisite mens rea for attempt under the minority common law rule.

MODEL PENAL CODE

[12] Given that Lilli's target offense is a result crime, the requisite mens rea is either purpose or belief. Purpose is defined as having the conscious objective of causing the result. Whether Lilli has the purpose or conscious objective of causing Clem's death is unclear for the same reasons as discussed above in [5]–[10].

[13] With respect to the alternative requisite mens rea of belief, the actor must believe that her conduct will cause the prohibited result. Whether Lilli has the requisite belief that her conduct will cause Clem's death is unclear. The facts in the Problem simply do not supply any information on what Lilli believes in that regard. One might argue that surely Lilli realizes (and thus believes) that if she delays long enough (much longer than eight seconds) in deciding what to do, her inaction accompanying the lengthy delay will cause Clem's death. But while this might be true, it does not establish that during her eight-second delay she forms the belief that her inaction for eight seconds will cause Clem's death. The relevant belief pertains to what her actual conduct (the eight-second delay) would cause; it is not belief as to what her conduct that she did not commit (a delay of much longer than eight seconds) would cause.

[14] As a result, it is unclear whether Lilli would satisfy the requisite mens rea for attempted murder under the MPC. The mens rea of purpose is unclear because it is unclear as to whether she ever formed a purpose to cause Clem's death. And even if she did form a purpose, it is unclear whether this purpose was sufficiently firm and fixed. As discussed above in [8]–[10], perhaps there is slightly more support for the conclusion that she lacked the requisite purpose. The mens rea of belief is unclear because the given facts in the Problem simply do not supply sufficient information as to her beliefs in this regard.

Actus Reus

COMMON LAW

[15] Whether Lilli satisfies the actus reus requirement may depend on which test a court employs. Although there are a wide variety of tests and perhaps no majority rule, the test enjoying the greatest plurality is the **substantial step** test. Under the test, the actor's conduct must both constitute a substantial step toward the commission of the offense and strongly corroborate the actor's mens rea. The analysis of the actus reus of attempt is a little trickier with respect to omissions, as is the case here, than with respect to affirmative acts. With an omission (a failure to act),

the actor is already doing all that is needed to be done to complete the offense—nothing. So, with respect to an omission, doing nothing is not only a substantial step, but it is *all* the steps necessary to complete the offense. On this basis, one might conclude that any omission necessarily constitutes a substantial step. To avoid this unfortunate conclusion, perhaps a substantial step in the omission context requires not only doing nothing but doing nothing for a sufficiently long period of time to come substantially close to completing the offense.

[16] The resulting issue is how long or how much of doing nothing suffices. There is no clear abstract or general rule that allows determining whether eight seconds is or is not a sufficiently long period of failing to act as to constitute a substantial step in an attempt by omission. Perhaps the analysis must be context sensitive. Where the death of the victim is a long way off, as in attempting to kill a child by failing to properly feed her sufficiently nutritious food, eight seconds would surely be insufficient as a substantial step. But in this case, where mere seconds are the difference between life and death, an eight-second delay in saving a drowning swimmer plausibly and perhaps likely qualifies as a substantial step.

[17] If the eight seconds of inaction does constitute a substantial step, to satisfy the actus reus requirement it must also strongly corroborate the actor's mens rea. Assuming that Lilli had the specific intent to cause Clem's death (under the majority rule) or gross recklessness with respect to Clem's death (under the minority rule), does her eight seconds of failing to undertake a rescue strongly corroborate the mens rea? It is not clear, but probably it does. Assuming both that Lilli had the requisite mens rea and assuming that eight seconds of inaction constitutes a substantial step, then the eight seconds probably strongly corroborates the mens rea. In Lilli's situation, failing to rescue a drowning swimmer is a fairly efficacious way to kill and is most likely consistent with either a specific intent to cause Clem's death or gross recklessness toward Clem's death.

[18] Besides the substantial step test, another test employed by courts is the **unequivocality or *res ipsa loquitur*** test. To qualify as the actus reus of attempt under this test, the actor's conduct must demonstrate or manifest the actor's mens rea to commit the target offense. That is, the actor's conduct must unambiguously speak for itself in establishing the actor's mens rea. This is a more difficult standard to satisfy than the substantial step test, which does not require the conduct to demonstrate the mens rea, but rather that it merely strongly corroborates the mens rea. Lilli's eight seconds of inaction most likely fails to satisfy this test. The eight seconds of inaction does not unambiguously demonstrate her intent to kill Clem or even her gross recklessness. The inaction per se could just as easily demonstrate or manifest that she panicked or froze or did not see Clem drowning or was carefully planning the most efficacious mode of rescue.

[19] **Dangerous proximity** is yet another test. To qualify, the actor's conduct must come dangerously close to completing the target offense. It is not clear that Lilli's conduct satisfies this test. On the one hand, in a context where mere seconds are the difference between life and death, the eight seconds of inaction is dangerously proximate. Moreover, the delay was sufficient to perhaps contribute to Clem lapsing into unconsciousness briefly. On the other hand, it was not dangerously proximate because Clem ended up walking away apparently unhurt. On balance, perhaps there is slightly more support for the view that Lilli's conduct does satisfy the dangerous proximity test.

[20] The last test we will consider, the **last step** test, is typically quite difficult to satisfy. To satisfy this test, the actor must complete all of the steps or actions necessary to complete the target offense. Typically, this would bar attempt liability until a very *late* stage in the actor's course of conduct. For this reason, the test has fallen out of favor by courts. But with an attempt by omission, this test is satisfied very *early* in an actor's stage of conduct. By failing to act, Lilli has already completed all of the steps necessary to kill Clem. She need not do (or fail to do) anything else. On this basis, every attempt by omission would satisfy the last step test. To avoid this unfortunate result, perhaps our application of the test would need to be altered as applied to omissions. Not only must the defendant fail to act, but the defendant must continue to fail to act for a sufficiently long period of time to complete the target offense. As reformulated, the first stage of failing to act would be the first step, and the last step would be the last instance of failing to act necessary to accomplish the target offense. On this basis, the outcome of the test as applied to Lilli's conduct is unclear. The analysis would be similar to the analysis in the dangerous proximity test, as discussed in [19].

MODEL PENAL CODE

[21] The MPC employs the substantial step test. Though nearly identical to the common law version discussed in [15] above, one difference is that the MPC provides a number of factual scenarios of an actor's conduct that, if strongly corroborative of the actor's requisite mens rea, cannot be found, as a matter of law, insufficient to qualify as a substantial step. Thus, these scenarios serve as plausible examples of what might be considered as substantial steps. None of these examples, however, apply to Lilli's conduct. See MPC § 5.01(2)(a)–(g). This alone does not support the inference that Lilli's conduct is not a substantial step. In fact, none of the examples include failures to act despite that the MPC specifically contemplates attempts by omission. MPC § 5.01(1)(b)–(c). As a result, with the one difference between the common law's substantial step test and the MPC's test inapplicable, the analysis of whether Lilli satisfies the MPC test will be identical to the common law analysis discussed above in [15]–[17].

Earliest Point Lilli Satisfies the Elements of Attempt

[22] Assuming that Lilli does satisfy the elements of attempted murder, what is the earliest point at which Lilli crosses the threshold from mere lawful preparation to unlawful attempt? The facts depict three possible stages: at two seconds, at five seconds, and at eight seconds. This is an exceedingly difficult determination, apparently lacking a bright-line rule of law. It is perhaps a question of fact for which there is no single right answer.

Defenses—Abandonment/Renunciation

The two principal defenses to attempt liability are impossibility and abandonment/renunciation. Impossibility is not applicable to these facts. Lilli's conduct in rescuing Clem, after her eight-second period of failing to rescue, arguably constitutes an abandonment/renunciation of any attempt to murder Clem.

COMMON LAW

[23] The abandonment defense is recognized in perhaps only a minority of jurisdictions. The principal elements of the defense, in the jurisdictions recognizing it,

are as follows: (i) the abandonment is voluntary; (ii) complete; and (iii) in some jurisdictions, the actor has not taken the last step necessary and has not caused significant harm to the victim.

[24] The voluntariness requirement is typically explained negatively. An actor's abandonment is *not* voluntary if it is motivated by unanticipated circumstances making completion of the target offense more difficult or capture by the police more likely. Here, Lilli satisfies neither of these negative conditions. Her abandonment appears to reflect her decision that she does not wish for Clem to die by her failure to undertake a rescue. It is most likely voluntary.

[25] The completeness requirement is also typically explained negatively. An actor's abandonment is *not* complete if it is motivated by a decision to either postpone commission of the target offense to a later time or commit the same crime on a different victim. Here, Lilli satisfies neither of these negative conditions. There is evidence neither that she plans to fail to save Clem at a later time nor that she plans to fail to save a different drowning victim. Her abandonment is most likely complete.

[26] It is less clear whether Lilli satisfies the requirement that she has not taken the last step necessary and has not caused significant harm to the victim. As discussed above in [20], she technically has taken the last step necessary to complete the target offense by simply doing nothing. But this understanding of the test is most likely inappropriate as applied to attempt by omission. The better version of the test is whether she has failed to act for long enough so that she need do nothing further to complete the target offense. Under this version of the test, it is unclear. She may well have failed to act for long enough but, because Clem did not die, perhaps she did not fail to act for long enough to be considered as having taken the last step. The other aspect of the requirement—not causing significant harm to the victim—she most likely did satisfy. Although her failure to act may well have contributed to Clem losing consciousness for a brief time, he did walk away apparently unhurt and without sustaining significant harm.

[27] Lilli most likely satisfies the requirements that her abandonment be voluntary and complete. She probably satisfies the requirement that her conduct was not the last step and did not produce significant harm. As a result, though it is not clear, Lilli probably satisfies the abandonment defense.

MODEL PENAL CODE
[28] The abandonment defense, termed renunciation, is recognized by the MPC and requires that the actor's abandonment be voluntary and complete. As discussed above in [24]–[25], Lilli most likely satisfies these requirements. A further technical requirement is that the defense is only available if the actor satisfies all the elements of attempt liability. Assuming satisfaction of that requirement, Lilli would most likely obtain the defense.

Conclusion
[29] Under the common law, whether Lilli is liable for the attempted murder of Clem will vary depending on the jurisdiction. Under the majority rule requiring specific intent, it is slightly more likely than not that she lacks the requisite mens rea. Under the minority rule requiring whatever mens rea that suffices for the completed offense, Lilli most likely satisfies the gross recklessness that suffices for murder.

Whether she satisfies the actus reus will vary depending on the jurisdiction. Lilli most likely satisfies the substantial step test (assuming that she satisfies the requisite mens rea), and it is slightly more likely than not that she satisfies the dangerous proximity and last step tests, but she most likely does not satisfy the unequivocality/ *res ipsa loquitur* test. Although many jurisdictions do not recognize the abandonment defense, in those jurisdictions that do, Lilli would most likely obtain the defense.

[30] Under the MPC, Lilli would probably not be liable. It is slightly more likely than not that she lacks the requisite mens rea of purpose or belief. Assuming that she does satisfy the requite mens rea, she most likely satisfies the substantial step test. But, even if she does satisfy the elements of attempted murder, she most likely would obtain the renunciation defense.

[31] Assuming that Lilli has satisfied the elements of attempted murder, the determination of the earliest point at which attempt liability attached is unclear. There is no bright-line rule of law that supplies an answer.

PROBLEM—2ND PART

After regaining consciousness and walking away apparently unharmed, Clem goes to sleep that night. The next morning he does not wake up. He has slipped into a coma caused by the loss of oxygen to his brain prior to being rescued.

Analyze and discuss how these additional facts alter, if at all, your analysis of Lilli's possible liability for attempted murder of Clem.

[32] Clem slipping into a coma is not dispositive in establishing Lilli's mens rea. Even with these new facts, it is far from clear whether Lilli did or did not have the mens rea of specific intent or purpose. And it does not dramatically alter the probable conclusion that Lilli had the mens rea of gross recklessness. But as a general matter, the requisite mens rea is more likely to be inferred the more harmful the result that the actor causes. On this basis, Clem's coma makes it somewhat easier (but perhaps not much) to infer the requisite mens rea.

[33] Depending on the particular test, Clem slipping into a coma has a comparatively greater effect on the analysis of Lilli's actus reus. The additional facts most clearly affect the analysis under the dangerous proximity test. If Lilli's conduct did place Clem into a coma, then her conduct is more persuasively dangerously proximate to causing the objective of the target offense—killing Clem. For the same reason, the last step test is comparatively more easily satisfied (albeit still unclear). It somewhat affects the substantial step test—conduct which places the victim into a coma would seem to be a substantial step. However, it does not clearly establish that the conduct strongly corroborates Lilli's mens rea. The analysis under the unequivocality or *res ipsa loquitur* test is least affected by the additional facts. Lilli's conduct, even though placing her victim into a coma, still does not unambiguously demonstrate her mens rea.

[34] The additional facts would alter the analysis of Lilli's possible abandonment defense under the common law. Some jurisdictions bar the abandonment defense where the actor has caused significant harm. Placing someone in a coma is most likely significant harm. As a result, in such jurisdictions, Lilli would most likely lose her abandonment defense. But Clem slipping into a coma would seemingly not affect the analysis of Lilli's renunciation defense under the MPC. Unlike the common law, the MPC does not preclude the defense where the actor has

caused significant harm. As a result, Lilli would still most likely obtain the renunciation defense.

TOOLS FOR SELF-ASSESSMENT

Go back to your written answer. Look for the issues identified in paragraphs [1]–[34] in the above Essay. Look also for the analysis that follows each issue, and mark your essay where you locate it. Do you fully describe the issue, identify the precise legal standard that applies, list the relevant facts, and show how the facts and law support a conclusion for each issue in a separate paragraph? Mark each conclusion in your essay. Are there sufficient reasons in the law and in the facts to support the conclusion?

1. Do what you are told. In the Problem, you are asked to analyze and discuss whether Lilli Lifeguard is liable for the attempted murder of Clem Nemesis. You need not analyze whether she is liable for any other offenses.
2. Do not analyze what is unnecessary. For example, it might be tempting to conduct an in-depth analysis of whether Lilli has a duty to save drowning swimmers, whether she is liable for some breach of her lifeguard contract, or whether she committed reckless endangerment. It also may be tempting to analyze whether Clem is contributorily negligent for his near drowning. Do not do so. It is not necessary under the instructions following the Problem.
3. Always remember to include an analysis of the MPC's approach unless you are instructed otherwise.
4. State the best possible arguments for alternative conclusions. Even as you reject possible conclusions as to why Lilli is or is not liable for the attempted murder of Clem, make the best possible argument first and only then explain why you are rejecting that conclusion.
5. Be on the alert for hypotheticals *without* red herrings. Do not assume that at least one piece of information in a fact pattern is necessarily irrelevant because you are expecting and anticipating a red herring. Sometimes all of the information in the fact pattern of a hypothetical may be relevant so as to mislead you into treating some of it as irrelevant. Simply because many fact patterns contain red herrings, do not assume that all fact patterns do so.
6. Be aware of the similarities and differences of attempt liability analysis under the common law and the MPC. Regarding the requisite mens rea, under the common law, the majority rule is specific intent, and the minority rule is whatever mens rea suffices for the target offense. Under the MPC, it is purpose or depending on the type of offense, purpose or belief. Regarding the actus reus, the common law uses a variety of tests. But the most common one is the same as used under the MPC—a substantial step that strongly corroborates the actor's mens rea. The only difference is that the MPC lists examples of what might qualify as substantial steps, if they strongly corroborate mens rea. Each principal defense for attempt liability— impossibility and abandonment/renunciation—are treated similarly under the MPC and common law. (For differences between the common law and MPC treatment of impossibility, see the next chapter.) The single difference with respect to the abandonment/renunciation defense is that the MPC does not explicitly limit the defense, as does the common law, to incomplete attempts. (For a discussion of the distinction between complete and incomplete attempts, see Tool # 10 below.)

7.   Keep in mind how mens rea is established. Unlike the Problem, in which we have access to Lilli's thoughts and mental processes, in many cases the defendant does not say what she was thinking. Even if she does, we cannot necessarily assume that she speaks truthfully. So, in such cases how does the prosecution establish the defendant's mens rea? In substantive completed offenses, often the prohibited result caused by the defendant affords an inference of the defendant's mens rea. But attempt cases are doubly difficult. First, an attempt, by definition, lacks a prohibited result from which to infer mens rea. Second, under the majority rule, attempt requires a higher level of mens rea. So, how is the mens rea of attempt established? It is established by inference from the actor's conduct, any words uttered by the actor, and the surrounding circumstances.

8.   The various tests for the actus reus of attempt may be separated into two general groupings. One group of tests finds the actor's conduct to suffice only if it serves to support or establish the actor's mens rea. Examples include the substantial step and the unequivocality/*res ipsa loquitur* tests. The other group of tests determines the sufficiency of the actor's conduct without regard to its relation to the actor's mens rea. Examples include the dangerous proximity test and the last step test.

9.   Maintain a perspective on whether each test for actus reus allows attempt liability to attach fairly early in a criminal course of conduct (that is, far from the commission of the target offense) or fairly late (close to the commission of the target offense). It may even be helpful to draw a time line showing at what point all the various tests would establish attempt liability. Of course, this can only be discussed in a general sense. Generalizations may be overturned in the application of the tests to particular facts. For example, the last step test would most likely establish attempt liability fairly late, perhaps the latest of any test. But as applied to an omission case, as in the Problem, it literally establishes attempt liability very early.

10.   Consider the scope of the abandonment/renunciation defense. Under the common law, abandonment is only recognized in perhaps a minority of jurisdictions. Even in such jurisdictions, it may not be applicable to all attempts. We might distinguish between two types of attempts—incomplete attempts and complete attempts. (Despite the confusing terminology, both types subject the defendant to attempt liability.) Incomplete attempts are eligible to be abandoned, but complete attempts are not eligible. An attempt is complete if the actor either has taken the last step necessary to complete the target offense or if she has caused significant harm. An attempt is incomplete if neither of those conditions is satisfied. Consider the following two examples illustrating the distinction. First, in the case of an actor intending to commit murder by gunshot, by the actor raising the gun and pointing it at her victim, attempt liability may attach. But the attempt is still incomplete. By the actor pulling the trigger, the attempt may become complete. (The substantive or target offense of murder, however, is not (yet) complete.) Second, in the case of an actor intending to commit murder by knife wound, by raising the knife to plunge it into the victim, attempt liability may attach. But the attempt is still incomplete. The attempt may become complete when the arm holding the knife moves forward toward the victim. (Football fans may see an analogy here to the rule that before the quarterback's arm moves forward any loss of the ball is a fumble, but once the arm starts moving forward it is an incomplete pass.) Outside of these two examples, the incomplete/complete attempt distinction is difficult to satisfactorily draw. And this difficulty is compounded when applied to attempts by omission, as is the case in the Problem above.

In contrast, the MPC does not explicitly limit application of the defense to incomplete attempts.

11. There are two approaches to the abandonment/renunciation defense. First, it is not technically a defense at all. That the actor abandoned casts doubt both on whether the actor ever had the requisite intent or mens rea to carry out the target offense and whether the actor's conduct proceeded far enough to qualify as the requisite actus reus of attempt. If the actor's abandonment casts sufficient doubt on the satisfaction of either the mens rea or actus reus, then all of the elements of the attempt offense are not satisfied. As a result, the actor has no need for a defense to avoid attempt liability. Second, abandonment/renunciation is technically a defense: it applies only if the actor satisfies all of the elements of an attempt. The MPC explicitly adopts this second approach. However, evidence of an actor's renunciation nonetheless remains relevant in assessing whether the actor satisfies the mens rea and actus reus requirements.

12. Remember that the abandonment/renunciation defense still applies even if the actor has crossed the threshold from mere lawful preparation to attempt liability. Under the common law, it is only after the actor both crosses that threshold and crosses the threshold from incomplete to complete attempt that the actor can no longer abandon. Under the MPC, an actor can still renounce until just before an attempt becomes the completed target offense.

13. Perhaps the most difficult aspect of analyzing the abandonment/renunciation defense is the requirement that the abandonment/renunciation be voluntary. It is not voluntary if, for example, the actor abandons because the actor encounters circumstances increasing the likelihood of detection or capture by the police. If the actor abandons because she hears police sirens or sees a police officer around the corner, the abandonment is not voluntary. But the actor may still voluntarily abandon if the actor does so due to the deterrent effect of punishment. The abandonment need not be motivated by a quasi-religious or moral awakening that the conduct is wrong. Even if the actor would ideally like to commit the crime but abandons due to a rational, self-interested motivation of not wanting to be punished, the abandonment is voluntary. In a sense, we want would-be criminals to be deterred by a rational fear of criminal punishment.

An actor's abandonment is also involuntary if motivated by circumstances making accomplishment of the objective more difficult. A victim's active physical resistance would clearly make accomplishment of the objective more difficult. But what if the victim or another person uses moral argument or persuasion that motivates the actor to abandon? Is this voluntary or involuntary? Courts are split. The basis for it being involuntary is that the victim's moral resistance made it more difficult. The basis for it being voluntary is not so much that the objective is more difficult to obtain, but rather, that the defendant has freely decided that he no longer wishes to attain the objective.

Yet another difficult class of cases for analyzing the voluntary component is when the actor abandons/renounces because the actor discovers that the objective of the crime is not as rewarding as anticipated. For example, a would-be robber discovers there is insufficient money to be stolen and abandons, a would-be rapist discerns his victim to be less than ideal because of disease or pregnancy and abandons, or a would-be drug purchaser determines the quality of the drugs to be lacking. Are these voluntary or involuntary? Courts are split on such cases.

The basis for them to be involuntary is that a circumstance unknown at the outset—that the crime would be less rewarding—made accomplishment of the criminal objective—a more rewarding transaction—more difficult. The basis for them to be voluntary abandonments is that the actors are "freely" choosing not to commit the crime. The unknown circumstance has not made commission of the crime itself more difficult but simply less rewarding than anticipated. How such cases are resolved may depend on how "criminal objective" is construed. If criminal objective is construed to mean attaining the anticipated, or a sufficient, benefit, then accomplishment of the criminal objective has been made more difficult by the unanticipated circumstance, and the abandonment/renunciation is involuntary. But if criminal objective is construed to mean commission of the crime, then the unanticipated circumstance does not make accomplishment of the objective more difficult, and the abandonment/renunciation is voluntary.

14. The following steps reveal the structure of the above Essay's analysis of Lilli's attempt liability under the common law. These steps are somewhat oversimplified so as to afford a better view of the forest without the obstruction of the trees. But this should not be mistaken for, or taken as a substitute for, in-depth knowledge of the trees. Perhaps with some modification, these steps could be utilized in answering Variations on the Theme.

COMMON LAW:

i. Did the actor commit conduct with the specific intent (under the majority rule) or whatever mens rea suffices for the target offense (under the minority rule) to complete the target offense?
ii. If no, then no attempt liability.
iii. If yes, does the actor's conduct go far enough toward completion of the target offense to satisfy whatever test (e.g., the substantial step test) for the actus reus of attempt the court or jurisdiction adopts?
iv. If no, then no attempt liability.
v. If yes, then there is attempt liability unless a defense applies (impossibility, which is discussed in the next chapter, or abandonment).
vi. If only the abandonment defense is plausible, does the jurisdiction recognize the defense?
vii. If no, then no abandonment defense and there is attempt liability.
viii. If yes, was the abandonment voluntary?
ix. If no, then no abandonment defense, and there is attempt liability.
x. If yes, was the abandonment complete?
xi. If no, then no abandonment defense, and there is attempt liability.
xii. If yes, did the actor commit an incomplete attempt?
xiii. If no, then no abandonment defense, and there is attempt liability.
xiv. If yes, then the actor has an abandonment defense, and there is no attempt liability.

MODEL PENAL CODE:

i. Did the actor commit conduct with the purpose of completing or with the belief that it will complete the target offense (if it is a result crime) or with the purpose of completing the target offense (if it is *not* a result crime)?
ii. If no, then no attempt liability.

iii. If yes, does the actor's conduct both constitute a substantial step toward completion of the target offense and strongly corroborate the actor's requisite mens rea?

iv. If no, then no attempt liability.

v. If yes, then there is attempt liability unless a defense applies (impossibility, which is discussed in the next chapter, or renunciation).

vi. If only the renunciation defense is plausible, was the renunciation voluntary?

vii. If no, then no renunciation defense, and there is attempt liability.

viii. If yes, was the renunciation complete?

ix. If no, then no renunciation defense, and there is attempt liability.

x. If yes, then the actor has a renunciation defense, and there is no attempt liability.

VARIATIONS ON THE THEME

For the following variations, assume that all of the facts from the original hypothetical obtain except as noted.

1. Assume that Lilli has not satisfied the elements of attempted murder. Clem dies without ever having come out of the coma. Does Lilli satisfy the elements of murder? That is, can Lilli commit murder without first committing attempted murder?

2. Immediately upon seeing the drowning swimmer, Lilli descends from the lifeguard observation platform. She runs toward the water in an effort to save the drowning swimmer, but she does not take the most direct route. Rather than a straight line, her path from the platform to the drowning swimmer might be described as a half-circle.

3. Immediately upon seeing the drowning swimmer, Lilli descends from the lifeguard observation platform. Rather than running, she casually saunters toward the water and the drowning swimmer.

4. Lilli mistakenly believed that the swimmer thrashing about in the water and crying out, "Help! Help! I'm drowning," was not actually drowning, but instead was only faking drowning as part of a practical joke.

5. Lilli correctly believed that the swimmer thrashing about in the water and crying out, "Help! Help! I'm drowning," was not actually drowning, but instead was only faking drowning as part of a practical joke.

6. The swimmer thrashing about in the water and crying out, "Help! Help! I'm drowning," was not actually drowning, but instead was only faking drowning as part of a practical joke. Lilli mistakenly believed that the swimmer was actually drowning.

7. Lilli's reason for eventually trying to save the drowning swimmer was her fear of being held liable for attempted murder.

8. Lilli's reason for eventually trying to save the drowning swimmer was that she heard police sirens and feared being apprehended.

9. Lilli's reason for eventually trying to save the drowning swimmer was that she saw someone else from far down the beach running toward the drowning swimmer and that Lilli realized that this person might end up saving the drowning swimmer if she (Lilli) did not save the swimmer.

10. Lilli's reason for eventually trying to save the drowning swimmer was that too many beachgoers were pleading with her to save the swimmer.

11. The time period between when Lilli first realized the swimmer required rescue and when Lilli decided to undertake a rescue was not eight seconds but rather fifteen seconds.

12. The time period between when Lilli first realized the swimmer required rescue and when Lilli decided to undertake a rescue was not eight seconds but rather one second.

13. During the interval between when Lilli first realized the swimmer required rescue and when Lilli decided to undertake a rescue, she was neither indecisive nor vacillating. Rather, during that time period, she desired that the drowning swimmer would die by her inaction.

14. During the interval between when Lilli first realized the swimmer required rescue and when Lilli decided to undertake a rescue, she was neither indecisive nor vacillating. Rather, she was merely indifferent as to whether the swimmer lived or died.

15. Immediately upon seeing the drowning swimmer, Lilli descends from the lifeguard observation platform. She initially walks away from the water before she runs toward the water in an effort to save the drowning swimmer.

ADDITIONAL READINGS

R.A. Duff, Criminal Attempts (1996)

George Fletcher, Rethinking Criminal Law 115–22, 135–84 (1978)

Paul Robinson, Criminal Law 623–41, 695–702 (1997)

Larry Alexander & Kimberly D. Kessler, *Mens Rea and Inchoate Crimes*, 87 J. Criminal Law & Criminology 1138 (1997)

Andrew Ashworth, *Criminal Attempt and the Role of Resulting Harm Under the Code and the Common Law*, 19 Rutgers L.J. 725 (1988)

Michael Cahill, *Attempt by Omission*, 94 Iowa L. Rev. 1207 (2009)

Russell Christopher, *Does Attempted Murder Deserve Greater Punishment than Murder? Moral Luck and the Duty to Prevent Harm*, 18 Notre Dame J.L. Ethics & Pub. Pol'y 419 (2004)

Douglas N. Husak, *The Nature and Justifiability of Nonconsummate Offenses*, 37 Ariz. L. Rev. 151 (1995)

Leo Katz, *Why the Successful Assassin Is More Wicked than the Unsuccessful One*, 88 Cal. L. Rev. 791 (2000)

Daniel G. Moriarty, *Extending the Defense of Renunciation*, 62 Temple L. Rev. 1 (1989)

IMPOSSIBLE ATTEMPTS

16

INTRODUCTION

Impossible attempts are a subset, or special category, of attempts. Of course, in all attempts the actor fails to complete the crime or consummate the harm. But, in impossible attempts, the actor's completion of the crime is impossible due either to a mistake about the means to effectuate the crime, a circumstance, or even the criminality of the actor's goal itself. For example, an actor who shoots at a victim but misses has committed a regular or "possible" attempt because it was quite possible for the actor to succeed and kill the intended victim. In contrast, an actor who points an *unloaded* gun at a victim and pulls the trigger, believing the gun to be loaded, commits an impossible attempt because the actor could not possibly have killed the intended victim by the means chosen of firing an unloaded gun.

The practical relevance of impossible attempts is that some types of impossible attempt supply a defense to attempt liability. Traditionally, the law distinguished between legal impossibility, which qualified for a defense; and factual impossibility, which did not. In turn, these two types spawned further types. The principal difficulty lies in situating a given impossible attempt within its particular type or category. Complicating matters even further, different jurisdictions term the categories differently in overlapping and confusing ways. This chapter will term the principal categories of impossible attempt as follows: General Factual Impossibility, Inherent Factual Impossibility, Pure Legal Impossibility, and Hybrid Legal Impossibility.

Perhaps following the MPC, a majority of jurisdictions have declared their abolition of the impossibility defense. But such pronouncements are surely overstated. All jurisdictions and the MPC recognize Pure Legal Impossibility (when the actor's desired or intended result or goal does not constitute a crime—e.g., engaging in consensual intercourse with a person above the age of consent under the mistaken belief that doing so is a crime) as a defense based on, at the very least, the legality principle. The MPC and probably most jurisdictions would also afford a defense for Inherent Factual Impossibility (when the actor utilizes completely inefficacious or absurd means to attempt to complete the crime—e.g., trying to kill by voodoo or witchcraft) because an actor employing such ineffective means poses little danger.

Neither the MPC nor a majority of jurisdictions supply a defense for the remaining types. No jurisdiction provides a defense for General Factual Impossibility (when the actor's mistake of a plain fact prevents completion of the offense— e.g., trying to kill by firing an unloaded gun, mistakenly believed to be loaded) perhaps because such actors are seen as no less dangerous or blameworthy than "possible" attempters. And, finally, only a dwindling minority of jurisdictions supplies a defense for Hybrid Legal Impossibility (when the actor's mistake of fact about a legal status regarding an element of the offense prevents completion of the offense—e.g., trying to kill a corpse under the mistaken belief that it is alive).

Perhaps a defense is allowed only due to these jurisdictions mistakenly conflating this type of impossibility with Pure Legal Impossibility.

The law of impossible attempts is surely not easy. One commentator declares, perhaps even with considerable understatement, that "no area of the criminal law is more confusing and confused than the common law of impossible attempts."[1] But it is surely not impossible. This chapter endeavors to bring new clarity and precision to the law of impossibility by utilizing a transparent, step-by-step analysis.

PROBLEM

Thirty-five-year-old Iago is sexually impotent. That is, Iago has been physically incapable of engaging in sexual intercourse for the past 15 years due to a medical condition. Iago tries to engage in sexual intercourse with Desdemona, who is 15 years old. Because of his medical condition, Iago is unable to engage in sexual intercourse.

Iago is charged with attempted statutory rape under the following statute:

> The offense of statutory rape consists of the following elements:
> 1. Sexual intercourse or penetration;
> 2. With a victim below the age of 16;
> 3. The defendant is at least three years older than the victim.

Analyze and discuss whether Iago has a defense of impossibility to attempted statutory rape under both the common law and MPC. Assume for the purposes of your analysis that Iago satisfies both the requisite mens rea and actus reus of attempt.

LIST OF READINGS

Weeks v. Scott, 55 F.3d 1059 (1st Cir. 1995)
United States v. Thomas and McClellan, 32 C.M.R. 278 (C.M.A. 1962)
People v. Thousand, 631 N.W.2d 694 (Mich. 2001)
MODEL PENAL CODE §§ 5.01, 5.05(2) (Official Draft and Revised
 Comments 1985)

ESSAY

Iago probably has no defense of impossibility to his charge of attempted statutory rape. Iago has probably committed an impossible attempt of General Factual Impossibility, which no jurisdiction recognizes as a defense. However, there are plausible arguments that Iago committed Hybrid Legal Impossibility or Inherent Factual Impossibility. Perhaps Iago has not even committed an impossible attempt of any type but only a "possible" attempt.

[1] While the criminal law still recognizes an impossibility defense, an increasing number of courts and codes purport to have abolished the defense of impossibility. Perhaps more accurately, the majority of jurisdictions has limited, rather than abolished, impossibility as a defense. Both the common law and MPC clearly do provide a defense for Pure Legal Impossibility. The MPC clearly does,

---

[1] JOSHUA DRESSLER, UNDERSTANDING CRIMINAL LAW 404 (5th ed. 2009).

and the common law probably does, provide a defense for Inherent Factual Impossibility. A minority of jurisdictions do recognize a defense for Hybrid Legal Impossibility.

[2] In order for Iago to have a defense of impossibility, he must have committed an impossible attempt. And in order to determine whether Iago committed an impossible attempt, one must first determine whether Iago was mistaken. Generally, impossible attempts involve mistakes.

[3] It is not clear from the facts that Iago made a mistake. If he is fully aware that his success is unlikely, then he is not mistaken about his prospect for successfully engaging in intercourse. And if he is not mistaken, Iago's attempt probably does not qualify as an impossible attempt. Rather, he has committed only a "possible" attempt. (If Iago truly believed it was impossible to succeed, he may not even have the mens rea sufficient for a "possible" attempt.) If, however, Iago believes he will succeed, then he is mistaken as to his prospects for success. And if he is mistaken, then he possibly has committed an impossible attempt. Let us assume that Iago has made a mistake.

[4] Impossible attempts involve inculpatory rather than exculpatory mistakes. An actor commits an exculpatory mistake when she actually causes harm but mistakenly believes her conduct is harmless. In contrast, an actor commits an inculpatory mistake when she commits harmless conduct but mistakenly believes it to be harmful.

[5] Iago has made an inculpatory mistake. Iago mistakenly believed that his conduct would be harmful, but it was harmless. That is, Iago mistakenly believed that he would successfully engage in intercourse with the underage victim, but he did not.

[6] Because Iago has made an inculpatory mistake, he most likely has committed some type of impossible attempt. But only certain types of impossible attempt provide a defense to attempt liability. In order to determine the specific type of impossible attempt, one must determine whether the actor has made a mistake about a fact or a law. And in order to determine that, it is helpful to determine *precisely* about what the actor is mistaken.

[7] Iago is mistaken about his ability or capacity to engage in sexual intercourse.

[8] Iago's mistake is about a fact. Iago is neither mistaken about the law under which he is charged nor any other law.

[9] One test for determining whether Iago has made a mistake about a law or a fact is to consider whether Iago could realize his mistake by referencing a law book. No law book would ever state that Iago or any other specific person is physically able to engage in sexual intercourse on the present occasion. Because Iago could not realize he was mistaken by referencing a law book, Iago has not made a mistake about a law. Because Iago has not made a mistake about a law, Iago's mistake must be about a fact.

[10] An alternative but similar rule for distinguishing between mistakes of law and mistakes of fact rests on who could best correct the mistake. If a lawyer could best correct the actor's mistake, then the actor has made a mistake about a law. If, however, a private investigator could better correct the actor's mistake, then the actor has made a mistake about a fact. Because a lawyer would have no particular expertise in helping Iago realize his mistake, Iago is making a mistake about a fact.

[11] That Iago has made a mistake about a fact helps narrow the specific types of impossible attempt that he might have committed. There are four principal types of impossibility:

i. General Factual Impossibility
ii. Inherent Factual Impossibility
iii. Pure Legal Impossibility
iv. Hybrid Legal Impossibility

Pure Legal Impossibility

[12] Because Iago has made a mistake about a fact, the category of Pure Legal Impossibility may be excluded. Pure Legal Impossibility involves the actor being mistaken about a law. This category applies where the actor's desired or intended result or goal does not constitute a crime. As an example, impossibility is a defense to a charge of attempted rape where the defendant, due to being under the age of 14, was conclusively presumed legally unable to engage in intercourse. The defendant's type of impossible attempt was Pure Legal Impossibility, and thus the defendant was not liable. One might argue, on this basis, that Iago's inability to engage in intercourse must also be Pure Legal Impossibility. Iago's inability, however, is medical or factual, not legal. Iago is mistaken about a fact, not a law. As a result, Iago has committed one of the remaining three types of impossibility—those which involve a mistake about a fact. We will now analyze each of the remaining categories in turn.

Inherent Factual Impossibility

[13] Iago's attempt probably does not qualify as Inherent Factual Impossibility. This type of impossibility arises when the actor's goal is criminal, but the actor utilizes completely unrealistic and ineffectual means to complete the crime under the mistaken belief that the means will succeed. Paradigmatic examples include killing by witchcraft or voodoo or trying to open a safe with magical incantations. These clearly suffice as ineffectual means because they are said to have a literally zero percent probability of succeeding.

[14] Various tests are used to determine the degree of ineffectuality necessary for Inherent Factual Impossibility. One test assesses whether the impossibility would be clearly evident to a reasonable person. Presumably a reasonable person would find the impossibility of killing by voodoo or witchcraft to be clearly evident. However, the impossibility of Iago succeeding might not be clearly evident because the cause of Iago's difficulty might not be clearly evident. And even if apprised of the details of Iago's medical condition, whether a reasonable person would regard Iago's prospects of succeeding as clearly impossible or merely extremely unlikely is unclear.

[15] The MPC standard is similarly unclear. Section 5.05(2) provides for a defense where the conduct is "so inherently unlikely to result or culminate in the commission of a crime that neither such conduct nor the actor presents a public danger." While Iago's conduct is extremely unlikely to result in the crime, is it "inherently unlikely?" Arguments could be made either way. A 15-year history of impotence surely suggests that Iago has an inherent difficulty. On the other hand, unlike voodoo or witchcraft, which will never work regardless of the claimed

potency of the voodoo or witchcraft, attempting to engage in intercourse with a minor by penetration of the male sexual organ is typically an efficacious means.

[16] One might question the adequacy of these tests and standards by considering *Weeks*. There, an HIV-infected defendant was charged with attempted murder for spitting in his victim's face. Does such conduct constitute a clearly evident impossibility to a reasonable person? Is it inherently unlikely? Again, it is difficult under these tests to definitively conclude one way or the other. The court upheld the conviction because the medical evidence suggested that the probability of killing by spitting HIV-infected saliva, while extremely low, was still slightly greater than zero percent and thus not impossible.

So how would Iago fare under *Weeks*? Probably Iago's attempt would not qualify as Inherent Factual Impossibility. Iago's 15-year incapacity does not necessarily preclude Iago from being able to succeed on this particular occasion. Though extremely unlikely, the probability of Iago succeeding is still greater than zero percent.

[17] *Weeks* suggests an alternative test for Inherent Factual Impossibility—when the actor's means chosen to effectuate the crime, when viewed in the abstract, has a zero percent probability of succeeding. While it might seem that Iago's chosen means to effectuate the crime has a zero percent probability of succeeding under the actual facts and circumstances, the test instead assesses Iago's chosen means in the abstract or in general. Because the chosen means of completing the crime (penetration with a male sexual organ) will generally succeed (that is, succeed in the abstract), Iago's chosen means has a significantly greater than zero percent possibility of succeeding. As a result, Iago's attempt probably does not qualify as Inherent Factual Impossibility under this test.

[18] The various tests for determining whether Iago's attempt is of the Inherent Factual Impossibility type conflict. Under the standard definition of this type of impossibility, the reasonable person test, and the MPC test, as discussed above in [13]–[15], the conclusion is unclear. In contrast, under the test suggested by *Weeks*, as discussed in [16]–[17], Iago's attempt is most likely not Inherent Factual Impossibility. Let us assume that the *Weeks* test is preferable and that Inherent Factual Impossibility may be excluded.

Hybrid Legal Impossibility

[19] Two types of impossibility remain. Iago has probably not committed Hybrid Legal Impossibility. This type arises when the actor's goal is illegal, but commission of the offense was impossible because the actor commits a mistake of fact regarding a legal status pertaining to, or an element of, the offense. (In addition, some special types of mistakes of law may be treated as Hybrid Legal Impossibility. See tool #7.) For example, *Thousand* most likely involves Hybrid Legal Impossibility. The defendant's mistake of fact regarding the identity and age of his intended victim pertained to whether the victim had the legal status of being a minor, which was an element of the offense. *Thomas* also involves Hybrid Legal Impossibility. The defendants' mistake of fact regarding whether their victim was alive pertained to whether the victim had the legal status of being a live human being, which was an element of the offense.

[20] Iago's mistake of fact is probably not about a legal status regarding an element of the offense. However, a weak argument may be made that Iago is committing Hybrid Legal Impossibility. Iago's goal is illegal (intercourse with a minor),

but commission of the offense is impossible due to a factual mistake (his ability to engage in intercourse), which is relevant to his conduct and relates to the element of intercourse. The problem with this argument is that Iago's factual mistake does not clearly regard a "legal status." Iago's ability or inability to engage in intercourse fails to constitute a legal status. Thus, Iago's mistaken belief that he can succeed does not regard a legal status. For clear examples of mistakes that do regard a legal status, consider the defendant's mistake in *Thousand* about whether a victim is below the age of consent or in *Thomas* about whether the victim is a live human being.

As courts have noted, distinguishing Hybrid Legal Impossibility from General Factual Impossibility is often itself impossible. Understandably, which type Iago committed may well be a close call. Although Iago's mistake does pertain to an element of the offense, it does not regard a legal status. As a result, probably the best conclusion is that Iago is not committing Hybrid Legal Impossibility. Assuming that Iago is not committing Hybrid Legal Impossibility, the only remaining type of attempt is General Factual Impossibility.

General Factual Impossibility

[21] The best conclusion is that Iago has committed an attempt of General Factual Impossibility—the actor's goal constitutes a crime, but the actor's mistake about a fact (*not* about a legal status regarding an element of the offense) prevents its completion. General Factual Impossibility provides no defense. Iago's goal, intercourse with a minor, constituted a crime, but Iago's mistake of fact regarding his capacity or ability to engage in intercourse prevented completion of the offense. Because Iago neither employed inherently unlikely means (when viewed in the abstract) nor was he mistaken about a legal status, as discussed above in [13]–[20], Iago's impossible attempt is best understood as General Factual Impossibility.

Conclusion

Iago's attempt probably qualifies as General Factual Impossibility. This type of impossibility is not recognized as a defense in any jurisdiction or the MPC. Plausible arguments may be made that Iago's attempt is either Inherent Factual Impossibility or Hybrid Legal Impossibility. If Iago committed an attempt of Inherent Factual Impossibility, then Iago would probably have a defense. However, there are too few cases regarding Inherent Factual Impossibility to know for sure. Under the Model Penal Code, §5.05(2), the court would have discretion to either dismiss such a case or mitigate the charges. If Iago's attempt qualifies as Hybrid Legal Impossibility, under the majority rule and MPC, Iago would not have a defense. But under the minority rule, he would have one. An argument might even be made that Iago has not committed an impossible attempt of any type. Rather, Iago has committed a "possible" attempt.

TOOLS FOR SELF-ASSESSMENT

Go back to your written answer. Look for the issues identified in paragraphs [1]–[21] above. Look also for the analysis that follows each issue, and mark your essay where you locate it. Do you fully describe the issue, identify the precise legal standard that applies, list the relevant facts, and show how the facts and law support a conclusion for each issue in a separate paragraph? Mark each conclusion in your essay. Are there sufficient reasons in the law and in the facts to support the conclusion?

1. Do what you are told. Here, you are to analyze whether Iago has a defense of impossibility to attempted statutory rape. A complete answer would identify the type of impossibility involved, if any, and explain what effect that type of impossibility will have on Iago's criminal liability—that is, does the type of impossibility involved supply a defense?

2. Do not analyze what is unnecessary. The Problem states that you are to assume that Iago satisfies the actus reus and mens rea for an attempt. So, you should not analyze whether Iago satisfies the elements of an attempt offense. The scope of your analysis is limited to whether Iago has a defense of impossibility.

3. Always analyze under the Model Penal Code unless you are instructed otherwise.

4. State the best possible arguments for alternative conclusions. Even as you reject possible conclusions as to what type of impossible attempt Iago may have committed, make the best possible argument first, and only then explain why you are rejecting that type of impossibility.

5. Be on the alert for red herrings. Some information in the fact pattern of a hypothetical may be irrelevant or even designed to mislead you. For example, suppose the hypothetical stated that Desdemona is 17 years old, but Iago mistakenly believes that she is 18. This is an irrelevant mistake under the supplied statute (designating the age of consent as 16). As long as he correctly believes that she is above the age of consent, it does not matter what *particular* age she is. Similarly, if Desdemona is 15 and Iago mistakenly believes that she is 14, this is also an irrelevant mistake under the given statute. As long as Iago correctly believes she is below the age of consent, it does not matter what particular age she is (of course, it might for other statutes).

6. Specify any necessary information that is lacking. In addition, assume any missing facts, proceed with your analysis, and argue in the alternative. For example, whether Iago believes he will succeed or whether he is aware of a low likelihood of success is not specified in the facts. So, assume it each way and explain how the assumption affects your analysis.

7. The following steps reveal the above Essay's analysis of what impossible attempt, if any, Iago has committed. These steps are somewhat oversimplified so as to afford a better view of the forest without the obstruction of the trees. But this should not be mistaken for or taken as a substitute for in-depth knowledge of the trees. Perhaps with some modification, these steps could be utilized in answering Variations on the Theme.

   i. Is the actor making a mistake?

  ii. If no, then the actor probably has not committed an impossible attempt.

 iii. If yes, is the mistake inculpatory?

    a. Does the actor commit harmless or innocuous conduct mistakenly believing it to be harmful or wrongful?

    b. If no, then the actor has not made an inculpatory mistake and probably has not committed an impossible attempt.

      c. If yes, then the actor has committed an inculpatory mistake and probably has committed an impossible attempt.
  iv. If inculpatory, identify exactly what the actor is mistaken about.
   v. Is it a mistake about a law or a fact?
      a. Could the actor best realize or correct the mistake by referencing a law book or consulting with an attorney?
      b. If yes, then the mistake is about a law. Go to vi.
      c. If no, then it is a mistake of fact, and three possible categories of impossibility remain. Go to ix.
  vi. Is it a mistake of governing/same law or nongoverning/different law?
      a. If the mistake is about the criminal law, more specifically, the offense with which the actor is charged, then it is a mistake about governing/same law.
      b. If the mistake is about noncriminal law, then it is a mistake about nongoverning/different law.
  vii. If governing/same law, then it is Pure Legal Impossibility.
 viii. If nongoverning/different law, then depending on the court, it is either Pure Legal Impossibility or Hybrid Legal Impossibility.[2]
   ix. If a mistake about a fact, does the means chosen to commit the crime, when viewed in the abstract, have a zero percent probability of success or a greater than zero percent probability?
    x. If zero, then it is Inherent Factual Impossibility.
   xi. If greater than zero, but extremely or inherently unlikely to occur, then the actor's attempt may be Inherent Factual Impossibility depending on the particular standard or test employed.
  xii. If greater than zero, and not qualifying as Inherent Factual Impossibility, does the actor's mistake concern a legal status pertaining to an element of the offense?
 xiii. If yes, then it is Hybrid Legal Impossibility.
 xiv. If no, then it is General Factual Impossibility.

8.   Analogize to other cases. In addition to applying the abstract rules, tests, and definitions of the various categories of impossibility, supplement your analysis with cases with similar facts. For example, in analyzing how to approach the attempted rape of a corpse, *Thomas* analogized to the attempted murder of a corpse. *Thomas* reasoned that because the latter scenario supplies no impossibility defense, neither should the former scenario.

9.   Do not be confused by the differing terminology used by courts and commentators. For example, *Thomas* includes both Pure Legal Impossibility and Hybrid Legal Impossibility under the single term "legal impossibility." And regardless of whether the term legal impossibility or Hybrid Legal Impossibility is used, both are misleading. What this chapter terms Hybrid Legal Impossibility most typically

---

[2] In some cases it can be exceedingly difficult to determine the precise type of inculpatory mistake of law. The distinctions between governing versus nongoverning law, same versus different, criminal versus noncriminal, and charged offense versus other criminal law is often ambiguous. Because of theses ambiguities, courts will vary in determining whether such mistakes qualify as Pure Legal Impossibility or Hybrid Legal Impossibility. For discussion of these distinctions in the context of exculpatory mistakes of law, see Chapter 4.

involves an actor making a mistake about a *fact*. This type of impossibility is none-theless designated as some form of legal impossibility because the actor's mistake about a fact concerns a legal status regarding an element of the offense. While *Thousand* does divide legal impossibility into the Pure and Hybrid forms, it uses the single term "factual impossibility" without distinguishing between the General and Inherent forms.

10. Be aware that the practical effect of a determination that Iago committed one type of impossible attempt might be the same as if Iago committed just a "possi-ble" attempt. For example, the practical effect of Iago committing General Factual Impossibility and a "possible" attempt is the same: criminal liability for attempt. In addition, under the majority rule and the MPC, the practical effect of Iago com-mitting a "possible" attempt, General Factual Impossibility, or Hybrid Legal Impossibility, will be the same: criminal liability. The distinction between those two types of impossible attempts only matters under the minority rule.

11. Consider not just what the law is but the direction or trend of the law. For example, the trend is to not grant a defense for Hybrid Legal Impossibility.

12. In analyzing whether an impossible attempt is Hybrid Legal Impossibility, look at the elements of the supplied statute to determine if Iago made a mistake about a legal status pertaining to an element of the offense. If a hypothetical does not provide a statute, try to imagine what the elements of the statute might be. If you are not sure what the elements of the offense are, then simply assume the requisite elements of the offense in order to undertake your impossibility analysis.

13. In analyzing whether an impossible attempt is Inherent Factual Impossibility, the key is to consider the probability of the actor's chosen means, not under the specific facts and circumstances of the case but rather in general and in the abstract. Consider, for example, an actor trying to kill someone by attempting to shoot an unloaded gun that the actor mistakenly believes is loaded. Under the specific facts and circumstances, the probability is zero. But in assessing the probability of the means chosen in the abstract or in general, we consider whether the general cate-gory of guns is an effective means to kill. Because guns will often actually contain bullets, the probability of killing with a gun is significantly greater than zero. In contrast, trying to kill someone by witchcraft is not only impossible under the actual facts and circumstances but also in general and in the abstract. While guns sometimes do work, witchcraft never does. Similarly, under the actual facts and circumstances, Iago perhaps has zero probability of succeeding. But when assess-ing Iago's chosen means in the abstract and in general, the probability is greater than zero. Unlike witchcraft, Iago's chosen means, when viewed in the abstract, often is efficacious.

14. Understand how to "manipulate" the *Weeks*-inspired test for Inherent Factual Impossibility. This will enable you to make arguments both in support of and against a given case being Inherent Factual Impossibility. To fully understand this test, let us consider its application to a number of variations on a perhaps difficult factual scenario for impossible attempt. Consider the following variations on an attempt to kill via the use of a gun that in various ways does not fully function:

a. Functioning Gun without bullets
b. Non-functioning Gun with bullets

c. Non-functioning Gun without bullets

d. Starter Gun (that "fires" blanks; used to start a race)

e. Prop Gun (as used on a movie set that looks, feels, and has the weight of a real gun)

f. Very Realistic Toy Gun (that looks very much like a real gun but lacks the weight and feel of a real one)

g. Toy Gun (it somewhat looks like a real gun from a distance, but is obviously not when viewed up close)

h. Very Unrealistic Bright Orange Nerf Gun (made of soft, spongy orange foam that "fires" soft, spongy orange nerf balls)

Assuming that the actor who tried to kill with each of the above guns was neither mistaken about a law nor a fact about a legal status pertaining to an element of the offense charged, the categories of Pure Legal Impossibility and Hybrid Legal Impossibility may be excluded. This leaves, as possible categories, General Factual Impossibility and Inherent Factual Impossibility.

Some of the variations are easy. Variations a, b, and c are generally considered clear examples of General Factual Impossibility. And variation h is generally considered to be a clear case of Inherent Factual Impossibility. But variations e–g perhaps could be argued either way. Again, the *Weeks*-inspired test is whether, given the means chosen to commit the offense, when viewed in the abstract, have a zero percent probability of succeeding. If zero, then Inherent Factual Impossibility; if greater than zero, then General Factual Impossibility. Of course, in some sense, any impossible attempt necessarily has a zero percent probability of succeeding—that is why it is an impossible attempt. (And, in some sense, even regular or "possible" attempts have a zero percent probability of succeeding; otherwise, the attempt would have succeeded and the actor's conduct would not be an attempt but rather a completed offense. For example, suppose an actor aims her gun at a victim and shoots and misses. Given the way that she aimed, it was not possible for her to hit the target.) As a result, a test for Inherent Factual Impossibility has to explain why a case of Inherent factual Impossibility is even "more impossible" than a case of General Factual Impossibility.

The *Weeks*-inspired test does this by assessing the means chosen *when viewed in the abstract* rather than under the actual facts and circumstances of the case. Under the actual facts and circumstances of variations a–c, the actor has zero percent probability of succeeding; shooting at someone with a nonfunctioning and/or unloaded gun has zero percent probability of succeeding. But when viewed in the abstract, the use of a real gun has a greater than zero percent probability of succeeding. This is because sometimes real guns do function and are loaded with bullets. In contrast, the means chosen in variation h has zero percent probability of succeeding both under the actual facts and circumstances as well as in the abstract. When viewed in the abstract, obviously fake, soft, spongy toy guns never function.

Let us consider the more difficult case of variation e. Depending on the abstract category employed in the *Weeks*-inspired test, this may be either Inherent or General Factual Impossibility. If the abstract category is broadly described as using means that look, feel, and have the weight of a real gun, then the probability of the actor succeeding is greater than zero, and thus the actor's attempt is General

Factual Impossibility. This abstract category includes real, loaded guns that sometimes will succeed in killing the target. If instead, the abstract category is described more narrowly as means that appear to be real guns but are not, then the probability of succeeding is zero, and thus the actor's attempt is Inherent Factual Impossibility.

Depending on how broadly or narrowly the abstract category is described, the means chosen may have either greater than zero percent probability of succeeding or zero, and thus the actor's attempt may be either General or Inherent Factual Impossibility. Appreciating the elasticity of the description of the abstract category allows you to make plausible arguments either way for the difficult cases like variations d–g.

VARIATIONS ON THE THEME

For the following variations, Iago is *not* impotent. Analyze whether Iago has an impossibility defense to statutory rape.

1. Iago engages in sexual intercourse with Desdemona who is 17 years old. Iago mistakenly believes Desdemona is 15.
2. Iago engages in sexual intercourse with Desdemona whom Iago correctly believes is 17. Iago, however, mistakenly believes that the law of statutory rape prohibits intercourse with those under 18.
3. Iago engages in sexual intercourse with Desdemona whom Iago mistakenly believes is 17, but Desdemona is 15.
4. Iago engages in sexual intercourse with Desdemona whom Iago correctly believes is 15, but Iago mistakenly believes that the law of statutory rape prohibits intercourse with only those under the age of 14.
5. Iago correctly believes that Desdemona is 15. He tries, but is unable, to have sexual intercourse with Desdemona by sticking pins in a voodoo doll.
6. Iago engages in sexual intercourse with 17-year-old Desdemona, whom Iago mistakenly believes is both alive and 15.
7. Because the bedroom is very dark, Iago mistakenly believes that he is engaging in intercourse with Desdemona, who is 15. Iago actually engages in intercourse with Desdemona's neighbor, Dora, who is 25.
8. Mistakenly believing that Desdemona is 14 and mistakenly believing that the age of consent is 18, Iago engages in intercourse with Desdemona. Desdemona is 17.
9. For this variation only, Iago is not 35. Rather, Iago is 17 and engages in sexual intercourse with Desdemona, who is 15. Iago mistakenly believes that Desdemona is 13.

ADDITIONAL READINGS

Joshua Dressler, Understanding Criminal Law 402–10, 416–19 (5th ed. 2009)
Anthony Duff, Criminal Attempts 76–115, 154–65, 206–33, 378–84 (1996)
Comment, 8 Hypothetical L. Rev. 1, 3–4 (1962–2007), in Sanford H. Kadish, Stephen J. Schulhofer & Carol S. Steiker, Criminal Law and its Processes 585 (8th ed. 2007)
Larry Alexander, Inculpatory and Exculpatory Mistakes and the Fact/Law Distinction: An Essay in Memory of Myke Balyes, 12 Law & Phil. 33 (1993)

Fernand N. Dutile & Harold F. Moore, *Mistake and Impossibility: Arranging a Marriage Between Two Difficult Partners*, 74 Nw. U. L. Rev. 166 (1979)

George P. Fletcher, *Constructing a Theory of Impossible Attempts*, 5 Crim. J. Ethics 53 (1986)

John Hasnas, *Once More unto the Breach: The Inherent Liberalism of the Criminal Law and Liability for Attempting the Impossible*, 54 Hastings L.J. 1 (2002)

Ira P. Robbins, *Attempting the Impossible: The Emerging Consensus*, 23 Harv. J. on Leg. 377 (1986)

Kenneth W. Simons, *Mistake and Impossibility, Law and Fact, and Culpability: A Speculative Essay*, 81 J. Criminal Law & Criminology 447 (1990)

Peter Westen, *Impossibility Attempts: A Speculative Thesis*, 5 Ohio St. J. Crim. L. 523 (2008)

ACCOMPLICE LIABILITY

17

INTRODUCTION

Liability in the criminal law comes in two principal forms. First, personal or direct liability—the actor is held liable for the conduct and/or harmful results personally attributable to and directly perpetrated by that actor. This form of liability comprises the bulk of our study of the criminal law. Second, complicity liability—the actor is held liable for the wrongful conduct and/or harmful results directly perpetrated and caused by another through the actor's contribution to, and association with, the direct perpetrator's commission of the offense. Under the common law, complicity liability itself comes in two distinct forms—conspiratorial liability and accomplice liability. Conspiratorial liability is based on an actor's agreement with one or more others to commit a crime. Because of the actor's agreement, the actor may be held liable for the crimes directly committed by the other conspirators. (Conspiracy, which can be the basis for both personal or direct liability and complicity liability, will be the subject of the next chapter.) Accomplice liability is based on an actor's aid to the direct perpetrator. By aiding or abetting another to commit a crime, an actor may be held liable for the crime. Under the MPC, only a specific type of conspiratorial agreement gives rise to accomplice liability.

Accomplice liability is derivative in nature. This has two distinct features. First, unlike conspiracy, there is no separate crime of being an accomplice (with one exception—an accomplice after the fact—as explained below). Rather, if an actor is held liable under principles of accomplice liability for a crime committed by the direct perpetrator (in common law terms, the principal), the actor is held liable for that crime. For example, if an actor is found liable as an accomplice to murder, the actor is guilty of murder. Second, accomplice liability stems from and is dependent on the direct perpetrator's commission (but not necessarily conviction) of a crime. If an actor aids a direct perpetrator, but the direct perpetrator fails to commit the crime, the actor is perhaps not liable as an accomplice because the direct perpetrator never committed the crime. (However, if the direct perpetrator fails to commit the completed offense but does commit an attempt, the actor may be liable as an accomplice for that attempt. Under the MPC, if the direct perpetrator fails to commit even an attempt, the actor can still be held liable for an attempt, but not as an accomplice.) A related feature of this derivative nature of accomplice liability is that generally, under the common law, the accomplice cannot be liable for a more serious crime than the principal.

In the early common law, the various modes of participation in a crime were assigned a wide variety of labels: principal in the first degree, principal in the second degree, accessory before the fact, and accessory after the fact. Under modern terminology, the surviving roles are principal, accomplice, and accomplice after the fact. Both principals and accomplices are generally held liable for the same offense and are subject to the same punishment. An accomplice after the fact (one who provides assistance *after* the commission of the crime) is both liable for a lesser, distinct offense (from the aided offense) and subject to considerably less punishment than the principal and accomplice.

PROBLEM

Snoop Cub is the street name for an undercover cop attempting to infiltrate Mr. Big's criminal gang. Sporting a black leather motorcycle jacket and very tight pastel T-shirts—"Shield-style, not Commish-style"—he believes he looks the part. He is street tough and street smart. Mr. Big's crew is well known for taking down major scores. Their "MO" is that they are good. The target of their planned heist is a jewelry store that has received a shipment of uncut diamonds. One of the members of the crew whom Snoop intensely dislikes, Mugsy, is well known for being a gun nut. Snoop shows Mugsy a limited-edition, hand-crafted, imported Glock with a beautiful rosewood handle. Knowing that Mugsy enjoys a reputation for waving his gun in other people's faces and being trigger happy, Snoop offers to let him use it during the heist. Mugsy accepts the gun. Because Mr. Big does not completely trust Snoop yet, Snoop is not brought along for the heist. As the crew departs for the burglary of the jewelry store, Snoop yells out to Mr. Big: "Bring me back a nice diamond solitaire pendant. Mother's Day is next week." After breaking into the store, Mr. Big tells Mugsy to neutralize the security guard, Doug Blart. Mugsy points his gun at Blart and tells him to drop his gun. As Blart is about to drop it, Blart quickly raises his gun and shoots at Mugsy. Blart misses. Believing that Blart will shoot at him again, Mugsy points his Glock at Blart and pulls the trigger. Nothing emanates from the gun except a click. Snoop had removed both the bullets and the firing pin before giving the Glock to Mugsy. Just after Mugsy pulled the trigger, and believing that Mugsy would kill him, Blart shoots and kills Mugsy. Mr. Big kills Blart. The crew then steals the diamonds. As they exit the store, swarms of police are waiting to arrest them. As it turns out, Mugsy was also an undercover cop from a different police unit. Both Snoop and Mugsy had notified their respective police units about the burglary. Neither Mugsy nor Snoop knew that the other was an undercover police officer.

Snoop is charged with the burglary and larceny of the jewelry store perpetrated by Mr. Big, the assault of Blart perpetrated by Mugsy, the murder of Mugsy perpetrated by Blart, and the murder of Blart perpetrated by Mr. Big.

Analyze and discuss Snoop's accomplice liability, if any, under both common law and MPC principles.

LIST OF READINGS

Riley v. State, 60 P.3d 204 (Alaska 2002)
Wilson v. People, 87 P.2d 5 (Col. 1939)
State v. Hayes, 16 S.W. 514 (Mo. 1891)
State v. Etzweiler, 480 A.2d 870 (N.H. 1984)
Bailey v. Commonwealth, 329 S.E.2d 37 (Va. 1985)
MODEL PENAL CODE § 2.06, 5.01(3) (Official Code and Revised Comments 1985)

ESSAY

Snoop is probably not liable as an accomplice to burglary and larceny or as an accomplice to the murder of Mugsy. It is unclear whether Snoop is liable for assault.

Snoop is probably not liable for the murder of Blart under the common law and clearly not liable under the MPC.

There are four general components of complicity to analyze: the actus reus, the mens rea, the relationship between the liability of the direct perpetrator and the accomplice, and possible defenses. The following general principles apply under both the common law and MPC. The actus reus is established if the actor aids, either physically or psychologically, the direct perpetrator's commission of the target offense. The requisite amount of aid is very minimal. Almost any aid suffices. The aid need not even be a but-for cause of the direct perpetrator's commission of the target offense. To satisfy the mens rea requirement, two different types of mens rea may be applicable: (i) specific intent or purpose to aid the direct perpetrator's commission of the target offense, and (ii) the mens rea required for commission of the target offense. The common law requires both types of mens rea; the MPC requires one or both depending on the type of element or offense. Because the nature of accomplice liability is derivative, an actor will only have accomplice liability if the direct perpetrator committed the target offense or an attempt. Of course, these general principles are subject to numerous exceptions and are the subject of significant variance between the common law and the MPC as will be discussed below.

Snoop's Accomplice Liability for Mr. Big's Burglary/Larceny

COMMON LAW

[1] The actus reus is satisfied by either physical or psychological aid. The only possible aid that Snoop provides to Mr. Big's burglary of the store and larceny of the diamonds is Snoop's request that Mr. Big bring back some jewelry for Snoop's mother. This arguably constitutes psychological aid. By his request, Snoop provides implicit encouragement and moral support of the burglary/larceny. Although Snoop's aid is quite minimal, it nonetheless suffices. The requisite amount of aid may be trivially small if it actually furnishes aid. The aid need not even be a but-for cause of the principal's commission of the target offense. As a result, Snoop most likely satisfies the actus reus requirement.

[2] The mens rea requirement consists of two different types of mens rea—the intent to aid the principal's commission of the crime and the mens rea required by the target offense. The feigning accomplice is a classic problem in the analysis of the mens rea of accomplice liability. As an undercover cop, Snoop is a feigning accomplice. As evidenced by his notifying his police unit about the heist, Snoop wants the principal to commit the crime so that the principal can be arrested, but he does not want the principal to enjoy the fruits of the crime, evade apprehension, or proceed sufficiently far in the criminal course of conduct that irreparable harm is committed. Because he wants Mr. Big to commit the crimes, he does provide the aid with the intent that it aid Mr. Big's commission of the crimes. As a result, the first component of the mens rea is satisfied.

[3] The more difficult issue is whether Snoop has the mens rea required by the target offenses. Let us consider larceny first. Larceny is typically defined as the taking and carrying away of the property of another with the intent to permanently deprive the owner of the property. Because Snoop wants Mr. Big to be apprehended after committing the larceny and the diamonds restored to the owner, Snoop lacks the requisite intent to permanently deprive the owner of her

property. As a result, Snoop lacks the requisite mens rea for the target offense and thus cannot be an accomplice to the larceny.

[4] Whether Snoop satisfies the mens rea for burglary is even more difficult. Burglary is typically defined as the breaking and entering of a structure with the intent to commit a felony inside. In one sense, he does satisfy the mens rea—he wants Mr. Big to commit the burglary so that Mr. Big may be arrested for burglary. On that basis, Snoop satisfies the requisite mens rea.

But in another sense, Snoop does not satisfy the mens rea. A requisite mens rea for the commission of burglary is the intent to commit a felony inside. The intended felony is larceny. As discussed above in [3], Snoop lacks the intent to commit larceny because he lacks the intent to permanently deprive the owner of the diamonds.

Working backward through the analysis demonstrates that Snoop may lack the mens rea for burglary. Because he lacks the intent to permanently deprive the owner of the diamonds, Snoop lacks the intent for larceny. And because he lacks the intent for larceny, he lacks the intent to commit a felony inside the structure. And by lacking the intent to commit a felony inside the structure, he lacks the intent for burglary. On this basis, Snoop is not liable as an accomplice to the burglary.

Most likely, courts would find that Snoop lacks the mens rea for burglary and thus cannot be liable as an accomplice to the burglary.

[5] Accomplice liability requires commission of a crime by the principal. Assuming that Mr. Big satisfies the elements of burglary and larceny and lacks a justification for committing those crimes, Snoop is eligible for accomplice liability.

[6] In conclusion, Snoop most likely lacks the requisite mens rea for the target offenses and thus is not liable as an accomplice to either burglary or larceny.

MODEL PENAL CODE
[7] The actus reus of accomplice liability may be satisfied by an actor aiding the direct perpetrator in the commission of the target offense. As discussed above in [1], Snoop aids Mr. Big's commission of the burglary and larceny. As a result, Snoop satisfies the actus reus requirement.

[8] The requisite mens rea varies depending on the nature of the element or offense. For conduct elements, the actor must aid the direct perpetrator with the purpose of aiding the direct perpetrator's commission of the offense. For result elements, the actor must have the requisite mens rea for the target offense. For attendant circumstance elements, the MPC gives courts the discretion as to whether the mens rea of purpose is required or merely the requisite mens rea of the target offense.

Neither burglary nor larceny contain result elements but each contain both conduct and attendant circumstance elements. With respect to the conduct elements, arguably Snoop does satisfy the requisite mens rea of purpose. As discussed above in [2], Snoop wants Mr. Big to complete the offenses of larceny and burglary so that Mr. Big can be arrested for those crimes. Though Snoop does not intend to permanently deprive the owner of the property, Snoop does want Mr. Big to so intend such that Mr. Big satisfies the elements for larceny and can be arrested. As a result, Snoop probably satisfies the mens rea of purpose to aid the direct perpetrator commit the target offenses.

[9] As discussed above in [5], Mr. Big's liability for the target offenses allows Snoop to be eligible for accomplice liability for those target offenses.

[10] Because Snoop arguably satisfies the elements of accomplice liability for the offenses of burglary and larceny, defenses should be considered. The MPC recognizes what is, in effect, an abandonment defense. To satisfy the defense, an actor must *both* terminate her complicity prior to the commission of the target offense *and* either (i) deprive the offense of effectiveness, (ii) timely notify the police, or (iii) make an appropriate effort to prevent the offense. Snoop clearly supplied timely notification to the police, but it is not clear that he terminated his complicity prior to the commission of the offenses. If he notified his police unit *after* his encouraging words to Mr. Big, perhaps the notification itself constitutes a termination of the complicity. But if instead he notified the police *before* his encouraging words, Snoop does nothing to affirmatively terminate his complicity. As a result, under a literal analysis of the defense, Snoop would obtain the defense if he notified the police after his aid but perhaps would not obtain the defense if he notified the police before his aid. Despite possibly not technically satisfying the defense, as a policy matter perhaps courts would grant Snoop the defense because of his status as a feigning accomplice whose efforts led to the apprehension of the direct perpetrator.

[11] In conclusion, Snoop most likely satisfies the actus reus element, probably satisfies the mens rea element, clearly satisfies the requirement that the direct perpetrator commit the target offenses, and probably satisfies the abandonment defense. Courts would probably not hold Snoop liable for burglary and larceny as an accomplice.

Snoop's Accomplice Liability for Mugsy's Assault of Blart

COMMON LAW

[12] The only aid Snoop supplied Mugsy was providing him with a gun. Because the requisite amount of aid is minimal, this would qualify as the actus reus.

[13] Whether Snoop supplied the gun to Mugsy with the intent or purpose to aid the crime of assault and with the mens rea for assault is unclear. It is unclear because the facts fail to state what Snoop was trying to accomplish. If Snoop wanted Mugsy to commit the crime either so that the police could arrest Mugsy for it or that someone would shoot him, then Snoop would both have the intent to aid the assault and the mens rea for the assault. (Assault is typically defined as to include intentionally placing another in imminent apprehension of physical harm.) Under either of those possible scenarios, Snoop would have the intent that Mugsy's victim be assaulted.

[14] But another possibility rests on the type of gun that Snoop provided—an unloaded gun with the firing pin removed. This fact supports the view that Snoop did not have the purpose of aiding Mugsy's commission of the assault. Rather, he might have been attempting to prevent Mugsy from killing anyone during the burglary, given Mugsy's reputation for being trigger happy. On this basis, Snoop lacked both the purpose/intent of aiding Mugsy and the mens rea required by the target offense.

[15] Even if Snoop lacked the purpose of aiding Mugsy's commission of the assault, a lesser mens rea may sometimes suffice. Some courts lower the requisite mens rea from purpose/intent to knowledge if the target crime is sufficiently serious.

Here, the facts plausibly support the view that Snoop gave the gun to Mugsy knowing that he would likely wave it around in front of other people. Even so, there are a number of obstacles to concluding that Snoop satisfies the mens rea of accomplice liability. First, it is not clear that Snoop had the requisite mens rea for the target offense of assault. Second, it is not clear that assault is a sufficiently serious offense. There is precedent for lowering the mens rea to knowledge for murder, but assault is a substantially less serious offense.

[16] Snoop's relationship to the principal raises a number of issues. First, the principal is dead and cannot be prosecuted for assault. But the nonprosecution of a principal (for any number of reasons, including the principal's death) is not a bar to finding Snoop liable as an accomplice. As long as the principal committed the offense, the principal need neither be prosecuted nor even alive in order for accomplice liability to attach.

[17] Second, Mugsy was an undercover cop. This raises the classic problem of the feigning principal (as well as raising a new twist on this problem—the feigning accomplice aiding the feigning principal). Typically, an accomplice is not held liable for aiding a feigning principal because the principal fails to commit the target offense. Because accomplice liability is derivative, there is no accomplice liability for aiding the lawful acts of the principal.

[18] But the instant case is different (and not just because the accomplice is also feigning). Here, the feigning principal actually commits the target offense. Mugsy actually does commit the crime of assault. While Mugsy may have had a beneficent motive in pointing the gun at Blart—following Mr. Big's instructions until the police arrested the crew outside or trying to prevent Blart from pulling his gun and getting injured—Mugsy nonetheless intended to, and did actually, assault Blart. On this basis, Mugsy's status as a feigning principal would not bar Snoop's accomplice liability.

[19] Even if Mugsy does satisfy the elements of assault, however, Mugsy's status may still bar Snoop's liability. Assuming that Mugsy was acting lawfully as a police officer and not "going rogue," Mugsy's assault may well be justified. An accomplice generally cannot be held liable for the justified acts of a principal.

[20] In conclusion, although Snoop commits the actus reus of aiding the principal by supplying a gun, it is unclear whether he has the requisite mens rea, and it is also unclear whether Snoop was aiding unlawful conduct. As a result, it is unclear whether Snoop will have accomplice liability for Mugsy's assault of Blart.

MODEL PENAL CODE
[21] As discussed in [12], Snoop aids the target offense by supplying the gun.

[22] Because the target offense of assault is a conduct crime, the actor's requisite mens rea is acting with the purpose of aiding the direct perpetrator's commission of the offense. As discussed above in [13]–[14], it is unclear whether Snoop satisfies this mens rea.

[23] As discussed above in [19], if Mugsy's assault is justified, then Snoop may not be liable as an accomplice. While the MPC conditions derivative liability on the direct perpetrator's commission of the offense, the MPC fails to specifically address the effect of a direct perpetrator's justification. If the direct perpetrator is justified, then she is not liable for committing the offense and thus, arguably, has not

committed the offense. If the direct perpetrator being justified does bar accomplice liability, and Mugsy was justified, then Snoop would not have accomplice liability for the assault.

[24] In conclusion, although Snoop commits the actus reus of aiding the direct perpetrator by supplying a gun, it is unclear whether he has the requisite mens rea, and it is also unclear whether Snoop was aiding unlawful conduct. As a result, it is unclear whether Snoop will have accomplice liability for Mugsy's assault of Blart.

Snoop's Accomplice Liability for Blart's Murder of Mugsy

COMMON LAW

[25] There is no evidence in the facts that Snoop either intended to aid Blart in killing Mugsy or that he did aid Blart in killing Mugsy. There is no nexus between Snoop and Blart. Snoop neither had contact nor communication with Blart. There is no evidence that Snoop was even aware of Blart's existence or that the jewelry store even had a security guard.

[26] However, there is evidence in the facts that Snoop hated Mugsy. While it is unclear why Snoop gave Mugsy an unloaded gun with the firing pin removed, it is possible that Snoop gave him such a gun with the belief that he would attempt to use it. And if he did attempt to use it against someone who did have a gun, Mugsy might well be killed. Even assuming this interpretation of the facts is true, it is still unclear how Snoop could be held liable as an accomplice to Blart's murder of Mugsy.

[27] One possible way of holding Snoop liable is the innocent instrumentality rule. The rule provides that an actor is liable for the conduct of another where, acting with the mens rea required for the commission of the offense, the actor uses, causes, or tricks an innocent or nonculpable party to commit the offense. The actor is not held liable as an accomplice but as a principal. As a result, the innocence or nonculpability of the direct perpetrator does not bar liability for the actor who uses the innocent. The rule arguably applies here. With the possible intent that Mugsy would be killed, Snoop possibly used Blart to kill Mugsy. One might argue that Snoop, in effect, tricked Blart into killing Mugsy by giving Mugsy an inoperable gun. (Had Blart known that Mugsy's gun was inoperable, presumably Blart would not have killed him.)

[28] There are a number of possible problems with applying the innocent instrumentality rule here. First, it is unclear whether Snoop had the intent that Mugsy be killed. Second, it is not clear that Snoop "used" Blart to kill Mugsy given the absence of a nexus between them. Third, the rule typically applies where the innocent lacks mens rea or is excused. There is little or no authority for extending the rule to action that is innocent because it is justified. Here, Blart's killing of Mugsy would seem to be justified in self-defense. Fourth, assuming the killing is justified, there is no murder or crime that is perpetrated by the innocent instrumentality.

[29] As a result, Snoop is probably not liable for Blart's killing of Mugsy either via principles of accomplice liability or the innocent instrumentality rule. (For a discussion of how Snoop might be held liable under other principles, see Tool #10 below.)

[30] The MPC also recognizes the innocent instrumentality rule. One explicit requirement is that the defendant must "cause" the innocent to commit the crime. As discussed above in [25], the absence of any nexus between Snoop and Blart makes it difficult to establish that Snoop did anything to Blart to cause him to kill Mugsy. If anything, Snoop caused Mugsy to act rather than Blart. On the other hand, there is an argument that but for Snoop's conduct, Blart would not have killed Mugsy. (See [27] above.)

[31] As discussed above in [28], Snoop is probably not liable for Blart's killing of Mugsy under the innocent instrumentality rule.

Snoop's Accomplice Liability for Mr. Big's Murder of Blart

COMMON LAW

[32] The only possible aid that Snoop supplied to Mr. Big that could serve as the actus reus of accomplice liability to the murder is the utterance of the encouraging words regarding the burglary/larceny. Although ordinarily this would not constitute aid for the different offense of murder, under the natural and probable consequences doctrine Snoop might be liable as an accomplice to the murder. This doctrine is typically analyzed as an aspect of the mens rea of accomplice liability and will be discussed below.

[33] While Snoop may have had the intent to aid Mr. Big's burglary/larceny, there is no evidence in the facts that he intended to aid Mr. Big's commission of murder. But the natural and probable consequences doctrine, recognized in most jurisdictions, may supply this missing mens rea. Under the doctrine, an accomplice to one crime committed by a principal, may be held liable as an accomplice to other crimes committed by the principal (even if these other crimes were neither intended, contemplated, or desired by the accomplice) if these other crimes were the natural and probable consequence of the original crime aided. Assuming that Snoop was an accomplice to the burglary/larceny, Snoop could be held liable as an accomplice to the murder if the murder was a natural and probable consequence of the burglary/larceny. When a criminal gang breaks into a jewelry store armed with guns, some resistance by an employee of the store that would be countered by the use of guns by the gang resulting in a murder is hardly surprising. Whether it rises to the level of a natural and probable consequence is less clear. But it is plausibly a natural and probable consequence. As a result, assuming that Snoop was an accomplice to the burglary/larceny, he possibly also could be held liable as an accomplice to the murder.

[34] Because Snoop is probably not an accomplice to the burglary/larceny as discussed above in [6], Snoop would probably not be liable as an accomplice to Mr. Big's murder of Blart under the natural and probable consequences doctrine.

MODEL PENAL CODE

[35] Because the MPC rejects the natural and probable consequences doctrine, Snoop could not be held liable as an accomplice to the murder.

Conclusion

Burglary/Larceny: Because Snoop is probably lacking the requisite mens rea for accomplice liability, Snoop is probably not liable under the common law. Under the MPC, despite Snoop probably satisfying the mens rea element as well as clearly satisfying the other requisite elements and possibly failing to satisfy an abandonment defense, most likely Snoop would not be held liable.

Assault: Because it is unclear whether Snoop satisfies the mens rea element for accomplice liability, and it is unclear whether the direct perpetrator's conduct was unlawful, it is unclear whether Snoop is liable under either the common law or MPC.

Murder of Mugsy: Because of the lack of a nexus between Snoop and Blart, Snoop probably neither aided nor intended to aid Blart kill Mugsy. The innocent instrumentality rule is also probably inapplicable. Under both the common law and the MPC, Snoop is probably not liable.

Murder of Blart: Because Snoop neither aided nor intended to aid the murder, he may only be liable under the natural and probable consequences doctrine of the common law. But the doctrine is probably inapplicable because Snoop was probably not an accomplice to the burglary/larceny. As a result, Snoop is probably not liable under the common law and clearly not liable under the MPC.

TOOLS FOR SELF-ASSESSMENT

Go back to your written answer. Look for the issues identified in paragraphs [1]–[35] in the above Essay. Look also for the analysis that follows each issue, and mark your essay where you locate it. Do you fully describe the issue, identify the precise legal standard that applies, list the relevant facts, and show how the facts and law support a conclusion for each issue in a separate paragraph? Mark each conclusion in your essay. Are there sufficient reasons in the law and in the facts to support the conclusion?

1.   Do what you are told. In the Problem, you are asked to analyze and discuss whether Snoop Cub is liable as an accomplice for Mr. Big's burglary/larceny, Mugsy's assault, Blart's murder, and Mr. Big's murder. You need not analyze whether Snoop is liable for any other offenses.

2.   Do not analyze what is unnecessary. For example, it might be tempting to analyze whether Mr. Big, Mugsy, and Blart are liable for any offenses. Do not do so. It is not necessary under the instructions following the Problem.

3.   Remember to include an analysis of the MPC's approach unless you are instructed otherwise.

4.   State the best possible arguments for alternative conclusions. Even as you reject possible conclusions as to why Snoop is or is not liable as an accomplice to a particular crime, make the best possible argument first, and only then explain why you are rejecting that conclusion.

5.   Be on the alert for red herrings. For example, both the type of clothing that Snoop wears and the type of gun that Snoop gives to Mugsy (limited edition, rosewood handle etc.) are irrelevant. But, of course, that the gun is unloaded and the firing pin has been removed are relevant.

6.   Be aware of the similarities and differences of accomplice liability analysis under the common law and the MPC. For examples, see Tools #7–9.

7.   Although not raised by the Problem, understand the relationship between accomplice liability and attempt. There are two different aspects, each of which differs under the common law and MPC. First, under the common law, in order to

suffice as the requisite aid for the actus reus of complicity, the actor's conduct must actually aid the principal's commission of the crime. Under the MPC, however, the actor need not actually aid the direct perpetrator; an attempt to aid suffices. Second, suppose an actor actually aids the direct perpetrator, but the direct perpetrator fails to commit the crime. Under the common law, the actor is not liable as an accomplice to the crime. The MPC agrees; it would also not impose accomplice liability. But the MPC would hold the actor liable for an attempt under § 5.01(3). Aiding a direct perpetrator to commit an offense that the direct perpetrator does not commit constitutes an attempt under the MPC but not the common law. The following chart summarizes this analysis:

Example 1: Actor actually aids direct perpetrator's commission of murder.

Outcome: <u>Common Law</u> <u>MPC</u>
Acc. Liab. for Murder Acc. Liab. for Murder

Example 2: Actor attempts, but fails, to aid direct perpetrator's commission of murder.

Outcome: <u>Common Law</u> <u>MPC</u>
No Acc. Liab. Acc. Liab. for Murder

Example 3: Actor actually aids direct perpetrator's commission of attempted murder.

Outcome: <u>Common Law</u> <u>MPC</u>
Acc. Liab. for Att. Murder Acc. Liab. for Att. Murder

Example 4: Actor attempts, but fails, to aid direct perpetrator's commission of attempted murder.

Outcome: <u>Common Law</u> <u>MPC</u>
No Acc. Liab. Acc. Liab. for Att. Murder

Example 5: Actor actually aids direct perpetrator's intended commission of murder, but direct perpetrator neither commits murder nor attempted murder.

Outcome: <u>Common Law</u> <u>MPC</u>
No Acc. & No Att. Liab. Att. Murder Liab., but No
  Acc. Liab.

Example 6: Actor attempts, but fails, to aid direct perpetrator's intended commission of murder, but direct perpetrator neither commits murder nor attempted murder.

Outcome: <u>Common Law</u> <u>MPC</u>
No Acc. & No Att. Liab. Att. Murder Liab., but No
  Acc. Liab.

8. Do not be confused by the mens rea of accomplice liability. This is an enormous source of confusion among both courts and commentators. The following

charts explain the general rule and the principal exceptions to the general rule under both the common law and the MPC:

COMMON LAW:

General Rule:	The actor must both (i) intentionally or purposefully aid the principal commit the offense, and (ii) have the requisite mens rea for the offense committed by the principal.
Exception #1:	Some (perhaps a minority of) courts lower the requirement of intent or purpose to aid the principal to the requirement that the actor knowingly aids the principal commit the crime, especially where the principal's crime is particularly serious: for example, murder.
Exception #2:	A majority of courts will attribute accomplice liability mens rea to an actor for a principal's crime that is a natural and probable consequence of another crime for which the actor did satisfy the mens rea for accomplice liability.

MODEL PENAL CODE:

General Rule:	The actor must aid or engage in other conduct with the purpose of promoting or facilitating the direct perpetrator's commission of the offense.
Exception #1:	Regarding a result element of a direct perpetrator's offense, the requirement of purpose is lowered to whatever mens rea suffices for commission of the offense. (But any conduct elements of that offense still require purpose.)
Exception #2:	Regarding an attendant circumstance element of a direct perpetrator's offense, courts have the discretion to require either purpose or the requisite mens rea for the target offense. (But any conduct elements of that offense still require purpose.)

9. Note the various types of conduct that can satisfy the actus reus requirement. Under the common law, there are three main types: (i) physical conduct, (ii) psychological encouragement or moral encouragement, and (iii) failing to act (when one is under a duty to act). An actor's mere presence does not constitute sufficient aid or assistance, but presence when coupled with encouragement or a prior agreement to assist does suffice. The MPC lists five different ways to satisfy the actus reus: (i) soliciting, (ii) aiding, (iii) agreeing to aid, (iv) attempting to aid, and (v) failing to aid (when one is under a duty to aid).

10. Did you conclude that Snoop was liable for Blart's killing of Mugsy? As discussed in the above Essay in [25]–[31], neither accomplice liability nor the innocent instrumentality rule supplies a strong basis for liability. If Snoop is to be held liable, then perhaps the preferable approach is under a theory of direct liability. Assuming that he intended that Mugsy be killed, he committed an act (giving Mugsy an inoperable gun) that was the but-for cause of Mugsy's death. It was also

the proximate cause. Blart's shooting was not a supervening act because it was involuntary (for the special meaning of involuntary for purposes of proximate causation, see Ch. 5) both because Blart was justified and because he lacked full knowledge of the circumstances.

11. Note the conceptual basis for the innocent instrumentality rule. Though the rule holds a defendant liable for the actions of another innocent actor, the defendant's guilt is not derivative. It is not derived from the guilty commission of the act by another. As a result, that the direct perpetrator cannot be held liable is not a bar for the defendant's liability. The defendant is thus not liable as an accomplice but rather as a direct perpetrator. The defendant has, in a sense, acted through the innocent, or used the innocent as an instrument, to commit the crime.

12. The following steps reveal the structure of the above Essay's analysis of Snoop's liability as an accomplice. These steps are somewhat oversimplified so as to afford a better view of the forest without the obstruction of the trees. But this should not be mistaken for, or taken as a substitute for, in-depth knowledge of the trees. Perhaps with some modification, these steps could be utilized in answering Variations on the Theme.

COMMON LAW:
 i. Did the actor engage in conduct that could have aided the principal?
 ii. If no, then no accomplice liability.
 iii. If yes, did the actor's conduct actually aid the principal?
 iv. If no, then no accomplice liability.
 v. If yes, was the amount or degree of aid sufficient?
 vi. If no, then no accomplice liability.
 vii. If yes, did the actor intentionally aid the principal's commission of the crime?
 viii. If yes, go to xiii.
 ix. If no, then did the actor knowingly aid a serious offense?
 x. If yes, go to xiii.
 xi. If no, then did the principal commit an additional offense that was the natural and probable consequence of the offense that the actor did intentionally aid?
 xii. If no, then no accomplice liability.
 xiii. If yes, did the actor have the requisite mens rea for the target offense?
 xiv. If no, then no accomplice liability.
 xv. If yes, does the principal both satisfy all the elements of the offense and lack a justification defense?
 xvi. If no, go to xx.
 xvii. If yes, does the actor have any applicable defenses?
 xviii. If no, then accomplice liability.
 xix. If yes, then no accomplice liability.
 xx. Does the actor satisfy the innocent instrumentality rule (and lack a defense)?

xxi.   If yes, then the actor is liable as a principal.

xxii. If no, then the actor is liable neither as an accomplice nor as a principal (under the innocent instrumentality rule).

MODEL PENAL CODE:

i.   Did the actor solicit, aid, agree to aid, attempt to aid, or fail to prevent (when under a duty to prevent) the direct perpetrator's commission of the offense?

ii.   If no, then no attempt liability.

iii.   If yes, did the actor engage in the conduct with the purpose of aiding the direct perpetrator's commission of the offense?

iv.   If no, then no accomplice liability.

v.   If yes, does the offense contain a result element?

vi.   If no, go to x.

vii.   If yes, does the actor have the requisite mens rea with respect to that result that is sufficient for the target offense?

viii. If no, then no accomplice liability.

ix.   If yes, go to x.

x.   Does the offense contain an attendant circumstance element?

xi.   If no, go to xiii.

xii.   If yes, courts have discretion to require either purpose or the requisite mens rea for the target offense.

xiii. Does the direct perpetrator both satisfy all the elements of the offense and lack a justification defense?

xiv.   If no, go to xviii.

xv.   If yes, does the actor have any applicable defenses?

xvi.   If no, then accomplice liability.

xvii. If yes, then no accomplice liability.

xviii. Does the actor satisfy the innocent instrumentality rule (and lack a defense)?

xix.   If yes, then the actor is directly liable.

xx.   If no, then the actor is liable neither directly nor as an accomplice (under the innocent instrumentality rule).

13. Keep in mind various possible organizational structures for your essay. While there may be no optimal structure, some structures are preferable to others depending on the particular features of the hypothetical to be analyzed. Because the instructions to this Problem require you to only analyze the liability of one actor for multiple possible crimes, it may be preferable to analyze the crimes one at a time, under both common law and MPC principles, before moving on to analyze the next crime. Within your analysis of each crime, consider organizing the discussion around four central components: (i) actus reus, (ii) mens rea, (iii) relationship between the direct perpetrator's liability and the actor's liability, and (iv) possible applicable defenses. Consider repeating this, for each crime, under each of the common law and MPC approaches, and in this order. This is the organizational structure featured in the above Essay. Structure #1

below depicts this organizational structure, and Structure #2 below depicts
an alternative:

Structure #1	Structure #2
Introduction	Introduction
General Principles of Complicity	General Principles of Complicity
Snoop's Acc. Liab. for Burglary/Larceny	Model Penal Code
Common Law	Snoop's Acc. Liab.for Burglary/Larceny
Model Penal Code	Snoop's Acc. Liab. for Assault
Snoop's Acc. Liab. for Assault	Snoop's Acc. Liab. for Murder of Mugsy
Common Law	Snoop's Acc. Liab. for Murder of Blart
Model Penal Code	Common Law
Snoop's Acc. Liab. for Murder of Mugsy	Snoop's Acc. Liab.for Burglary/Larceny
Common Law	Snoop's Acc. Liab. for Assault
Model Penal Code	Snoop's Acc. Liab. for Murder of Mugsy
Snoop's Acc. Liab. for Murder of Blart	Snoop's Acc. Liab. for Murder of Blart
Common Law	Conclusion
Model Penal Code	
Conclusion	

Structure #2 analyzes Snoop's accomplice liability for all the different crimes
first under the common law and then, only after analyzing each offense, doing the
same under the MPC. The possible advantage would be that you would not have to go
back and forth between common law and MPC principles. But the clear disadvantage
would be a loss of efficiency where the common law and the MPC are the same.

VARIATIONS ON THE THEME

For the following variations, assume that all of the facts from the original Problem
obtain except as noted.

1.   Mr. Big fails to hear Snoop's request that Mr. Big return with jewelry for
Snoop's mother.
2.   Snoop is charged as an accomplice to Mugsy's attempted murder of Blart.
3.   Mugsy is not an undercover cop and thus is not a feigning direct perpetrator.
4.   Snoop is not an undercover cop and thus is not a feigning accomplice.
5.   Snoop does not remove the firing pin of the gun that Snoop supplies to
Mugsy.
6.   Snoop gives Mugsy a loaded and operable gun, with the firing pin intact.
Rather than Mugsy's gun not firing when he tries to shoot Blart, the gun fires but
Mugsy misses.
7.   Snoop knew that Mugsy was an undercover officer before he gave him
the gun.
8.   Snoop failed to notify his police unit of the burglary/larceny of the jewelry
store.
9.   Rather than uttering the request to Mr. Big to bring him back some jewelry for
Mother's Day, Snoop gives Mr. Big a lucky penny as a good luck charm.

10. Rather than uttering the request to Mr. Big to bring him back some jewelry for Mother's Day, Snoop requests to accompany Mr. Big and the crew on the heist.

ADDITIONAL READINGS

GEORGE FLETCHER, BASIC CONCEPTS OF CRIMINAL LAW 188–200 (1998)

GEORGE FLETCHER, RETHINKING CRIMINAL LAW 581–85, 634–82 (1978)

LEO KATZ, BAD ACTS AND GUILTY MINDS: CONUNDRUMS OF THE CRIMINAL LAW 252–60 (1987)

CHRISTOPHER KUTZ, COMPLICITY: ETHICS AND LAW FOR A COLLECTIVE AGE (2002)

PAUL ROBINSON, CRIMINAL LAW 321–55 (1997)

Joshua Dressler, *Reassessing the Theoretical Underpinnings of Accomplice Liability: New Solutions to an Old Problem*, 37 HASTINGS L.J. 91 (1985)

Markus D. Dubber, *Criminalizing Complicity: A Comparative Analysis*, 5 J. INT'L CRIM. J. 977 (2007)

Douglas N. Husak, *Justifications and the Criminal Liability of Accessories*, 80 J. CRIM. L. & CRIMINOLOGY 491 (1989)

Sanford H. Kadish, *Complicity, Cause, and Blame: A Study in the Interpretation of Doctrine*, 73 CAL. L. REV. 323 (1985)

Michael S. Moore, *Causing, Aiding, and the Superfluity of Accomplice Liability*, 156 U. PA. L. REV. 395 (2007)

Robert Weisberg, *Reappraising Complicity*, 4 BUFF. CRIM. L. REV. 217 (2000)

CONSPIRACY

18

INTRODUCTION

The offense of conspiracy, as we know it today, was not recognized by the early common law. The scope of conspiracy was limited to groups of persons bringing false claims or making false accusations in court. It was not until the seventeenth century that the offense of conspiracy expanded to prohibit groups agreeing to commit a criminal offense. In the nineteenth century, the scope of conspiracy again expanded to include agreements to commit lawful acts by unlawful means. Though some jurisdictions still retain this latter expansion, the essence of conspiracy today is the agreement by two or more persons to commit any criminal offense.

The two primary rationales for prohibiting conspiracy stem from conspiracy's close relationship with the doctrines of attempt and complicity. Conspiracy, it might be said, is an attempt by committee or a group attempt. The crime of conspiracy addresses the special and enhanced danger posed by groups of persons planning to commit a crime. This special danger is not only greater than the same conduct by an individual, but it is also greater than the combined effect of each individual in the group committing the same conduct separately. In other words, the whole is greater than the sum of its parts. The law of conspiracy combats the synergistic effects of group criminality. And because of this special danger, the crime of conspiracy, like attempt and other inchoate crimes, is complete even if the target offense is not committed. This provides an early opportunity for police intervention. Moreover, conspiracy allows police intervention at an even earlier stage than attempt law, precisely because of the enhanced danger posed by groups of persons agreeing to commit a crime. That is, the greater the danger, the earlier the intervention.

Situating conspiracy between the laws of attempt and accomplice liability heightens our appreciation of the central features of conspiracy law. Like attempt, but unlike accomplice liability, conspiracy is a separate offense from its target offense. Conspiracy is a separate offense from the criminal object of the conspiracy. But unlike attempt, a defendant can be convicted and punished under the common law for both conspiracy and the target offense. For example, one may be convicted and punished for both conspiracy to commit murder *and* murder; but one may only be convicted and punished for attempted murder *or* murder. Like attempt, but unlike accomplice liability, conspiracy is generally punished less than the target offense. For example, both conspiracy to commit murder and attempted murder are punished less than murder, whereas an accomplice to murder may be punished as much as the direct perpetrator of the murder.

The slippery and elusive nature of the offense has both fueled its popularity among prosecutors and courted controversy among critics. Judge Learned

Hand has termed conspiracy "the darling of the modern prosecutor's nursery."[1] But conspiracy has been criticized as "so vague in its outlines and uncertain in its fundamental nature . . . [that] it is a veritable quicksand of shifting opinion and ill-considered thought."[2]

PROBLEM

Billy Bilker, Don Duper, and Sven Swindler are real estate salesmen in a shady company specializing in selling almost-worthless parcels of Arizona's desert. The office manager has called them in for a sales meeting. The company has called in a guest motivational speaker, Alec B. Cobbler. After insulting them as worthless losers, Cobbler offers motivational platitudes such as "Always Be Closing" and "Get them to sign on the line which is dotted." Cobbler announces the terms of this month's sales contest: "First prize is a Vespa scooter; second prize is a set of salad tongs; and, third prize is you're fired." After visually demonstrating the sort of brass required to be a good salesman, Cobbler also dangles the new customer leads in front of them—the GlenLarry GlenMoss leads. Cobbler says, "To you they are golden, but you cannot have them. These leads, like the coffee, are for closers and will be kept in the company safe until after the sales contest."

Meeting with Gerry Grifter, the head of a rival real estate company, Bilker tells Grifter about the GlenLarry leads. After some discussion, Grifter agrees that if Bilker can steal the leads, Grifter will buy them from him at a lucrative price.

Bilker, Don Duper, and Sven Swindler later gather at the donut shop across the street and complain that their present leads are all deadbeats and how they desperately need the high-quality GlenLarry leads. Bilker proposes that someone should steal the leads and sell them to Grifter. The following dialogue ensues:

Duper:	"Are we talking about stealing the leads or are we just talking?"
Bilker:	"Isn't it only right that, as men, we should sometimes take what men need?"
Duper:	"Yes. Sometimes . . . yes . . . sometimes a man. So, are we going to steal the leads?"
Bilker:	"Your end will be $10,000."
Duper:	"So you've already talked to Gerry Grifter?"
Bilker:	"Yes. You bring me the leads and I will take them to Grifter."
Duper:	"So, I guess we're stealing the leads? I bet they'll be steamed at corporate."
Bilker:	"Those jerks deserve it. They've been breaking my rice bowl for years."
Swindler:	"Yeah, it would be great to give Cobbler a kick right in the brass."
Duper:	"So, we're really going to steal the leads."
Bilker:	"No, you're gonna steal the leads."
Duper:	"Me? Why me? Why not us?"
Bilker:	"I'm the one who put the deal together with Grifter, so you should be the one who breaks in."

---

[1] Harrison v. United States, 7 F.2d 259, 263 (2d Cir. 1925).

[2] Francis Bowes Sayre, *Criminal Conspiracy*, 35 HARV. L. REV. 393, 393 (1922).

Duper:	"I don't want to do it by myself. I'll get caught and I don't want to go to jail."
Bilker:	"Well, you're already liable for conspiracy. You'll go to jail for conspiracy."
Duper:	"Conspiracy? But I haven't done anything."
Bilker:	"Doesn't matter, you listened."

Swindler has also listened but has said nothing further. Later that night with the office empty, Swindler breaks into the office, steals the GlenLarry leads, and takes them to Bilker. Bilker sells the leads to Grifter.[3]

Analyze the criminal liability, if any, of Billy Bilker, Don Duper, Sven Swindler, and Gerry Grifter for conspiracy and any completed target offense using both common law and MPC principles. You should not discuss in detail the elements of the target offenses—burglary, selling stolen goods, and purchasing stolen goods—but do state whether the actors are liable for their commission due to their conspiratorial liability.

LIST OF READINGS
Iannelli v. United States, 420 U.S. 770 (1975)
Kotteakos v. United States, 328 U.S. 750 (1946)
Pinkerton v. United States, 328 U.S. 640 (1946)
Braverman v. United States, 317 U.S. 49 (1942)
People v. Lauria, 59 Cal. Rptr. 628 (Cal. Dist. Ct. App. 1967)
Kilgore v. State, 305 S.E.2d 82 (Ga. 1983)
MODEL PENAL CODE § 5.03 (Official Code and Revised Comments 1985)

ESSAY
Bilker, Duper, Swindler, and Grifter are all possibly liable for conspiracy to commit burglary and selling and purchasing stolen goods as well as each completed target offense under both common law and MPC principles.

[1] The typical elements of conspiracy under the common law are as follows: (i) an agreement to commit a criminal offense or a lawful act by unlawful means, (ii) the intent to agree, (iii) the intent that the object of the agreement be achieved, (iv) a corrupt or wrongful motive (increasingly irrelevant, but still formally recognized in some jurisdictions), (v) the commission of an overt act in furtherance of the conspiracy (in some jurisdictions), and (vi) there is at least one other conspirator (in some jurisdictions).

[2] Possible defenses under the common law to conspiracy-related liability include the following: (i) impossibility (in some jurisdictions), (ii) abandonment/withdrawal with some limitations, and (iii) Wharton's rule (in some jurisdictions only a presumptive defense).

---

[3] Aspects of the Problem are inspired by, and some of the dialogue is a pastiche of quotes and paraphrase from, the film, *Glengarry GlenRoss* (Artisan 1992).

[3] The elements of conspiracy under the MPC are as follows: (i) an agreement to commit a criminal offense, (ii) with the purpose of promoting or facilitating its commission, and (iii) the commission of an overt act in furtherance of the conspiracy (for lesser offenses).

[4] The only applicable defense to conspiracy liability under the MPC is renunciation.

Bilker

COMMON LAW

[5] The first element, agreement, requires evidence of at least two parties who agree. Conspiracy is a bilateral concept: it is an agreement, and an agreement requires two or more people. Agreement is established either directly or through circumstantial evidence supporting an inference of agreement. There is arguably evidence of express agreement here. The facts state that Grifter "agrees that if Bilker can steal the leads, Grifter will buy them from him at a lucrative price." At the very least, this is evidence that Grifter is expressly agreeing with Bilker. In addition, after proposing that the leads be stolen and sold to Grifter, Bilker says to Duper, "You bring me the leads and I will take them to Grifter." Bilker also states: "I'm the one who put the deal together with Grifter." While there is no crystal clear statement—"I agree"—by Bilker, the above facts and statements are evidence of an express agreement between Bilker and Grifter. In the alternative, most courts would likely infer the agreement from the entirety of the circumstances and conversations.

[6] The second element, intent to agree, is established by much of the same evidence as in [5]. Bilker meets with Grifter and secures Grifter's agreement that Grifter will buy the stolen leads. Bilker also proposes to Duper and Swindler that the leads be stolen and sold to Grifter. These facts strongly support an inference of Bilker's intent to agree to commit a criminal offense.

[7] The third element, intent that the object of the conspiracy be attained, is established by much of the evidence discussed in [5] and [6] above. More specifically, this intent is evidenced by Bilker's solicitation of Duper and Swindler to actually break into the office and steal the leads. Furthermore, Bilker's actual receipt of the stolen leads and subsequent sale to Grifter strongly supports an inference of his intent that the conspiratorial objective be attained.

[8] The fourth element, a corrupt motive, is easily satisfied when the target offense is *malum in se*. Here, the target offenses of burglary and the sale and the purchase of stolen property are clearly *malum in se*. Given the absence of evidence that Bilker failed to appreciate that these crimes were unlawful, courts would safely presume that Bilker acted with a corrupt motive, thereby satisfying the element.

[9] The fifth element, an overt act, is established by any party to the conspiracy committing an overt act in furtherance of the conspiracy. The act need not constitute a substantial step or rise to the level of an attempt to commit the target offense. Even a trivial or lawful act suffices. Under the facts, the following overt acts would suffice: planning the meeting with Duper and Swindler, proposing that Duper and/or Swindler steal the leads, receipt of the stolen leads, and sale of the stolen leads.

[10] The sixth element, the plurality requirement, is established by evidence of more than one person conspiring. As Justice Cardozo declared, "It is impossible

for a man to conspire with himself."[4] The requirement is fulfilled when two or more persons satisfy the requisite mens rea for conspiracy. The facts discussed in [5]–[7] support satisfaction of the plurality requirement. Grifter and Bilker agree, intend to agree, and intend to attain the conspiratorial objective.

[11] The only possible defense that Bilker might plausibly assert is based on Wharton's Rule, which is discussed below in [41].

MODEL PENAL CODE

[12] The first element, agreement, is easier to satisfy under the MPC than under the common law. While the common law utilizes a bilateral conception of agreement, the MPC adopts a unilateral conception of agreement in which only one party need agree. (For an explanation of the bilateral/unilateral distinction, see Tool #16.) This element is clearly satisfied, as discussed in [5]. The second element, having the purpose of facilitating or promoting the target offense, is also satisfied, as discussed in [7]. The third element, the commission of an overt act, if applicable, is satisfied as discussed in [9]. The defense of renunciation is inapplicable.

Duper

COMMON LAW

[13] The first three elements, agreement, intent to agree, and intent to achieve the objective of the conspiracy, are not as easily satisfied with respect to Duper. The issue of whether Duper agrees differs from that of Bilker. With respect to Bilker, that he agreed was comparatively clear, and the only issue was whether his agreement was direct and express or indirect and inferred. In contrast, whether Duper has agreed is based on statements of nominal agreement followed by disagreement, both of which are express. The difficulty is in what conclusion to draw: (i) he agreed and then attempted to abandon, or (ii) he never did agree.

[14] In support of the first view that Duper agreed with Bilker and then attempted to abandon, Duper stated, "So, we're going to steal the leads." This is as express a statement of agreement as we are ever likely to encounter, especially given the typically clandestine nature of conspiracy. In some jurisdictions, the conspiracy is complete upon utterance of this express statement of agreement. And once complete, abandonment is not a defense to conspiracy. As a result, Duper's subsequent statement, "I don't want to do it by myself," occurs after the conspiracy is complete and therefore fails to preclude conspiratorial liability.

[15] In other jurisdictions, however, the offense of conspiracy is not complete until an overt act has been committed in furtherance of it. If Duper's subsequent statement, "I don't want to do it by myself," is uttered prior to any overt act committed in furtherance of the conspiracy, then the conspiracy is not complete, and Duper's statement constitutes an effective abandonment. On this basis, Duper would have no liability for conspiracy. In contrast, if Duper's statement was uttered after such an overt act, the conspiracy is complete, thereby precluding an abandonment defense. There is an overt act prior to Duper's statement—Bilker planning to meet with Duper (and Swindler). Bilker's overt act is attributable to Duper because the overt act of one party to a conspiracy is attributable to all members of

---

[4] Morrison v. California, 291 U.S. 82, 92 (1934).

a conspiracy (even those who join the conspiracy subsequent to the commission of the overt act). As a result, Duper's statement attempting to abandon, uttered after the overt act and thus after the completion of the conspiracy, was ineffective. On this basis, Duper satisfies the first three elements.

[16] In contrast to the first view that Duper agreed and then attempted to abandon, the second view is that he never did agree. In support of the second view, Duper's statement of nominal agreement was based on Duper's mistaken assumption that he and Bilker together would commit the burglary. The very statement that purports to express his agreement explicitly expresses a necessary condition for the agreement: "So, *we're* going to steal the leads." To the extent that he agreed, he only agreed to commit burglary with Bilker. He never agreed to commit the burglary without Bilker. As soon as Bilker made clear that he (Bilker) would not directly commit the burglary, Duper clearly expressed nonagreement: "I don't want to do it by myself." On this basis, Duper fails to satisfy the first three elements.

[17] On balance, it is unclear whether Duper satisfies the first three elements. Under the first view, that he agreed and then attempted to abandon, Duper does satisfy the first three elements (in both overt act and nonovert act jurisdictions). Under the second view, that he never did agree, Duper satisfies none of the first three elements. Because of the difficulty of reconciling these opposing views, it is unclear whether Duper satisfies the first three elements.

[18] With respect to the fourth element, corrupt motive, courts will most likely find that Duper had a corrupt motive for the same reason as discussed in [8].

[19] As discussed in [15], Bilker's commission of an overt act even before Duper joins the conspiracy suffices to satisfy the fifth element.

[20] Because it is unclear whether Duper satisfies the first three elements, it is equally unclear whether the plurality requirement is satisfied. Under the assumption that Duper does satisfy the first three elements, the plurality requirement is satisfied. Bilker is Duper's coconspirator. Bilker is clearly soliciting Duper to commit the crime. Bilker clearly intends to enter into an agreement with Duper and intends that the conspiratorial objective be attained. As a result, under the assumption that Duper does satisfy the first three elements, the plurality requirement is satisfied.

Even under this assumption, one might argue that the plurality requirement is not satisfied because Bilker and Duper never agreed to the same thing at the same time. Bilker "agrees" that Duper alone should steal the leads, and Duper "agrees" that Bilker and Duper together should steal the leads. But perhaps this argument merely revisits the irreconcilability of whether Duper satisfies the first three elements as discussed in [13]–[17] above.

[21] If Duper satisfies the elements of conspiracy, the only defense that he might plausibly assert is abandonment. But as already discussed in [15]–[16] above, in both overt act jurisdictions and nonovert act jurisdictions, the conspiracy was already complete upon his statement expressing agreement, and his attempted abandonment is ineffective. (Although Duper lacks an abandonment defense to conspiracy itself, his abandonment/withdrawal may be effective with respect to his liability for the target offenses as discussed in [43] below.)

MODEL PENAL CODE

[22] The first element, agreement, is clearly satisfied. Duper's statement, "So, we're really going to steal the leads," establishes his agreement to steal the leads with

Bilker. That Bilker never agreed to steal the leads with Duper and only agreed that Duper alone should steal the leads fails to preclude Duper's agreement under the MPC's unilateral conception of agreement.

[23] The second element, with the purpose to facilitate or promote the commission of a criminal act, is established for the same reasons as discussed in the previous paragraph [22].

[24] The third element, the commission of an overt act in furtherance of the conspiracy, only applies with respect to misdemeanors or felonies of the third degree. If burglary, under the circumstances here, constitutes a misdemeanor or such a felony, the overt act requirement applies. (Under the facts here, burglary is a third-degree felony.) The requirement may be satisfied by an overt act committed either by Duper or another conspirator. It is unclear whether the MPC follows the common law rule that a previous overt act suffices, as discussed above in [15]. If a previous overt act does suffice, then Bilker's previous overt act satisfies the requirement. If not, then perhaps Bilker's subsequent overt act of accepting receipt of the stolen leads suffices. Either way, this requirement is satisfied.

[25] Duper might plausibly assert the renunciation defense. Unlike common law abandonment, renunciation is a defense to the crime of conspiracy itself. In order to qualify for the defense, a conspirator must both renounce his criminal purpose and thwart the completion of the target offense. Duper arguably renounces by stating, "I don't want to do it by myself," but fails to take any steps to thwart completion of the target offense. As a result, Duper most likely fails to qualify for the renunciation defense.

Swindler

COMMON LAW

[26] The first three elements, agreement, intent to agree, and intent to attain the conspiracy's objective, may be established indirectly by inference. When the target offense is committed in a manner consistent with the previously choreographed scheme, courts will typically infer agreement, intent to agree, and intent to attain the conspiratorial objective, even in the absence of express and direct evidence of these elements. Here, Swindler completed the target offense and turned over the leads to Bilker, consistent with the plan. As a result, these three elements are plausibly satisfied.

[27] One might argue that Swindler satisfies none of these elements. First, there is no direct evidence of his agreement or intent. Second, his only statement— "Yeah, it *would* be great to give Cobbler a kick right in the brass"—suggests hypothetical or abstract agreement but not actual agreement. Third, his completion of the target offense as per Bilker's proposed plan at most affords a basis to infer his intent to agree and the intent to attain the conspiratorial objective but not necessarily his actual agreement. However, most likely, courts will infer that Swindler satisfies the first three elements.

[28] The fourth element, corrupt motive, is most likely satisfied as discussed above in [8].

[29] The fifth element, the commission of an overt act, is easily satisfied by Swindler's burglary of the office.

[30] The sixth element, plurality, requires two or more persons agreeing with each other and satisfying the mens rea of conspiracy. Bilker is Swindler's

coconspirator. As discussed in [5]–[7] and [26], Bilker and Swindler agree with each other, and each plausibly satisfy the requisite mens rea. As a result, the plurality requirement is plausibly satisfied.

[31] The only possible defense that Swindler might plausibly assert is based on Wharton's Rule, which is discussed below in [41].

MODEL PENAL CODE

[32] Swindler satisfies the first two elements, agreement and purpose to promote the conspiratorial objective, on the same basis as discussed above in [26]. Swindler also satisfies the third requirement, the commission of an overt act, as discussed above in [29]. The defense of renunciation is inapplicable.

Grifter
COMMON LAW

[33] The first three elements, agreement, intent to agree, and intent to attain the conspiratorial objective, are easily satisfied by the statement in the facts that "Grifter agrees that if Bilker can steal the leads, Grifter will buy them from him at a lucrative price." That Grifter does actually buy the leads from Bilker further evidences Grifter's satisfaction of these elements.

[34] The fourth element, corrupt motive, is satisfied as addressed above in [8].

[35] The fifth element, the overt act requirement, is easily satisfied by any number of acts including Bilkers's solicitation of Duper and Swindler to steal the leads and Grifter's purchase of the leads from Bilker.

[36] The sixth element, the plurality requirement, is satisfied. Bilker is Grifter's coconspirator. As discussed in [5]–[7] and [33], Bilker and Grifter agree with each other and satisfy the mens rea of conspiracy.

[37] The only possible defense that Grifter might plausibly assert is based on Wharton's Rule, which is discussed below in [41].

MODEL PENAL CODE

[38] The first two elements, the agreement and the purpose to promote the conspiracy, are satisfied by Grifter as discussed in [33] above. The third element, the overt act requirement, is satisfied by Grifter as discussed in [35] above. The renunciation defense under the MPC is inapplicable.

Conspiracy Structure & Scope of Liability
Analyzing the structure of the conspiracy is necessary for determining the scope of each conspirator's conspiratorial and target offense liability. (The following analysis will assume that Duper is a party to the conspiracy. This is unclear as discussed in [13]–[17].)

COMMON LAW

[39] This conspiracy will most likely be prosecuted as a single chain conspiracy. In a chain conspiracy, each party has a specific task or responsibility that links together the individual criminal acts to form the larger criminal objective. Bilker needs either Duper or Swindler to steal the leads, and he needs Grifter to buy them; either Duper or Swindler needs Bilker to sell and Grifter to buy the leads; Grifter needs Duper or Swindler to steal the leads and Bilker to sell them.

Each of them is linked together and necessary for the ultimate success of the conspiratorial plan.

[40] As conspirators in a single conspiracy, each conspirator is liable for conspiring to commit all of the various target offenses. Thus, each actor is criminally liable for conspiracy to commit burglary, sell stolen property, and purchase stolen property.

[41] One possible defense for the conspirators is Wharton's Rule. It bars conspiracy liability for any offense that requires the criminal participation of two or more persons. Both selling stolen property and buying stolen property necessarily require criminal participation of two or more persons. As a result, under Wharton's Rule, none of the four coconspirators could be prosecuted for conspiracy to commit the sale and purchase of stolen property. However, there is an exception to Wharton's Rule, the so-called "third-party exception," which allows for conspiracy liability where the number of conspirators exceeds the minimum number of persons necessary to commit the offense. Here, the minimum number of persons necessary to commit the target offenses of sale of stolen property and purchase of stolen property is two. The number of conspirators is four. As a result, Wharton's Rule does not apply, and all four conspirators are subject to liability for conspiracy to commit burglary, sale of stolen property, and purchase of stolen property.

[42] As conspirators in a single conspiracy, each conspirator is liable for every reasonably foreseeable target offense committed by every other conspirator in furtherance of the conspiracy. This is known as the *Pinkerton* doctrine. Under this doctrine, each of the four conspirators would be subject to liability for the target offenses of burglary, sale of, and purchase of stolen property. However, a minority of jurisdictions reject the doctrine. In non-*Pinkerton* jurisdictions, a conspirator's liability for target offenses committed by coconspirators is generally limited to accomplice liability. That is, a conspirator would only be liable for target offenses that the conspirator aided. (For an analysis of target offense liability for each conspirator based on accomplice liability principles, see [48]–[52] below.)

[43] As discussed in [14]–[15] and [17], Duper's arguable abandonment was ineffective with respect to his conspiratorial liability, but it nonetheless may provide a defense to his target offense liability. Courts generally require that the abandoning actor communicate the abandonment to the coconspirators and sometimes require the abandoning actor to persuade the other conspirators to abandon. Duper communicated his arguable abandonment to Bilker and Swindler but not to Grifter. Duper also failed to persuade the other conspirators to abandon. As a result, Duper's abandonment defense will not preclude his target offense liability.

MODEL PENAL CODE

[44] There are two broad principles the MPC employs to determine the structure and scope of a conspiracy. First, as discussed above in [12], it utilizes the unilateral conception of agreement. Second, if a conspirator "knows that a person with whom he conspires to commit a crime has conspired with another person or persons to commit the same crime, he is guilty of conspiring with such other person or persons, whether or not he knows their identity, to commit such crime." MPC § 5.03(2).

[45] The first principle allows a conspiratorial link between a party who agrees with another and that other. Because Grifter agrees with Bilker, Grifter is

conspiring with Bilker; because Bilker agrees with Grifter, Bilker is conspiring with Grifter. Because Bilker agrees with Duper, Bilker is conspiring with Duper; because Duper agrees with Bilker, Duper is conspiring with Bilker. Because Bilker agrees with Swindler, Bilker is conspiring with Swindler; because Swindler agrees with Bilker, Swindler is conspiring with Bilker.

[46] Application of the second principle affords additional links among the conspirators. The first additional link is Duper and Swindler to Grifter. Duper and Swindler have each conspired with Bilker to commit burglary, the sale, and the purchase of stolen property. Duper and Swindler each know that Bilker has conspired with Grifter to commit the sale and purchase of stolen property. As a result, Duper and Swindler have each conspired with Grifter only to commit the sale and the purchase of stolen property. Those are the only crimes they have conspired with Grifter to commit because those are the only crimes that both (i) Duper and Swindler each conspired to commit with Bilker, and (ii) Bilker conspired to commit with Grifter. See MPC § 5.03(2) as discussed above in [44]. (But because Grifter does not know that Bilker has conspired with anyone else, Grifter is liable for conspiring with neither Duper nor Swindler.)

The second additional link is Swindler to Duper. Swindler and Bilker have conspired to commit burglary and the sale and the purchase of stolen property. Swindler knows that Bilker has conspired with Duper to commit the same offenses. As a result, Swindler has conspired with Duper to commit burglary and the sale and the purchase of stolen property. (But because Duper does not know that Swindler has conspired with Bilker, Duper has not conspired with Swindler.)

[47] By operation of the first and second principles, Bilker, Duper, and Swindler are each subject to liability for conspiracy to commit burglary, sale of stolen property, and purchase of stolen property. Grifter, however, is only subject to liability for conspiracy to commit the sale and purchase of stolen property. (As discussed in [46], Grifter is not liable for conspiracy to commit burglary because Grifter does not know that Bilker has conspired with anyone else.)

[48] Under the MPC, conspiratorial liability merges into liability for substantive offenses. That is, one cannot be liable for both the conspiracy offense and the target offense. If liable for the target offense, one is not liable for conspiracy to commit that target offense. A conspirator is subject to liability for target offenses in two ways: (i) target offenses directly committed by the conspirator, and (ii) via accomplice liability for target offenses committed by coconspirators. (Accomplice liability requires one to solicit or aid the commission of the offense by another.)

[49] Some of each actor's conspiratorial liability merges into his target offense liability. As discussed in [47], Grifter is subject to liability for conspiracy to commit the sale and purchase of stolen property. Grifter is possibly subject to liability for two target offenses. First, he may be liable for the sale of stolen property as an accomplice. Though he solicited the commission of the sale of stolen property, he is nonetheless not liable as an accomplice because his conduct is "inevitably incident" to the offense. MPC § 2.06(6)(b). The sale of stolen property is inevitably incident to its purchase. Under this rule, as a direct perpetrator of the purchase of stolen property, Grifter cannot be an accomplice to the sale of that very same stolen property. Because Grifter lacks liability for the target offense of the sale of stolen property, his conspiratorial liability for the sale of stolen property does not merge and thus remains.

Second, he directly committed the purchase of stolen property. Grifter's liability for conspiracy to commit the purchase of stolen property merges into the target offense, and thus Grifter will have no conspiratorial liability for that offense.

[50] Some of Bilker's conspiratorial liability merges into his target offense liability. As discussed in [47], Bilker is subject to liability for conspiracy to commit burglary, the sale, and the purchase of stolen property. Bilker has possible target offense liability for all three crimes. First, he directly committed the sale of stolen property. Second, by soliciting the target offense of burglary he is liable for burglary as an accomplice. As a result, Bilker's liability for conspiracy to commit burglary and the sale of stolen property merges into the target offenses, and thus Bilker will have no conspiratorial liability for those offenses.

Third, though he solicited the purchase of the stolen property, he is nonetheless not liable as an accomplice because his conduct is "inevitably incident" to the offense. MPC § 2.06(6)(b). As discussed above, the purchase of stolen property is inevitably incident to its sale. Under that rule, as a direct perpetrator of the sale of stolen property, he cannot be an accomplice to the purchase of that very same stolen property. Because Bilker lacks liability for the target offense of the purchase of stolen property, his conspiratorial liability for the purchase of stolen property does not merge and thus remains.

[51] Also, some of Swindler's conspiratorial liability merges into his target offense liability. As discussed in [47], Swindler is subject to liability for conspiracy to commit burglary, the sale, and the purchase of stolen property. Swindler has possible target offense liability for two crimes. First, he directly perpetrated the target offense of burglary. Second, by providing the stolen leads to be sold, he arguably aided the target offense of the sale of stolen property, and thus is liable as an accomplice. As a result, Swindler's liability for conspiracy to commit burglary and the sale of stolen property merges into the target offenses, and thus Swindler will have no conspiratorial liability for those offenses. But because he lacks target offense liability for the purchase of stolen property, his conspiratorial liability for the purchase of stolen property does not merge and thus remains.

[52] And finally, some of Duper's conspiratorial liability merges into his target offense liability. As discussed in [47], Duper is subject to liability for conspiracy to commit burglary, the sale, and the purchase of stolen property. Duper has possible target offense liability for burglary and the sale of stolen property. By encouraging the burglary of the leads and the sale of the stolen leads to Grifter, Duper has accomplice liability for those two target offenses. As a result, Duper's liability for conspiracy to commit burglary and the sale of stolen property merges into the target offenses, and thus Duper will have no conspiratorial liability for those offenses. But because he lacks target offense liability for the purchase of stolen property, his conspiratorial liability for the purchase of stolen property does not merge and thus remains.

Conclusion

Bilker: Under the common law, in *Pinkerton* jurisdictions, Bilker has conspiratorial and target offense liability for burglary, sale of stolen property, and purchase of stolen property. In non-*Pinkerton* jurisdictions, Bilker has conspiratorial liability for all three offenses and target offense liability for burglary and sale of stolen property. Under the MPC, Bilker has conspiratorial liability for the purchase of stolen property and target offense liability for burglary and the sale of stolen property.

Duper: Under the common law, it is unclear whether Duper has any conspiratorial or target offense liability because it is unclear whether he agreed, intended to agree, or intended that a target offense be achieved. Under the MPC, Duper probably has conspiratorial liability for the purchase of stolen property and target offense liability for burglary and the sale of stolen property.

Swindler: Under the common law, Swindler probably is a party to the conspiracy. Assuming he was a conspirator, in *Pinkerton* jurisdictions, Swindler has conspiratorial and target offense liability for burglary, sale of stolen property, and purchase of stolen property. In non-*Pinkerton* jurisdictions, Swindler has conspiratorial liability for all three offenses and target offense liability for burglary and sale of stolen property. Under the MPC, Swindler has conspiratorial liability for the purchase of stolen property and target offense liability for burglary and the sale of stolen property.

Grifter: Under the common law, in *Pinkerton* jurisdictions, Grifter has conspiratorial and target offense liability for burglary, sale of stolen property, and purchase of stolen property. In non-*Pinkerton* jurisdictions, Grifter has conspiratorial liability for all three offenses and target offense liability for purchase of stolen property. Under the MPC, Grifter has conspiratorial liability for the sale of stolen property and target offense liability for purchase of stolen property.

TOOLS FOR SELF-ASSESSMENT

Go back to your written answer. Look for the issues identified in paragraphs numbered [1]–[52] above. Look also for the analysis that follows each issue, and mark your essay where you locate it. Do you fully describe the issue, identify the precise legal standard that applies, list the relevant facts, and show how the facts and law support a conclusion for each issue? Mark each conclusion in your essay. Are there sufficient reasons in the law and in the facts to support each conclusion?

1.   Do what you are told. Here, you are to analyze the criminal liability, if any, of the four specified actors as well as any applicable defenses.
2.   Do not analyze what is unnecessary. The focus of this Problem is conspiracy law. It is not concerned with an in-depth analysis of the elements of the target offenses.
3.   Always analyze under the MPC as well as the common law unless you are instructed otherwise.
4.   State the best possible arguments for alternative conclusions. For example, if you conclude that Duper does agree to commit a crime, also make the best possible argument that he does not agree.
5.   Be on alert for red herrings. For example, you should not treat Bilker's declarations on conspiracy law as authoritative and binding.
6.   Consider the best organization for your answer. The above Essay's organization analyzes the elements of conspiracy for each actor, one actor at a time: first under the common law and then under the MPC. In analyzing each actor's conspiratorial liability, first, each element of the conspiracy is analyzed followed by a consideration of any possible applicable defenses. Only then, after each actor's conspiratorial liability is analyzed, does the above Essay analyze the overall structure of the conspiracy. Alternatively, one could start with the structure of the conspiracy first

and then work backward determining whether each participant is an actual conspirator. Neither organizational approach is necessarily preferable in answering all hypotheticals. The organization of the above Essay is, however, preferable for this particular hypothetical. This particular hypothetical raised substantial issues as to whether each participant satisfied the agreement element. In other hypotheticals, where the agreement of the participants is less in doubt, it may be preferable to begin the analysis with the structure of the conspiracy. Yet another approach would be to analyze all of the actors under common law principles and then all of the actors under MPC principles. In some ways, this approach would be easier because it would not be necessary to jump back and forth between MPC and common law for the analysis of each actor. For most hypotheticals, however, this approach might be too lengthy and cumbersome.

7. In general, structuring your essay by analyzing one actor at a time will be particularly helpful whenever a hypothetical features many criminal actors. Hypotheticals involving issues of conspiracy will typically feature more criminal actors than any other type of hypothetical. As a result, it will often be particularly helpful to structure your essay answer accordingly.

8. The following steps reveal the structure of the above Essay's analysis of the actors' possible liability for conspiracy. These steps are somewhat oversimplified so as to provide a better view of the forest without the obstruction of the trees. But this should neither be mistaken for nor taken as a substitute for in-depth knowledge of the trees. While these steps are specifically suited to answer this particular hypothetical, this general structure with perhaps some modification might be useful to analyze any fact pattern involving conspiracy.

COMMON LAW
  i. Did the defendant agree (with another) to commit a criminal offense or a lawful act by unlawful means?
  ii. If no, then no conspiracy liability.
  iii. If yes, did the defendant intend to agree?
  iv. If no, then no conspiracy liability.
  v. If yes, did the defendant intend that the conspiratorial object be attained?
  vi. If no, then no conspiracy liability.
  vii. If yes, did the defendant have a corrupt motive?
  viii. If no, then no conspiracy liability (in some jurisdictions).
  ix. If yes, did the defendant or a coconspirator commit an overt act in furtherance of the conspiracy?
  x. If no, then no conspiracy liability (in some jurisdictions).
  xi. If yes, did the defendant satisfy the plurality requirement?
  xii. If no, then no conspiracy liability (in some jurisdictions).
  xiii. If yes, then the elements of the offense of conspiracy are satisfied, and the defendant is liable for conspiracy subject to the application of any defenses.

MODEL PENAL CODE
  i. Did the defendant agree to commit a criminal offense?
  ii. If no, then no conspiracy liability.
  iii. If yes, did the defendant have the purpose of promoting the commission of the crime?

iv. If no, then no conspiracy liability.

v. If yes, did the defendant or a coconspirator commit an overt act in furtherance of the conspiracy?

vi. If no, then no conspiracy liability if the target offense is a misdemeanor or third-degree felony. If the target offense is a first- or second-degree felony, then the defendant has satisfied the elements of conspiracy and is liable subject to the application of any defenses.

vii. If yes, the defendant has satisfied the elements of conspiracy and is liable subject to the application of any defenses.

(The above step-by-step processes fail to include an analysis of possible defenses, an analysis of the structure of the conspiracy as well as each conspirator's responsibility for agreements entered into, and crimes committed by, coconspirators. This was done to preserve the advantages of simplicity. For an illustration of these aspects of the analysis, please see the above Essay.)

9. Generally, a prosecutor will wish to establish a single large conspiracy rather than multiple small conspiracies. The advantages for the prosecutor are numerous: (i) each conspirator may be criminally liable for the substantive criminal offenses committed in furtherance of the conspiracy by any conspirator; (ii) all coconspirator statements are admissible against fellow conspirators as an exception to the hearsay rule; (iii) all of the conspirators in a single conspiracy may be tried together in a joint trial, promoting efficiency and the effect on the jury of guilt by association; and (iv) greater choice of venue—conspirators can be tried in any jurisdiction where any of the conspirators committed any act in furtherance of the conspiracy.

10. Note the three different types of conspiratorial structures: (1) the wheel in which there is one person or group (the "hub") who deals with two or more other persons (the "spokes") who are connected by a commonality of objective (the "rim"); (2) the chain, involving several layers of people dealing with a single subject matter; and (3) the chain-wheel, typically a very large conspiracy, containing aspects of both chains and wheels.

11. Remember that criminal conspirators do not speak like contract law attorneys. Criminal conspirators rarely declare in legalistic and formalistic terms: "I agree unreservedly and with sound mind and body do hereby declare my purpose and intention to undertake this criminal objective, faithfully and with due diligence. . . ." Instead, even a casual viewer of crime shows on television might realize that criminal conspirators speak ambiguously, elliptically, and rarely include the magically transformative words "I agree." The Problem features a dialogue between conspirators that is murky, ambiguous, and nonlinear. Statements by the actors are often nonresponsive to the previous actors' statements, leaving much room for interpretation. The dialogue exemplifies, however stylistically, the typical difficulty that arises in trying to establish agreement among would-be conspirators.

The best approach with hypotheticals that obscure and bury agreements among conspirators in copious amounts of irrelevant dialogue is to be like a sleuth sifting through bits and pieces of dialogue. That is, as in [5], even though express agreement cannot be established through a single unambiguous statement, express agreement can be established by combining two or three ambiguous pieces of dialogue, which together form an unambiguous whole expression of direct agreement.

12. This typical lack of direct evidence of express agreement that is due, in part, to the clandestine nature of conspiratorial agreements, has had a surprising effect. Typically, one might think that this lack of direct evidence favors the defendant and leads to acquittals. In contrast, however, because this lack of direct evidence of express agreement is so pervasive, it has lowered the bar for what suffices as sufficient evidence of agreement. As a result, keep in mind that courts will most often find agreement through indirect circumstantial evidence and inference.

13. Note that there are multiple mens rea requirements for conspiracy under the common law. The actor must intend to agree and intend that the conspiratorial objective be attained. Generally, the analysis of each will be similar. That is, if an actor satisfies one intent, then he will typically satisfy the other intent. For example, as can been seen in the above Essay, none of the actors satisfied one intent but not the other. But occasionally this does occur. For example, if an undercover police officer poses as a drug cartel kingpin and agrees with *D* to supply *D* with drugs for resale, courts will find that the officer satisfies the mens rea of intent to agree but nonetheless lacks the intent that the conspiratorial objective be attained.

14. Sometimes the corrupt motive doctrine is actually relevant. When the conspiratorial objective is a *malum in se* offense, the mens rea requirement of a corrupt motive will generally be easily satisfied. For example, in the above Essay, the target offenses of burglary, sale of stolen property, and purchase of stolen property are *malum in se*. As a result, the analysis need only be superficial in that courts will presume that such actors had the requisite corrupt motive. But where the conspiratorial objective is a *malum prohibitum* offense, the corrupt motive doctrine may provide an actual defense. While ignorance of the law is generally no defense, it is a defense via the corrupt motive doctrine for the crime of conspiracy. For example, if *D1* and *D2* commit *malum prohibitum* substantive offense X, not realizing that X is a crime, they generally would have no defense. But, if instead, *D1* and *D2* merely agree to commit the same crime, X, then their lack of knowledge of the unlawfulness of X does provide a defense to liability for conspiracy because they lack a corrupt motive.

15. Avoid this common mistake: confusing agreement with the group that agrees. Conspiracy refers to the agreement, not the group. Sometimes courts will blur the two together but this is incorrect. You should avoid this misuse of the term.

16. Keep in mind the distinction between the bilateral conception of agreement and the plurality requirement under the common law. The two doctrines are often confused. The bilateral conception requires at least two persons to agree. (The MPC adopts a unilateral conception that merely requires one party to agree and does not contain a plurality requirement.) In contrast, plurality requires not only that two or more persons agree, but also that two or more persons satisfy the mens rea requirements for conspiracy. Both the distinction and the confusion surrounding it are best illustrated by the classic problem of the feigning conspirator. For example, suppose *D* discusses with *P*, an undercover police officer, their joint commission of crime X. *P* plans to arrest *D* before the target offense is completed. While almost all agree that *D* is not liable for conspiracy to commit crime X, authorities disagree as to the reason why. Citing the bilateral conception of agreement, some would conclude that *D* fails to satisfy the agreement element because *P* is only feigning agreement, and thus *D* is not agreeing with anyone. Citing the

plurality requirement, other authorities argue that D and P agree, but P lacks the intent to agree. Also citing the plurality requirement, still other authorities find that D and P both agree and intend to agree but that P lacks the intent to attain the conspiratorial objective. Though the conclusion may be the same, keep in mind the distinction and the differing views on how the distinction is drawn. (Note that under the unilateral conception, as applied to the feigning conspirator example above, D would be eligible for conspiracy liability.)

VARIATIONS ON THE THEME
For the following variations, assume that all of the facts from the original hypothetical obtain except as noted.

1. Shortly before Duper indicates his reluctance to steal the leads alone, Bilker purchases a pair of gloves for Duper to use during the burglary so as not to leave fingerprints.
2. Shortly before Duper indicates his reluctance to steal the leads alone, Bilker purchases a pair of gloves for Duper to use during the burglary so as not to leave fingerprints. Duper tries on the gloves to ensure a proper fit.
3. Duper communicates his withdrawal to Grifter.
4. Duper successfully dissuades Bilker from pursuing the target offense.
5. Duper successfully dissuades all parties from pursing the target offense.
6. Gerry Grifter merely feigns agreement, planning to inform the police. Upon receipt of the leads, he informs the police.
7. Bilker does not inform Duper and Swindler about Gerry Grifter's involvement. Neither Duper nor Swindler is aware of Grifter's involvement.
8. Grifter is aware of Swindler's involvement.
9. Rather than jointly discussing the theft of the leads with Duper and Swindler, Bilker discusses it with each separately. Neither Duper nor Swindler is aware of the other party's possible involvement in the plan to steal the leads.
10. On his way to steal the leads, Swindler robs a liquor store.
11. When Swindler breaks and enters the office, Cobbler is unexpectedly present, and Swindler knocks him unconscious with a blow to the head.
12. Bilker merely feigns agreement, planning to inform the police. Upon receipt of the leads, he informs the police; and, rather than selling them to Grifter, he surrenders them to the police.

ADDITIONAL READINGS
Joshua Dressler, Understanding Criminal Law 429–64, 493–95, 497 (5th ed. 2009)

George P. Fletcher, Rethinking Criminal Law 218–25 (1978)

Leo Katz, Bad Acts and Guilty Minds: Conundrums of the Criminal Law 260–75 (1987)

Wayne R. LaFave, Criminal Law 648–99 (5th ed. 2010)

Paul Marcus, The Prosecution and Defense of Conspiracy Cases (5th ed. 2002)

Paul H. Robinson, Criminal Law 643–69 (1997)

Phillip E. Johnson, *The Unnecessary Crime of Conspiracy*, 61 CAL. L. REV. 1137 (1973)

Neil Kumar Katyal, *Conspiracy Theory*, 112 YALE L.J. 1307 (2003)

Paul Marcus, *Criminal Conspiracy Law: Time to Turn Back from an Ever Expanding, Even More Troubling Area*, 1 WM. & MARY BILL RTS. J. 1 (1992)

Paul Marcus, *Conspiracy: The Criminal Agreement in Theory and in Practice*, 65 GEO. L.J. 825 (1977)

MISTAKE OVERVIEW

19

INTRODUCTION

Mistakes arise in a variety of contexts and forms and affect the possible criminal liability of actors in a variety of ways. Exculpatory mistakes of both fact and law may negate mens rea or otherwise provide a defense, inculpatory mistakes trigger an impossible attempt analysis, and mistakes relating to defenses may preclude an actor from successfully asserting the defense. Each of these mistakes has been discussed in separate chapters, as if in a vacuum. But on a law school exam or in criminal law practice, exam fact patterns and clients do not necessarily pre-identify the type of mistake at issue. As a result, it is crucial to develop the ability to identify which type of mistake you are confronting.

Before distinguishing among the different type of mistakes, the threshold inquiry is whether an actor is mistaken. Mistakes and accidents are easily confused. Consider these two examples. First, an actor shoots at and kills a human being, believing it is a tree. Second, an actor shoots at a tree, correctly believing that it is a tree, but the bullet ricochets and hits and kills a human being. In the first example, the actor has killed by mistake. In the second example, the actor has killed by accident. Intuitively, we can sense the difference in the examples and distinguish mistake from accident. But articulating this intuitive difference is surprisingly difficult. Some scholars suggest that mistakes pertain to circumstance elements, and accidents pertain to result elements. Another possible articulation of the distinction is that mistakes occur internally, inside the actor's mind. Accidents occur externally, outside the actor's mind. Perhaps neither of these somewhat abstract and ambiguous articulations of the distinction is helpful. Perhaps neither of these attempts to formalize the distinction is as reliable and as helpful as our intuition.

The importance of this distinction is that mistakes and accidents are often treated differently and involve different rules, principles, and doctrines. Although accidents are not subject to the rules governing mistakes, they will perhaps find relevance in the analysis of both mens rea and causation. This chapter will focus on mistakes.

This chapter sets out 16 variations on a central fact pattern. Each variation tests your ability to identify the mistake, if any, and analyze its possible relevance to the actor's criminal liability. This approach serves two functions. By illustrating the wide variety of types of mistakes all in the same factual context, it is easier to see the differences in the types of mistakes than if they appear in disparate factual scenarios. Second, by utilizing multiple mini-fact patterns, you receive ample practice in analyzing all, not merely some, of the various types and forms of mistake.

The analytical framework that we present and suggest you adopt simplifies and clarifies the often bewildering and overwhelming maze of differing rules for different types of mistakes. The suggested approach helps you navigate this maze by taking you step by step through the analysis. By precisely ordering the steps, this approach to analyzing mistakes achieves an optimal balance of simplicity, clarity, and accuracy.

PROBLEM

Christopher Moonwalken and Robert DeFaro go deer hunting in a jurisdiction that includes, but is not limited to, the following offense:

1. Killing or attempting to kill deer
2. At any time except during the month of September.

The mens rea for this offense is unspecified.

Analyze and discuss the criminal liability, if any, of the actor(s), as well as any applicable defenses, under both the common law and MPC in the following scenarios:

(1) Correctly believing that it is not hunting season, but incorrectly believing that there are bullets in his gun, Christopher Moonwalken points his gun at a live deer and pulls the trigger.

(2) Incorrectly believing that the date is September 15, Moonwalken shoots at what he incorrectly believes is a tree. In fact, the date is September 16, and he has shot and killed a deer.

(3) Due to a brain injury sustained from playing too many games of Russian Roulette (and losing), Moonwalken mistakenly believes that it is always hunting season. Moonwalken kills a deer on January 25.

(4) Incorrectly believing that there are three bullets in his gun, Robert DeFaro attempts to kill a deer on September 30 believing that hunting season is limited to October. In fact, his gun only contains two bullets.

(5) Moonwalken intentionally shoots at a tree on September 30. The bullet ricochets off the tree and hits and kills DeFaro who has camouflaged himself to look like a deer. Moonwalken incorrectly believes deer hunting season is limited to December. DeFaro correctly believes deer hunting season is limited to September.

(6) DeFaro mistakenly hears a deer talking to him. DeFaro replies, "You talkin' to me? I don't see anyone else around, you must be talkin' to me. You talkin' to me?" Mistakenly believing that killing a talking deer, even outside of hunting season, is not a crime, DeFaro kills the deer on July 17. DeFaro suffers from a brain injury sustained from too many car accidents that he was in during his days as a taxi driver.

(7) Moonwalken kills a deer on September 8, incorrectly believing the date is August 8.

(8) Correctly believing that the date is August 8 and that it is not hunting season, DeFaro shoots a fake deer incorrectly believing it to be a live deer.

(9) Due to a brain injury sustained from playing too many games of Russian Roulette (and losing), Moonwalken mistakenly believes that the current month is always October, and he kills a deer on September 25.

(10) Incorrectly believing that hunting season is in October, Moonwalken kills a deer in October.

(11) Honestly, but incorrectly, believing that DeFaro is imminently trying to unlawfully kill him, Moonwalken, unable to retreat in safety, kills DeFaro. The bullet, however, passes through DeFaro and kills a deer. The shooting takes place on September 30.

(12) Moonwalken tells DeFaro that he enjoys looking at the deer and the trees; he does not wish to take the life of a beautiful creature of the forest. DeFaro jokingly tells Moonwalken that he (DeFaro) will kill Moonwalken unless Moonwalken kills a deer. Honestly, but unreasonably, believing that DeFaro will kill him unless he kills a deer, Moonwalken kills a deer on October 1.

(13) Correctly believing the date to be October 1, Moonwalken, who is of average size and strength, attempts to kill a deer 100 yards away by picking up DeFaro and throwing him at the deer.

(14) Incorrectly believing the date is October 1 and incorrectly believing that hunting season is limited to the month of October, Moonwalken kills a deer on September 30.

(15) Correctly believing that there is one deer that is either rabid or has "mad deer" disease and will imminently infect and kill the rest of the deer population in the area, Moonwalken kills the suspected deer on August 24. Moonwalken honestly and reasonably, but mistakenly, killed the wrong deer. He killed a healthy deer.

(16) Seeing his wife, Vicki, engage in sexual intercourse out in the woods with another man whom DeFaro mistakenly believes is Moonwalken, DeFaro becomes enraged. Cursing that his gun is out of bullets, DeFaro runs back to the hunting lodge to reload. On his way back to the trysting spot, DeFaro sees Moonwalken and kills him.

LIST OF READINGS

Review the chapters on Mistake of Fact, Mistake of Law, Impossible Attempt, and any other chapters that you think the scenarios implicate.

ESSAY

(1) Moonwalken is mistaken as to whether there are bullets in his gun. Because there are no bullets in his gun when he tries to shoot at a deer, his conduct is harmless. But because he correctly believes it is not hunting season, he mistakenly believes that his conduct is wrongful or harmful. By committing harmless conduct mistakenly believing it to be harmful, Moonwalken has committed an inculpatory mistake. An inculpatory mistake raises the issue of an impossible attempt. Moonwalken's inculpatory mistake is about a fact. One cannot determine whether a gun is loaded by referencing a law book. Because the mistake does not pertain to an element of the offense or a legal status, the attempt does not qualify as hybrid legal impossibility. Because the probability is greater than zero that Moonwalken could attain his goal (killing a deer) given the means chosen (shooting it with a gun), when viewed in the abstract, the attempt does not qualify as inherent factual impossibility. Rather, it qualifies as general factual impossibility, which is not a defense under either the common law or MPC. As a result, Moonwalken is criminally liable for attempting to shoot a deer outside of hunting season.

(2) Moonwalken has made two mistakes—about the date and his target. Because both the believed date and the actual date are both within hunting season, his mistake about the date is irrelevant. His mistake about the target is also irrelevant—both the actual target (a deer during hunting season) and the intended target (a tree) were both lawful targets at which to shoot. Because he killed a deer during hunting season, his conduct is harmless. Because he (mistakenly) believed he was shooting at a tree, he correctly believes that his conduct is harmless. Because he believes that his conduct is harmless and it is harmless, he has committed neither an inculpatory nor an exculpatory mistake. Moonwalken has no criminal liability.

(3) Moonwalken is mistaken that "it is always hunting season." By killing a deer outside of hunting season, his conduct is harmful. By mistakenly believing that the killing occurs during hunting season, he mistakenly believes that his conduct is harmless. By committing harmful conduct mistakenly believing it to be harmless, Moonwalken has committed an exculpatory mistake. It is not entirely clear from the ambiguous description of his mistaken belief whether he is mistaken about a law or a fact. His mistake that it is always hunting season could be due to a factual mistake, perhaps due to his brain injury, that the month is always September. (Think of the character played by Bill Murray in the film, *Groundhog Day*, who believes (correctly) that every day is Groundhog Day.) That is, he might be entirely aware that hunting season is limited to September but believe that the current month is always September. Alternatively, his mistake that it is always hunting season could be a mistake of law. That is, he might be entirely aware that the current month is January but mistakenly believe that hunting season is *not* limited to September. The indeterminacy of whether Moonwalken has made a mistake of fact or law is not due to the inadequacy of the tests for distinguishing between them. Rather, the indeterminacy is due to the Problem's ambiguous description of Moonwalken's mistake. Whether mistaken about law or fact, Moonwalken's mistake pertains to the element of killing a deer outside of September. The following analysis will first assume that the mistake is about a fact and then, subsequently, assume that it is a mistake of law. Finally, whether Moonwalken qualifies for the defense of insanity will be considered.

a. MISTAKE OF FACT

Under the common law, whether Moonwalken's mistake provides a defense depends on the requisite mens rea of the element. If the mens rea of this element requires specific intent, then a reasonable or unreasonable mistake is eligible to negate this mens rea. Even if his mistake is unreasonable, his mistaken belief that the current month is always September precludes having the intent to kill a deer outside of September. Thus, the mistake would negate this mens rea. If the mens rea of this element is general intent, then only a reasonable mistake is eligible to negate this mens rea. Though the facts do not state whether Moonwalken's mistake is reasonable or unreasonable, mistakenly believing that the month is always September is presumably unreasonable and thus would fail to negate this mens rea. Because his mistake is unreasonable and does not otherwise preclude liability, the moral wrong and legal wrong doctrines are inapplicable. If his mistake pertains to a strict liability element, then the mistake would not negate this mens rea (with strict liability there is no mens rea to negate).

Under the MPC, whether Moonwalken's mistake provides a defense depends on the requisite mens rea of the element. His unreasonable mistake would be eligible to negate the mens rea of purpose or knowledge. Killing a deer under the mistaken belief that the current month is always September precludes having the purpose to kill, or knowledge of killing, a deer outside of September. Therefore, the mistake would negate each of those mens rea. If the mens rea was recklessness, then only a faultless or a negligent mistake would be eligible to negate the mens rea. That is, only a reasonable mistake or an unreasonable but nonreckless mistake would suffice. Because there is no evidence that Moonwalken was consciously aware of the possibility that he was mistaken, his unreasonable mistake might well be nonreckless and thus would be eligible to negate recklessness. Moonwalken killing a deer under the unreasonable belief that the current month is always September, without conscious awareness that the current month might not be September, precludes his killing a deer with recklessness as to the current month being outside of September. If the mens rea of the element is negligence, then only a faultless or reasonable mistake is eligible to negate the mens rea. Moonwalken's unreasonable mistake would not be eligible to negate negligence. If the element is strict liability, then the mistake would not negate this mens rea (with strict liability there is no mens rea to negate). (The element is most likely not strict liability because the MPC, with only a few exceptions, rejects strict liability.) Because Moonwalken's mistake does provide a defense, depending on the mens rea of the element, MPC § 2.04(2) may apply (the MPC's correlate principle to the Moral and Legal Wrong doctrines of the common law). The provision assesses whether the actor would be guilty of another offense had the situation been as the actor supposed. That is, under the facts as Moonwalken believed them to be, was he committing a crime? No. He believed that he was killing a deer during hunting season, which is not an offense. Thus Moonwalken would not be liable for another offense under MPC § 2.04(2).

b. MISTAKE OF LAW

Under the common law, Moonwalken's exculpatory mistake of law provides a defense if one of the following three situations apply: (i) reasonable reliance on an official statement of law later determined to be invalid or erroneous, (ii) the mistake negates the requisite mens rea of an element of the offense, and (iii) lack of fair notice of the law's existence. There is neither evidence of (i) nor (iii). With respect to (ii), under the common law, if the mens rea of the element of the offense to which the mistake pertains (hunting season being limited to September) is wilfulness (defined as the knowing violation of a known legal duty) or a specific intent mens rea, then Moonwalken's mistake, even if unreasonable, would be eligible to negate his mens rea. Because he believes that he is killing deer during hunting season and thus is unaware that his conduct is unlawful, his mistake would negate wilfulness. But his mistake would not negate any other type of specific intent mens rea. Moonwalken's mistaken belief that he is killing during hunting season does not negate a specific intent to kill deer outside of September. That is, his mistaken belief that the law allows hunting season year-round is compatible with a specific intent to kill deer outside of September. For example, Moonwalken may both believe that hunting season is year round and have the purpose, intent, and knowledge as to killing a deer in January. Because the mistaken belief and the requisite mens rea are compatible, the former does not negate the latter. The next type of mens rea to consider is general intent. Mistakes of law generally do not negate general intent mens rea. But even if they are eligible to do so, Moonwalken's mistake would not. As discussed above, Moonwalken's mistake of law is compatible with a general intent mens rea. As a result, the mistake would not negate a general intent mens rea. Likewise, if his mistake pertains to a strict liability element, then the mistake would not negate his mens rea (with strict liability there is no mens rea to negate).

Under the MPC, a mistake of law provides a defense in the same three situations as described above. There is neither evidence of (i) nor (iii). With respect to (ii), under the MPC, if the mens rea of the element was purpose or knowledge, then any mistake—reasonable or unreasonable—would be eligible to negate either mens rea. But Moonwalken's mistake negates neither. His mistaken belief that he is killing during hunting season does not negate a purpose to kill, or knowledge of killing, a deer outside of September. As discussed above, because the mistaken belief and the requisite mens rea are compatible, the former does not negate the latter. If the requisite mens rea is recklessness, either a faultless or negligent mistake would be eligible to negate it. That is, either a reasonable or a nonreckless unreasonable mistake suffices. The facts fail to state whether Moonwalken's mistake is reasonable or unreasonable. Presumably, the mistaken belief that it is always hunting season is unreasonable. Because there is no evidence in the facts that Moonwalken was consciously aware that hunting season might be limited to September, his unreasonable mistake might well be nonreckless. Even so, his unreasonable nonreckless mistake that it is always hunting season does not negate killing a deer with recklessness as to the current month being outside of September. He may well be entirely aware that he is killing outside of September—in January. Thus his mistake would not negate recklessness. If the requisite mens rea was negligence, then only a faultless (reasonable) mistake would be eligible to negate it. Moonwalken's presumably unreasonable mistake would not be eligible to negate negligence. And even if it was, his mistake of law would fail to negate killing a deer with negligence as to the killing being outside of September. Moonwalken's belief that he was killing a deer during hunting season does not preclude that he should have known that he was killing outside of September. If the element is strict liability, then the mistake would not negate this mens rea (with strict liability there is no mens rea to negate). (The element most likely is not strict liability because the MPC, with only a few exceptions, rejects strict liability.) Because Moonwalken's mistake does not otherwise provide a defense, MPC § 2.04(2) is inapplicable.

c. INSANITY

Moonwalken's mistake raises the issue of an insanity defense. Let us assume that his brain injury constitutes the requisite mental disease. Due to his mental disease, he believed that it was always hunting season and thus did not realize that his actual conduct of hunting deer out of season was wrong. Therefore, due to his mental disease, he failed to know or appreciate that his conduct was wrong, thereby possibly satisfying most of the tests for the insanity defense under the common law as well as the MPC test for insanity.

(4) DeFaro makes two mistakes—about the number of bullets in his gun and the time period of hunting season. His mistake about the number of bullets is

irrelevant. His mistake about deer hunting season is relevant. DeFaro's conduct is harmless (attempting to kill a deer on a day that is, in fact, during hunting season). But because he mistakenly believes that it is not hunting season, DeFaro mistakenly believes that his conduct is harmful. By committing harmless conduct mistakenly believing it to be harmful, DeFaro's mistake is inculpatory. An inculpatory mistake raises the issue of an impossible attempt. Because he could realize his mistake by referencing a law book, he has made an inculpatory mistake of law. Because DeFaro is mistaken about the criminal law, more specifically, the law governing his possible offense, DeFaro's mistake is a mistake of same law or governing law. This type of impossible attempt is pure legal impossibility, which is always a defense. DeFaro is not liable for an attempt under either the common law or MPC.

(5) Moonwalken is mistaken as to when deer hunting is permissible. Moonwalken's mistake is irrelevant because Moonwalken was neither hunting deer nor killing deer. Shooting DeFaro was not a mistake; it was an accident (it involved a result, not a circumstance). So, there is no relevant mistake. Because DeFaro has camouflaged himself to look like a deer, arguably Moonwalken is neither reckless nor negligent and would have no liability. However, if Moonwalken was reckless or negligent, then Moonwalken would be liable for involuntary manslaughter under the common law and either manslaughter (if reckless) or negligent homicide (if negligent) under the MPC.

(6) DeFaro makes two mistakes—first, that a deer is talking to him and second, that it is not a crime to kill a talking deer outside of hunting season. The first mistake is only indirectly relevant in that it contributes to his second mistake, which is relevant. By killing a deer outside of hunting season, his conduct is harmful. But because he mistakenly believed that killing a talking deer beyond hunting season was lawful, he mistakenly believed that his conduct was harmless. By committing harmful conduct mistakenly believing it to be harmless, DeFaro's mistake is exculpatory. Because by referencing a law book he could realize his mistake, DeFaro has made an exculpatory mistake of law. He satisfies neither the reasonable reliance nor the lack of fair notice exceptions to the general rule that mistake of law is no defense. And because his mistake pertains to neither element of the offense, his mistake would fail to negate even a specific intent element. (Of course, he would have a defense if the requisite mens rea of the offense was wilfulness— a knowing violation of a known legal duty.)

Despite probably not prevailing on an exculpatory mistake of law defense, DeFaro's mistake might nonetheless support an insanity defense. DeFaro failed to know or appreciate that his conduct was wrong. Assuming that his brain injury constitutes the requisite mental disease, and that his mistake is due to his disease, he thereby possibly satisfies most of the tests for the insanity defense under the common law as well as the MPC test for insanity.

(7) Moonwalken is mistaken about the date. His conduct is harmless (he killed a deer during hunting season). But because he mistakenly believes he killed a deer outside of hunting season, he mistakenly believes that his conduct his harmful. By committing harmless conduct believing it to be harmful, DeFaro has made an inculpatory mistake. Because the actual date may be determined by looking at a calendar, not a law book, his mistake is a mistake of fact. Because the factual mistake pertains to an element of the offense—the duration of deer hunting

season—the type of impossible attempt is hybrid legal impossibility. Under the majority common law rule and the MPC, this is not a defense. Under the minority common law rule, it is a defense. Moonwalken will be liable for the attempted killing of deer out of season under the common law majority rule and MPC; Moonwalken will not be liable for any crime under the common law minority rule.

(8) DeFaro is mistaken about whether his target is a live or fake deer. His conduct is harmless (shooting at a fake deer). But because he mistakenly believes he is shooting a live deer outside of hunting season, he mistakenly believes that his conduct is harmful. By committing harmless conduct believing it to be harmful, DeFaro has made an inculpatory mistake. An inculpatory mistake raises the issue of an impossible attempt. Because whether DeFaro's target is a live or fake deer is a question of science, not law, DeFaro has made a mistake of fact. His mistake of fact pertains to an element/legal status of the deer hunting offense—the killing of a deer (meaning an actual live deer). This type of impossibility is hybrid legal impossibility. Under the majority common law rule and the MPC, this type of impossibility is not a defense. Under the minority common law rule, it is a defense. DeFaro will be liable for attempting to kill a deer out of season under the common law majority rule and MPC; DeFaro will not be liable for any crime under the common law minority rule.

(9) Moonwalken is mistaken about the month. His conduct is harmless (killing a deer during hunting season). But because he mistakenly believes he is killing a deer outside of hunting season, he mistakenly believes that his conduct is harmful. By committing harmless conduct believing it to be harmful, Moonwalken has made an inculpatory mistake. An inculpatory mistake implicates an impossible attempt. Because he cannot realize his mistake by referencing a law book, his mistake is factual. But because his mistake about the fact of what month it is pertains to an element of the offense—the element stating that hunting season is limited to the month of September—Moonwalken has committed the hybrid legal form of impossible attempt. Only under the minority rule of the common law is this type of impossibility a defense.

Despite not obtaining the impossibility defense in most jurisdictions, Moonwalken might raise an insanity defense (assuming that his brain injury qualifies as the requisite mental disease). Unlike the actors in Scenario 3 and 6 above, who were unaware that their conduct was wrong, Moonwalken believes that his conduct is unlawful. Thus he fails to satisfy that aspect of the test for the insanity defense. Moonwalken also fails to satisfy the other common criteria—failing to know or appreciate the nature and quality of his act or failing to be able to control his conduct. As a result, Moonwalken fails to satisfy almost all tests for insanity.

But there is one insanity test that he may satisfy—the Product test. It requires that his crime was the product of his mental disease. That is, the mental disease is the but-for cause of the crime. One might argue that the mental disease is not the but-for cause. His mental disease did not cause him to be willing to kill a deer out of season. He believes that it is out of season, and he is willing to kill anyway. His mental disease only causes him to not know the month. As a result, one might argue, his crime is not the product of his mental disease.

But perhaps the better argument is that his mental disease is the but-for cause of his crime. But for the mental disease he would not have mistakenly believed that it was October. (Instead, he would have known that it was September and that he was lawfully killing a deer.) And but for his mistake, he would not have committed the crime of an impossible attempt. Thus, but for the mental disease he would not have committed the crime. As a result, Moonwalken possibly satisfies the Product test for insanity, which may only apply in one jurisdiction.

(10) Moonwalken is mistaken about when deer hunting is permissible. His conduct is harmful (he kills a deer outside of hunting season). But because he mistakenly believes it is hunting season, he mistakenly believes that his conduct is harmless. By committing harmful conduct mistakenly believing it is harmless, Moonwalken's mistake is exculpatory. Because he would realize his mistake about the duration of hunting season by referencing a law book, he has made a mistake of law. Moonwalken's exculpatory mistake of law provides a defense if one of the following three situations apply: (i) reasonable reliance on an official statement of law later determined to be invalid or erroneous, (ii) the mistake negates the requisite mens rea of an element of the offense, and (iii) lack of fair notice of the law's existence. There is neither evidence of (i) nor (iii). With respect to (ii), under the common law, if the mens rea of the element of the offense to which the mistake pertains is wilfulness (defined as the knowing violation of a known legal duty), then Moonwalken's mistake will negate the mens rea. If the element prohibiting killing deer outside of September requires any other mens rea than wilfulness, then Moonwalken's mistake will not negate it. Despite Moonwalken's mistake of law, he is entirely aware that he is killing a deer outside of September. Under the MPC, the same analysis would apply. (See discussion in (3), above.)

(11) Moonwalken is mistaken as to whether DeFaro poses an imminent, unlawful, and deadly threat. This is not a mistake pertaining to an offense but rather the defense of self-defense. If charged with murder, under the common law, Moonwalken's mistake will not bar his self-defense justification if his mistake is reasonable. If unreasonable, under the majority rule, Moonwalken will not prevail on a defense of self-defense and may be liable for murder. Under the minority rule, however, the unreasonable belief supports a mitigation defense (under the doctrine of imperfect self-defense) reducing liability for murder to a type of manslaughter. Under the MPC, Moonwalken's mistaken belief also does not necessarily preclude his self-defense claim. If Moonwalken's mistaken belief (in MPC terms— that force is immediately necessary) is neither reckless nor negligent, then he will be justified in self-defense. If his mistaken belief is reckless, he will be justified if the mens rea of the offense charged is greater than recklessness. Assuming he is charged with murder, and murder requires a mens rea of purpose, knowledge, or a gross form of recklessness, Moonwalken will be justified. But Moonwalken could be liable for manslaughter or negligent homicide. If his mistaken belief is instead negligent, then he is justified if the mens rea of the offense charged is greater than negligence. Assuming he is charged with murder, he would thus be justified. But Moonwalken could be liable for negligent homicide.

With respect to the deer, Moonwalken's conduct and mens rea are innocent. Moonwalken neither shot a deer outside of hunting season nor intended to shoot a deer outside of hunting season. There was no mistake and no crime.

(12) Moonwalken is mistaken that DeFaro would actually kill him if he failed to kill a deer. This is not a mistake pertaining to the offense with which he is

charged—killing deer out of season. Rather, his mistake pertains to a defense that he might assert to the charged offense—the defense of duress. That Moonwalken is mistaken does not bar his duress defense. An actor may obtain a duress defense if he mistakenly, but reasonably, believes the threat is genuine. What does bar Moonwalken's duress defense is that he was *unreasonably* mistaken that DeFaro would carry out the threatened harm. Under the MPC, Moonwalken would also not obtain the defense. Because Moonwalken unreasonably believed that DeFaro's threat was genuine, Moonwalken would most likely not satisfy the standard for duress that a person of reasonable firmness would be unable to resist the threat. (See MPC § 2.09, Comment at 380 n.50.) As a result, Moonwalken lacks a duress defense under both the common law and MPC and would be liable for the offense of hunting deer out of season.

(13) Assuming that Moonwalken is mistaken, his mistake regards his ability to kill a deer by throwing DeFaro at the deer. His conduct is harmless (inefficaciously throwing an object at a deer). But because he mistakenly believes that he might succeed in killing a deer out of season, he mistakenly believes that his conduct is harmful. By committing harmless conduct believing it harmful, Moonwalken's mistake is inculpatory. An inculpatory mistake raises the issue of an impossible attempt. Because he cannot realize his mistake by referencing a law book, Moonwalken has made a mistake of fact. Because the mistake does not pertain to an element of the offense, Moonwalken's attempt does not qualify as hybrid legal impossibility. Depending on how the test is employed, the probability of Moonwalken attaining his goal (killing a deer), given the means chosen (hurling DeFaro at it), when viewed in the abstract, is either zero or greater than zero. Most likely, the probability is zero. If so, then this attempt qualifies as inherent factual impossibility. Under the common law, this is probably a good defense. Under the MPC, the court would have the authority to either dismiss the charge or diminish Moonwalken's punishment if convicted.

Another possible view of the facts is that Moonwalken is not mistaken. The facts supply no explicit evidence of a mistake. Perhaps Moonwalken knows he will be unable to succeed. If so, then there is no mistake and thus no inculpatory mistake. And if there is no inculpatory mistake, then there arguably is no impossible attempt.

Under the common law, different courts and jurisdictions might treat Moonwalken's mental state differently. Some courts would treat Moonwalken's mental state as a hope that is insufficient for intent. For those courts, there would be no attempt liability. Other courts, however, might find that Moonwalken still has the specific intent to kill even though he knows he will be unable to do so. For the latter courts, Moonwalken would be eligible for attempt liability. If so, Moonwalken might raise the defense of inherent factual impossibility (despite the absence of an inculpatory mistake).

Under the MPC, the mens rea for attempt is purpose or belief. Purpose is defined as "conscious object" to cause the result. Thus, under the MPC, even if Moonwalken does not believe that he will succeed, he might still have purpose. Moonwalken would be subject to attempt liability but might escape by asserting the MPC's version of the inherent factual impossibility defense—the conduct is "so inherently unlikely to result" in the offense that the actor does not pose a "public danger." § 5.05(2).

With respect to any crime potentially committed against DeFaro, Moonwalken might face liability for assault and battery.

(14) Moonwalken has made two mistakes. First, he is mistaken as to the calendar date. Second, he is mistaken as to when hunting season is permissible. His first mistake is inculpatory. His conduct is harmless (killing a deer during hunting season). But because he mistakenly believes that he is hunting on a date that is outside of hunting season, he mistakenly believes that his conduct is harmful. By committing harmless conduct believing it harmful, Moonwalken has made an inculpatory mistake. An inculpatory mistake raises the issue of an impossible attempt. Because he could not realize his mistake by referencing a law book, this is a mistake of fact. Because it is a mistake of fact that relates to an element of the offense (defining the duration of hunting season), Moonwalken's attempt qualifies as hybrid legal impossibility. Under the MPC and a majority of jurisdictions, this is not a good defense, and Moonwalken would be liable for attempted deer killing out of season. Under the minority rule, this is a good defense, and Moonwalken would not be liable.

Moonwalken's second mistake is also inculpatory. His conduct is harmless (killing a deer on a day that is during hunting season). But because he mistakenly believes that the day is outside of hunting season, he mistakenly believes that his conduct is harmful. By committing harmless conduct believing it harmful, Moonwalken has made an inculpatory mistake. An inculpatory mistake raises the issue of an impossible attempt. Because he could realize his mistake by referencing a law book, this is a mistake of law. Moonwalken's mistake is about the criminal law, more specifically, the law governing his possible offense. Therefore, he has made a mistake of governing law or same law. Such an inculpatory mistake of law involves pure legal impossibility, which is always a good defense, and Moonwalken would not be liable under either the common law or the MPC.

However, it is still unclear how this situation should be analyzed. Moonwalken has committed one act but with two different mistakes, each one involving a different type of impossibility. Has Moonwalken committed one impossible attempt or two? If Moonwalken has committed only one impossible attempt, then is it hybrid legal or pure legal impossibility? Under the minority rule, perhaps it would not matter because both types are good defenses and there is no liability. But under the majority rule and the MPC, hybrid legal impossibility is not a good defense, and pure legal impossibility is a good defense. So which one is it?

To avoid this apparent conflict, another approach might be to consider the mistakes together. His conduct is harmless (he actually killed a deer on a day that was during hunting season). Considering his mistakes in the aggregate, Moonwalken mistakenly believed that he was killing a deer on a day (October 1) that he believed was during hunting season (the month of October). Thus, Moonwalken correctly believes that his conduct is harmless. By committing harmless conduct correctly believing it harmless, Moonwalken has made neither an inculpatory nor an exculpatory mistake. And by committing harmless conduct correctly believing it harmless, Moonwalken arguably has no attempt liability.

Ultimately, it is not entirely clear how such a situation should be analyzed.

(15) Moonwalken is mistaken about which deer is rabid or has "mad deer" disease. This is a mistake pertaining not to the offense with which he is charged—killing deer out of season. Rather, his mistake pertains to a defense that he might

assert to the charged offense—the defense of necessity. That Moonwalken is mistaken may not bar his necessity defense. An actor may obtain the necessity defense if he mistakenly, but reasonably, employed means to avert the greater harm. Although Moonwalken's conduct did not avoid a greater harm than he caused, his conduct may still be justified because he reasonably employed means to avoid the greater harm. Under the MPC formulation, an actor is eligible for the choice-of-evils defense if the harm sought to be avoided is greater than the harm sought to be prevented by the offense. The harm sought to be avoided was the death of the entire deer population (in that area). That harm was greater than the harm of killing one deer out of season. As a result, despite Moonwalken's mistake, he is eligible for the defense of necessity/choice-of-evils to a charge of killing deer out of season.

(16) DeFaro is mistaken about his wife's sexual partner in the woods. This is a mistake pertaining not to the offense with which he might be charged—the murder of Moonwalken. He purposefully and intentionally killed Moonwalken. Rather, his mistake pertains to a defense that he might assert to the charged offense—the defense of provocation/EMED. Under the common law, that DeFaro is mistaken does not necessarily bar his provocation defense. At least in some jurisdictions, an actor may obtain a provocation defense if he mistakenly killed a nonprovoker. The MPC does not explicitly allow the defense under such circumstances but probably would not preclude it. As a result, DeFaro's mistake does not necessarily bar his provocation/EMED defense to the murder of Moonwalken. If successful, the defense would reduce his liability from murder to manslaughter.

TOOLS FOR SELF-ASSESSMENT

Go back to your written answer. Look for the issues identified in paragraphs numbered (1)–(16) above. Look also for the analysis that follows each issue, and mark your essay where you locate it. Do you fully describe the issue, identify the precise legal standard that applies, list the relevant facts, and show how the facts and law support a conclusion for each issue? Mark each conclusion in your essay. Are there sufficient reasons in the law and in the facts to support each conclusion?

The above Essay tracks fairly closely the following analytical steps:

   i.   Is the actor making a mistake, or has there been an accident?
  ii.   If an accident, analyze its effect on the issues of mens rea and causation.
 iii.   If a mistake, is it a relevant or irrelevant mistake?
  iv.   If irrelevant, the mistake will have no bearing on the analysis of the actor's liability.
   v.   If relevant, does the mistake pertain to an offense or a defense (e.g., self-defense, defense of others, necessity, duress, provocation/EMED)?
  vi.   If pertaining to a defense, then go to rules of that specific defense to determine the effect the mistake may have.
 vii.   If pertaining to an offense, is it inculpatory or exculpatory or neither?
viii.   If neither, determine whether there is both mens rea and actus reus (and thus the actor is eligible for liability) or whether there is neither (and thus the actor is not liable).
  ix.   If an inculpatory mistake, then Impossible Attempt principles apply.
   x.   If an exculpatory mistake, is the mistake about law or fact?

xi.   If the mistake is about law, then Mistake of Law principles apply.

xii. If the mistake is about fact, then Mistake of Fact principles apply.

1.   Do what you are told. Here, you are to analyze the criminal liability, if any, of the actor(s), as well as any applicable defenses, under both the common law and MPC in each of the 16 scenarios.

2.   Do not analyze what is unnecessary.

3.   Always analyze under the MPC unless you are instructed otherwise.

4.   State the best possible arguments for alternative conclusions.

5.   Be on alert for red herrings. For example, in problem (5), the facts state that DeFaro correctly believed hunting season was in September. Because DeFaro was neither attempting to hunt, nor hunting, nor killing deer, whether his belief about hunting season was correct or incorrect is irrelevant.

6.   Specify any necessary information that is lacking. In addition, assume any missing facts, proceed with your analysis, and argue in the alternative. For example, in scenario (3), whether Moonwalken has made a mistake of fact or law is unclear and may well be indeterminate. The best approach to such a situation is to explain why it is unclear and/or indeterminate and then assume the issue each way. That is, assume that the mistake is about a fact, and proceed with your analysis. Then, assume that the mistake is about a law, and proceed with your analysis.

7.   Do not let the specific inclusion of the deer hunting statute mislead you. Other offenses might also be at issue. Note that the Problem states that the jurisdiction's offenses *include* the deer hunting offense but are not limited to that offense. In addition, the instructions direct you to analyze *any* criminal liability that the actors may incur. As a result, your essay should contain an analysis of the actors' commission of, and/or defenses to, offenses apart from the deer hunting offense.

8.   **Accident v. Mistake**

The first step of the analysis is determining whether an accident or mistake is involved. One way to draw the distinction is that mistakes are about circumstances, and accidents are about results. For example, if an actor shoots at a human being thinking it is a tree and the human being dies, the actor has killed by mistake. The actor is mistaken about a circumstance—whether the object at which he is shooting is a human being or a tree. Conversely, if an actor shoots at a tree, correctly thinking that the tree is a tree, but the bullet ricochets and hits and kills a human being, the actor has killed by accident. The actor is not mistaken about anything. He intends to shoot at a tree and he does, in fact, shoot at a tree. The bullet ricocheted and accidentally hit a human being. The accident pertains to the result of the death of a human being. Another possible test for distinguishing mistakes from accidents is that mistakes occur internally, inside the actor's mind. In contrast, accidents occur externally from the actor. However, perhaps neither of these tests is entirely satisfactory. The best method of distinguishing them may be the use of your intuition and common sense.

The significance of the distinction is that accidents are not subject to the rules that govern mistakes. While both may affect or negate mens rea, specific rules have evolved to handle mistakes. For example, under the common law, honest and reasonable exculpatory mistakes of fact possibly exculpate despite the type of mens rea. In contrast, whether an accident exculpates requires a fact-specific, case-by-case analysis.

9. Irrelevant Mistakes

Some mistakes are irrelevant. It is helpful to identify them as such at the beginning of your analysis of a problem so they do not distract you from the analysis of other mistakes that are relevant. For examples of irrelevant mistakes, see scenario (2) where Moonwalken mistakenly believes the date is September 15, but it is actually September 16. Because both dates are within hunting season, the mistake is irrelevant. In senario (4), DeFaro mistakenly believes that there were three bullets in his gun when actually there were only two. The mistake is irrelevant as long as there is at least one bullet in his gun when he tries to shoot a deer. In scenario (5), Moonwalken intentionally shoots at a tree in September (during hunting season) mistakenly believing that hunting season was in December. Because he neither attempted to kill a deer nor did he kill a deer, his mistake is irrelevant.

10. Offense v. Defense

If you identify that the mistake is honest and possibly relevant, the next step is to determine whether the mistake pertains to a defense or an element of an offense. The most likely defenses to which a mistake would pertain would be justification defenses such as self-defense, defense of others, or necessity. But as the above scenarios illustrate, mistakes can also play a role in the defenses of duress, insanity, and provocation/EMED. Mistakes about such defenses are relevant because the mistake may or may not preclude the defense. If the mistake pertains to a defense, then go to the particular rules regarding mistakes for that particular defense. If instead, the mistake pertains to an element of an offense, then go to Tools #11-13 for the analysis of such mistakes.

11. Mistakes That Are Neither Inculpatory nor Exculpatory

Some mistakes are neither inculpatory nor exculpatory. These will typically arise in two situations. First, where both the actor's conduct is harmless and the actor believes it harmless, the actor will not be liable for an offense. For example, in problem (2), Moonwalken mistakenly believes that he is shooting at a tree on September 15, but he has actually shot a deer on Sept. 16. Because hunting season is during September, Moonwalken both believed that he was doing something lawful and it actually was lawful. Second, where both the actor's conduct is harmful and the actor believes it harmful, the actor is eligible to be liable for an offense. For example, suppose that Moonwalken mistakenly believes that he has three bullets in his gun and shoots and kills a deer on October 15, but he actually only has two bullets in his gun. Both Moonwalken's conduct is harmful (he does kill a deer out of season) and he believes it harmful (he believes that he is killing a deer out of season). Thus, he is eligible to be found liable for the offense. His mistake as to the number of bullets in his gun is neither inculpatory nor exculpatory. His mistake is irrelevant.

12. Inculpatory v. Exculpatory Mistakes

Once you have determined that the actor made a relevant mistake pertaining to an offense, the next step is determining whether the mistake is inculpatory or exculpatory. Inculpatory mistakes arise when an actor's conduct is harmless, and the actor mistakenly believes it harmful. Inculpatory mistakes are so named because they possibly make the defendant worse off by virtue of having made them. Inculpatory mistakes will possibly inculpate or incriminate the defendant.

That is, but for the inculpatory mistake the criminal justice system would have no interest in the actor's innocuous, harmless conduct. Exculpatory mistakes involve just the opposite—the actor's conduct is harmful, but the actor believes it harmless. Exculpatory mistakes are so named because they make the defendant possibly better off by virtue of having made them. Exculpatory mistakes will possibly exculpate, or lead to an acquittal for, the defendant. But for the exculpatory mistake, the defendant would clearly satisfy the requisite mens rea.

But do not make the mistake of assuming that because a mistake is inculpatory that the actor will necessarily be liable for an offense. And similarly, do not make the mistake of assuming that because a mistake is exculpatory that the actor will necessarily not be liable for an offense. Not all inculpatory mistakes inculpate; not all exculpatory mistakes exculpate.

13. Mistakes of Law v. Fact

After identifying a mistake as either inculpatory or exculpatory, the next step is to determine whether it is a mistake of law or fact. Consider applying one or both of the following tests. First, if the actor could realize that he or she was mistaken by referencing a law book, then it is a mistake of law. If the actor could not, then it is a mistake of fact. Second, if the actor could better realize that he or she was mistaken by consulting a lawyer rather than a private investigator, then it is a mistake of law. If not, then it is a mistake of fact.

Despite these helpful tests, differentiating between a mistake of law and a mistake of fact is not always easy. There are two distinct types of cases where drawing the distinction is difficult. The first type arises where the description of the mistake is ambiguous, as in scenario (3), and/or there is not sufficient information to make an adequate determination. In such cases, explain the ambiguity or lack of information, and then analyze the mistake both ways—as a mistake about a fact as well as a mistake about a law. Note that in these cases, the difficulty of the determination is not due to the inadequacy of the tests themselves.

But there is a second type of case where the analysis of whether the mistake is of fact or law is indeterminate, which does pose a challenge to the adequacy of the tests. Suppose a jurisdiction contains a deer hunting statute that forbids deer hunting when a red flag is flying over the Forest Ranger station and permits deer hunting when a green flag is displayed. Cal goes deer hunting and kills a deer on a day that a red flag is flying (making deer hunting unlawful). Cal mistakenly believed that the flag was green and thus that deer hunting was permissible. (Perhaps Cal is color-blind.) Is Cal's mistake one of fact or law? The seemingly obvious answer might well be that he is mistaken about a fact. Cal could not determine the color of the flag on that day by looking in a law book. Consulting with a lawyer rather than a private investigator would not be the best way to realize the mistake. But Cal's mistake might well be a mistake of law. (This is either instead of or in addition to it being a mistake of fact.) The deer hunting statute, contained in that jurisdiction's Official Code, explicitly incorporates by reference the color of the flag on any particular day. As a result, being mistaken about the color of the flag is literally being mistaken about the law. Thus distinguishing between mistakes of law and fact, in some unusual cases, may well be indeterminate in principle. (For a further, and perhaps the original, discussion of this issue, see Larry Alexander's article in the list of additional readings.)

VARIATIONS ON THE THEME

1. Incorrectly believing that the date is September 30, DeFaro kills a deer on October 1.

2. Honestly but unreasonably believing that DeFaro is about to unlawfully kill him, Moonwalken kills DeFaro.

3. While walking through the woods, Moonwalken meets another hunter, Meryl. Mistakenly believing that Meryl is consenting, Moonwalken engages in intercourse with her.

4. While hunting, DeFaro spots a fire in the woods. Mistakenly believing that the fire threatens to kill all 1000 people in a nearby town, DeFaro sets a firebreak to divert the fire. The fire never posed a threat to the nearby town. DeFaro destroys private property and is charged with the offense of destruction of property by fire.

5. On October 8, Moonwalken mistakenly believes that an actual, live deer is a fake deer set up for target practice. Moonwalken shoots at the deer and misses.

6. DeFaro meets Meryl's niece, Sheryl, walking in the woods. Reasonably believing that Sheryl is above the age of consent, DeFaro and Sheryl engage in intercourse. Sheryl is below the age of consent.

7. Moonwalken mistakenly believes that Meryl is about to unlawfully kill DeFaro. To save DeFaro, Moonwalken kills Meryl.

8. Moonwalken correctly believes that DeFaro reasonably, but mistakenly, believes that Meryl is about to unlawfully kill DeFaro. Just as DeFaro is about to shoot Meryl, Moonwalken shoots and kills Meryl.

9. For this and the next question, suppose that in addition to the offense of hunting deer out of season, there is also the more serious offense of aggravated deer hunting out of season involving the killing of a female deer. Mistakenly believing that the date is October 2 and that he is killing a male deer, Moonwalken kills a female deer on September 30.

10. Mistakenly believing that the date is September 29 and that he is killing a male deer, DeFaro kills a female deer on October 4.

ADDITIONAL READINGS

Joshua Dressler, Understanding Criminal Law 153–80, 216–18, 402–10 (5th ed. 2009)

George P. Fletcher, Basic Concepts of Criminal Law 148–67 (1998)

George P. Fletcher, Rethinking Criminal Law 683–758 (1978)

Leo Katz, Bad Acts and Guilty Minds: Conundrums of the Criminal Law 165–86 (1987)

Paul H. Robinson, Criminal Law 259–68, 301–307, 544–54 (1997)

Larry Alexander, *Inculpatory and Exculpatory Mistakes and the Fact/Law Distinction: An Essay in Memory of Myke Balyes*, 12 Law & Phil. 33 (1993)

Rosanna Cavallaro, *A Big Mistake: Eroding the Defense of Mistake of Fact About Consent in Rape*, 86 J. Crim. L. & Criminology 815 (1996)

Russell L. Christopher, *Mistake of Fact in the Objective Theory of Justification: Do Two Rights Make Two Wrongs Make Two Rights...?* 85 J. Crim. L. & Criminology 295 (1994)

George P. Fletcher, *Mistake in the Model Penal Code: A False, False Problem*, 19 Rutgers L.J. 649 (1988)

Kenneth W. Simons, *Ignorance and Mistake of Criminal Law, Noncriminal Law, and Fact*, __Oнıo Sт. J. Cʀıм. L.__(forthcoming 2012)

Kenneth W. Simons, *Mistake of Fact or Mistake of Criminal Law? Explaining and Defending the Distinction*, 3 Cʀıмıɴᴀʟ Lᴀᴡ ᴀɴᴅ Pʜıʟᴏsᴏᴘʜʏ 213 (2009)

Kenneth W. Simons, *Mistake and Impossibility, Law and Fact, and Culpability: A Speculative Essay*, 81 J. Cʀıм. L. & Cʀıмıɴᴏʟᴏɢʏ 447 (1990)

TABLE OF CASES

TABLE OF MODEL PENAL CODE PROVISIONS AND STATUTES

CPSIA information can be obtained
at www.ICGtesting.com
Printed in the USA
LVHW100213080119
603122LV00011B/108/P